OF BODY & BRUSH

40

OF BODY

Grand Sacrifice as Text/Performance in Eighteenth-Century China

BRUSH

ANGELA ZITO

The
University of
Chicago Press
Chicago &
London

ANGELA ZITO is assistant professor of religion at Barnard College of
Columbia University. She is the co-editor of *Body, Power, and Subject in
China,* also published by the University of Chicago Press.

The University of Chicago Press, Chicago 60637
The University of Chicago Press, Ltd., London
© 1997 by The University of Chicago
All rights reserved. Published 1997
Printed in the United States of America
06 05 04 03 02 01 00 99 98 97   1 2 3 4 5
ISBN 0-226-98728-0 (CLOTH)
ISBN 0-226-98729-9 (PAPER)

Library of Congress Cataloging-in-Publication Data

Zito, Angela.
    Of body and brush : Grand sacrifice as text/performance in
eighteenth-century China / Angela Zito.
        p.   cm.
    Includes bibliographical references and index.
    ISBN 0-226-98728-0 (cloth : alk. paper)—ISBN 0-226-98729-9
(paper : alk. paper)
    1. China—Politics and government—18th century.   2. Rites
and ceremonies—China.   3. China—History—Ch'ien-lung,
1736–1795.   4. Imperialism.   I. Title.
DS754.17.Z58   1997
951.032—dc21   97-12362
                                                    CIP

⊗ The paper used in this publication meets the minimum requirements of
the American National Standard for Information Sciences—Permanence
of Paper for Printed Library Materials, ANSI Z39.48-1984.

To my parents
Anthony John Zito & Joanne Angelo Arena Zito

Contents

Illustrations

Prologue: Clothing, Carrying, and Codifying

A slim volume from the Qianlong reign, entitled simply *On Wardrobe* (*Chuandai*), detailed the emperor's days around his clothing and movements in space.[1] According to this record, on the eighth day of the eleventh month in the twenty-second year of his reign (1757), the Qianlong emperor commenced the week-long ceremony of Grand Sacrifice to Heaven.

He wore a round cap in a neutral shade of sable and satin;[2] a cashmere and woven silk calf-length robe, trimmed in black fox; a sable fur short formal jacket, dangling a diamond on a yellow cotton floss necklace; an ordinary girdle; white cotton stockings and black sheepskin-lined boots. After breakfast, he went out Jiyang gate in a four-bearer palanquin, crossing to Biyang Palace where he rested inside the Jianfu Palace. Later he mounted the Great Palanquin and was borne out of Duanzi Gate and into Jihua Gate to stop at the Hall of Abstinence to prepare for the Sacrifice to Heaven three days hence. He was proffered his dinner. (*On Wardrobe*, 265–66)

This style of description records each day. On the next day of his fasting, for instance, the emperor added to his dangling cloisonné ornament a turquoise medallion announcing the fast. He put on his same plain sable hat but changed into "a sienna silk and black fox-fur trimmed calf-length robe; a black panther-skin short formal jacket" (*On Wardrobe*, 266), retaining the usual white socks and sheepskin-lined boots. After his ritual bath at noon, however, he switched his jacket and ornaments. What distinguished this day of sacred preparation was the fact that he went nowhere, crossed no thresholds borne aloft on the shoulders of his bearers.

A few days later, mention of the Sacrifice to Heaven lies buried, the actual ritual enrobed in the loving minutiae of sable and silk, lost in circuitous routes through double gates and palanquins carried by as many as sixteen men (*On Wardrobe,* 268–69). Let us leave the emperor poised for what must be the main event of this book and try to make some sense of this sort of document.

In this welter of sartorial, transportational, and architectural detail lay themes examined in this study. First, *On Wardrobe* is a "daily book," and everything the emperor wore, every change of clothing was recorded, beginning with the solar New Year. His ceremonial thus appears, from this vantage point, deeply contextualized in the everyday life of the court: days of greeting his mother at dawn, giving audience, eating, and being carried around the Forbidden City. Importantly for my purposes, we see how the emperor's body provided to his courtiers an occasion, oddly, for writing. Indeed, dynastic histories take as their first level of information gathering the "Diaries of Rising and Repose," the *Qijuji.* This imperial body, living a three- (even four-) dimensional existence, was constantly turned into two-dimensional text. The kingly body lived a double existence as both site of corporeal practice and occasion for production of inscriptions for the imperial archive. In turn the emperor was enjoined to perform the scripts produced out of his own, and his ancestors', orchestrated lives—the ritual handbooks and dynastic canons that will be examined here (see chapters 3 and 4). His doubly animated existence can be understood as the heart of text/performance.

That courtiers closely documented clothing, the layers of significant surfaces that overlay the emperor's flesh, was not accidental. The imperial body provided a body of surfaces that were made to signify (see chapter 1). That they emphasized gates and palanquins also becomes sensible if the imperial city is understood as itself a sensuous embodiment in brick, mortar, and wood of the imperial ritual process. Gates control movement between inner and outer domains; palanquins require constant mounting up and down (see chapter 5). Finally, in texts of this sort—anonymous, excessively fussy—we have little sense of the awesome might of Qianlong as a military strategist or an engaged administrator. The emperor, carefully watched, clothed, "invited," "led," "carried," appears instead as the eunuch's fantasy king: utterly at the mercy of his handlers. That this image of the king hardly exhausts the political import of the Qianlong reign should be obvious. Yet ironically, it was not unimportant. In his scrupulous attention to Chinese protocols of the text/performances of *li,* or ritualization, the Qianlong emperor showed himself quite aware of how this smothering process could be countershaped to the ends of the throne. The meanings embedded in the practice of Grand Sacrifice were important to his rule. He and his imperium labored together with men expert in the history of *li* to fashion ceremonial forms that provide twentieth-century readers with not only a glimpse of ideology in the narrow "will-to-power" sense, but also a possibility of understanding the metaphysics that made such meanings plausible at all.

This book provides a reading of the "invisible" structures and logics of the language and gesture that formed the practice of Grand Sacrifice in the eighteenth century in China. But such a project bears its own irony because it can only be carried out through strict attention to the actual material traces of those practices: paintings, handbooks, treatises, calendars, floor plans of temples, diagrams of vessels, and illustrations of clothing, robes, and vessels that exist today. I think the central paradox of theorizing social life rests here: without such visible practicalities, we can know nothing and do nothing. Yet, without understanding how palpable things and events become arranged through invisible logics, how they acquire sense *in relation* to one another in space and time, those practicalities would remain forever meaningless and thus lack force to organize *us*.

Once I recognized how the things of that imperial ritual universe, my historical sources, were produced *within* the same structures and logics that I was trying to decipher, certain adjustments had to be made. Even though the things, my sources, exist in physical materiality, they provide no hard stepping stones through a swamp of meaning. They do not give a privileged vantage point *upon* their structuring system, having been constantly performed into being within it, but only varying points of view *inside* it. Thus this book should not only inform us on the possibilities and limitations of the practices that produced its sources, but change our view of the sources themselves.

In a roundabout way, I am restating an axiom of Chinese ritual (and social) life: that the visible and invisible worlds are mutually dependent. One does not exist without the other; to become solely preoccupied with one side means committing the "sins" (so hurled by each team at the other in Chinese religious life) of being either too "Buddhist" (other-worldly) or too "Confucian" (pragmatic). (Visible) people must have their gods as surely as (invisible) gods require the palpable sign of incense. For the modern historian, abandoning the mutuality of seen/unseen might be expressed as overly empiricist versus too idealist.[3] In fact, to assume such a binary at all means misunderstanding their nondual nature, how they form a shifting hierarchicizing whole. Or even better, it would be to reinforce what Bruno Latour (1993) has called the "modern constitution": the separation of the world of materiality and the world of thought that underlays and founds the great binaries of the post-Enlightenment European world.

I show in the pages that follow how Chinese ritualists who focused their energies upon imperial ceremony simply did not operate within that metaphysics. In Latour's terms, they were distinctly "non-modern" in allowing and appreciating the proliferation of hybrid forms of agency that actively sought to harness the cosmos for human social purposes. They made these tasks far more explicit than our own current modern arrangements allow. Perhaps it is their open recognition of these strategies that conveys a strangeness to us. Their problems— of forming and naturalizing hierarchies of value in society; of working through inclusion in, and exclusion from, the powers of agency; of accounting for similarity and difference in social life—are all ones we share. I think we gain by recognizing the differences in the politics they brought to bear in forming ritualist solutions.

Many people have advised, assisted, and cheered this project onward. I will try to name a few. My first teacher in Chinese social history, to whom I will always feel the grateful debt of *xiao* and to whom I can only offer my poor emulation: E-tu Zen Sun. The faculty at the University of Chicago launched me into this double engagement with Others and my own intellect: Harry Harootunian, Philip Kuhn, Michael Dalby, Edward Ch'ien (now deceased), Susan Mann, Ronald Inden, David Schneider, Nancy Munn, Terence Turner. At Chicago I also met James Hevia, whose interest in ritual, to my delight, paralleled my own. His ideas have consistently challenged and sustained me though many years of discussion. It is rare to find a kindred mind attached to the generosity that makes collaboration possible. I thank the collective of *positions,* many of whom have been collaborators and interlocutors for over a decade, especially Tani Barlow, James Hevia, Judith Farquhar, and Lisa Rofel. Late and very helpful readings of the manuscript were provided by Dorothy Ko and Christian Depee.

My colleagues at Barnard and Columbia welcomed me into their midst and provided wonderful support, especially Jack Hawley, Natalie Kampen, Atina Grossman, Alan Segal, Celia Deutsch, and Randall Balmer. My writing group has read these chapters, sometimes twice: Maggie Sale, Judith Weisenfeld, Karen Van Dyck, Zita Nunes, Linda Green, and Priscilla Wald. My students and teaching assistants made my teaching life not only bearable but often even interesting. I wish I could buy you all a drink now that the ones among you who were too young have graduated.

I thank my professors in the Philosophy Department at Beijing University, Deng Aimin in Song thought, sadly, now deceased; and Liu Yulie and Wang Shouchang in history of Chinese philosophy. My tutor, Zhu Jiajin of the Palace Museum, spent hours with me reading ritual texts. Many *tongxue* read and talked for hours, especially Tang Xiaofeng, Hu Jingping, Geng Youjun, and my roomate Zhang Lixi. For the opportunity to study in Beijing for those years, I am grateful for grants from the Committee on Scholarly Communication with the People's Republic of China (now the Committee on Scholarly Communication with China) and the Social Science Research Council.

In 1992 I spent some months at the Number One Historical Archives in the Forbidden City in Beijing under a grant from the CSCC. My thanks to Yin Shumei, who provide invaluable assistance. I was hosted by the Institute for Research of Qing History at Renmin University and thank my adviser, Wang Sida, for the institute's hospitality and scholarly assistance. The 1994 NEH summer seminar at the University of Michigan, "Reading the Manchu Summer Palace at Chengde: Art, Ritual and Rulership in 18th Century China and Inner Asia," organized by Donald Lopez, James Hevia, Ruth Dunnell, and Evelyn Rawski, provided a chance to pore over visual materials and meditate on the central Asian components of the Qianlong reign. I especially thank Phillipe Foret, a fellow member, for producing the computer graphics used here.

I am grateful for permission to reprint a number of materials in this volume. Part of chapter 1 originally appeared as Angela Zito, "Silk and Skin: Significant Boundaries," in *Body, Subject, and Power in China,* ed. Angela Zito and Tani E. Barlow (Chicago: University of Chicago Press, 1994), pp. 103–30, © 1994 The University of Chicago, reprinted by permission of the University of Chicago Press. Part of chapter 5 originally appeared as Angela Zito, "Re-presenting Sacrifice: Cosmology and the Editing of Texts," *Ch'ing-shih wen-t'i* 5, no. 2 (December 1984): 47–78, reprinted by permission of Johns Hopkins University Press. Part of chapter 7 originally appeared as Angela Zito, "City Gods, Filiality and Hegemony in Late Imperial China," *Modern China* 13, no. 3 (July 1987): 333–71, © 1987 by Sage Publications, Inc., reprinted by permission.

My editor, T. David Brent, at the University of Chicago Press has known my work and encouraged it for many years, always putting it into a wider intellectual context. I can only hope that the effort proves to be worth the patience he has shown. The readers of the manuscript, Ken Dean and anonymous, offered useful and learned suggestions.

People produce their meanings and so produce themselves. But a self requires a great deal of nurturance. My parents, Tony and Joanne, now know all about the intricacies of academic life. My brothers and their families grow wiser with every year. My brother Chuck is an indispensable font of advice and dining companionship. I thank Carol Ockman, Helga Druxes, Gail Hershatter, Claudia Pozzana, and Lella Heins. My friend in all things intellectual and domestic, John Calagione, spent precious hours of his life with me on this and many other projects. I cannot thank him enough.

Having shown that, although "I" put my name on the cover, in fact a web of teachers, colleagues, friends, and family in some sense produced this work collectively through me, I will now proceed to negate that insight into social life by the usual ritual claim to final responsibility. For these (provisional) fruits of our long association, for the form of this particular writerly intervention in the process, only I can be blamed. You can all relax.

Abbreviations

DQHD	*Da Qing huidian* (Assembled Canon of the Qing)
DQTL	*Da Qing tongli* (Comprehensive rites)
ECCP	Hummel, *Eminent Chinese of the Ch'ing Period*
HDT	*Da Qing huidian tu* (Illustrations for the Assembled Canon)
HDZL	*Da Qing huidian zeli* (Examples attached to the Assembled Canon)
LJYS	*Qinding Liji yishu* (Imperial edition of the analysis of meanings in the Record of Rites)
LJZY	*Liji zhengyi* (Verification of meanings in the Record of Rites)
LQTS	*Huangchao liqi tushi* (Illustrations of dynastic ritual paraphernalia)
QSG	*Qingshi gao* (Draft history of the Qing)
RXJWK	*Rixia jiuwen kao* (Revised edition of *Legends of old about the capital*)
SKQSWYG	*Siku quanshu* (Wenyuange edition of the Library of the Four Treasuries)
SKQSZM	*Siku quanshu zongmu* (General catalogue of the Library of the Four Treasuries)
WLTK	*Wuli tongkao* (Comprehensive investigations of the Five Rites)

Introduction

But I am sure we do end up with better, more explanatory histories, if we have comprehended, more abstractly, some of the forms and relations which constitute them.   RICHARD JOHN-SON, "What Is Cultural Studies Anyway"

The eighteenth century in China has been as famous for its imperial displays and ceremonial performances as for its literati scholarship and vast text-editing projects. The Manchu Qianlong emperor (r. 1736–1799), who ruled an Inner Asian empire that included China, labored never to miss a single solstice Sacrifice to Heaven in sixty years, made six inspection progresses south from Beijing to the Yangtze Valley, and fought battles with competing peripheral domains throughout his reign. The kingly displays were arranged by his imperium, the group of men entrusted with the governance of the realm by virtue of their noble Manchu birth or, if they were Han Chinese, their success in the elaborate rite of passage of examination in the classics.[1]

From the point of view of the Manchu throne, it was fit and right that such scholars should live their lives speaking in the emperor's voice, carrying out his tasks, representing and orchestrating the spectacle of his majesty. From the point of view of literate and ambitious men, service to the throne was honorable. By the eighteenth century, there were few "eremitic" abstainers who eschewed to serve the conquerors out of loyalty to the previous Han Chinese dynasty. But for these scholars, the emperor was one patron among many who fed them while they read and clothed them while they collated. They developed the scholarly standards of the time away in the rich regions of the south and brought them to Beijing to impress the throne.

Among these scholars, commentary upon and exegesis of the classics reached a summarizing apogee in the eighteenth century. Interest in retrieving the details of the institutions of monarchy likewise peaked. The essence of true government was thought to inhere in the concrete ceremonial prescriptions of the past. Thus, the study of *li* (usually translated as ritual) held a particular fascination for Chinese scholars in the eighteenth century. These scholars paradoxically saw no contradiction in spending enormous energy researching the history of *li* in (or out of) service to the throne, while simultaneously criticizing the classics that were thought to provide ultimate sanction for the rites. One culmination of imperial ritualization and literati scholarship lay in the Grand Sacrifices (*Dasi*),[2] the four most important rituals of a full imperial ceremonial year.

In the Qing period, these comprised the foremost category of three kinds of sacrifice: The Grand (*Da*), Middling (*Zhong*), and the Miscellaneous (*Jun*). There were four Grand Sacrifices: to Heaven at the Round Mound at the Southern Boundary (*nanjiao yuanqiu dasi*); to Earth at the Square Pool at the Northern Boundary (*beijiao fangzi daji*); to the Imperial Ancestors in the Grand Temple (*zongmiao sishi daxiang*); at the Altar of Soil and Grain (*sheji*).[3]

Together these four ceremonies formed a set that took the emperor out of his palace in each of the cardinal directions around the capital: south to worship Heaven at the winter solstice, north to sacrifice to Earth at the summer solstice, east to the Ancestral Temple in each season, and west to the Altar of Soil and Grain again every spring and autumn. The Grand Sacrifices were the most important events in a full, yearlong ritual cycle that also included court audience, guest rituals, rites of mourning, and ceremonies associated with military conquest.

All levels of sacrifice shared an identical ceremonial order. They began with as many as five days of preparation (in the case of Grand ones), during which participants were secluded, animals killed, and things placed in prescribed fashion upon altars, while people's places were marked. On the day of the ceremony, the emperor moved in procession toward the appropriate altar and himself offered each of the Three Oblations (*sanxian*) of jade, silk, and cups of liquor. Music and dance accompanied his movements, interspersed with the recitation of hymns.

The repetition of Grand Sacrifice throughout the year constituted the emperor and his imperium spatially and temporally in three aspects: The Sacrifice to Heaven and Earth showed the emperor as the link between the two. In the cosmic triad of Heaven, Earth, and Humanity so familiar in Chinese think-ing, the emperor persistently claimed status as the one man who connected the cosmos.

The Sacrifice to the Ancestors at the Grand Temple displayed the emperor in the eyes of his realm as the prime exemplar of filiality, and thus a model for the relations between emperor and subject, father and son. The Sacrifice at the Altar of Soil and Grain cast him as the whole of his imperial parts, social and geographic. This was the highest-ranked sacrifice to be performed outside the capital and it was carried out simultaneously by the emperor in Beijing and by members of the imperium at provincial, prefectural, and county levels.

Grand Sacrifices were particularly important because they were designed to unite the entire realm, its visible (*ming*) and invisible (*yu*) portions. By providing a special and sacred space where certain people could call upon the power of the unseen world of the spirits, sacrifice formed a recurrent mode of political discourse. It supplied a vocabulary of action that ultimately aimed at the power to govern the realm itself as it displayed and materialized the metaphysics of hierarchy upon which that realm rested.

This book frames a number of arguments through which to grasp Grand Sacri-fice as a technique of imperial rule. These four frames nest within one another and provide an ever-widening context for understanding Grand Sacrifice. The narrowest concerns the form of sacrifice: that it poses the problem of ruling through the brush or the body, by virtue of virtue or of kinship descent, as a sage or as a son. A wider frame concerns the throne's management of the *li* of Grand Sacrifice as it rested upon its relationship with the literati imperium out-lined above. The third frame for understanding Grand Sacrifice investigates how it produced the throne/imperium's relation to the populace at large. Finally, the study as a whole must stand framed by the implicit comparison with Euro-pean modes of power/knowledge and state formation.

First, and most internally to the form of the ritual, I argue that in mobilizing this sort of ceremonial, the Manchu throne was able to seize upon existing dis-courses that emphasized the production of authority simultaneously through text and performance, ruling through the brush and the body. These discourses were Han Chinese and, mediated by what we might call a pan-Asian sensibility steeped in Buddhism and an ongoing frontier exchange through marriage and material culture, were fruitfully enfolded into the Manchu imperium.

Rites of sacrifice accomplished the symbolic construction of the king (and cosmos, and filiality, and the imperium with its servants) by providing, in the materials and movement of the ritual process, a setting in which certain "solutions" to important contradictions in social life became plausible.[4] Foremost among these for a foreign clan-based monarchy like the Manchu presiding over a country ruled by scholars was the mediation between two models for the inheritance of power: through biological sonship of the body and meritorious achievement "of the brush," emblematized by the literati as scholarly in nature.

In the details of its form, Grand Sacrifice allowed the throne to display and control the contradictions of the reproduction of its own power: Should power be inherited by filial sons or by knowledgeable scholars? To restate their problem: Who is more important—those who produce *wen,* "cosmic text-pattern," available to those who can discern it and materialize it in building, writing, music? Or those who produce *xiao,* filiality, through bearing and raising sons and inculcating the bodily performances of rituals?

A further second framing context: the throne's management of the *li* of Grand Sacrifice rested upon and formed its relationship with the literati imperium. The throne and the scholar-editors who researched and wrote handbooks of *li* articulated themselves in a mutually constituting relation of the production and circulation of power and meaning. In a particularly intimate linking of what sociologist Paul Connerton (1989) calls "inscription and incorporation," the imperium produced Grand Sacrifice as a performance of texts and a textualizing performance.

However, the action of sacrifice proceeded doubly. While it produced the majesty of the king, at the same time it stood as a sign of its own production. This production was one intimately linked to the practice of writing and signification itself, which was reified at every level. The Ministry of Rites (*libu*) began the process, through the examination system (*keju*), recruiting the members of the imperium who were then responsible for the ritual construction and maintenance of the realm. Writing itself formed their "rite de passage," to borrow Van Gennep's useful construct, from the periphery of the domain (outside or *wai*) toward its inward center (*nei* and *zhong*), from below (*xia*) upward (*shang*) toward the emperor (Van Gennep 1960).

Thus the production of a set of sensuous signs through action designed to situate the human within the cosmic began with editing and writing. Text and performance together formed a set.[5] If texts preserved ritual in the medium of language, it was only through that language that the rest of the performance took place. This text/performance form had important implications for imperial rule and for the retrospective understanding of China's monarchy by modern Han Chinese.

The imperial rituals I examine here have usually been dubbed the "state cult" and associated with Confucianism. It is literati Confucianism's intermittent, if long, association with imperial power (especially since the imperium was reconstituted under Sui Wendi from C.E. 581 to 604) that has resulted in its status as the (declared) natural background, the ground upon which the heterodoxies of Daoism, Buddhism, and secret society activity were figured. In turn, this profoundly political connection has prompted a retrospective claim for "Confucianism" by twentieth-century Chinese interested in providing a genealogy for their nation-state as a clearly readable, instrumentally rational, this-worldly point of view. Thus have the inner, value-creative workings of the imperium as the "natural ancestor" of the modern state eluded sustained critical scrutiny by both Chinese and Western scholars.

In China, the written records of the imperial formation, the nascent "state" if you will, not only reflected the utilitarian will to rule of the emperor but also partook of a sacred quality that the written word in general possessed. This sacred quality, so richly exhibited in various imperial editing projects on *li*, provided a peculiar power to move and persuade that extended to writing an active role in ritual performance, beyond one of mere representation. A linguistic optimism or feeling that written signs could be brought into harmony with the things of the world was a central component of the "ritualist metaphysic" that will be discussed at great length later.

How powerfully did this metaphysics shape literati and imperial perspectives on governance? Why did the literati who lived far away in the wealthy Yangzi Delta region, with their own networks of patronage, nonetheless spend so much time focused socially and intellectually on imperial concerns, especially researching and writing about kingly ritual? What implications did this fact have for the forging of a scholarly community separate from imperial patronage and thus for the eventual relationship between the twentieth-century state and the intelligentsia? At an even deeper level, masters at controlling inscriptions of all kinds, scholars nonetheless were faced with the necessity of featuring an (imperial) performing body at the center of the imperium. What legacy did this emphasis upon bodily practices mediated through the hegemonic scripts of *li* leave for twentieth-century political campaigns?[6]

The third, wider frame for understanding Grand Sacrifice lies in how it produced the throne/imperium's relation to the populace at large. More highly condensed sorts of occasions like imperial ceremonies provided crystallizations of otherwise dispersed "meaning." As rituals of imperial sacrifice bridged material and thoughtful life by embodying only certain philosophic propositions about humanity and its cosmos on its altars, the emperor and his imperium produced, and attempted to control, meaning and value that ramified into every corner of Chinese life.[7] The imperial body and personae were at its center. I have called this imperial centering form the body of yang power. In the final chapter I will briefly explore some ramifications it might have for thinking about gender distinction.

The monarchy drew its power from its participation in categories significant in everyday life, embodying such morally charged imperatives as filiality (*xiao*) through use of a shared repertoire of gesture, architecture, and language. The hugely expensive, seven-day Grand Sacrifice that Qianlong performed was just a more extravagant version of ritual prescribed for clan hall and family altar.[8] Domestic architecture mimicked in its basic materials (wood and plaster) and structure (tile roofs supported by pillars on platforms, arranged in courtyards) the architecture of the Forbidden City. Temples were also similar to one another and to residences.

The emperor became, at the center of his ritualization within the discourses of *li, wen,* and *xiao,* a privileged exemplar of correct embodiment and perfect practice. But he was never divine to any of the peoples he ruled; a man among other men (and the perfection of yang masculinity), he provided the model of how to model for others who would emulate him. This chain of emulation was formed through the bodies of his imperium, his governors, his district magistrates who ruled in his place out in the provinces.

The throne thus spent an immense amount of energy seeking to establish itself as the foremost exemplar of *wen.* Particularly in the eighteenth century, the Qianlong emperor sought obsessively to hold the most splendid rituals, to collect the finest paintings, renovate and build on a grand scale and, of course, to re-present the Chinese and Manchu past by editing them together with a seeming spatial and temporal seamlessness.

Historian Harold Kahn describes the Qianlong emperor as cultural patron and producer:

The emperor on the throne was both part of the high culture he patronized and above it. He had license to be both greater and different. . . . The Qianlong emperor created a legacy of taste for unshakable imperial pomp, massive projects and occasional displays of what can only be called elephantine delicacy. It was practically an imperial requirement to awe—to sponsor that which was monumental, solemn and ceremonial, literally to be bigger than life. . . . Universal kingship after all, embraced the cosmos, and that posture demanded suprahuman scale in architecture, ritual and the manifold roles required of the emperor. (Kahn 1985: 291)

Imperial ritual must be viewed in this context of very material production, especially in an era of such prosperity as the eighteenth century. The process of *wen* left its significant trace upon many *things* and *activities* that were part of the good life (books, paintings, music), a good life that was not necessarily consciously connected to the imperium. Indeed, historians have argued cogently that the eighteenth century saw the rise of alternative centers of cultural legitimacy in the southern Yangzi Valley (Elman 1980 and 1984; Chow 1994). One of the questions that must be raised in conjunction with their view, however, is whether or not the value (in all its senses as meaning and material) produced through *wen* activities did not generate, as it were, a surplus that was constantly diverted toward empowering the imperium.

A fourth and widest context for undertaking this study lies in comparison between China and Europe. The comparative mode forces itself upon any cross-cultural reading, and I hope I have made it a reflexive element of the entire book. Chinese forms of organizing embodiment, expressivity, and production of the self differed from the model of classical subjectivity and representation dominant in Europe in the eighteenth century.

Recent critiques of representation and of the unitary subjects thought to be its authors have provided clues for approaching a social formation like China that conceived itself, and its "selves," quite differently from Europeans. It is especially crucial for cross-cultural historians working through Euro-American discourses to be aware of this grounding of most social theory.[9] I am interested in retrieving those Chinese forms and techniques and in investigating them because they underlay and shaped politics as it is more traditionally conceived by historians. However, this study has also allowed me to read the Chinese material back into European social scientific and hermeneutical theory's face, contributing to the ongoing constitution and critique of received categories for analyzing societies and power.

Thus, this book has a double agenda: to learn more about the constitutive discourses of eighteenth-century Chinese society through a study of imperial authority and to do so using a critical cultural-historical method that allows for self-reflection upon our categories as historians. Such a method emphasizes the social uses of form as we find it in the ritual handbooks and encyclopedias, clothing, altar spaces, paintings, and vessels. Such forms materialized and shaped conceptual choices, and taking them into account allows two things for analysts: first, we move beyond a history of ideas, allowing a glimpse of the materiality of performance and embodiment. Second, they open space for the materialization of language itself. We are reminded that ideal choices are always formed and constrained by a material and formal repertoire, whether grammar or gesture; and that expressive form provides the context within which social selves create and act.[10]

Subjectification, or the establishment of sites from which people can speak/act and assume agency, also works through the material forms of language and gesture and is thus intimately connected to embodiment.[11] The objects listed above constitute for us the historical record of the protocols of *li,* and *li* provide a rich source for the history of such "subjectification" in China.[12] The subjects discussed here include, first and foremost, the imperial personae, body and voice. But implicated within this model of human agency (perforce unattainable by anyone else, but a desired goal insofar as the imperium held up the monarch as perfect male father/son/sage/ruler) were the men whose editing and management both empowered and constrained them. I return to these interpretive frames in the final chapter, but the book itself is organized to present first "text" and then "performance." As Norbert Elias puts it in his own elegant preface to *The History of Manners,* "To gain access to the main questions, it is necessary first to obtain a clearer picture." To address the issues raised within these frames, we must immerse ourselves in the details of the editing and ceremonial of Grand Sacrifice. Accordingly, the book is divided into three parts:

Part 1, "Ruling Boundaries," expands on the theoretical issues outlined above, introducing the Qianlong emperor's reign and my reasons for taking up the cultural historical study of monarchy. It sets forth the major terms and discourses germane to this study: *li, wen, xiao,* hierarchy, polarity, centering.

Part 2, "Text: Editing the Ritual Corpus," discusses editing as a site for the constitution of social and political power that would accrue to those who sought discursive control of *li.* The many handbooks on exactly how to perform *li* of all sorts are not philosophy or discussion about *li;* they are a text of a different order. They describe spaces, clothes, vessels, and the whole material apparatus of how ideas about *li* would take form. Intellectual historians who have examined classical scholarship in the Qing have not so far concentrated upon writing and editing themselves as part of a larger practice aimed at such discursive control. Instead they have employed a history-of-ideas approach, emphasizing the philosophical discourse of orthodox neo-Confucianism. By recontextualizing philosophy as a moment within editing practice, itself a part of ritual performance, I bracket received distinctions between politics, aesthetics, religion, and philosophy. I thus redirect attention from the role of bureaucratic rationality in the workings of the Qing state to the practice and the micropowers of ritualization.

Once the domain of philosophical speculation enlarges, the performing body reappears, wearing embroidered robes, chanting hymns, filling ceramic and wicker vessels, burning carcasses of sheep and oxen, entering and exiting temples gates, bowing at the foot of stairs. The emperor's *li* were simply the most splendid examples of *li* in general—they drew upon and, in turn, provided models for ritual events at other locations in society, especially ancestral veneration in clan halls or family homes. That similarity of form linked the imperial center with everyday life.

Part 3, "Performance: The Ritualizing Body Inscribes," delineates the ceremonial form of a Grand Sacrifice to Heaven in detail. Understanding what sorts of bodies were engaged in these ritualizing activities thus became crucial to a project that was first conceived as only "symbolic." Carried out through the material forms of language and gesture, practices of subjectification are intimately bound to carnality. As an exemplary set of rituals, the Grand Sacrifices featured the imperial body as a more general pattern available for emulation throughout the realm. I argue that arrangement of space and movement within it, recitation of hymns, and the deployment of objects all produced certain positions for the actors, especially showing how manipulation of high/low and inner/outer produced the emperor as the embodiment of yang power.

The imperium placed texts on its altars and endlessly transcribed the actions of the emperor. This mutual relationship between ritualized texts and textualized performances harnessed the more obvious artifice of writing to the less self-conscious realm of deeply learned and remembered bodily gesture. Paradoxically, the entire complex of Grand Sacrifice, a highly artificed practice, may also be thought of as a sophisticated imperial attempt to naturalize through ritualization, and thus reify, its own activities. That I *describe* processes of reification will not, I hope, be mistaken for reification itself on my part. My respect for the complexity, indeed beauty, of imperial ritual technology will not, I hope, be mistaken for either naive belief in its unmediated efficacy or for wholesale admiration of its more dubious, because successful, power.

PART 1

Ruling Boundaries

1

SIGNIFYING EMPERORSHIP

Of Portraits and Princes

The grandiose ambitions of the Qianlong emperor in the cultural sphere were embroiled with problems of authenticity and deception: centrally, in the Qianlong literary inquisition where scrupulous philological research was joined with political repression . . . and more obliquely in the transparently fraudulent claims of Qianlong imperial portraiture, where the emperor had himself portrayed in a universe of inflated roles ranging from paragon of bucolic simplicity to living Buddhist deity.   RICHARD VINOGRAD, *Boundaries of the Self*

In the many portraits that survive, the Qianlong emperor appears in various guises. Warrior, Buddhist deity, Taoist monk, writer, father, son, recluse, hunter, banquet host, beardless youth, future ancestor—he surfaces in attempts to be all things to all his many peoples. Hardly surprising for a monarch who "faced" in many directions to rule an enormous empire: northwest to the homeland of his once-nomadic Manchu ancestors; west to Mongolia and Tibet, Buddhist societies whose loyalty was never utterly certain; south to the huge population of China, conquered by the armies of his great-grandfather in the early seventeenth century.

Is it sufficient to relegate to the status of deceitful plot, as art historian Richard Vinograd does in the above quotation, this complex deployment of expressive technology, the brush, in its depiction of the imperial body? Significantly, Vinograd also refers to Qianlong's "literary inquisition," linking another use of the brush, this time as instrument of writing and editing, to the same imputed imperial conspiracy. In this regard he is hardly alone.[1] The eighteenth century has been excoriated by generations of Chinese, along with foreign scholars who have followed their lead, as decadent and repressive. The Qianlong emperor's patronage of the arts, and his sponsorship of many encyclopedic editing projects that were also occasions for surveillance of publishing, seems to have been particularly resented retrospectively by Han Chinese intelligentsia of the twentieth century. This reduction of culture to politics simplifies both terms, misrecognizing both the politics of culture and the culture of politics.

Underlying Vinograd's rather typical dismissal is a particular view of the relation between representation and its politics, one shared by most critics of the Qianlong era and indeed most sinological scholarship. The theory of "representation" as it has been bequeathed to the modern human sciences (and, I would argue, Euro-American common sense) assumes a prior "real" object to which language refers. The mainstream development of such a relationship between perception and world can be traced to various discourses of mimesis. Marxism's nineteenth-century intervention in this cozy relationship of "what you see is what you ought to get" politicized it as "ideology" but never challenged its fundamental epistemology. For early Marxists, "ideology" mystified that which was prior and constitutive of social life; the economic and social class base produced a cultural superstructure. In this view, cultural artifacts participate in the lie of masking power.

This quite mechanical view of the relationship of culture and ideological function has been under revision by later Marxists for most of the twentieth century.[2] Even more profoundly, however, the assumption that "representation" reflects a preexisting reality has been challenged by the notion of "signification." This innovation takes language and expressive, semiotic activity to be productive of the very "reality" in which human beings find themselves.[3] Along the same lines, Michel Foucault's theories of discourse seek to "substitute for the enigmatic treasure of 'things' anterior to discourse the regular formation of objects that emerge only in discourse" (Foucault 1972: 47). Foucault's later notion of power/knowledge considers cultural practices to be the very mode of becoming human that produce not lies that mystify power but truth effects that channel and enable the operations of power.[4]

The business of ruling never proceeds easily; it is a stuttering process that seeks always to define and control the sources of its power. As ruling formations, monarchies of the past share with modern-day governments by the "people" (be they democratic or socialist) the necessity to found themselves within a declared natural order of people and things. The more closely allied rulership and authority are perceived to be with everyday commonsense views of the ways things simply are, the more invisible their control becomes.[5] The events of politics in the narrow sense (the battles of court factions, the machinations of priests against the throne, parliamentary infighting over foreign policy, local elections) are but one visible measure of invisible discourses within which "politics" emerges as a possible object at all.[6]

It is this view of the political I wish to extend to the Qianlong reign, the longest in Chinese history. The emperor did not rule so long *despite* his extraordinary ego[7] but because the projects he patronized stamped his epoch with a certain tenor and organized visibly many aspects of the life of the imperium. Any of the many ways he invested his time (his Buddhist practice remains one of the most notoriously debated issues, argued to this day between Tibetan and Chinese nationalists) can be interpreted in narrow, utilitarian fashion as contributing to an "ideology" mystifying the "real" politics of rule, much as Vinograd dismisses imperial artistic, literary projects as subordinate to a "politics" of autocratic interest. But to do so would be to miss the point of the "invisible" ways that any monarchy organized itself in order to organize its realm; it would ignore the systematicity, patterns, conventions, and discursive advantages the monarchy enjoyed by virtue of its position.

Any ruling formation, including monarchy, becomes deeply invested in perfecting the formal means for producing naturalizing discourses. By "naturalizing discourses" I mean those that normalize the contingent into the typical along two axes: people's relation among themselves and with a larger horizon beyond which human agency cannot reach (call it Nature, Cosmos, Science, God, Dao, or the State). It is only within these categories of the declared "natural" or "real" that action is possible and conceptions of power and its legitimate use operate. The notion of "what is" dictates "what is possible." In other words, reifications that fix social life are utterly necessary to that life.[8] Just as it is the business of the ruling formation to seek control of the technologies for "fixing" life, so it is the business of critique to catch them in the act. It is not, however, our task to fantasize life without reification, when the state withers and language becomes finally transparent and all existence shines through as unmediated experience. Foucault's resolutely pessimistic concept of power/knowledge captures the sense that *what* we know, and *how* we come to know it, often dictates the possibilities for action. Control of such knowledge then, ipso facto, becomes part of the machinery for channeling power. Critique of such control points the way (hopefully) to a better way of channeling power, but not to power's end.

For Chinese of the eighteenth century, one of the local discourses that produced power/knowledge concerned *li* (usually translated as "propriety" or "ritual"). *Li* summarized the way of being human that was necessary to the cosmos, the principle by which the interpenetration of visible (*ming*) and invisible (*yu*) portions of that world was maintained. The concept of "hegemony," which, like power/knowledge, goes beyond "ideology," also helps to understand *li*.

What is decisive is not only the conscious system of ideas and beliefs, but the whole lived social process as practically organized by specific meanings and values. . . . [The hegemonic] thus constitutes a sense of reality for most people in the society, a sense of absolute because experienced reality beyond which it is very difficult for most members of the society to move.[9]

For the people living within the hegemonic of *li,* the appropriateness of feeling and perception, the coincidence of affective and cognitive fitness generated a ground of "normality" or "naturalness." The Manchu dynasty that ruled China for 267 years participated in the Chinese discourse upon *li,* laboring to make itself an absolute arbiter of this important formation. Through the patronage of its editors, the throne tried to position itself to mediate its texts and performances, and thus the sorts of subject positions possible in its universe of practice. Grand Sacrifice provided one site for the production of *li* that combined surveillance of the form of ceremony and the messages facilitated through bodily ritualization with the textual mediums through which *li* were transmitted.

Analyzing how the discourse of *li* produced the power of its ritualizing round presents us with a number of problems. We cannot simply fall back upon our repertoire of favorite human science reifications such as "society," "individual," "state," "representation," "culture," "nature," "body." Each of these concepts possesses a rich history of its own; each has come into being as a means of thinking within the history of post-Enlightenment, colonizing Europe. Each naturalizes the concerns of a particular history. The Chinese literati, the throne, and its imperium operated within different reifications altogether: concepts such as *li* itself, *wen* or "text-pattern," *xiao* or filiality; processes such as yin-yang polarity, hierarchy, *zhong* or centering. Grand Sacrifice as text/performance took these reifications, these discursive objects, for granted. Through an analysis of it, we can learn more about the throne's role in creating both expressive forms and the subjects who found themselves hailed within those forms. This creation entailed elements of both "inscription" and "incorporation," text and performance. It provides us with one strand in the genealogy of modern state-formation in China. As a means of introducing these basic categories, these productive re-ifications, and before turning to the text/performances of Grand Sacrifice, I would like to return to those "deceptive" portraits.

The Military Manchu: On *Wen* and *Wu*

Qianlong's portraits have long caught scholars' eyes: Historian Harold Kahn illustrated his classic *Monarchy in the Emperor's Eyes* with a number of them. Art historian Maxwell Hearn feels that the Manchus needed to assert their identity in multiple forms in order to rule effectively. Thus they were attentive to what Hearn calls "roles" or "paradigms" (1980: 108).

Indeed, reading the portraits "representationally" we might assume that they mediate between the emperor's self and a single role—one role at a time. Thus in figure 1 the emperor (fourth from the left) hunts in military armor. And in figure 2 he rides after a hare. In figure 3 he fills the center of a thanka-style painting as the Buddhist deity Manjusri; in figure 4 he attends a debate between two Tibetan lamas (he is in the upper right); in figure 5 he hosts a banquet; in figure 6 he plays with his children; and in figure 7 he serves his mother. In figure 8 he appears as a recluse, in 9 as a youth with an older companion. In figure 10, we see him among the accoutrements of a literatus.

A representational reading can make these depictions of Qianlong transpar-ent, allowing us to see right through his clothing, settings, and gestures to the role referent in the extratextual social world. Leaving aside theological issues such as the existence of Boddhisattvas to act as referents for Qianlong's arroga-tion of that role, we might rest content that a certain kind of multifaceted social "reality" was being mediated through imperial portraiture. Knowing what we know about the complexity of his task as king, we might be more forgiving than Vinograd about his arrogance and applaud the sophistication and the stamina of his imagination and that of his imperial court painters.

But if we look more closely at the portraits *as a set* that refers within itself and to other practices, a different and more complex reading emerges. As art historian James Cahill mentions, Chinese critics had, since the tenth century, constantly rejected "life-likeness and visual fidelity to nature" in favor of captur-ing the energy or spirit of things (1982: 8). Thus it is not obvious, even in the crudest sense of general painterly convention, that Qianlong's artists should have felt confined by visual fidelity to social "nature" and portrayed the emperor's actual behavior. As "fictions," however, they produced interesting truth effects: as a set, the portraits convey some profound insights into the eighteenth-century imagination of self and social formation.

I will first describe a distinction in the depiction of "hierarchy" between portraits that speak of Qianlong's Manchu-ness and those that produce him as Han Chinese. This will allow me to introduce the Manchu bid for hegemony over Mongol and Tibetan Buddhists, and over the Han. Then I will discuss how the portraits seemingly designed more specifically for Han Chinese consumption display the monarchy as encompassing the shifting subject positions of the polarities of superior and submissive. Hierarchy and polarity are important, if abstract, components of the discursive logic of *li* and figure strongly in Grand Sacrifice. Finally I will discuss forms of embodiment figured in portraiture as integral to understanding ritualization.

Images of Qianlong at the hunt contrast with the other portraits. By the eighteenth century, the Manchu hunt was cast as a necessary drill for soldiers gone soft from peacetime comfort. Such martial pictures show Qianlong among his men. In figure 2 little sets him off from them besides the color of his coat and the fact that he is shooting the hare. In Figure 1 he is recognizable only because of the detail of his face, and his horse. (He was pointed out to me by someone familiar with the painting.) Nothing in the arrangement of these paintings conveys his distinctiveness as Son of Heaven, a Chinese designation out of place in portraits that construct him as "Manchu."

By the eighteenth century, this very category of identity had come to be a vexatious problem for the throne. The following discussion will tack between the necessity of providing information for readers unfamiliar with Central Asian history, and recognition that this very material is often highly contested today within a genealogy of "information" shaped by the Manchu throne and especially the Qianlong emperor himself.

The Manchus were known as the Ruzhen tribes, descended from the same Tungusic stock as the founders of the Jin dynasty (1122–1234) that had threatened the Southern Song only to be conquered themselves in the end by the Mongols in the thirteenth century. As they assembled the elements of their kingly center of conquest during the late sixteenth and early seventeenth centuries, the Manchus incorporated the social usages of the peoples with whom they allied or whom they overcame by force. However, they began with an attitude toward social order different from the Chinese to the south. According to many

1. The Qianlong emperor whistling for deer. In the detail, he is the first rider. By Giuseppe Castiglione. Hanging scroll; color on silk; 223.4 cm × 426.2 cm. Palace Museum, Beijing. From *Qingdai gongting huihua*, 109.

2. The Qianlong emperor shooting a hare. From *Qingdai dihou xiang*. Courtesy of the C. V. Starr East Asian Library, Columbia University.

scholars, an association of relative equality among (the ruling) parts underlay many Manchu customs.[10] From the time of Nurhaci (1529–1626), the first emperor of the Manchu Qing conquest dynasty who began uniting the Ruzhen tribes, to his grandson Fulin (1638–1661), the first of his line to sit on the Han Chinese throne, the generally accepted narrative of "sinicization" describes how the Manchus moved from this notion of equal parts to a Chinese idea of hierarchy as encompassment of parts clearly ranked in importance.

Chinese, Manchu, and Mongol peoples shared the idea of a heaven-designated king, but their notions of heaven differed. For Manchus and Mongols, heaven canopied many domains, all equivalent. Furthermore, the same designation referred to the parts of the domain and to the domain itself. The whole was merely and literally the sum of its parts; it did not encompass and transcend them. Following the same logic, the word *han* in Manchu and *qan* in Mongol denoted simultaneously the emperor of the Mongol empire and the heads of the great appanages into which that empire was divided (Farquhar 1968: 200–201).

For the Chinese, heavenly singularity contrasted with earthly diversity in a relation of encompassment and subordination that ranked domains and their people in an order of importance. Andrew March calls this "Confucian geography's central myth" (1974: 15). Earth was subordinate to heaven as a whole, but its parts were different. The significance of this "myth" for social life was dual: on the one hand, all humans shared the same "heavenly" nature (they could be governed by the same set of principles) and the representative of Heaven, its Son, was the best bearer of this summary of all good for humankind. He was not one king among many but the supreme emperor of all. On the other hand, the Chinese earthly system was a hierarchy in another sense: a principle by which the elements of the whole are ranked in relation to the whole. Doing full justice to the implications of this fundamental difference in the way the two groups imagined whole/part relations would require a pair of full-scale ethnographies, not my purpose here. Since the rest of this book will attempt to explicate Chinese notions of hierarchical order in the eighteenth century through an analysis of Grand Sacrifice, I will leave the Chinese vision until later and turn first to a short version of the Manchus'.

As the Manchus conquered the East Asian continent, the elaboration of their own domain's ritual paralleled the destruction of their neighbors' domains. While waging wars at the periphery of their expanding territory, battles that continued through the Qianlong reign (1736–1796), they defined and redefined their center.[11] In so doing, the Manchu provide us with one of the best examples of the abstract "dynastic realm" as Benedict Anderson terms it:

Kingship organizes everything around a high center. Its legitimacy derives from divinity, not from populations, who, after all, are subjects, not citizens. In the modern conception, state sovereignty is fully, flatly, evenly operative over each square centimeter of a legally demarcated territory. But in the older imagining, where states are defined *by centers,* borders were *porous and indistinct,* and sovereignties faded imperceptibly into one another. (Emphasis mine.)[12]

The interrelated process of empire building described by Anderson calls to mind the traditional Chinese terms *wen* and *wu.* As a *wu* or military monarch, the Qianlong emperor was never content to limit his sovereignty, but campaigned the span of his reign not so much to sharpen his borders as to extend the umbrella of his rule so that all the known world faded in its shade. By the end of his 60-year reign, 160 years since Fulin, the Shunzhi emperor, had passed through the Great Wall, the Qianlong emperor presided over an Asian empire larger than any ever headed by a Han Chinese (larger than either the Han or the Tang dynasties) and second only to the Mongol domain of the thirteenth century.

In tandem with military or *wu* conquest, the Manchus as lords sought to "organize everything around a high center," to borrow Anderson's phrase. If their goal was the creation of a hierarchy of domains with themselves as supreme overlords, then the incorporation of the social and ritual forms of others can be read as attempts to incorporate the modes for organizing and producing those societies themselves (Hevia 1989). Such would be the *wen* aspect, the "civilizational" facet of rule. Manchu relationship with Mongol clans as it was mediated through the banner system[13] and Buddhism provided practices to create a new hierarchy of dominance that would eventually incorporate both Mongols and Tibetans.[14]

The Manchus' kingly titles provide a précis of the stages of their hierarchizing ambition. As Nurgaci united the Ruzhen tribes in Liaodong, he was known in Manchu as the *sure beile* or "Wise Prince." The implication: maybe the best prince but a prince among many. He accepted the title *Kundulun Qan* in 1607 from his Mongol Five Qalqal allies.[15] In 1616 he declared himself the Heavenly Designated King (*Tianming han*) of the Later Jin, signaling that he was an open contender for universal king (Farquhar 1968: 201; *ECCP* 597). Thus, by 1616 Nurgaci had progressed from unifier of the Ruzhen to envisioning a conquest of Asia in the image of the Mongol Khanate. It remained, however, for his son Hung Taiji (r. 1626–1643), with the surrender and marrying in of the son of Ligdan Khan of the Mongolian Chahars, to capture the great seal of the Mongol Khanate (Wakeman 1985: 203).[16] Staking such a claim to succeed Ghenghis Khan allowed Hung Taiji to bid symbolically for the Chinese emperorship by declaring himself the Son of Heaven in 1636 and proclaiming an altogether new dynasty, the Qing.

Nurhaci may have declared himself the Han of Qans, clearly signaling danger to the Chinese of the south. Nevertheless, he operated within a Manchu-Mongol idea of social polity until he died. How was this polity imagined and how did it differ from the Chinese model to which his son Hung Taiji turned with such ferocious energy? The influence upon decision-making exerted by the shift to Chinese-style organization provides a directly relevant example:

Nurgaci had shared power with some other members of the Aisin Goro clan: four senior banner chiefs rotated as administrative assistants. He envisioned a "collegial" rule after his death with all the banner princes having an equal voice in policy.[17] With his death in 1626, however, Chinese influence became more marked.[18] As elected leader, in Kessler's words the "first among equals" envisioned by his father, Hung Taiji swore an oath together with other princes to carry forward Nurhaci's plans. But within ten years, he had moved toward unitary imperial rule.[19]

A good illustration of the contrast between a Chinese notion of hierarchy and the "collegial" society of central Asia is provided in the Chinese saying "A city equal to the domain is the root of disorder" (Kessler 1971: 10; Roth Li 1975: 132). Another example of the "encompass and rule" of Chinese hierarchical thinking, it was used by Chinese advisers counseling Hung Taiji on modifying clan rule. Toward that end, "Imperial clan leaders were brought into a state council and subordinated to it" (Fairbank 1970: 215).[20] Hung Taiji disgraced the senior princes on pretexts, finally deciding in 1632, with the advice of Chinese aides, that they could no longer sit beside him facing south in the traditional Chinese kingly manner, but had to sit below. (Kessler 1971: 10; *ECCP* 562–63; *Qingchao wenxian tongkao* chap. 125, "Wangli" 2; Roth Li 1975: 125).[21] Furthermore, in 1631 Six Boards modeled on the Chinese Ming dynasty's Six Ministries were established. They were initially supervised by *beile* princes, but probably by 1636 the *beile* were discharged and the boards controlled by executive officers and censors, a mixture of Han, Manchu, and Mongol appointees (Wakeman 1985: 167–68). The question of the sharing of power remained a vexing one for the throne even much later. When we encounter it again below as one of the chief paradoxes displayed by Grand Sacrifice, in the parts rewritten for emperor and district magistrate, the parallels to the problem of the princes should be clear.

By the eighteenth century, the *wu* or martial aspect of Manchu identity (as hunter and soldier) emerged as a problem. Efforts were made under Qianlong to shore it up in the face of slacking.[22] Only further research would show if, and how closely, the signification of this *wu,* or martial, identity was intertwined with an idea of relative equality among parts, like the old Manchu confraternity of princes. One is tempted, looking at the emperor in the first two portraits, to answer affirmatively, yet we might be dealing less with a description of an accomplished eighteenth-century Manchu identity than with a signification that seeks to accomplish that identifying link with a "traditional" past.[23]

The throne's relations with its Mongolian and Tibetan subjects proceeded in the idiom of Buddhist practice. Figure 3 shows the emperor as the Bodhisattva Manjusri, or Wisdom, a designation that he received from both Tibetan and Mongol sources (*DCJMBP* 320–22 and passim; Farquhar 1968). Insofar as Buddhist practice was also an element of Manchu-ness, we note that in figure 4, Qianlong sits at the left hand, the eastern position of most honored "guest" among the other "guests" who are attending a debate before a Buddhist altar. Instead of putting himself in the position of centered host, in Han Chinese style, he is among the others, higher in prestige but nonetheless appearing in that Manchu-style company described above. Certainly this image presented a rhetoric of togetherness in the dharma (the Buddhist teaching) visible to any who would like to read it that way. That the Han Chinese literati were notoriously unwilling to do so was not the emperor's problem. He had other attitudes to model for them.

Portraiture of the emperor for Han consumption depicted him in *wen* mode, the constructor of the kingly center rather than the destroyer of borders through their expansion. *Wen* is usually taken to mean "writing" or "literature." More literally and precisely it is text-pattern, signs of cosmic order accessible to those who can discern them.[24] Certainly the Manchus actively sought to mobilize the resources of *wen* in founding their kingdom through techniques that included writing and editing, building, and the ritualizations of *li.* It is the emperor in *wen* mode that concerns this study.

With the exception of Qianlong as the Bodhisattva Manjusri, the remaining portraits included here were produced within and aimed at consolidating the

3. The Qianlong emperor as the bodhisattva of wisdom, Manjusri. From *Zijin cheng dihou shenghuo*, 117.

4. The Qianlong emperor, upper right, receiving Wobaxi, head of the Tuerkute tribe of the Mongols in the Wanfa Guyi Hall in Chengde. Screen painting; color on silk; 164.5 cm × 114.5 cm. Palace Museum, Beijing. From *Qingdai gongting huihua*, 234.

Han cultural imaginary. They portray the emperor as a man of *wen,* and the hierarchy they model differs from that constructed in terms of his self-as-Manchu.

Banqueting and Hosting: Hierarchy in the Han Mode

The emperor of China occupied the center of a web of rituals designed to establish and maintain the social realm. The imperial ritual schedule had varied in each dynasty in its details, but never in the seriousness or opulence with which it was fulfilled.[25] In eighteenth-century China, the Qianlong emperor performed the yearly cycle of Grand Sacrifice as well as other, less spectacular rituals such as planting the first seed. His filial obligations included observing ancestral death anniversaries with smaller versions of Grand Sacrifices, visiting his mother daily, as well as arranging the enormously expensive and complex southern tours for her delight (Kahn 1967; Gao Jin 1771). His hunting expeditions to the Summer Palaces to the north of the Forbidden City were likewise carried out with much pomp in a prescribed fashion. He held audience each day, and gave periodic feasts to celebrate the New Year, the success of military campaigns or the acceptance of gifts from emissaries of peripheral domains. The emperor also presided over examinations of officials and was the center of a number of prescribed rites for the presentation and exchange of written texts. His reign name was on the coin of the realm, and social time itself was calculated within its parameters as such-and-such day, month, year of the Qianlong reign. His city was an intricate cosmic center reproduced in miniature in district magistrate's headquarters in every corner of the realm.

In figure 5 the emperor hosts a banquet. Such occasions often accompanied the audience ceremonies that the throne held for visiting dignitaries. These rites were prescribed in the *Comprehensive Rites of the Great Qing* (or *Da Qing tongli* 1756). This handbook (our main formal source on Grand Sacrifice) on how to do rituals at court was commissioned by the Qianlong emperor in 1736, the first year of his reign, and completed by his ritual editors in 1756. Hosting and the uses of foods figure in all five sections.[26]

Feeding the Forbidden City was complex and expensive—the cost for 1757 has been estimated at 9,540 ounces of silver. The court was away from Beijing for a portion of that or any year (Wang Shuqing 1983: 58). The emperor's table, a matter of great concern, was overseen by the Bureau of the Imperial House-

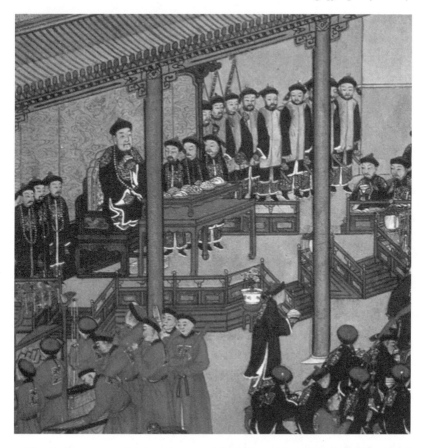

5. The Qianlong emperor hosting a banquet—he's the largest figure behind the pillar. Detail of the painting *Banquet at the Ziguang Pavilion*. Palace Museum, Beijing. From *Zijin cheng dihou shenghuo,* 62.

hold's (*Neiwufu*) Imperial Tea and Meal Office (*Yucha shanfang*). Qianlong ate breakfast between 6 and 7 A.M. and dinner between noon and 2 P.M. He seems to have snacked rather lightly in the evenings (Wang Shuqing 1983: 60; Li 1988: 83). He always ate "alone," that is, at his own small table, as was the custom for everyone who dined at court.

As with so many matters, he seems to have been the occasion for a whole panoply of activities that far exceeded the task at hand, in this case, feeding just one human being. For example, after each meal the Imperial Tea and Meal Office recorded for the archive what was eaten, the setting and style of tableware and cloths, what special requests the emperor made, even the cook's name

(Li 1988: 83). Thus thousands of menus are preserved, such as this breakfast recorded for an autumn morning in 1779 at *Bishu shanguang,* the northernmost summer palace outside the Wall:

On the table we find a bird's nest soup containing pork and duck; sauteed chicken with soft bean curd; a stew of duck, dogmeat and pork; bamboo shoots; Fu Lu'an served a bird's nest soup with chicken and noodles; various minced meats; deep-fried duck with meat; quickfried pork; quick-sauteed chicken eggs; sauteed chicken feet; *Xian* pork; "oil cakes"; chicken dumplings; diced lamb scalded with sesame seeds; and fruit congee (the latter two untouched).

On another table: Fourteen dishes of bobo cakes—filled with the eight delicacies; four dishes of yellow greens; three dishes of *naizi* milk curds. On a third table some baked goods; and on a fourth table eight plates of meats. (Li 1988: 82)

This appears to be a modest imperial breakfast. Sometimes imperial menus featured more than ninety dishes (Wang Shuqing 1983: 61). It was recorded in 1779 that the Qianlong emperor, who liked poultry, went through 140 ducks and chickens in one month (Li 1988: 84). How could he have eaten all this food and lived?

He didn't eat it all himself. Our breakfast record goes on to report that the emperor sent five dishes to named concubines (Li 1988: 83). In fact, "leftovers" from the emperor and the empress were sent, according to a prescribed form, to concubines, princes, princesses, high officials, and occasionally visiting dignitaries, and record was made of these bestowals.[27] Apparently the emperor "touched" the food and then passed it on to his court. In other words, the food was first assembled as a whole, presided over by the emperor, and only then divided out among the other eaters.

In Grand Sacrifices, and indeed in any commoner ancestral sacrifice (which in form was a miniature of Grand Sacrifice), the food was first assembled as a meal and offered to the spirits. After they descended and "inspired" their meal, the human participants parceled out the food among themselves, preserving a strict order of precedence for how much and what sort of food people would get. The "Jitong" chapter of the *Record of Rites* discusses the point of this

way of disposing of the leftovers whose every change is marked by increasing numbers of people eating them. Thus the distinction between noble and mean was marked, and a simulacrum of the graces dispensed by the sovereign was manifested. Through the four vessels of millet, we see an imitation of the centering in the temple, a temple that itself provides a simulacrum for all within our borders. (*LJZY* 49/2:1604; Legge 1885: 2:243)

This theorization of hierarchy as a whole containing many, unequally valued but equally necessary parts, featured the emperor. In both cases, Grand Sacrifice and a banquet, the emperor acted as *zhuren*—translated as either sacrificer or host. (Should we perhaps say sacrificial host?) In each case he presided over the creation of a whole made of many distinctive parts. Without him as its center it could not come into being. Those people who accepted food from his table literally took in parts of this whole and thus signaled their embodied position in this hierarchy of encompassed parts.

To clarify how this "hierarchy" works, we might contrast it to a ritual meal more familiar: the Roman Catholic Mass. Although a clear distinction is established between priest and congregation, each member eats a small white host, a bit of unleavened bread, believed to be the body of Christ. These hosts, unlike the Sacred (mutton, beef, or pork) Flesh and other foods of Grand Sacrifice, or the many and varied dishes from the emperor's table, are all exactly alike. In Eucharistic theology, those who ingest them embody positions of precise spiritual equality vis-à-vis the body of Christ, whose agents of incorporation they have become. The Catholic Mass was designed to eliminate distinction and to create not a human hierarchy but the possibility of embodiment of direct relation with godhead in each person, regardless of his or her social or physical differences from others.[28]

The emperor's sacrifices and meals, as well as his more formal hosting occasions, were quite different. These occasions produce "encompassed hierarchies," a term I borrowed from the sociologist of India, Louis Dumont, in my earlier writing on ritual (Zito 1984, 1987). Hierarchy for Dumont does not mean a series of mutually exclusive statuses but a whole that contains its parts while exceeding them in importance as their sum total and organizing ground (Dumont 1980: 239–45).

In the case of a Qing emperor, he did not literally embody the hierarchy but cast himself as the most important facilitator for bringing it into being. A sacrificial host mediated, or centered (Chinese term *zhong*), the ritual around himself, positioning other spirits, people, and things so as to include them in a whole that embodied simultaneously his own power and their relative importance vis-à-vis that power. What interests us here about this mode of social engagement is how it acts not to overcome Others by force but to include them in its own projects of rulership. Other peoples in this world, the invisible world of spirits, were openly admitted as being absolutely necessary to the king's rule—they constituted it in a relation of yang-yin logic, where yang not only complemented yin but contained it as a necessary part of itself.

Polarity and Position in Social Life

In his portraits, Qianlong himself models enough of these yang-yin positions to make the important point that he is not exempt from their necessity: Although as banquet host in figure 5 he is yang, as a guest among guests before the Buddha in figure 4, he is yin-positioned to the Buddha's yang.

Yang-yin was a form of logic that classified and related things, relationships and processes as encompassing asymmetries. This logic posited the world as operating in terms not of equally poised, binarized, harmoniously balanced "dualities" (the current modern cliché about yin-yang) but rather as complementary polarities.[29] *Zhong* as "centering" was the management of hierarchically ordered, encompassed sets of asymmetries such as Grand Sacrifices.

In ritual usage, the word *zhong* (center) does not mean "inside" (that is *nei*, whose antonym is *wai*, "outside"; *zhong* has no proper opposite term). As a noun it means "middle," but an empty one, found between the inner and outer, where the upper and lower meet and where there is no movement in the four directions. As a verb, *zhong* means to hit the center. "Centering" thus constantly creates itself through the correct separation of upper and lower, the correct bounding of inner and outer. Conceived of in this manner, it is the mediate third that makes meaningful difference possible. When people "make the triad with Heaven and Earth" they *zhong,* providing meaningful connection between these two constantly related forces.[30]

The double meaning of *zhong* as nominative and verbal perfectly indicates an act captured by a topographical metaphor, space constantly created and indicated through process. Humans are the beings who *zhong* most excellently because within themselves they ideally "follow the mean." This process has been discussed primarily in philosophical and ethical terms; its cosmic-ritual significance has been little explored.[31] As we will see, one of the things that *li,* and especially sacrifice, accomplished through their enactment was to *zhong* through complex relations of encompassment that organized cosmic bipolarities. I also use *zhong* here to indicate the activity of interfacing between written and performed orders of signification, the texts and performances of *li.*

In social relations, the yang position of power and authority never reigned exclusively in isolation but required its Other in a yin position to complete its initiatives: the Five Bonds in Chinese social life—father/son, ruler/minister, husband/wife, elder/younger siblings, friend/friend—provide the framework for this shifting hierarchy. In the "Jitong" chapter of the *Record of Rites,* the Five Bonds are subsumed within an even larger system of polarity:

Sacrifice comprises Ten Bonds: One can see the service to spirits, the appropriate signi-fication between Lord and Minister, the bond of father and son, the degrees between noble and mean, the distance between close and far relatives, the bestowal of reward and rank, the distinction between husband and wife, measure in governing the realm, precedence between older and younger, and the boundaries of high and low.

Here we see the social bonds embedded in a continuum between spirits and governance that finally makes explicit the topography obtaining as a boundary between high and low, a yang-yin polarity.

In figure 6 the emperor images yang fatherhood and husbandhood, seated in the center of the veranda of a house, his children cavorting around him, two women (wives?) behind. This picture provides an especially nice example of the nesting effect of polarity: the masculine yang Qianlong is, in fact, visiting the yin women's quarters; they contain him, functioning in this instance as yang.

In contrast to his image as father, in figure 7 the emperor offers a goblet of wine to his mother: she is seated within the building, in the yang-host position while he walks below her, in the yin-submissive position of son. The occasion was her birthday; Qianlong was particularly assiduous in the public performance of his filiality, or *xiao.*

In figure 8 the emperor sits in the open air at a low table, displayed on a hillside before a pavilion. He is completely alone in a setting of mountains and water (the Chinese for landscape is *shanshui,* "mountain/water"), except for a nearly invisible, tiny attendant out of his sight at the foot of the hill. The painting typically thematizes the reclusive enjoyment of wild scenery. In doing so, it points to another mode of polarity: the neo-Confucian notion that humanity exists within a larger cosmos (portrayed as "nature") as a necessary but hierar-chically encompassed portion. In this case, the mountain cosmos contains the emperor, positioning him as yin. Again, however, the pivoting tendencies of polarity are displayed. While Qianlong may be yin to the greater cosmic yang, he is simultaneously yang to his diminutive (and lower) attendant.

Finally, one last ambiguous and fascinating example of this sort of polarity. Figure 9 depicts Qianlong as a young man (on the right) with an older com-panion. Once again, the emperor embodies for the painter the yin position of

6. The Qianlong emperor with his family during Spring Festival. Hanging scroll; color on silk; 277.7 cm × 160.2 cm. From *Qingdai gongting huihua*, 119.

7. The Qianlong emperor serving his mother on her birthday. Detail of the painting *The Empress Dowager's Birthday.* Palace Musuem, Beijing. From *Qingdai gongting shenghuo,* Taibei: Nantian Shuju.

"younger" to a yang elder. Harold Kahn says the old man may represent a projection of the emperor's older self, although a recent catalogue entry on the portrait makes no mention of this interpretation (Kahn 1971: 77; Rogers and Lee 1988: 182). Palace Museum curator Zhu Jiajin identifies the older man as the Yongzheng emperor, Qianlong's father (1988: 80). The inscription in the em-

8. The Qianlong emperor "passing the summer day in pine tree shade." By Dong Bangda. Hanging scroll; ink on paper; 194.3 cm × 157.7 cm. Palace Museum, Beijing. From *Qingdai gongting huihua*, 162.

peror's own hand identifies the artist as the European Giuseppe Castiglione (1688–1766), a Jesuit court painter, saying: "In portraiture Shi-ning (Castiglione) is masterful; he painted me during my younger days. The white-headed one who enters the room today does not recognize who this is" (Rogers and Lee 1988: 182).

These various interpretations are rich. If the emperor was depicted as both

高真世等擁續我少
年時入室臨池者不
知此是誰
壬寅暮春御筆

9. The Qianlong emperor as a youth with a companion. Attributed to Giuseppe Castiglione and entitled "Happy Spring Tidings." Hanging scroll; color on silk; 68.8 cm × 40.6 cm. Palace Museum, Beijing. From *Gongting huihua,* 103.

yang/elder and yin/younger in a sort of two-dimensional time warp, it restates the point made by figures 6 and 8: subjectivities could pivot between yin and yang moments. Or, alternatively, if the older man is Yongzheng, we can still note that the inscription inserts Qianlong as a "white-headed one" in the same frame as his young self. In this case, the writing emperor manifests as older than his own father, taking the role of both son and grandfather. The grandfather-father-son triad is important in sacrifice and will be discussed in detail below. If indeed only the younger man renders the emperor, then the portrait nonetheless shows that it did not impinge upon the imperial dignity to be depicted in the position of submissive, yin completer.

We might suspect that the imperial point was in fact to encompass all possible positions in the five bonds, to provide the ground upon which all subjectivity was figured, made visible, and *included*. His many surviving portraits present this monarchical view of social reality quite straightforwardly. But this "wish" of the throne was only possible in a social formation that proposed, upheld, and ritualized through *li* the Five Bonds in the first place.

Significant Boundaries

Figure 10 is famous—the emperor sits on a low divan, backed by a freestanding screen upon which a landscape is painted (figure 10). Another portrait of himself hangs upon and partially covers this bit of framed nature. The emperor on the divan and the emperor in the hanging portrait face each other. Both are encompassed by the effect of the inscription in Qianlong's hand, whose first line titles the picture, "Is It One or Two?" The emperor signs himself "Cave of Narayana," a three-faced Buddhist deity, and so draws attention to the writing self that faces this painting of himself posed before his own portrait. It is an arresting image, one well-suited to focus further investigation of signification and subjectivity in eighteenth-century China.[32]

The portrait presents a form of imperial embodiment that epitomized the (usually male) literatus who combined in one person the privileges of both inscription (the creation of signification) and incorporation (distinctive forms of body discipline). I have called it the "body of yang power." Certainly it was not the only form of incarnate practice in the eighteenth century—there must have been other resistant and alternative modes of subjectification. But its tremendous power to incite emulation bears witness to its compelling ideological strength.

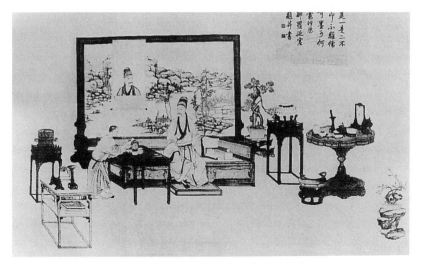

10. "Is It One or Two?" From *Qingdai dihou xiang.* Courtesy of the C. V. Starr East Asian Library, Columbia University.

Successful intervention in cosmic process, or correct *li,* depended upon the peculiarly human ability to provide the site for the emergence of ordered pattern from chaos. Discourses on painting, medicine, and ritual that had originated in the Han still converged in emphasizing the site of this emergent pattern, which was then accessible as various forms of knowledge through an ever-shifting boundary or surface. These "sites" formed boundaries that produced both the subject/body as source of signification and the texts which constructed that subject and provided it with historicity. This "body in between" resonated perfectly in an era obsessed with anxiety about boundary breakdown brought about by social and economic shifts.

From the late sixteenth century, the Chinese economy expanded, buoyed by importation of Japanese and Mexican silver until the 1630s, when Spain and Japan restricted trade.[33] But the resulting deflation, while probably a factor in late Ming crisis, interrupted neither China's long-term involvement in the world economy nor her domestic economic trends (Rawski 1985: 4; Wakeman 1986: 19 note 76). Those trends were characterized by the commercialization of agriculture and concomitant development of markets in three macro-regions of China: North China, along the Grand Canal, the Lower Yangzi and the Southeast Coast (Rawski 1984: 5).[34] An increasing monetization of the economy was reflected both in government policies (from tax reform, which commuted levies in kind into silver, to subcontracting for supplies previously supplied through corvee labor) and in local growth in cash-cropping, rural and urban handicraft production, wage labor, and absentee landlordism (Rawski 1985: 5–7). Thus, the rise of a money economy was accompanied by changes in social relations among villagers, between villagers and townspeople, and between local elites and the imperium. Such developments in the economies of exchange have been linked to a profound sense of fragmentation and competition in society.[35] At the least, the new economy set the scene for the emergence of a "fluid and flexible status system, largely free of effective legal barriers to status mobility," while at the same time encouraging a proliferation of ever-finer categories of social distinction (Rawski 1985: 8). New practices of exchange and status were, in turn, mediated by new intellectual and religious practices. The late Ming concern with accounting and calculability, even in morality, has been seen as a sign of the breakdown of traditional hierarchy in the face of market-oriented models for human interaction.[36]

From late Ming to mid-Qing, an era of profound social change manifested itself as boundary anxiety through class competition, gender negotiation, and ethnic suspicion. The "soul-stealing" crisis of 1768, when the throne hunted down people accused of sorcery, provides rich evidence of these fears. In his elegant analysis, Kuhn draws attention to the social attitudes that accompanied the economic expansion, the "long slow inflation" that resulted in "flourishing investment" and better tax retrieval (1990: 32). As "free labor" went up for sale in a buyer's market, there was often a "scant margin of survival in a competitive and crowded society" (35–36). Constant movement resulted in breakdown of traditional community ties such as the Five Bonds celebrated by the emperor's portraits, and a population of "migrants, sojourners, merchants and mountebanks, monks and pilgrims, cutpurses and beggars" (41). We might add that the very thing the circulation of money had made possible, relations of exchange with strangers, became a source of social aggravation. Such out-of-place people were the ones most often suspected of sorcery (41).

Gender relations afforded another arena in which the fierce competition for status and wealth, and their attendant anxieties, could be articulated. As Susan Mann remarks succinctly of new discussions on marriage and dowry in the eighteenth century: "Anxieties about blurred boundaries of all kinds—including between 'respectable' (*liang*) and 'polluted' (*jian*) women—informed the conversations" (1991: 206). Widow chastity and suicide, which grew in popularity during the seventeenth and eighteenth centuries, provide perhaps the most poignant and dramatic example. The virtue of women's bodies was policed and protected as the visible badge of honor for their families and communities

(Mann 1987). Footbinding also increased steadily in popularity during this period. Its literal binding effects upon mobility, ideally confining women to the inner chambers of the home, were burst by its value as class boundary marker. So powerful was the status conferred by bound feet upon prospective brides that by the nineteenth century the practice had seeped much beyond the literate elite (Gao 1995: 30–38).

The throne continued to feel uneasy before that elite. Kuhn notes that, in prosecuting soul-stealing cases, Qianlong reacted to the twin evils of sedition (by the Han) and assimilation (by the Manchus). In other words, the throne suffered an apprehension of boundary failure between Manchu and Han. The notorious book-burnings that accompanied the editing projects sponsored under Qianlong were likewise motivated by fear of disloyal glorification of the former native dynasty and anger at snide comments by Chinese writers about non-Han "barbarians" (Woodside 1990: 160; Goodrich 1966).

As Mary Douglas (1966) pointed out long ago, no form of human embodiment can be considered apart from the social body that produces it and for which it often stands as a symbol. To restate: the social and personal bodies stand in relations of mutual productivity. The body often stands as symbol for society; however, it also acts as the site upon which social relations reproduce and transform through the body's gestures and memories.

An era of boundary anxiety such as existed in eighteenth-century China would very likely produce a style of embodiment that highlighted boundary making and breaking, investing it with a quality of naturalness and inevitability. Just so, we will see how the imperial body was constructed within Grand Sacrifice as a mobile mediator and boundary controller. To introduce this body of surfaces, we return to figure 10.

"Is It One or Two?"

The portrait "Is It One or Two?" differs in important ways from a post-Renaissance European realist portrait, a self objectified and re-presented. It has little in common with that modern consciousness of the self as interior, separate from a world constituted as exterior and objective. The emperor did not paint it, yet he participated in its production by the supplement of his calligraphy. Thus we have a writing self, a self posed and a self portrayed; the memorialization of the appreciation of a representation. The work is perfectly emblematic of a century when scholars were scrutinizing older epistemological traditions in order to question past forms of representation.

Portraiture in general enjoyed a revival in the seventeenth century after an eclipse by landscape that James Cahill connects to the Song preoccupation with patterns underlying all cosmic phenomena. Song artists thought these patterns were best expressed through extrahuman motifs of landscape (Cahill 1982: 106). By the eighteenth century, the few profound studies of faces that rely upon its physical expression to convey the inner being of the subject were influenced by visiting European painters such as Castiglione. The sense they convey of a body/person isolated in empty space only highlights the difference of portraiture within the social formation we are examining here.

As Steven Goldberg has shown, since the pre-Han period, Chinese painters portrayed human beings within specific *topoi* that provided them with an identity. This identity, however, is a shifting, contextual phenomenon, denoting a relative point of convergence among culturally and historically specific sets of determinant relations (Goldberg n.d.: 9). Goldberg discusses the contextual *topoi* of gardens, palaces, hermitages, and trees and rocks beside rivers. Thus, instead of the portrayed body bearing the burden of representation of singular identity, it is the relationship of a figure to its context that constructs the body as something occurring between them. The figure is often surrounded by objects that suggest an inner life (Cahill 1982: 115).[37] Qianlong sits among the accoutrements of an artist and man of letters, a *wenren:* painting and screen, scrolls and albums, brushes and inkstone. In an amusing reversal of the usual portrait convention of the person sitting beneath a tree, we see trees beneath the man; miniaturized pine and prunus indicate Qianlong's love of microcosmic reproduction.[38]

In other words, the things pictured in a portrait of this sort signal inward traits, brought to visibility and displayed upon the surface of the painting. The interior of the emperor's self is not a space marked off sharply from an exterior, a private sanctum for secret thoughts appropriate to that space. It is instead the origin for readable, external signs. In this portrait, those signs may be personal and not particularly important. However, in ritual, the king's body becomes both source and site of cosmically key representations.[39] This way of depicting the relations of the interior and exterior body in painting resonates with the constructed body of traditional medicine in China.

The body in traditional medical practice was (and is) thought of as a complex network of patterns of matter/energy known as *qi*. This network is an organization of all the observable manifestations of the body into an integrated set of functions and relationships (Kaptchuk 1983: 52; Porkert 1974: 25–37). Boundaries between interior and exterior are conceived dynamically as the interface where the two meet, and this changes according to point of view or function. For instance, the whole system of acupuncture meridians depends on patterns of energy deep in the body's interior being palpable on its surface.[40] These points happen to coincide with the skin. In contrast, there is a kind of *qi* called *feng* that circulates between the microcosmic body and the macrocosm, providing an interface beyond the barrier of the skin (Hay 1983b: 92). What I wish to emphasize is that the interface of interior and exterior, the surface formed as the site of their interaction, is also the privileged site of signification in the overlapping discourses of art, medicine, and ritual.

These three discourses had their founding moments in the Han period (200 B.C.E. to C.E. 200) with the rise of yin-yang theory and correlative thought. At that time, the natural and human world was conceived systematically as a vast plane of resonating sets of perceptible correlations by cosmic thinkers like Dong Zhongshu (179?–93 B.C.E.). During the complex performance of Grand Sacrifice, it could be said that the eyes of participants saw the intricately decorated clothing and the colors and patterns of vessels; that their mouths ate and their tongues tasted the cooked meat and wine; that their noses smelled incense and their ears heard music. But according to the logic of correlation and resonance, it was just as reasonable to say that the eye called forth beautiful pattern, the mouth good food, the tongue proper taste, the nose correct smells, and the ear perfect music. The portraiture convention that turned the emperor inside out through the objects arrayed beside him provides an eighteenth-century example of the "planar": a surface-oriented signification that assumes no fixed boundaries between the internal self and the external world. Instead, self and world are contextualized in a web of interconnection, leading to a fascination with texture and text.

The dynamic and relative relationship between inner and outer is also portrayed through the two portraits themselves. They are a temporal series; in his mind's eye, is not the first, hanging portrait furthest from the emperor? Yet, as we look at the painting and imagine the emperor inscribing it, paradoxically it is the hanging portrait that is most encompassed. In this case, the innermost portrait exists as a portion of the whole, not just as its complement but rather its microcosm. It contains the exterior as the exterior encompasses it. (It is a portrait, after all, of the man holding its "frame" painting.) More important, the first painting was a necessary element in the design of the second painting. As a metaphor for interiority, it does not assert itself against the world but participates in its creation.

Another important portrait convention we notice is the invisibility of the corporeal body behind folds of clothing. While Chinese painters chose not to display the body's flesh in painted form, they leave constant traces of their own body's effort in the brushstrokes that animate the silk.[41] John Hay has persuasively argued that the aesthetic vocabulary that anthropomorphizes calligraphy into possessing bones, flesh, sinew, blood, vein, and breath derives from traditional medicine (1983b: 78). These usages are not only metaphorical since calligraphy is, in Hay's words, "A line of energy materializing through the brush into the ink trace" (88). In fact, it is a vein *mo* of ink that pulses in the rhythm of the painter's own arteries (also *mo*), an extension of the painter's real body. The emperor's calligraphy transforms into a metonymy (a relation of contiguity) the metaphors of similitude that are the two portraits by connecting them to his fleshly body. The calligraphy calls attention to the heart/mind—the embodied consciousness—that has produced the painting. This performative aspect of calligraphy provides interesting insights into ritual.

In his calligraphic entitlement, the emperor names himself, but does not describe himself. His writing is fundamentally an act, not a portrayal, and this distinction would stand even if we were dealing with an actual self-portrait by his own brush. But can we so easily separate calligraphic "act" and painterly "representation"? It is just this performative quality of the Chinese notion of the written word that led me to propose that ritual, especially Grand Sacrifice, be thought of as text/performance, communicative activity as a continuum composed of objects, writing, gestures, and oral presentation (Zito 1989; 1994).

A question also suggests itself: which heart/mind is indicated, the emperor's own or the original painters'? It seems that those poor men have had the honor of elision in service of the imperial ego. Now this single painting may seem a petty example. But even while making a wishful and whimsical joke (the inscription is, in fact, a little satire on the inability to distinguish representational difference; its answer to its own question, "Is It one or two?" can be summed up as "It doesn't matter!"), the emperor cannot escape the conventions of monarchy, although his irony is a perfectly mid-Qing response. His subsumption of the painters' work under his own inscription was not only royal prerogative, it was fundamental to the creation of the monarchical form whose king had also to play the sage, who summarized as the One Man the voices of the realm before heaven.

In fact, a third and final convention of portraiture will allow us to further expand this point. Qing literati enjoyed picturing themselves as famous people of the past. The painting in figure 10 follows another portrait of the Yuan dynasty painter Ni Zan.[42] The Qianlong emperor has replaced the landscape artist on the couch, and dressed himself the same way. Thus, three painters have been displaced from the portrait—the emperor is pictured *as a painter, of* a portrait he didn't paint, *in* a painting he didn't do. His act of entitlement, that calligraphic trace (as a king whose brush carried the power of life and death) can have no meaning for himself as a writer without an accompanying trace of himself as the ultimate writer-artist of the kingdom, present and past. The agency of that writing body could not be "represented"—it was the principle of monarchy itself, glimpsed in the traces of his brush, or in the partial portrayals of his embodiment of the subject positions of the Five Bonds in *li* uncovered earlier. The emperor was everywhere and nowhere.

The portrait constitutes a plane that carries the patterns of *wen* and brings them to visibility. It is the place where inner and outer take physical form (following Hay 1985). We can now move from the surface of a painting that displays the emperor to the sacrifices where his body provided a mobile site that both displayed and motivated a surface of signs. (Is this an inversion, or the other side of a surface?)

Silk and Skin: The Body Between

Grand Sacrifice to Heaven, performed by the emperor in his capacity as Son of Heaven, took place yearly at the winter solstice—a cold and bleak time in Beijing. It was held outdoors on an enormous three-tiered and balustraded white marble altar, in an area called the *jiao*. Usually translated "suburban," *jiao* in fact means "boundary." Thus we note that the physical site of the sacrifice was between the city and the countryside, just as its sacrificial action mediated Heaven above and Earth below.[43]

Most of the year, the altar of Heaven stood bare; only for ritual performance were the carpets unrolled, torches fired, the tents, spirit tablets, and vessels of food offerings readied. Yet, the vast open space must have combined with the size and permanence of the altar to dwarf these objects, and by far the most impressive sight on it must have been the emperor and his officialdom in their dragon robes and fur-trimmed, jewel-topped hats.

To make the transition to ritual performance from painting, I will first discuss another silk surface, that of clothing as surface of motifs, then explore why the ceremonially garbed body was so often compared to sacrificial vessels.[44]

Manchu clothing was designed for mobility on horseback, in pieces: a short jacket over trousers covered with aprons back and front. This composite style was translated into *chaofu* (see figure 11), to be worn on all ceremonial occasions, and men who passed the *jinshi* examination were presented a complete set by the emperor (Miyazaki 1981: 87). Court dress was made of silk, its motifs either embroidered on or woven in as tapestry. *Chaofu* shared the same decorative motifs of the more commonly produced *qifu* or *longpao* (dragon robes), whose unbroken surface makes it easier for us to study the symbolism.

Both robes are covered with cosmic signs. Earth, sea, and sky are represented: The hem is covered with water, at the four axes of the robe (the four cardinal directions), mountains jut upward into a cloud-filled sky, where dragons fly and other symbols associated with king and cosmos float (Cammann 1952: 81). When the robe was worn and the head emerged from above the clouds on the collar, the observer was presented with a mobile microcosm of the eighteenth-century Chinese universe. It is not surprising or a coincidence that all members of the imperium wore dragon robes.

The emperor's clothing, however, added to this overall structure the ancient Twelve Emblems (*shi er zhang*) (Yun Jing 1883): the sun, moon, stars, mountains, small dragons, birds, a *fu* symbol (denoting his civil power to adjudicate), an ax (his power to punish), sacrificial cups, water weeds, fire, and grain (Cammann 1952: 87–88). In the Qing period, the Twelve Emblems appear only after 1759, with the promulgation by the Qianlong emperor of the *Huangchao liqi tushi* (Illustrations of dynastic ritual paraphernalia). The Twelve Emblems had always been closely associated with sacrifice. By the eighteenth century they were thought to refer not only to the extrahuman cosmos (the four principle sacrifices, animate nature, the five phases) but also to the qualities of a model sovereign. (These included enlightenment, protectiveness, adaptability, filiality, purity, and so on) (Cammann 1952: 90–91). Their double reference to the larger cosmos and the inner man marks their wearer, the emperor, as the chief centerer in these rituals.

The 1759 *Illustrations* also prescribed another layer of clothing for court occasions that further differentiated the members of his imperium from the emperor: a dark, short-sleeved coat worn over the dragon robe. This coat displayed the wearer's rank as a square insignia sewn on the front, back, and shoulders. The nine civil ranks were denoted by birds, the nine military ones by fierce, four-legged animals. Only the emperor exposed his dragon robe's symbols.

11. The Qianlong emperor as a young man wearing his dragon robes and cap. Unidentified artist; color on silk. Courtesy of the Metropolitan Museum of Art, Rogers Fund, 1942 (42.141.8).

Thus the Qianlong emperor asserted the power of the throne to recover, as it covered, the power of cosmic signification for itself.

But although the emperor was differentiated by the colors he wore and the Twelve Emblems, in fact, his clothing rather tended to blend in with that of his courtiers, a fitting reminder that the Son of Heaven was, above all, an accessible model—of sageliness, of filiality, of human perfection. Indeed, the period of *bei*, "perfecting" or "preparation," before the day of sacrifice, included all participants, not just the emperor. During this period, the careful research of the members of the Ministry of Rites into proper ritual procedure materialized as the appropriate objects for sacrifice were assembled. In the stables, oxen, sheep, and pigs were inspected by appropriate ritualists. They were killed "offstage" and their hair and blood removed.

Intricately decorated porcelain replicas of Shang and Zhou bronze ritual vessels were filled with a variety of foods, some cooked, some uncooked. These too were examined before the sacrifice. The fasting participants, who had been literally emptying their stomachs and figuratively emptying their heart/minds, were also inspected. These procedures established a homology between victims, participants, and vessels. Not only were all three subjected to the same ordering gaze of various inspectors, they were also divided into "inner" and "outer" portions and interrelated by a series of inversions. Vessels were "overfull" of food and patterns, while victims were conspicuously empty and blank. The people performing sacrifice, however, bearing their inner calm within their sumptuous robes, combined the traits of victims and vessels. The "Ritual Vessel" chapter of the *Liji* (*Record of Rites*) provided the theory for this practice: "The Ritual Vessel and thus, Grand Preparation. The Grand Preparation is the heightening of exemplary power *de*. Commentary: 'Ritual Vessel' refers to *li* turning people into vessels [*qi* also meaning 'the means whereby something is accomplished']." A vessel is a boundary between its inside and its outside. As such, it is indeed the perfect metaphor for *zhong*, "to center," to mediate between two opposites.[45]

We can visualize the members of the imperium kneeling and prostrating themselves after the ceremony began, gazing over the vessels lined up in rows, just as they themselves were, before the spirit tablets of heaven. In the Qing case, the jeweled hats they wore even seem to imitate the lids of vessels (see figure 12). But more important, if a man was a perfect vessel, then what he bore within himself, his reverence (*jing*) and integrity (*cheng*), were the perfect gifts. And indeed, the highest praise the Qianlong emperor bestowed upon men in regular personnel reviews was the heretofore cryptic "A Great Vessel!"[46]

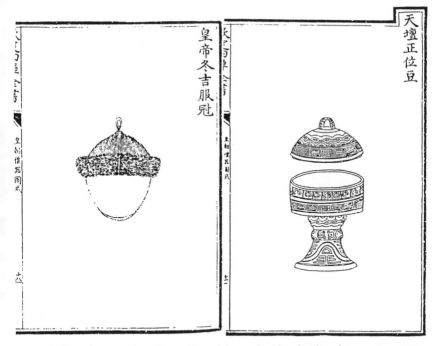

12. Woodcuts of ceremonial jewel-topped hat and *dou* vessel used on the Altar of Heaven. From *LQTS* 1.11a and 4.16a.

"Mediation," or the generation of a principle of thirdness whereby opposites are brought into proximity, proceeds in sacrifice by the act of "centering."[47] The human body *cum* vessel is clothed in a tissue of silk whose symbolic web marks the participant as the "centerer," the site of transformation between inner emotion (*qing*) and outer cosmos. In passing we must note that silk was also the preferred surface for painting and calligraphy. But even more pertinent for our purposes is the plethora of editorial metaphors that contrast webs and networks of knowledge to the single connecting thread of analysis.

This construction of the body as interfacing membrane, taking up its life "in between" as it were, had (and has) an analogue in everyday life: the concept of "face."[48] Hu Hsien Chin (1944: 45–64) points out that there are two words for face in mandarin: *lian,* which refers to physiognomy, and *mianzi,* the "social skin," as Terence Turner might put it (Turner 1980). According to this dichotomy, *lian* is the more fundamental layer; it is that claim to dignity which all human beings share. Thus to "tear one's face" (*polian*) is very serious and results in shame. *Mianzi,* on the other hand, is additional, accruing upon one's *lian* as one grows in social influence and power.[49] Both layers of interfacing self depend for their construction upon interaction with others (an active illustration of the ideographic depiction of the Confucian virtue *ren* as "two people"). In other words, in creating "face," a surface meets a gaze.

These gazes are hierarchizing because, while everyone ideally possesses the same *lian,* how far one's *mianzi* extends is a matter of the importance attached to one's social role. The perfection with which one fulfills these roles, primary among them that of the filial son or daughter, dictates how "big" is one's *mianzi.* One can *mian* others, that is "face" them, as when in the eighteenth-century novel *The Scholars* Bailiff Huang is described as "One who can speak face-to-face with the Magistrate" (Wu Jingzi 1981: 16). But equality is not necessarily implied in this way of describing the two men's relationship. Here *mianzi* is a site from which communication is possible, communication that takes place within a social hierarchy.

In fact, Chung-yin Cheng defines face as "the presentation by means of which a person stages his social existence and communicates its meaningfulness" (1986: 330). Cheng's choice of words resonates strikingly with the various humanly created signifying surfaces under discussion. With the concept of face, we see the aesthetic considerations of the discourses of *wen* (calligraphy, painting, literature) extending and transforming directly into social-political ones, through ritual and particularly sacrifice, which creates perfectly filial sons. As Hall and Ames put it:

> The process of becoming an exemplary person in Confucian thought entails both the dissolution of a delimiting and retarding distinction between self and other, and the active integration of this liberated self into the social field through the disclosure of significance (*yi*). (1987: 93)

I do not produce these philosophical generalizations about Chinese personhood in order to explain portraiture or *li.* Rather such propositions only acquire flesh when embedded in discursive processes like the classification, editing, and ritualization entailed in Grand Sacrifice.

This opening chapter has been an exercise in uncovering patterns that would make sense of a body of artifacts. Much more could be said of these portraits, but this examination introduced some key eighteenth-century concepts: *li*/ritualization, *wen*/text-pattern, *xiao*/filiality, yang-yin polarity and *zhong*/centering, as well as some processes such as hierarchization, subjectification as multiple and shifting positions, and embodiment as the layering of surfaces always already within a social-historical field. We have ranged through painting, clothing, writing, ideology of the body, and political economy in order to uncover their deeply embedded and reciprocal "naturalness."

These named patterns and concepts acted as founding reifications. They were some of the taken-for-granted, naturalized concepts within which the imperium constructed the routines of the early modern state. They indeed formed part of the logic of *li,* but were, in the paradoxical manner of all reifications, produced within those same practices.

The remainder of this study discusses how, in eighteenth-century imperial ceremonies, two-dimensional orders of signification produced in texts by a small segment of Chinese society—male literati—were incorporated in three-dimensional bodies, and how those bodies produced signification in turn. Within the ritualist metaphysics, subjectivity and language were organized to operate *within* the world rather than *upon* it. Human consciousness as agent constantly performed itself into being through actions of significance, the set of practices called *wen.* Grand Sacrifice specifically provided the intersection of the discourse upon filiality (*xiao*) through ancestor veneration with discourses upon history and its retrieval through texts (*wen*), two potent forms of social power. It thus allows us to explore how the circulation of meaning (in writing and ritual) and the production of subject positions (in the form of filial sons) coincided at the imperial level to produce a powerfully productive/coercive formation.

The reproduction of the social takes place through the reproduction of sites of subjectification; it is the re-creation of a community engaged in constant discursive negotiation about very basic notions of what constitutes itself. *Li* allows us to see that constructions of the social and its limits are politically significant because they connect the person and a larger collectivity in a way that seems "natural" to participants. Taking a positive, constructive approach to *li* will not depoliticize it. On the contrary, we draw attention to its role in constituting a sense of reality for the people living within its meaningful horizon, and thus its contribution to the particular hegemony of imperial China.[50]

Through "ritual" or *li,* we glimpse the fundamental modes of construction of identity for members of the Chinese polity as these modes are implicated in the meaning of particular institutionalized structures of power. One of these foci of power was the monarchy, which formed an important cultural model and motive for mid-eighteenth-century Chinese society. Even if its monarch was not

Chinese in his kinship genealogy, there were many other sorts of genealogies and modes of participation in the Chinese past that the Manchu throne could activate to its advantage when it faced the Han. I am interested in those that "centered" sociality through *li,* and it is to the further theorization of that discursive object that we now turn. That theorization also entails, of course, an investigation of the necessary reifications upon which this study founds itself.

2

METHOD, MONARCHY, AND RITUAL

To do, not to think about doing; to fashion the stuff of life, not to contemplate it; . . . The Chinese creative faculty remains within the plane of certain organic habits, failing to rise from the formalism of rules to the freedom of the idea.   SAMUEL JOHNSON, *Oriental Religions and Their Relation to Universal Religion*

In 1878, as part of his series on universal religion, American scholar Samuel Johnson differentiated the Chinese mind from the Hindu: Hindus are "cerebral" while Chinese are "*muscular*" (Johnson 1878: 5; emphasis in the original).[1] The "formal rules" that "immobilized" the Chinese in petty detail, preventing them from getting any transcendent distance from life, were *li*.

As a branch of ceremonialism which makes so important a part of Chinese life, these fine-spun courtesies serve to mark what grotesque transformations may befall the higher elements of character when absorbed by an intense interest in concrete details. (13)

The "grotesque transformation" that Johnson most decries is the replacement of "progress" as a social goal by "*propriety*," "descriptive of the mutual obeisance to which the life of all human aspiration is reduced" (17). Johnson uses a number of terms to characterize Chinese *li:* formal rules, ceremonialism, courtesy, propriety. He emphasizes the concreteness of their detail and, by way of criticism, their mutual and hierarchical nature. By framing his descriptions within unselfconsciously self-serving judgments about national character, Johnson seems to signal his distance from us. Yet the dualism that most profoundly underlies and organizes Johnson's discussion of Chinese social life, that of the cerebral and the muscular, the mind and the body, remains central to present analysis of *li* as ritual. We seem unwittingly to share many nineteenth-century presuppositions about human nature.

Opposing Reifications in Ritual Studies

Two or three generations of cultural anthropologists have attempted to reject models for understanding human life based upon such universal concepts of human nature, but this particular bifurcation seems to be especially difficult to theorize into abandonment. Even as anthropologists set off in search of "native categories" instead of "universal nature," they seemed unaware that their new-found sensitivity to local mores might still be underwritten by old presuppositions.

Social science approaches in some anthropological studies of China have followed the major post-Cartesian fault line of mind versus body in bifurcating *li* as ritual into either meaning or performance. (Alas, Mr. Johnson carried on his suspicious project within a since well-worn groove.) I propose instead that we think of *li* as a *discourse* that, rather than *being* ritual, in fact contained "ritualization" as one of its parts.[2] An alternative cultural-historical approach that grounds itself in the local specificities of *li* would emphasize the production of subjects and their circulating meanings in situations of domination or resistance.

In the recent volume *Death Ritual in Late Imperial and Modern China,* anthropologist and co-editor James L. Watson argues for primacy of performance over belief while co-editor historian Evelyn Rawski disagrees, seeing belief and performance as both necessary to ritual life and necessary for its control by the state (Watson and Rawski 1988).

Watson insists on the prevalence of "orthopraxy" in Chinese ritual life, maintaining that the state did not concern itself with belief, only with correct performance: "The internal state of the participants, their personal beliefs and predispositions, [were] largely irrelevant" (6) (he means "irrelevant" to the Chinese state, not to his own understanding). Watson outlines a performance sequence for funerary rites common in the Ming dynasty (1368–1644), consisting of public notification of death, mourning dress, bathing of the corpse, transfer of goods from living to dead, preparation and installation of the spirit tablet, use of paid professionals, music, encoffining of the corpse, and finally expulsion of the coffin. According to Watson, the state, having abandoned control of the "ideological" as too complex, sought to prescribe and intervene in the performative domain. The elite espoused, exemplified, and encouraged this orthopraxy.

Watson's split between belief and performance seems to me to restate the long-standing division in positivist social science of thought and action, theory and practice. Sherry Ortner's essay "Theory in Anthropology since the Sixties" shows that tendencies to divorce meaning from performance, minds from bodies have run deep in anthropology (1984). Ortner charts the move from symbolic and structural models of social life[3] to practice-oriented ones, in other words, from models that located meaning at a level other than experience to models that include the actor. In studying ritual, anthropologists turned from the cognitive, symbolic aspects of a ceremony to emphasize its active performance, not merely its display of symbols for analysis analogous to a text.[4]

The most sophisticated of performance-oriented practice theories, for instance Pierre Bourdieu's, has promised a transcendence and reincorporation of meaningful structure into action; of belief with performance (Bourdieu 1977). Yet when we see performance theories in context and in conjunction with the symbolic and structural models of social and ritual life they mean to replace, we notice their own partiality. Performance theories merely counterpose the willing body to the curious, anxious mind. Instead of rituals that solve cognitive or emotional angst by providing meaning, we have rituals that solve social conflicts by organizing docile bodies in performance. In studies of Chinese *li,* the rough equivalent to the meaning/performance and mind/body split in anthropology lies between philosophers and institutional historians.

The earliest work on *li* was done in philosophy. Concentrating upon texts, these writers are interested in what *li* meant for writers. Many modern philosophers have interpreted *li* in the context of something they call "Confucian humanism." They see Confucius's writings as marking a turn from the supernatural toward the ethical in a classificatory move that rests upon an analogy made between Confucianism's immanentalist anthropocentrism and European Renaissance humanism. Furthermore, these philosophers have often translated *li* as "propriety," emphasizing its abstract quality as a rational standard of value for individuals.[5] In doing so they have opposed Confucianism to Daoism as the cultural and ethically obsessed opposes the natural and innocent (Munro 1985).

The creation of these dual categories bases itself in yet another analogy with European experience, a Cartesian framework that posits an internally consistent, psychological subject who exists in tension with external society and then opposes the social order to the natural.

These philosophers share a tendency to neglect or de-emphasize the ceremonial practices associated with *li* in favor of a "meaning-centered" approach reminiscent of symbolic anthropology. In unconscious collusion with the philosophic texts they study, they make the material circumstances of the productions of such textuality, along with the performing bodies of ritualists, disappear.

And those interested in performance? In studies of Chinese *li,* institutional historians have emphasized ceremonial performance with far less attention to meaning. Treating *li* as a code for conduct, they explain the coherent systems developed by rulers in imperial China to accomplish certain tasks without questioning wider beliefs in practice that provided the "bureaucracy" with the very context of its functioning.[6]

In fact, rather than turning to anthropology when studying Chinese imperial ritual, Western scholars have often preferred models drawn from sociology for two reasons: first, historians of China have worked in the long shadow cast by the work of Max Weber, whose connecting of Confucian literati and bureaucratic government has provided an overwhelmingly powerful model in the field.[7] Second, they harbor a creditable wish to give China its due as a complex society, to rescue it from any contamination of the "exotic" or "colonialist" aura surrounding anthropology. The list of works that proceed by analyzing the political function of imperial ritual as narrowly conceived through the sociology of legitimation is long.[8]

In analyzing kingly ritual, historians tend to be interested in ceremonial over a long time span, relating it to other institutional trends. Anthropologists operate in a shorter timeframe and analyze precisely what ceremonies meant and accomplished for participants.[9] As David Cannadine puts it:

> The historians ask about structures of power, whereas the anthropologists ask about structures of meaning. The historians want to know how the ceremonial image and the stability of the state relate to each other, whereas the anthropologists want to know how a society constructs a transcendent symbolic idiom, and how human beings are transformed into divine kings. (Cannadine and Price 1987: 14)

The division noted above by Cannadine, between historical study of "structures of power" and anthropological study of "structures of meaning," is too simple. "Structures of meaning" are part of the production of value and the structuration of power, fundamentally shaping and limiting the forms that domination will take in any society. Thus the usefulness of cultural anthropological method to my task: To grasp the workings of the imperial hegemony in China (and thus to be able to recognize true challenges to this particularized power that sought to generalize itself throughout Chinese life), it is necessary to analyze precisely and concretely *how* the imperium (as monarchical power through its officials) sought to define and organize fundamental categories and aspects of existence, how it coped with many of the naturalizing reifications, the basic organizing categories of everyday life introduced in chapter 1, especially *li*.

At this point we might conclude that theories of ritual (or *li*) that either reify the mind or overemphasize the body are useless by virtue of their incompleteness. The skeptical might even wonder if these opposing reifications of "mental" versus "performance" in fact require one another for their analytic existence at all. Once we connect them in this fashion, it becomes easier to understand them as mutually necessary moments in a discourse that, like all discourses, creates the very objects it then purports to analyze. Following Bourdieu, I would call this discourse "objectivist" (Bourdieu 1977: 1–30).

By "objectivist" I mean the powerful Cartesian vision of a world objectified as meaning, available for representation by all knowing minds, whatever their color, gender, or class (Bordo 1988). In the objectivist universe, symbolism is possible because mind and its meanings are forever separate from the world and its facts. (Thus we have invented the sign and its referent.)[10] The Cartesian division between mind-reduced-to-knower facing a world-objectified-as-knowledge separates first, body from mind and, second, actor from the world.[11] The performative critique at least seeks to restore the body to the mindful person. But performance approaches fundamentally do nothing for the actor divided from the world's wider context because of the lurking theatrical metaphor: The actor remains stranded upon a stage. Furthermore, imagining ritual as performance "naturalizes" the position of the analytic observer into a member of the audience, confounding an act of interpretation with an act of participation while still confining native ritualists to the status of actors instead of thinkers (Bell 1992: 39, 42). Can we avoid "ritualizing *li*"?

Catherine Bell observes that analysts often see ritual as "behavioral" while myth and doctrine are seen as "conceptual." She points out that this way of thinking about ritual fits very neatly with the act of theory building itself; ritual becomes the behavioral object of our own conceptualizations. The category ritual, far from existing as a "thing" separate from the analyst's eye, is to a great extent brought into being *as* analysts seek satisfying answers to their questions about phenomena like social integration, conflict resolution, meaning, and culture. She implies that we then project these concerns upon the ritualists we study. These questions are, of course, *already* based upon points of view, theories, and epistemological necessities. Thus Bell positions us to understand the *process* of classification and categorization that is the *practice* of our own theorizing. If she is right in proposing a homology between ritual as our created object and our theories of it, then she is also right in proposing that we must "grasp differentiation itself as an activity, and to begin to appreciate the activity of theory-making" (Bell 1992: 112). In some cases is it not also possible that native ritualists indeed might be working through meditations upon the operations of social life similar to our own in form and sophistication if not in the particulars of content?

Literate Chinese concerned with *li* were also theory builders. Correct encoding, propagation, and performance of *li* were mostly monopolized by literati men and considered the purview of those who ruled.[12] *Li* were textually transmitted from ancient times. Thus historian Evelyn Rawski maintains, contra Watson, that the state did try to link orthopraxy to orthodoxy and that "belief and performance [were] very hard to separate" (Watson and Rawski 1988: 22). Now we can read Watson's actually quite important insight that the two were separated in a different light. The question to ask is not *whether* or not belief and performance were linked but rather *how* they were linked, in what contexts, and to what ends.

In making the countercase that belief and performance were tightly knit in Chinese ritual, Rawski rightly points out that during their enforcement of standardized ritual performance, officials and local elites explicitly tried to disseminate values and beliefs (Watson and Rawski 1988: 20–36).[13] That is, they linked belief and performance very closely. Clearly, *li* were early connected to ancestor veneration, and thence to a constellation of beliefs and practices tied to family life, group historical continuity, and correct rule. By the eighteenth century, with classical commentary all the rage, scholars carefully examined the ritual prescriptions of past dynasties in order to produce handbooks and encyclopedias for the current emperor. Thus, the study of *li* held a particular fascination for the ruling members of the scholar-gentry (Elman 1984: 116).

Grand Sacrifice as an important instance of *li* relates text and performance as processual moments within a discursive formation of great power. In other words, the nonseparation, the conflation, the intimate interpenetration of body and mind, meaning and action were precisely an effect of *li*. Any mode of analysis that automatically "ritualizes" *li* by separating these aspects from one another does it great disservice.

Li as Discourse

Fitting *li* into either of the categories of meaning or performance generated by the analytics of ritual studies limits its power. I propose thinking of *li* as a discourse. According to Timothy Reiss, "The term discourse refers to the way in which the material embodying sign processes is organized. Discourse can thus be characterized as the visible and describable praxis of what is called 'thinking'" (1982: 9).

In other words, material and thoughtful life are produced simultaneously: Within any social formation, the relationships between words and things, and the practices whereby those conventions are instituted, imply subjectivities who will understand and "find" themselves through those practices. (By subjectivities I mean positions within which identities form that provide grounds for practice, that is, acts in the world [Smith 1988; Henriques et al. 1984].) Discourse is a constitutive practice whose traces we find in its products, one of which is subjectivity itself. Appropriate subjectivities are produced as meaning is created and circulated as part of the materiality of building a world to live in. The equation of these discursive factors differs from place to place and epoch to epoch. I would thus take the investigation of the discursive production of subjectivities to be a key task for cultural historians (Foucault 1982: 224; Farquhar and Hevia 1993: 514).

So broadly defined, "discourse" seems almost a shorthand term for social production itself. To be useful it must be narrowed. Unlike a strictly dialectical approach (e.g., Berger and Luckman 1966), as Foucault has used "discourse," it also allows that such processes include certain aspects of life and exclude others. Room is made for slippage, contradiction, and resistance.[14] For example, modern discourses of natural science (there are many) exclude discourses of religion as they, in the words of Hayden White (who is speaking here of discourse generally), "*constitute* the ground whereon to decide *what shall count as a fact* . . . and to determine *what mode of comprehension* is best suited to the understanding of the facts thus constituted" (1978: 3; emphasis in the original). To follow our proposed example, religious discourses are thought to be useful only for explaining "religious" facts, not "natural phenomena." Hence when creationism seeks to take on scientific evolutionary theory in the latter's terms, providing statistics and research data, worse than being merely wrong, it can seem epistemologically inappropriate and impossibly wacky.

As discourses constitute the grounds upon which a sense of lived reality can be figured, they also facilitate the transport of that sense through human time.

Sociologist Paul Connerton (1989) proposes that societies remember in two ways: through inscription and through incorporation. The former stores information for retrieval in external sources, the latter in the sedimented practices of bodily disposition and gesture. What I think a discourse does most importantly is install inscription and incorporation in ways that mutually produce powerful formations for generating social life. Thus classification schemes, genres of writing, conventions, and metaphors (meaning) combine with social organizations of bodies in space (institutions) to produce such forms as biomedicine, education, the juridico-prison system, youth culture, religion, sexuality, etc. (Note we have already straddled the meaning-versus-power dichotomy that has bedeviled anthropologists and historians.)

Emperorship in China had been cast as a *culturally* constructive political institution in the broadest sense even before the Han.[15] Certainly by that period, the imperial claim to mediate literature and ceremony as features of the everyday life of its imperium was well-staked (Loewe 1994). The throne brought the written record into being and had ever since tried to assert a special power to arbitrate standards of human expression in the crucial and interpenetrating categories of *li, wen,* and *xiao.* But these three "discourses" are culturally productive in ways that go far beyond a definition of "culture" as superstructural and expressive.[16]

We have defined *li* as the ways of being human that are considered necessary to the workings of the cosmos as well as its embedded social order, including everything from how to dress to how to venerate ancestors. *Wen* in a narrow sense meant "text" or "writing" and, more expansively, cosmic patterning that included activities such as painting and music in order to mobilize the human sensorium beyond the eye. *Xiao,* filiality, achieved its status as organizing trope for connecting cosmic and social hierarchies through polar yin-yang logic by the Han dynasty. All three have been associated closely with the Confucian school of Ru.

In China the discourses of *wen, li,* and *xiao* likewise organized both incorporation and inscription in ways that interpenetrated and complicated their relationship. They overlapped and appeared in one another's domains as ritualized inscription and scripted ritualization, often in the service of an ethos of filiality. The categories of inscription and incorporation have often been opposed in sociological theorizing (Connerton 1989), or imagined in evolutionary scale, where writing replaces speech and record-keeping replaces the rituals of mnemonic recitation (Goody 1987). In Chinese monarchical ritual practice, they were fruitfully combined in novel and powerful ways until the twentieth century.

Regarded in this light, *li* as a discourse first posited a whole that preceded and organized its parts historically: call it a cosmology or a discursive ground, it provided the ongoing validation for social dispositions through its text/performances. It also organized protocols for the training of people to retrieve correct *li* from the past and re-present them in the present imperium. The eighteenth-century textual traces of *li* were of four sorts: sets of ceremonial prescriptions in handbooks, object of exegesis for scholar-literati, code for conduct in materials like the Sacred Edict, and reservoir of appropriate means for discussing political life (Zito 1984). As the sum of the perspectives of its performed texts, *li* provided the articulation that gave them effect.

Second, *li* organized strategies for forming subject positions. Theorization about social life within discourses of *li* constantly emphasized the Five Bonds of father/son, ruler/minister, husband/wife, elder/younger siblings, and friend/friend. These subject positions (ruler, minister, father, mother, son, daughter, friend of higher status, friend of lower status, elder, younger) were practically embodied in varieties of ways that produced reciprocal hierarchical relations.[17]

In the seventeenth century, display of knowledge of *li* through proper ceremony was good, but by the eighteenth century not as good as writing books about *li*. Far from being an abstract and transcendent standard of behavior imposed upon all people equally, *li* included finely differentiated practices that created a network of relationships, thus enabling situated subjectivities. Not all of these possible positions were equally important nor equally available to all people, but all were necessary to reproducing Chinese social life.[18]

Third, *li* also specified a "perfect person," an "ideal subject" in all senses of that word: one who not only performed practically and bodily the appropriate ceremonial *li* but reflected upon that performance in various sorts of permanently expressive media—texts, paintings, music. This person both produced texts that were performed and performed texts. They lived trans-temporally: through literacy able to retrieve a sagely past for enactment in the present, with an eye for hurling their re-presentations into a future when they themselves would be ancestors.

In other words, *li* provided a model for what we might call perfect praxis in the embodied subject positions of ruler/subject and father/son. But we must not mistake these for a general Chinese embodied self—that would be a misrecognition of a body of ideology that sought to generate a desire of imitation for the whole of social life. For the analyst, it is to fall victim to the imperium's own vision of itself. The emperor's power lay in the distance of longing his imperium could create between this body of yang power and the bodies of everyday life that could only approximate that position carefully crafted for the king. Because imitation was itself considered a form of profoundly meaningful participation in late imperial life, the imperium sought to provide above all a modeling of modeling.

The Discursive Labor of Becoming King

If the king modeled human life, he shares that life's basic problematics and becomes a template upon which various solutions are tried out. Monarchies in Europe and Asia shared one such problematic: the king's body and his mortality (i.e., how to imagine his relation to an extrinsic, eternal order).[19] For European monarchies, the situation was complicated by sharing sovereignty with that other divine king clothed in human flesh, Jesus Christ.[20] Chinese monarchies never took stage explicitly with so intrusive a counterforce as God in human form. In their Confucian moments, they acted on behalf of "Heaven," an entity conspicuously without a body. In their Buddhist moments, they acted as Cakravartin kings in concerted partnership with dharma teachers of the sangha, in a supposed symbiosis of enlightenment. In neither case was a possibly superior human body available for modeling, leaving the field clear for imperial control of the crucial resource of the power of exemplary virtue or *de*. Everyone who sat on the throne availed himself of this resource.

The history of monarchy in Europe as well has been shaped through a series of complex claims upon divinity. Roman ceremonies of apotheosis after the burial of a dead emperor released his soul to lodge with the gods, henceforward to be worshipped as one of them (Price 1987). Christianity's insistence that no man was god was accompanied by a parallel claim to ritual mediation with the One God who was left. In everyday life, this meant real questions of jurisdiction over beings who were, after all, creatures with souls who belonged to God, even if their taxes were rendered to Caesar.

With Constantine's fourth-century founding of Constantinople and recognition of Christianity as the imperial religion, imperial monarchy once again approached the divine, but this time with the church firmly between the king and God and very much on God's side (Cameron 1987: 107). Henceforward, one of the principal matters of concern in monarchical ritual was the contradiction of divine and secular power, the church and the state. Slowly, monarchy won this struggle for ceremonial precedence, and kings who had once been crowned by the pope ultimately ended up crowning themselves (literally so, in the case of Napoleon).[21] It was not that kings acceded their divine right to rule; they simply no longer acknowledged the church as mediator between themselves and that ultimate source of power. The ramifications in everyday life were profound as the way was cleared for modern European monarchical states to make

their power visible not only through ritual performance and dramatic display, but through the gradual extension of "officializing" procedures and routines, through the capacity to bound and mark space, to record transactions, to count and classify its populations, to gradually replace the religious institutions as the registrar of the life-cycle facts of birth, marriage, and death. (Cohn and Dirks 1986)

Monarchy in the Classical Age presided over the foundings of modern states: in fact, in the case of Louis XIV (whose reign has been credited with the beginning of modern media), the state and the monarch were declared equivalent.[22] The triumph of the state over the church was complete, and it had been carried out through monarchy.

The Chinese monarchy also had a relationship to an extrahuman source of power, although the idea of "Heaven" was not the same as the self-willed creator who was the Judeo-Christian godhead. The principle of the Mandate of Heaven (*tianming*) was first invoked by the Duke of Zhou to explain how his people had conquered the Shang (1600–1100 B.C.E.): Heaven bestows the mandate to rule upon a deserving man and his lineal descendants.[23] Never did the Chinese monarchy have to share Heaven's ear with another arbiter (although a case might be made for the Buddhist fulfilling of this function at certain times in Chinese history), but the relationship was still fraught with difficulty.

From the very first recounting of the Mandate, it was contradictory: The initial bestowal was made on merit, but its further inheritance took place through descent. Thus was set one of the problems that would absorb monarchical theorists and ritualists in China: shall power be passed to sons or to meritorious officials, the heir or the sage?[24] The institutional contradiction that this problem expressed lay between the state and the family.

In the dynastic founding myth of the Manchus, a similar problem was rehearsed. Pamela Crossley recounts the tale of how the hero Bukuri Yongson was conceived when his mother Fekulen held a fruit that had fallen from the mouth of a sacred crow, thus making him the embodiment of his clan's totem animal. The child Bukuri was barely grown when he pacified the warring factions of the many clans and was elected *beile* by them, later naming them *manju* (1985:13).

Crossley points out that in his person, Bukuri united his people and his own clan. In a series of part-for-whole substitutions, the myth establishes its hero as the personification of the single Aisin Goro clan who came to rule as emperors and, in turn, establishes the Aisin Goro clan as the manifestation of the newly unified Manchu people (19, 21). In the eighteenth century, Hongli, the Qianlong emperor, was quite devoted to both the myth and the recuperation of Manchu history in general. The documentation of the Manchu past, rendering it "visible, manageable and standard" (Crossley 1987: 747), included a text on Aisin Goro clan rituals. Other clans were urged to adopt the clan's rites.

We might read these textual encodings as efforts to surmount the contradictory claims of family and empire. What at the beginning had been the necessity of incorporating all clans into "Manchu-ness" had become by the eighteenth century a problem infinitely more complex. There had never been any point trying to incorporate the Han Chinese in those terms; but other, equally interesting and efficacious ways had by then been found in the Chinese ritual repertoire to mediate the difficulties of ruling a nation of scholars through a confederation of clans.

As *Chinese* lords, Manchu efforts to create a hierarchy of subordination among domains was accomplished through temple-building, ceremonial, and the editing of texts, discourses of *xiao, li,* and *wen* (in its narrow sense—writing) long associated with the civilizing *wen* aspect of kingship.[25] Hence it is no coincidence that the building of a ritual center in the Manchu homeland to rival Beijing should precede the occupation of the Chinese city itself.

Before they entered Beijing upon another's invitation in 1644, to remain upon their own design, the Manchu rulers had established in northern Shenjing a replica of that ceremonial center.[26] On May 14, 1636, Hung Taiji proclaimed that the new dynasty was to be called *Qing* (*ECCP* 2; Zheng Tianting 1980b: 166; Xiao Yishan 1963: 1:175; Meng Sen 1981: 1:386–87). That year, "the tenth year of the Tiancong period, [the emperor] measured the ground in Shenjing, established a Round Mound (*yuanqiu*) and Square Pool (*fangze*), sacrificed to announce to Heaven and Earth, and changed the year designation from Prime to *Chongde*."[27]

Hung Taiji also established an Ancestral Temple or *Tai Miao* (*QSG* 86.61/2573; *ECCP* 595). He filled it with ascendants of his father Nurhaci, going back as far as the fifteenth century and awarding the posthumous title of *Ziwang* to Monge Temur (d. 1433). When Hung Taiji's son, Fulin, actually took up the imperial throne, he also took over the Altars of Soil and Grain abandoned by the Ming as they fled Beijing, and he sacrificed to announce the fact.[28]

The Manchus showed their eagerness to manifest the suasive, civilizing "patterns" of *wen* in another fashion. In 1629 Hung Taiji established the *Wenguan* or

Literary Office. Its purpose was to record the affairs of the kingdom, understand past kingly experience, and produce reliable histories (Xiao Yishan 1963: 1:233). In 1636, the year that the dynasty's name was changed, the Literary Office was reorganized into the *Nei sanyuan,* or Three Inner Courts. The *Guoshi yuan,* or Office of Domainal Affairs, recorded, commented upon, and issued imperial proclamations and collected and compiled historical materials. The *Bishu yuan* handled correspondence with foreign domains, command-edicts, and provincial memorials. The *Hongwen yuan* was responsible for Imperial clan education.[29]

As an illustration of how effective Chinese techniques of hierarchization were for the building of empire, we turn to the founding moment of Qing rule. In 1636 Hung Taiji claimed the title of Son of Heaven. In the spring of that year, the tenth year of the Tiancong reign, Prince Daisan (1583–1648), Hung Taiji's elder brother, along with the princes of the Inner and Outer Dependencies, and the civil and military officials in Shenjing, presented a "petition" requesting that he take the throne.

The Princes and the Grand Ministers, Civil and Military, along with the Princes of the Outer Regions respectfully think an emperor should ascend and mount Heaven. Giving special care and protection as though to his family, he should respond to this initiative and arise. When the sub-celestial realm is in chaos, cultivate virtuous power and embody Heaven. Overawe with troops those who are against you; cherish with virtuous power those who are with you. The fame of your extensive kindness manifests in all directions. Your compelling of Korea to submission by Kingly force, and the unification of the Mongols, give you an even greater claim upon the Imperial seal. Inner and Outer transform in perfection, Above is in harmony with Heaven's intention, Below agrees in popular feeling. Therefore the ministerial ranks looking upward to Heaven to embody its heart/mind respectfully proffer this reign name. Each and every ceremonial thing is already thoroughly prepared. We humbly desire that you grant this request to your servants and not render false and empty the hopes of so many. (Xiao Yishan 1963: 1:174)

Some points about this text and its presentation will help us to understand Manchu attitudes toward Chinese kingship at this crucial moment of transition.

The text was written in three languages, Manchu, Mongol, and Chinese, and proffered simultaneously by native representatives of each group. A *biaowen,* literally a "text of expression," is usually translated "petition," which captures the sense of its movement from below upward to the throne. *Biaowen* figured importantly in the Guest Rituals (*binli*) from at least the Tang period. Princes or their envoys presented them along with *fangwu,* or "local products," as part of *gong,* or "precious things."[30]

By virtue of the *biaowen,* the Chinese were cast as "petitioners" to a new emperor who was a member of a group previously enfeoffed by the Han Chinese Ming emperor.[31] Thus was enacted an inversion of their relations of dominance. Under these new terms, China was placed with other subordinate domains petitioning the soon-to-be Son of Heaven. Ironically, the contents of the *biaowen,* with allusions to the sub-celestial realm, the integration of the four directions of Inner, Outer, Above, and Below, are quite Chinese in character.

The difference between Manchu and Han visions of social order, barely touched upon here, can be viewed as a contradiction between the two societies before the Shunzhi emperor entered Beijing. Once the Manchus sat upon the throne, these differences were not simply resolved by a transcendent "next phase" of "bureaucratic rationalization." On the contrary, many of the themes remained as contradictions *within* the polity of the Qing domain, especially the problem of authority inherited through kinship as *xiao* or through merit as *wen.* It was these sorts of paradoxes and puzzles that the spectacular ritual text/performances such as Grand Sacrifices sought to resolve—and in the imperium's favor.

Writing, ceremony, and building provided sensuous embodiments of the king's power that made visible the king and his imperium. Modern Chinese historians call it *wenzhi,* "rule by *wen,*" something for which the Qianlong emperor was particularly famous (Wu Zhefu 1970: 1; Luo Ming 1986: 167). As for the contributions of the throne to an early modernizing of the state archive through such practices (like Louis XIV?), the next chapter discusses the relationship forged between the literati and the imperium through the writing and editing of *li.*

PART 2

Text: Editing the

Ritual Corpus

3

CLASSIFYING *LI*

Time and Agency

In the winter of 1755, Qin Huitian put us all to shame by coming out with the *Wuli tongkao* [Comprehensive investigation of the Five Rites]. Having served in the Ministry of Rites, he was familiar with reading the precedents. . . . Material from above, created within the milieu of the court, will extend down to the debates of the *Ru* scholars. Nothing remains unearthed or hidden. All is laid out, in order, like administrative divisions. LU JIANZENG, preface to *WLTK*

Such editing projects as the *Comprehensive Investigation of the Five Rites* (*Wuli tong-kao*),[1] carried out independently by men who served constantly in the imperium, were the corollary in the gentry sphere of massive editing projects sponsored by the throne. Many of these projects centered upon *li*. This chapter places this editing activity in context and concentrates upon how *li* was categorized by the editors of the *Siku quanshu* (Library of the four treasuries).[2] The metaphors used by Lu to describe Qin's editing success, how he "unearthed" the "hidden" and ordered the words of the past, will be found to be quite common descriptions of both editing and ritual. In fact, we will see how the editor's visual function was enshrined in the eighteenth-century versions of Grand Sacrifice, as its grammar alternated activities of "ordering" and "classification" with "examination" and "inspection."

The Eighteenth Century: Graveyard of Modernity?

Modern interpretation of the eighteenth century in China has been vexed by a number of stereotypes and misreadings that for many years eclipsed its positive importance. The century in which the Manchus completed their military dominion under the sixty-year reign of the Qianlong emperor was famous among European observers for the "pax sinica" that allowed for an unprecedented development of commercial and cultural sophistication in the empire. The eighteenth century in China, victim of its own success as a time of Manchu-led prosperity and relative peace, has tended to be reviled by later observers, Chinese and foreign, as the cause of, or ignored as mere background to, the more exciting and deadly events of the nineteenth.

First, Chinese views: Since the mid-nineteenth century, intellectuals from the majority Chinese population that eventually inherited the Qing empire have been unhappy with their recent past. After the Opium War of 1840, in the wake of the Taiping Rebellion, in the midst of economic depression and European victory, Chinese literati looked askance at the previous one hundred years as a time of corruption, extravagance, and irresponsibility (Naquin and Rawski 1987: x). Twentieth-century Chinese historians, whether bourgeois nationalists or Maoist nationalists, have often (conveniently) blamed the specifically Manchu ethnicity of the rulers for their country's woes.

The autocracy of the Manchu throne was condemned for stunting the cultural and political life of China, leaving it rigid and unprepared for contact with imperialist Europeans.[3] The intellectual life of the eighteenth century, dominated by a movement called "evidential scholarship" (*kaozheng*), which emphasized the study of *li*,[4] has been excoriated as mere philology, a safe pastime for Han Chinese scholars in fear of their lives from a Manchu monarch who persecuted them relentlessly with literary inquisitions.[5] Until quite recently, the eighteenth century was thought to have been, in Quinton Priest's words, "the graveyard of the promising intellectual trends toward a modern sensibility which had emerged in the Ming-Ch'ing transition period."[6]

Where the Chinese have seen a cultural desert—decadent, wasteful, and a block to modernization (Xiao Yishan 1963: 2:593–96; Leung 1977: 7–10)— United States historians have seen a garden of blooming economic trends. The era, however, was then shelved by these foreign scholars as the glorious back-ground, the baseline of civilization from which China fell into nineteenth-century overpopulation and decadence (Feuerwerker 1976; Hsu 1970).

Recently, in both Chinese and foreign scholarship, efforts have been made to see the period as laying complex foundations for today's agrarian state.[7] Revi-sionist approaches in intellectual history have pointed to continuities between seventeenth-century statecraft reformers and nineteenth-century New Text scholarship reformers, linked through the eighteenth-century evidential schol-arship movement (Mann 1975: 28–32; Priest 1986: 20–23; Yu Ying-shih 1975: 105–110; Chow 1994: passim). Others have attacked the literary political repression thesis, notably R. Kent Guy (1987) in his important work on the *Library,* maintaining that throne and literati/gentry worked closely together. An alternative social-historical approach stresses that the professionalization of nonimperial scholarship and library building in the eighteenth century began extra-intellectual trends that would culminate in nineteenth-century transfor-mation of the literati (Elman 1984).[8]

Indeed, the zeal with which eighteenth-century scholars turned upon texts showed philology to be, as Elman says, "more than just an auxiliary tool" (1984: 34; Guy 1980: 192, 260–78). Kai-wing Chow has convincingly argued that eighteenth-century ritual textual scholars were as obsessed with ethical prob-lems as their predecessors (1994: 187–204). If self-cultivation toward the goal of the moral goodness of sagehood was no longer the primary road to knowl-edge, then perhaps in knowledge through certain, painstaking method lay true self-cultivation. That this method was coincidentally the purview of a tiny elite and thus also functioned as a class marker only makes it important to appreciate as precisely as possible the form and meaning it took for those subjected to its rigors.

Classical Studies

The eighteenth century saw the rise of what Yu Ying-shih has called the scrip-tural tradition.[9] Yu points out that editing, collating, writing, and textual studies had always been important Confucian and later Cheng-Zhu school activities. In the eighteenth century, they became paramount, and the moment of tension shifted from one between morality and intellection to a thoroughly intellectu-alist preoccupation with types of knowledge (Yu 1975: 123; 1977: 41–44).

For these men, the act of editing texts can be seen as a centrally meaningful process. I use "editing" here in its original English sense, from the Latin *editus: e* meaning "out" and *dare* meaning "to give"—to bring forth or give out. That definition gives a nice sense of the avowed purpose of both editing and ritual in the eighteenth century, that is, to manifest, show, or display that which had been hidden—in this case, the wisdom of the sages. In the vocabulary of the Qing editor, one term describing textual preparation occurs again and again. *Xiu* means to embellish, correct, repair, study, cultivate, or practice. In its last sense, the word was used as part of "self-cultivation" (*zixiu*) by devotees of Song learning. As *xiudao* for Daoist and *xiuxing* for Buddhists, it conveyed a similar sense of improvement, refashioning, and restoration of the self through a pre-scribed set of practices. *Xiu* is the patterning of disorder, always according to old standards but actually incorporating the new. *Xiumiao,* to "renovate temples," was worthy of mention in gazetteers and commemoration in stelae.

If *wen* became the main mode for sustaining the *dao* in human time, then eighteenth-century endeavors so often compartmentalized by modern histori-ans into art, philosophy, politics, or ritual can be seen as a related constellation of practices. In their own time, they produced the material signs of the order within which was embodied the substance of the *dao* and through which it func-tioned. So contextualized, both *xiushen* (an incorporated performance) through quiet sitting and *xiuwen* (editing texts), neo-Confucian practices, can be under-stood as aspects of the same sacred quest for the *dao.* Quiet sitting was deli-berately supplemented, by mid-Qing, with another sort of performance, *li,* es-pecially ancestral sacrifices.[10]

The goal of reaching sagehood through editing culminated a movement that maintained and even elevated the status of the skills of the *wenren,* or literate person. The foundations of this trend lay deep in transformations occurring in economy and society in the sixteenth and seventeenth centuries that created great anxiety in the ruling elite, shaping in new ways desire for and access to education. By the seventeenth century, the rise of literacy among people uncon-nected to the imperium (and its literati extension at the local level) could be seen as a serious threat to its monopoly of the discourses based upon *wen,* which had been culturally defined as fundamental to the operation of power and au-thority. The literati solution was to recuperate its position as interpreters and creators of authority through text by reconnecting writing and obscure ancient ritual practice. By approaching *li* through texts, they embedded sacrificial *li* within the practices of *wen* and forged a connection between the *wenren* scholar and the filial son, the sage and the heir. Sacrifice as text/performance in the eighteenth century united the universalist ethics of the imperium's meritocracy (sageliness through learning) with the particularist ethics of kinship (power inherited through clan descent). No wonder that study and practice of *li,* both its texts and performances, formed a particularly supple arena for the display and construction of gentry power.

Classical studies, or *jingxue,* flourished in the eighteenth century as never before. A general boom in publishing (Ko 1994: introd.) buttressed the efforts of throne, imperium, and private scholars. More books were produced during the Qing dynasty than heretofore in Chinese history (Shi Meicen 1966: 131). Because woodblock printing required low-skilled labor and little capital outlay, and paper was cheap in China, Qing publishing rested upon Ming technological advances that kept costs low (Rawski 1985: 19). The publishing explosion affected urban elites while penetrating the countryside as well. Quantitatively, the increase in book production derived mostly from growing demand for basic textbooks as education became more available in times of prosperity (20–21). Among the wealthy, however, a network of collectors amassing libraries drove up the value of rare books tenfold from the seventeenth to the eighteenth centuries (Elman 1984: 284). Thus, both book distribution and collection reached its pre-twentieth-century apogee in the Qing.

The throne contributed to this general textual mania by sponsoring large-scale editing projects as imperial printing likewise reached new heights under the Qing. Projects included the encyclopedic *Gujin tushu jicheng* (Synthesis of illustrations and books past and present) under the Kangxi (r. 1661–1722) emperor, but it was from 1736 to 1795, during the reign of the Qianlong emperor, that court book production peaked. Many more titles were printed during this sixty-year period than during previous reigns.[11]

Previous dynastic publishing enterprises had concentrated on reproducing the classics, histories, and philosophy of former eras. With the Qing, however, the emphasis in court printing shifted to works by and for the reigning emperor: government records and statutes, and compilations (Shaw 1983: 63–64). Works commissioned by the throne were compiled and published with captions like "Under Imperial Auspices" (*Huang chao*) or "By Imperial Order" (*Qinding*).[12] In fact, the increasing number of printed books in circulation seems to have provided the government with the opportunity of consolidating for itself the role of unifier and judge of the many and often inaccurate versions of a book in circulation.[13]

The throne staked a very serious claim to the prerogatives of chief collector and arbiter of knowledge in the form of the *Siku quanshu.* This book-collecting and editing project began with an initial edict in the winter of 1772 ordering a search for valuable and rare books. In March of the next year, the administrative apparatus was created in Beijing to evaluate the works collected. The project eventually encompassed more than 700 staff who edited over a 22-year period an annotated catalogue of 10,680 extant titles and produced a huge compendium that reprinted 3,593 titles in 36,000 volumes (Guy 1987: 1; *ECCP* 121; Wu Zhefu 1970: 1–4).

As the search for worthy texts spread through the empire, a parallel, more ominous shadow project took shape, dubbed the "literary inquisition" (*wenzi yuanyu*) in modern scholarship. The throne wished to suppress works that impugned the Manchus or their history. For about seven years, from 1776 to 1782, the censorship campaign gathered steam as the editors, collators, and officials involved turned the throne's zeal to their own ends. Entire families were ruined because of writerly and publishing indiscretions (Goodrich 1966; Guy 1987: 157–200; Zhou Yuanlian 1991: 737–40). While historians have usually linked the campaign closely to the *Library* itself, Kent Guy has persuasively argued for separating the work of the *Library* proper from this other crusade:

Both projects demonstrated the Qianlong emperor's profound belief in the importance of the written word as source of ideological justification. . . . But the two efforts were not related as pretext and reality; they were two distinct outgrowths of the combination of power and vulnerability, pride and sensitivity that characterized the rule of Manchus, and particularly the Qianlong emperor, in China. (1987: 166)

We can further appreciate the importance of the written word as source of "ideological justification" by linking it to ritual practice. As I will show in the rest of this chapter, under the aegis of the scholars who were in charge of the *Library,* new ideas about the histories and classics were developed and a new place was found for works on ritual, in a category overlapping these two classifications.

The scholars who will appear in these pages shared a pattern of life that undoubtedly contributed to common discursive concerns. They were all male. Virtually all of them successfully completed a rite of passage (the examination system) and served in various capacities in the imperium. Many began their careers in the Hanlin Academy in Beijing, where editing projects were undertaken and literary compositions for formal occasions were written (Lui 1981). They then went on to serve in one of the Six Ministries or in the provinces as administrators or educational officers. They combined this official career in the imperium with time off for mourning parents, offending the throne, and finally, retirement to their home districts. While in office and at home, these scholars pursued studies of many sorts, especially the written protocols of the past in *li*.

Eighteenth-century scholars inherited an accretion of nearly two millennia of annotation, emendation, abridgment, commentary, and dispute over a body of "classic" texts that were fixed at thirteen in number by the Song period (Fan Wenlan 1979a: 302). Even when the actual authenticity of a text was not held in question, bitter controversies over nuance of meaning in the classics divided the scholarly community (Fan Wenlan 1979b: 265–69; Yu Ying-shih 1975: 105–46; Shi Jin 1973). The community of scholars in the Jiangnan (or the Lower Yangzi) region had developed by the mid-eighteenth century an epistemological perspective that underlay the neat grids of traditional classification by "schools."[14] The concentration of wealth in the Jiangnan region could support many academies, libraries, and wealthy patrons, providing an alternative to Beijing for intellectual and social prestige (Elman 1984: 8–13). The cities of Suzhou, Nanjing, Yangzhou, and Hangzhou were particularly important, and each served as the nominal center for an academic "school."

The epistemological perspective that the scholars of the Lower Yangzi academic community shared grew out of something later known as "evidential studies" or the Han Learning movement. Han Learning scholars preferred to return to the original sources of classical commentary in the Han (206 B.C.E. to C.E. 220), circumventing especially Song (960–1278) and Ming (1368–1628) writers. Above all, eighteenth-century classical scholars felt that the way to a true revival of the wisdom of the sages lay in careful reconsideration of those sages' original texts, insofar as these could be reconstructed through linguistic glosses upon archaic Chinese provided by Han commentaries. They bypassed later Song reinterpretation that had pursued a line of inquiry opened in the late Tang and brought to fruition in the Song with the Cheng brothers and Zhu Xi. Known as *xinglixue* (the study of nature and coherence)[15] or *daoxue* (the study of the way) in Chinese, in English this resynthesis of classical scholarship is referred to as Neo-Confucianism. A powerful synthesis of Buddhist and Taoist practices, the Cheng-Zhu wing of the school reconnected humankind with cosmic process in a new fashion, reinterpreting the Han classics in accordance with *its* new metaphysics (Henderson 1984: 119–36). From the Ming period onward, the Cheng-Zhu school provided the throne with an orthodox interpretation of the classics that was used in the examination system.

Qing Han Learning evidential scholars raised intellectual objections to this Song-Ming metaphysics, which they felt to be tainted by Daoist and Buddhist practices and concepts. But their critique was not limited to hair-splitting matters of intellectual filiation. It had a distinct political component as well. During the late Ming and early Qing, the elite felt that overconcentration upon Daoist-influenced Buddhist-style abstract speculation and personal cultivation had distanced intellectuals so far from reality that a kingdom fell to the Manchus while philosophers sat, glazed in contemplation of bamboo (Qian Mu 1963: 1:134). Within Han Learning thus developed a "tougher" mode of scholarship, "concrete studies" (*shixue*), "unadorned studies" (*puxue*), or "evidential studies" (*kaozheng xue*), one that scholars hoped would be more in touch with reality, as they "sought truth from facts" and "investigated evidence." The evidence was culled through new methods like philology and epigraphy: hence the label "evidential."

These methods in turn affected most scholarship in the eighteenth century and especially marked the massive book-collecting project of the *Library*, carried out between 1771 and 1784. The evidential standards of minute attention to philological arguments in investigating a text's provenance, exhaustive comparison of all available editions of texts, and incorporation of evidence from stone stelae and bronze inscriptions were applied by editors of the *Library*. From within Han Learning circles, however, grew a reaction to what was perceived as its excessive specialization. These dissenters came to be known as "Song Learning" scholars.

The differences between the two schools were not simply reducible to a Song Learning defense of Cheng-Zhu orthodoxy in the face of a Han Learning challenge to return to earlier sources. They disagreed in their concepts of truth and how it could be verified. For adherents of both orientations, truth lay with the sages, but Han Learning scholars felt it was discoverable only as textual evidence. Song Learning scholars, on the other hand, felt truth was a more subjective question of personal judgment, or as Guy elegantly puts it, "more often experienced than documented" (1987: 155).

For Han Learning scholars, as attention honed in more tightly upon text, speech and writing separated in the interests of a new unity. Qian Daxin (1728–1804) describes the moment well in his preface to a work on phonology by his contemporary, Xie Qikun (1737–1802):

The wisdom of the six classics is expressed in writing. Without phonology, the language of the six classics is unclear. . . . [As for etymology] Cang Jie created language and the Yellow Emperor, following him, gave the 100 things their names. The ancient names are modern words. Although the forms of ancient script have changed and their shapes and meanings have been divided, [the meaning] transmitted by the ancients is still implicit in them. . . . Through the script we can ascertain the sounds. Through the sounds, we can establish the meanings. Phonology is the one method of uniting all three [wisdom, sounds, and script]. It is the one-tenth that unites the whole.[16]

Once writing and speech had been split, scholars saw a new connection between the two, and the word itself doubled into spoken and written parts. Any direct link between visual sign and meaning was now mediated by recourse to speech. But, paradoxically, they reconstructed ancient speech itself through written characters. Thus eighteenth-century Chinese scholars ultimately never sacrificed the primacy of writing to speech, in a movement counter to that described for western Europe by Jacques Derrida. In *Of Grammatology* (1976) Derrida notes that in the post-Platonic western philosophical tradition, a metaphysics of speech-as-being has subordinated writing to a merely supplementary role, as the sign of an already and forever present signified.[17] I raise this point to highlight what I find to be a persistent theme in Chinese philosophical discourse: the resistance to transcendence and subject/object splitting (Hall and Ames 1987: introd.). Derrida sees these splits as fundamentally fostered by the suppression of writing in favor of speech, of a fetishization of speech to the point that it has installed a metaphysics of (false) "presence" (Derrida 1976). I think Chinese philosophical speculations never fully escaped reckoning with writing, precisely because of its constant implication in ritual performance and thus connection with the body. That text/performance was such a powerful social and political form further insured that writing would remain a material concern. Let me elaborate.

For eighteenth-century scholars, this detour through the oral/aural did (albeit only briefly) raise doubts reminiscent of Derrida's unwanted metaphysics. Simultaneously called into doubt were the connection between speaker and spoken (the evidential obsession with the question of personal authorship, of whether or not words were truly uttered by the sages) and between the word and its referent (the research into *mingwu,* or "words and things"). For phonologists who founded philology, writing was seen as an imperfect reflection of the spoken word, encompassed by discourse (in the narrow sense of "the spoken"). Writing was thought to change more slowly than speech, hence the doubt about referents of characters. But, and again paradoxically, in practice this intense doubt (*yi*—a methodological prerequisite for evidential scholarship) was first applied to shift away from reliance on the Song-Ming *yulu,* writing based upon an actual spoken record. Writing showed speech, but speech did not precede and induce writing.

A *yulu* was the record by his students of a master's words. It was favored by Song-Ming students of the Cheng-Zhu neo-Confucian School of Nature and Coherence, and its referents were the master's words that had been uttered with didactic intent. Speech and writing were held together tightly by this intent and encompassed the writer himself in an elision enabled by anonymous transmission. The result was a fixed text, one that could only be supplemented by commentary.

Evidential scholars rejected this emphasis upon "lecturing" (*jiangxue*) and "question and answer" (*wenda*) styles of teaching popular with neo-Confucianists (Elman 1984: 48; Chow 1994).[18] As Naquin and Rawski note:

> The introversion of this specialized community, seen in its rejection of Socratic modes of discourse or any kind of lectures (to the public or one another), was in deliberate contrast to those Ming neo-Confucian schools inspired by the sixteenth century philosopher, Wang Yangming. (1987: 66)

In other words, face-to-face teaching aloud was abandoned for writing; the "specialized community" became far more interested in communication within itself and less inclined to speak across the barrier of literacy to commoners.

Their methodological doubt broke the intentional connection between speech and writing. Evidential method required that the writer be a separate observer, writing down what he had seen or overheard. Phonologists such as Jiang Yong (1681–1762) disagreed with earlier assumptions that language was a "moral, social, and political tool" (Elman 1984: 395). Writing was thought to reflect observation directly, and the writer inserted him*self* as the author of this process. In other words, as observer and object split, author and text separated. Battles raged in the scholarly world over author-ity in issues such as who had answered certain questions first. It did not matter if the object under scrutiny was a book, an inscription, or an astronomical event. Thus, in the eighteenth century, it was not so much that the idea of what constituted a "classic" changed as it was that the very idea of what could stand as a proper text itself changed. Classical scholars had created texts that could be shared, amended, and plundered *as data* by other scholars (Elman 1984: 221–228). What interests me here is the deeper implications of this evidential shift in the perspective upon how truth could be verified and its contrast to what we will call the "ritualist metaphysics" in the next chapter.

To anticipate, the ritualist metaphysics, unlike evidential scholarship, posited an analogical relation between words and things, signs and referents, while human subjectivity was organized as resonant with the larger universe. Later we will see how, within the imperium, Grand Sacrifice as text/performance likewise posited a seamless fit between the emperor's word and action. The signifying practice of editing texts imitated as it constituted the form of its signified. That ritualist view of language was akin to what Gu Yanwu (1613–1682) called an "ideal vision of language as a tool to revive the past" (Elman 1984: 219). Indeed, both ritualist and evidential agendas shared the goal of manifesting, showing, or making visible that which had been hidden, obscure, and invisible. But the skepticism of evidential scholar Jiang Yong about the possibility of ever restoring the ancient language contrasts strikingly with what I hope to show is the linguistic optimism of the ritualist.

Han Learning evidential methods were founded within the crack between the spoken and written. Epigraphy, notation books, paleography, and philology crowded into the space opened by the phonological critique. However, at the same time that they pursued these exciting representational alternatives, many evidential scholars were heavily involved in the editing of imperial ritual texts. The centrality that *li* occupied for eighteenth-century scholarship has been pointed out by many scholars.[19] Their own preoccupation with the subject was, to some extent, an inheritance from the heroic era of the transitional generation of critical seventeenth-century statecraft thinkers, but they pursued ritual studies in a different fashion.

In the seventeenth century, Yan Yuan (1635–1704) had wished to wrest *li* from any connection to texts.

Take the case of someone who seeks to understand rituals. Allow him to read a book on ritual hundreds of times, allow him to discuss and inquire about rituals tens of times, or allow him to think about and mentally distinguish them ten times over—still he cannot be considered knowledgeable about rituals![20]

Others, like Wan Sida (1633–1683), seemed to have inadvertently continued this trend. Wan devoted a lifetime to the written record on *li,* but by his careful scholarship proving the *Zhouli* inauthentic, he too seems to have implied that *li* existed beyond the word (either originally spoken or later forged in text).[21] By the eighteenth century, however, evidentialists were more impassioned by the *written record* of the performance of *li.* Almost every classicist studied the written "institutions" (*zhi*) of rituals, dwelling upon clothing, vessels, and ceremonial form with intimidating thoroughness. Their faith that they could retrieve the institutions of the sages sustained many detailed and daunting projects. As long as the writing and editing practice of the literati revolved closely around *li*, especially but not solely imperial *li*, it would tend to reproduce a relation of hierarchical dependence upon the throne.

One center for ritual studies was Yangzhou, but many of the scholars associated with this group were from surrounding areas, and on the whole, the school grew up in the shadow of the influence of Han Learning scholar Hui Dong (1697–1758), who was from Suzhou.[22] Most of the men whose work we will concentrate upon here were associated at one time or another with the 1761 *Five Rites* encyclopedia on ritual by Qin Huitian (1702–1764), whom we met in the opening of this chapter. Yet many of them also served as imperial editors, producing, for example, the imperial ritual handbook *Da Qing tongli* (Comprehensive Rites of the Qing, hereafter *Comprehensive Rites*), completed in 1756, or the compendium of domainal regulations, *Da Qing huidian* (Assembled Canon of the Qing, hereafter *Assembled Canon*), completed in 1763. These men comfortably straddled the two worlds of private and imperial patronage.

For instance, Qin himself collated various works on ritual at imperial behest while serving in the Ministry of Rites. At the time, he was also working on the *Assembled Canon*.[23] He served in the Ministry of Rites from 1745 to 1750, under Wang Anguo (1694–1757), with time off for mourning his father (*ECCP* 167). Other contributors to the *Five Rites* included Fang Guancheng (1698–1768), Lu Jianzeng (1690–1768), and younger men like Lu Wenchao (1717–1796), Wang Mingsheng (1722–1798), and Qian Daxin (1728–1804). Dai Zhen (1724–1777), brought into the project by Qian, lived at the home of Wang Anguo when he taught in Yangzhou from 1756 to 1762. At that time, Wang had just finished supervising the editing of the *Comprehensive Rites* and was still involved with the editing of the third edition of the *Assembled Canon* (*ECCP* 803).

Two Edicts: Shared Metaphors of Editing and Ritual

In his edict of 1771 calling for the editing of the *Library,* the emperor made it apparent that he should and would defend the truths of classical teaching as he saw them and could affect by edict the organization of knowledge in his realm (Guy 1984: 136). This edict introduces a constellation of terms often encountered in Chinese writing on scholarship and ritual, terms indicating that both should bring to light the hidden and give form to chaos.

The emperor began by asserting that he was a student himself, thus setting up an implicit solidarity between himself and his editors. (The convention in

English of translating the imperial first-person designation *zhen* as "we" in this case exposes the underlying logic of the solidarity.)[24]

We have always been mindful of precedent, revered the writings of the past, and ruled in accordance with the principle of coherence. We have been diligent from day to day in our study. (*SKQSZM* 1963: 1:1)

As part of showing that he could effect the connection between knowledge and the power to rule that would bear witness to his dynasty's deservance of the Mandate of Heaven, an emperor who collected books maintained that he did so not only for the throne but for the sake of the realm.[25] In an oblique way, the edict claimed that the throne provided the context for facilitating all scholarship:

But the only goal of study is to obtain guiding principles and know more of the words and deeds of the past in order to gain virtue. Only if book collections are broad and encompassing can research be fine and precise. (*SKQSZM* 1963: 1:1)

The Qianlong emperor wanted a project at least the size of the Kangxi era encyclopedia, *Gujin tushu jicheng,* one that would give scholars a "broad view" (*daguan*) of policymaking in the past, one in which "the unity of scholarship past and present will be made manifest [*zhang*]." Then, the work of those scholars "who know only a small subject and compile narratives so detailed that [the thread] of every last fact or phenomena is gathered and followed [*jianzong tiao-guan*] will each be fitted into their proper tradition." "Any surviving books that clarify [*chanming*] essential methods of government" should be collected. Thus, works that have been lost in past obscurity or that are in the hands of scholars "still hidden in the mountains" will be "brought to light [*faming*]."

The *Library*'s founding edict uses "clarify" (*chanming*), "bring to light" (*faming*), and "make manifest" (*zhang*) to articulate the theme of making visible the hidden. It employs "to gather and follow" (*jianzong tiaoguan*) to convey a second important theme of editing and ritual alike, that of bringing form to chaos. The first set of usages serves to privilege the eye, the second belongs to references to weaving, threading, and connecting. Other examples of such terminology that we will see occurring below include for showing, or displaying, *xian, zhu, shi, shi, xian;* for "examining and inspecting," *kan, yue, yan, kao, guan, sheng, sheng, shi;* for weaving and connecting, *ji, guan, jing, tiao.* The implications of these two tropes will be taken up in the next chapter and in part 3 below.

The short edict calling for the compilation of the *Comprehensive Rites* was promulgated in the first year, the sixth month of the Qianlong reign (1736). It likewise discusses how things that have remained hidden will now come forth.

Since the time of the Han and Tang, although the ceremonies of the Boundary Sacrifices and the Court have been sketched in order to facilitate preparation, the whole set of their designations [has] remained hidden with those who carried the [direct] responsibility. Now they will emerge into use. (*DQTL* 1756: 1a, woodblock ed.)

The emperor laments upon how difficult it has been in the past to bring order to details of ritual such as architecture, carriages, clothing, drinking and eating, marriage, and sacrifice. For although scholars had books, "as times differ, so did institutions." The problem was compounded by the realization that society was not homogeneous, but rather made up of hierarchically differentiated groups. "What the gentry and ministers can follow is difficult to show [*shi*] to the masses of commoners" (*DQTL* 1756: 1a).

The edict of the *Comprehensive Rites* dwells upon *li* as a vehicle for perceiving and reinforcing continuity and connection where none is readily apparent either to scholars who wish to learn from the distant past or to an emperor contemplating the social diversity of an empire. The intensive ritual research of the eighteenth century resulted in the production of handbooks that would standardize ritual procedure and create consistency of practice across class lines (Naquin and Rawski 1987: 90; Ebrey 1991a; Chow 1994).

Indeed, the edict goes on to tell us that the "complex and heavy" chapters of the *Assembled Canon*, along with past books on ritual, must be consulted in order to produce the *Comprehensive Rites*, a "complete ceremonial systematization for Capping, Marriage, Funerals, and Sacrifice. It must be hoped that it will be of clear [*mingbai*] simplicity so that both gentry and commoners will easily welcome it."[26]

We see once again a cluster of terms privileging the eye, this time describing what ritual will do. The two edicts, the first discussing editing practice, the second ritual performance, connect through their similar metaphors. The common term *zhu,* which begins the last line of the edict and is usually translated "Let [so and so do such and such]," (in this case, princes and grand ministers who are in charge of such matters), takes on added richness because the word *zhu* also means to show, make manifest, or to write, edit (Fairbank 1970: 39, 42, 47). In this edict calling for the editing of a ritual handbook, it conveys the imperial command that begins both those processes and, in fact, begins the text/performance of ritual.

Text/performance of *li* began with classification and continued to feature this literate claim to control of knowledge as a prominent feature of performance itself. The rest of this chapter discusses the classifications of texts on *li* in the *Library* and their implications for notions of time and human agency.

History's "Books on Governance"

The texts used in this study are filed in the *Library* under two main categories: history[27] and classics.[28] Editorial comment in the *Library* can serve to orient us on the question of how history and classics were constructed as categories in the late eighteenth century and how ritual texts came to bridge the two.[29]

Any bibliography provides a convenient summary or map of basic culturally defined categories whereby knowledge and experience are defined and analyzed. The Qianlong emperor laid down the basic classificatory framework for the *Library* merely by so naming it and thus bestowing upon it the famous "four category" (or *siku*) system (figure 13). They consist of classics (*jing*), history (*shi*), philosophy (*zi*), and *belles lettres* (*ji*).[30]

After the four categories were institutionalized under the Tang with the imperially sponsored *Suishu* "Essay on Classical Collections," classics, history, philosophy, and *belles lettres* became the basic categories most employed by bibliographers until the late eighteenth century. Rather than simply imitating and reproducing past practices, however, *Library* editors did make changes.

Within classics, scholars added the category *Wujing zongyi* (general summarizing works) for texts that provided an overview of the Five Classics (*SKQSZM* 1:33–34/169–89). Their most important changes, however, centered around the subcategory *xiaoxue*, literally "lesser learning," usually simply called philology (Guy 1987: 227; Elman 1984: 163). The editors excluded the works on elementary education and child training they felt had been mistakenly included in the Song, and narrowed the category to include only works on philology, etymology, phonology, and studies of the vocabularies of individual classics (Guy 1980: 227–28; *SKQSZM* 1:40/338). By these changes, evidential editors sought to obviate the influence of the Cheng-Zhu school while consolidating their own position as interpreters of textually born truth. By narrowing the scope of the *xiaoxue*, they widened the use of this category as repository and organizer of their new methodology for dealing with *all texts*: classics, histories, or philosophies.[31]

In contrast, the history section was more tightly controlled and carefully

I. CLASSICS	**III. PHILOSOPHY** *(zibu ch.91–147)*
Book of Changes	Confucians
Book of Documents	Military Startegies
The Poetry	Legalists
Rites*	Agriculturalists
Spring and Autumn Annals	Medicine
Classic Filiality	Astronomy and Mathematics
General Summarizing Works	Calculating Arts
Four Books	Arts
Music	Repositories of Science
Philology	Miscellaneous Writers
	Encyclopedias
II. HISTORY *(shibu ch. 45–90)*	Novelists
Dynastic Histories	Buddhism
Annals	Daoism
Records of Affairs	
Unofficial Histories	**IV. LITERATURE** *(jibu ch. 148–200)*
Miscellaneous Histories	Elegies of Chu
Edicts and Memorials	Individual Collections
Biographies	General Anthologies
Historical Records	Songs and Drama
Contemporary Records	
Chronography	
Official Registers	
Books on Governance*	
Epigraphy and Bibliography	
Historical Criticism	*Books used in this study.

1 3. Sections under the four categories in the *Library,* based on Elman, *From Philosophy to Philology* (1984), 164.

edited (Guy 1987: 61). According to Kent Guy, none of the newer developments in historical writing—local histories, epigraphy, notation books—influenced the organization of the collection. A new category was created for the
memorials to the throne filed in the *belles lettres* section of earlier bibliographies.
And a special category was created to accommodate larger encyclopedic works
such as the *Wenxian tongkao* and the various *Tongdian.* This new section was called
zhengshu, or Books on Governance.[32] In Guy's opinion, the section's two innovations reflected imperial and not private concerns.[33] This new category is particu-

larly revealing precisely because it "excited little interest among eighteenth century intellectuals" (Guy 1980: 233). In other words, the actual creation of the
category crowned unspoken consensus upon it as a normal way of classifying
together this particular set of texts. What was included in the Books on Governance section?

The *Library*'s *General Catalogue* lists six subsections of "Books on Governance,"
including Comprehensive Institutions, Canonical Rituals, Money, Military Governance, Laws, and Public Works (figure 14). The largest subsection was
"Canonical Rituals" (*dianli*), which contains twenty-four works. But works filed
under the subsection "Comprehensive Institutions" likewise consisted mostly of
the technical details of performance of ceremonies whereby every area of imperial governance was carried out.[34] In fact, Books on Governance as a whole was
overwhelmingly preoccupied with *li,* and here we find the ritual texts that are
of special interest to this study.[35]

In the subsection of Books on Governance concerned with Canonical Rites,
we will find the *Comprehensive Rites,* the *Illustrations of Dynastic Ritual Paraphernalia*
(*SKQSZM* 1:82/701–8, see p. 706). In the subsection on Comprehensive Institutions, we find the *Assembled Canon* and the *Examples Attached to the Assembled
Canon* (*SKQSZM* 1:81/693–701). Figure 14 lists those texts under their relevant
subsections. Was this division into Canonical Rites and Comprehensive Institutions meaningful?

In the history category, as a whole, texts are classified according to the Han
period division into "chronologies" (*jizhuan,* descriptive narratives) or "essays"
(*zhi*), which analyze topics.[36] The first nine sections under history (figure 13)
are chronologies of one sort or another; the remaining sections contain essays.
Filed as they are with other books of essays, we would expect all Books on
Governance to be analytic in form, whereas in fact they are not. The texts that
are exceptions to this classificatory priority are the ritual handbooks filed under
Canonical Rites. Let me elaborate.

The ideal Books on Governance were the Comprehensive Institutions such
as the *Wenxian tongkao.* These texts sought to present all human time in one
book, accomplishing this task through selected examples, isolated from an original temporal sequence and framed for discussion by analytic subject headings.
The *Assembled Canon,* preserving the principle if not the scale of such massive
works of "Comprehensive Institutions," sought to present all relevant govern-
mental information for one dynasty, the Qing, since its beginning (Jin Yubi
1962: 116).

The ritual handbooks under Canonical Rites differ. Qing editors of the *Com-*

Subsection	Total Entries
Comprehensive Institutions *tonghzhi*	*19*
Da Qing huidan*	[Assembled canon of the Qing]
Da Ming huidan*	[Assembled canon of the Ming]
Xu Wenxian tongkao*	[Continuation of the Comprehensive investigations of *wen*]
Canonical Rituals *dianli*	*24*
Da Qing tongli*	[Comprehensive rites of the Qing]
Huangchao liqi tushi*	[Illustrations of dynastic ritual paraphernalia]
Ming jili*	[Collected rites of the Ming]
Da tang kaiyuan li*	[Rites of the Tang Kaiyuan period]
Money *bangji*	6
Military Governance *junzheng*	4
Laws *faling*	2
Public Works *kaogong*	2

*Texts used in this study.

14. Subsections of the "Books on Governance" section under the category "History." Compiled from *SKQSZM* 1:81–84.

prehensive Rites handbook drew upon the *Assembled Canon* as a source (*SKQSZM* 82/1:706; *DQTL* 1756: imperial preface, 1a), but they thought of the two texts as complementary.[37] "The *Comprehensive Rites* and the *Assembled Canon* are to be taken mutually like a coat and its lining [*biaoli,* outer/inner, external/internal]" (*DQTL* 1756: *fanlie,* 1a). In fact, the *Comprehensive Rites* took its model texts from a divergent genealogy, one that related texts differently to history and time than did the *huidian* or *tongkao* "Comprehensive Institutions" traditions. This divergent genealogy included handbooks edited since the Tang to aid in the actual performance of rites in their respective eras, works that reproduced iconically in their form aspects of the ritual logic they were to aid to fruition in performance.[38]

Although its editors were bidden to consult extensively the historical record of ritual, as a finished product the Qing *Comprehensive Rites* seems to have existed wholly in and for the present. As its *Library General Catalogue* colophon states: "The *Comprehensive Rites* only sets down the hierarchical differences between the great and humble, the order of the proceedings [*jiemu zhi xianhou*] without extending into changes over time" (*SKQSZM* 82/1:706). The *Comprehensive Rites* was designed to facilitate actual ritual performance by emphasizing the ceremonial usages in carrying out ritual (*xingli yijie*), and these usages were written out in detail for convenient following.[39] The *Library* editors praised the handbook's editors for being selective in their inclusion of past ritual usages and emphasizing what was truly appropriate for present-day needs:

Changing events [*shi*] require suitability [to circumstance]. [The editors] did not rigidly follow in the footsteps of previous people. Timeless example [*fa*] calls forth that by which it can be maintained [in the present]. In putting together historical records, there will always be an excess that cannot be brought wholly to perception in manifest practice. When arranging the historical record of ritual texts of previous eras, everything that cannot be actually used should be discarded. (*SKQSZM* 82/1:706)

What the *Comprehensive Rites* accomplished, in fact, was the materialization for present dynastic practice of the best and most suitable from ritual in the past. The Qianlong emperor's *Comprehensive Rites,* small as it was at only fifty chapters, took more than twenty years to complete, an expensive distillation. Since perfect ritual in the present reflected perfect access to ritual past (perhaps today we would subsume such knowledge under the heading "history"), much material had to be examined, but only with an eye to actual practice. The emperor's preface concludes thus:

This piece is clear and complete, detailed without being overly wordy and complex. It treats the Classics as its model and supplements the *Assembled Canon*. Let families recite it and households practice it so that the Five Relationships will be extended. In daily use, it will cause a surge of filiality and will correct customs. (*DQTL* 1756: preface, 1b)

The *Comprehensive Rites* was to be a convenient aid to actual performance. Its emphasis lay upon "ceremonial usages in carrying out rituals" (*xingli jieyi*) and not upon the historical background of the items used in the rites.[40] While texts like Du Yu's *Tongdian,* or Ma's *Wenxian tongkao* or even, on a smaller scale, the Qing dynasty's own *Assembled Canon* encompassed the past by listing it, the *Comprehensive Rites* was prepared as a substitute for the past. The *Comprehensive Rites,* as repository of the editing choices of the eighteenth century, would help ensure the continuation of society through time by facilitating *li* as performance. It *was* history in a way that texts that *list* events could not be. Its contribution to a ritual corpus heavily weighted toward the encyclopedic was a narration of ceremonies that gave a step-by-step (hence *xing*) account of their unfolding in time. It restored their temporal dimension through a narrative that assembled bits and pieces of other times to facilitate the enactment of ritual in the lived time of the eighteenth century.

Chinese historiographers have speculated at great length upon various classifications. Here we have explored one recurring aspect of textual form that may have been meaningful for classifiers when viewed in a larger ritual context—that is, how texts reflect and construct time.[41]

According to the *General Catalogue*'s headnote of this subsection of history, "Books on Governance" deserved a special category because it combined features of both histories and classics (*SKQSZM* 82/1:693). They recorded ritual time that combined the timeless (the encompassment of all ritual in the encyclopedic Comprehensive Institutions) with the timely, and the well-timed, in the handbooks of Canonical Rites. It is just this rescue of human example as temporal experience from its enshrinement as timeless classical value that ritual texts facilitated.

Li Mediating Classics and History

Qing scholars had been preoccupied by the question of the relationship between classics and histories at least since the seventeenth century. In fact, it has been argued that an important inaugural point in the debate rests with the Ming philosopher Wang Yangming, who is credited by historian Cang Xueliang with the phrase "the Six Classics are all history" (Cang 1984: 106). Wang was objecting to the commonplace Cheng-Zhu view that the classics spoke of the principles of coherence of things, while the histories recorded their actuality. It was objection to the dualisms between the *dao* and material force or *qi,* and *li* as coherence and "things," that underlay Wang Yangming's, and later Zhang Xuecheng's, most radical critique of the misconceptualization of the classics as timeless.[42]

The position articulated by Yan Ruoju (1636–1704) on the question in the seventeenth century furthered in an unwittingly literal fashion Wang's project to connect the classics with material concerns. Yan drew attention to the classics' fundamental identity with other texts *qua* text.

What Classics? What Histories? What Commentaries? My concern is only with what is true. If the Classic is true and the History is false, then it is permissible to use the Classic to correct the History and the Commentary. If the History and the Commentary are true and the Classic is false, then can it be impermissible to use the History and the Commentary to correct the Classic?[43]

How was this truth discerned? Through the methods of comparative philology pioneered by Yan himself and enshrined later in the Philology section of the *Library,* a ground of identity for all texts was established upon the shared fact of their being formed within language. The profound similarity between classics and histories was seen to lie in their textual nature. Yet it would be a mistake to conclude that such "rigorous analysis" and "collection of impartial evidence" implied a Baconian scientific revolution.[44] When scholars after Yan Ruoju took up the question of the relationship between classics and history, they discussed them first as physical texts, as objects that had been authored, manipulated through classification, miscopied, or forged.

In Zhang Xuecheng (1738–1801), we find clearly articulated the political implications of the recovery of the classics as authored human artifacts. The question of the actual origins of the classics as human productions was one of his chief preoccupations.[45] If the classics were nothing but the original historical records of ancient governments, as Zhang claimed, then one could conclude that the original sages were, in fact, historians (Nivison 1966: 66). It is only a short step to revise this proposition and declare passionately that the route to sagehood lay in the writing of history. Thus, Zhang's and others' claim that the classics were history, while the outcome of the creation of new standards for comparability of texts, was also a way of "investing history itself [and its writers] with the near-sacred character of classical writings" (204).

Headnotes collected in the *Library*'s *General Catalogue* reflect these concerns. In the headnote beginning the classics section, the editors describe these texts as unreachable by any single writer.

The Classics are the distillation of the Sages' formulations that provide a model for ten thousand generations. The purport of their collection is like the sun centering itself in the sky. There is no one who can add anything to their narrative. Those who would say they have done so are still only commenting upon what the Classics have said. (*SKQSZM* head *juan*/ 1:1)

Here the social nature of the classics is recognized as a reification. The editors feel that no commentary can measure up to the standards of the sages. Indeed, they listed the shortcomings of each school of classical studies, starting with the Han period itself. Those scholars were accused of rigidity because teaching was passed strictly within schools. Although evidential studies are complimented, a tendency to triviality within them is also noted. Both "Han Learning" and "Song Learning" are criticized. Finally having placed everyone on an equally lowly footing, the editors suggest:

> We must stop viewing through "Schools," take the best from each, banish private coherence principle, allowing public coherence principle to emerge. When public coherence emerges, then the meaning of the Classics will be clarified. The Classics are not private, but are the public coherence of all under Heaven. (Ibid.)

The classics as model (*xing*) are the property of the community as a whole.[46] The classics instantiate the principle of coherence and have appeared, and continue to appear, like the very sun whose timely reoccurrence is necessary to life itself. We are here presented with a view of the classics as eternal verities, and individual initiative in studying them seems to be discouraged.[47]

In contrast to this view of the classics as out of reach by any one scholar, or single school, the histories are described as more accessible. Rather than facing the texts in question entirely as a collective audience, the intellectual community is divided into those who write history and those who read it. History's modeling function is never raised explicitly, only implied in a discussion of how correct history allows judgments of praise and blame.

In the headnote to the history section of the *General Catalogue,* we find that the process of writing history begins with observation (*guan*) of the traces of events (*shiji*), from their beginning to end (*shimo*).

> The Way of History lies in seeking simplicity through choice of narrative, and detail through investigation of evidence. None is simpler than the *Spring and Autumn Annals,* none more complex than *Zuozhuan.* What the historians of Lu recorded encompassed was the beginning and end of each event. (*SKQSZM* 45 / 1 : 397)

The actual process of "fixing" history in text then follows:

> When the sages observed [*guan*] from beginning to end, they attained a knowledge of the truth and falsity of events, and were able to fix judgement about praise and blame by means of a single word [*zi*]. This is why writers of history value "investigating evidence" [*kaozheng*]. (Ibid.)

And just as the writing of history depends upon observation, so does its reading.

Qiu Ming recorded through annals and later people observed them in their entirety [*shimo,* translated above as "from beginning to end"] attaining a knowledge of the truth and falsity of events, thus comprehending the judgement about praise and blame born by a single word. This is why readers of history value "investigating evidence." (Ibid.)

For the editors of the *Library,* observation was an active process that led to a morally satisfying judgment. It pertained to events and to texts equally and, as we will show below, is a central activity in the ritual process of Grand Sacrifice. But it had its origin in the events of the world, surviving as "traces" (*ji*):

If there were no traces of events, even the sages could not have written the *Spring and Autumn Annals.* Without knowing the traces of events even sages reading the histories could not make judgments based upon the characters. (Ibid.)

The literal translation of the word *ji* is "track or footsteps," reminding us that these "traces" are already very human, very inside "culture," and not part of an objective, separate "natural" reality. For the editors of the *Library,* history as event, and its writing, were both situated within a social discursive space.

Editors conceptualized histories and classics as simultaneously similar and different. Both were the words of the sages. Scholars spoke of both genres with optimism about the possibility of knowing the past and the wisdom of the sages through textual evidence. In the case of history, text itself functioned for the observer much as did the original "traces of events" for the writers of history. In the case of classics, text was the vehicle allowing access to the models of the sages. Classics and histories were similar insofar as both were text or *wen,* the *words* of the sages.

On the other hand, human agency (defined here as the capacity to act) was depicted differently in relation to each category. An active role is imputed to the men who can create (*zuo*) the texts of history. Not every historian's work was judged as similarly worthwhile. Evidential methods will allow historians to choose the best. In contrast, the scholarly community was portrayed as collectively passive as it faced the classical canon. Insofar as they considered classics and histories to be different, scholars emphasized that they were words of (different) *sages.* Thus, Lu Wenchao (1717–1796), the respected collator whose edition of the *Yili,* or *Ceremonial Rites,* was considered definitive in its time, formulated the point I am making here when he said: "The histories have different uses from the classics, but they derive from the same sources . . . the historical records of the sages."[48]

As the words of the sages came to preoccupy eighteenth-century scholars as *written records,* writing itself came to be viewed as an historical act. This convergence implied a rejection of the former distinction between *yan,* words, and *shi,* events as writing subsumed speech.[49] As Zhang Xuecheng put it in his essay "The Teaching of History": "Words, as historical utterances, are themselves events; and events are complexes that always involve words" (Nivison 1966: 225; Zhang Xuecheng 1985: 1.7a).

Herein lies the importance of the category Books on Governance, repository for so many texts on ritual, for understanding the conjuncture of writing about past *li* and performing *li* in the present. In their headnote, the *Library* editors point out that the Books on Governance are most salient for their combination of models to be imitated (*fa,* usually associated with classics), and events (*shi,* associated traditionally with history).

Essays in the Standard Histories on Arts and Letters [where bibliographies are found] contain the category "Narratives" [*gushi*]. [What is contained in these narratives?] How the progenitors created models [*fa,* to be imitated], and for many generations observed them carefully, makes up what is known as the Narratives of a Dynasty [*yichao zhi gushi*]. (*SKQSZM* 82/1:693)

In other words, the events recorded in Books on Governance are the creation of models for governance. Since we have noted already that ritual texts occupied most of this category, we may conclude that *li* were conceptualized as the means whereby the models of the Classics were reworked and reenacted through each dynasty. (Remember that Canonical Rites handbooks were designed to expedite the reproduction of ritual time in historical time.)

The initiation of a category in the 1770s that recognized books combining the classical standards and historical events indicates how closely classics and history were by then considered to be allied. Why did editors and ritual experts place *li* at the nexus of history and classics, as indeed a proving point that the two were fundamentally identical? I think their conception of the nature of ritual itself entered into their decision.

In the Cheng-Zhu tradition (already nearly eight hundred years old by this time), classics were thought to provide the timeless standard of order and meaning.[50] History, on the other hand, dealt with contingent facts and events in the world. Put another way, classics embodied the realm of normative *value* while histories chronicled *action.*[51]

Yet these discontinuities and contradictions between an imagined "ought" and a lived experience must be mediated in any social formation. Often rituals accomplish this task because they both expose and construct the implicit grounds of the declared "natural," which everyone shares. As Murphy puts it:

Ritual and the sacred do not express the solidarity of the social group nor do they symbolize the constraint of its norms upon the individual. Rather, they *bridge the contradiction between norm and action and mediate the alienation of man from his fellow man*. (1971: 243; emphasis added)

In eighteenth-century China, *li* in general, and rites of sacrifice in particular, did accomplish such mediation. Lu Wenchao's colophon, dated 1763, to Qin Huitian's encyclopedic *Five Rites* begins:

The intertwining coils of ritual are everywhere between Heaven and Earth bounded by the uses of the Five Rites as the completion of the year is bounded by the Four Seasons and Five Phases. If we wish to divide them roughly, the Felicitous Rites [*jiali*] are closely related to spring; Guest Rites [*binli*] to summer; Military Rites [*junli*] to autumn, and Funerary Rites [*xiungli*] to winter. The Auspicious Rites [*jili*, rites of sacrifice] *flow through and link the center* of the four others, as the earth is entrusted with the sovereignty of the Four Seasons.

Heaven is above and earth below. The myriad things are scattered and differ. When people are born, as children they know love. As they grow a bit, they know respect. Is it that the Three Ways of Heaven, Earth and Humanity [*san cai*] having been established, the *li* followed?[52]

In Lu's cosmology, the *li* have a simultaneous social and extrahuman origin. As *li* intertwine (*pan*) through the universe, the Five Rites correspond to the Five Seasons. Rites of sacrifice, however, are the *central* (*zhong*) and *connecting* (*guan*) rites. The social origins of *li* lie in providing the ground of similarity for correspondence between seemingly disparate things and people. Lu goes on to praise the *Five Rites* because it presents ritual as a living link between past and present:

One studies the Three Ages of the past for the ritual that future generations will follow . . . Ponder [these rites], arrange them, research their transformations, and the *dao* which cannot change will manifest itself. The sages created a clear narrative and, of course, much of that is included here. (*WLTK* prefaces 1a–b/2)

The word translated here as "manifest" is *zhu,* which I noted above also means "to write," equating once again writing and ritually induced transformation.

It is not too surprising, then, that ritual was chosen as the most fitting subject for texts that would serve as emblem and embodiment of the identity of classics and histories. The texts of *li,* its inscriptions, accomplish much the same things that were imputed to performance: bridging and connecting. According to its headnote, Books on Governance are included in the *General Catalogue*'s "standard table of contents to be able to perceive the meaning of the comprehensive connectedness of the past and present" (*SKQSZM* 82/1:693). Books on Governance, that is, texts on ritual, make the past present. They also bridge the gap between high and low, rulers and ruled, since their production is accomplished collectively by throne and officialdom. "Our Emperor on high, systematizing, renews daily, handing down plans for appointments. [In response,] We have already respectfully presented upward the new book boxes" (ibid.). Thus are the texts themselves included in the connection that correct ritual forges between value and action, the timeless and the timely, past and present, rulers and ruled.

The Editing Eye

Li or ritual was a set of principles for ordering and connecting that was both cosmically dictated and humanly maintained. By the eighteenth century, an emphasis upon textual studies coincided with a mania for the retrieval and representation of historical ritual.[53] With signification and communication raised to such a level of cosmic necessity, there clearly existed the potential for the editing of texts to become also the centrally meaningful, sacred process described by Yu Ying-shih earlier in this chapter.

The eighteenth-century ritual handbook, the *Comprehensive Rites,* highlighted the textual aspect of Grand Sacrifice so that the event became not only a celebration of the monarchy, but also a display of the ability of its servants to re-create the king in a fashion perfectly consonant with the original intentions of the sages *as these could be read from their written traces.* Their division of ceremonial order differed from that of past editors: they explicitly introduced good evidential practices into the period of Preparation. These included "ordering" (*zhizhai*) and "classification" (*she*) that alternated with "examination" (*shi*) and "inspection" (*sheng*) (figure 15, segments 1–12).

In eighteenth-century prefaces to ritual handbooks, the ritual classics, and the introductions to sections of the Qianlong editing project, the *Library,* notions of clarifying (*ming*), manifesting (*xian*), and displaying (*shi*) often occur, drawing attention to the eye as chief means whereby people apprehend latent patterns.[54] The eye was not always so privileged: Kenneth DeWoskin's work on music in the Han and Six Dynasties period makes a case for the ear (1982: 24–36). The

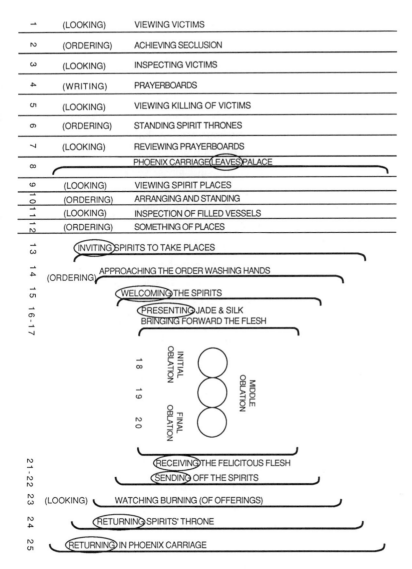

1	(LOOKING)	VIEWING VICTIMS
2	(ORDERING)	ACHIEVING SECLUSION
3	(LOOKING)	INSPECTING VICTIMS
4	(WRITING)	PRAYERBOARDS
5	(LOOKING)	VIEWING KILLING OF VICTIMS
6	(ORDERING)	STANDING SPIRIT THRONES
7	(LOOKING)	REVIEWING PRAYERBOARDS
8		PHOENIX CARRIAGE (LEAVES) PALACE
9	(LOOKING)	VIEWING SPIRIT PLACES
10	(ORDERING)	ARRANGING AND STANDING
11	(LOOKING)	INSPECTION OF FILLED VESSELS
12	(ORDERING)	SOMETHING OF PLACES
13		(INVITING) SPIRITS TO TAKE PLACES
14	(ORDERING)	APPROACHING THE ORDER WASHING HANDS
15		(WELCOMING) THE SPIRITS
16-17		(PRESENTING) JADE & SILK / BRINGING FORWARD THE FLESH

INITIAL OBLATION — 18

MIDDLE OBLATION — 19

FINAL OBLATION — 20

21-22		(RECEIVING) THE FELICITOUS FLESH / (SENDING) OFF THE SPIRITS
23	(LOOKING)	WATCHING BURNING (OF OFFERINGS)
24		(RETURNING) SPIRITS' THRONE
25		(RETURNING) IN PHOENIX CARRIAGE

15. Grammar of Grand Sacrifice. Based on the Sacrifice to Heaven in *DQTL* 1756: chap. 1.

question of whether or not this eighteenth-century privileging of the gaze signals a shift comparable to the momentous one in European hierarchies of perception after the invention of the telescope, vanishing point perspective, and the development of the Cartesian cogito, remains for research (Bryson 1983: chaps. 1–2; Lowe 1982: chap. 1; Alpers 1983). Judging from the coherence and importance of the ritualist metaphysics under discussion, one is tempted to conclude not, and to decide that the intellectual innovations of evidential scholars were encompassed and halted precisely because of their close articulation with imperial ritual. Nonetheless, room must be left for analysis of their effort as a negative factor operating from within the constructive positivity of the ritualist metaphysics. The evidential obsession with observation and order based upon humanly invented criteria of proof that only obliquely connected with the operation of the *dao* was important. It doubtless contributed, along with the fall of the monarchy and the continuous widening of alternative, extra-imperial forms of prestige and power in Chinese society after the eighteenth century, to the transformation of the ritualist metaphysics.[55]

In emphasizing the eye, what were these editors trying to see? Eighteenth-century descriptions of the *Comprehensive Rites* always draw attention to its narrative shape and, hence, to its structuring of time. I have diagrammed the ceremonial order to highlight the echo-like arrangement of the action (see figure 15, noting paired actions like segment 8, "leaving," and segment 25, "returning"; segment 15, "welcoming," and segment 22, "sending off").[56] Participants could preview the ritual because its sequence instantiated a series of miniature cosmic cycles whose beginnings implied and contained their ends—a sort of "what goes around comes around." It is as though neither term of such paired actions could be enunciated or imagined without evoking its opposite as its condition of possibility. The deliberate division of the segments of action in sacrifice into beginnings and endings, all of which were encompassed within each other, constructed time not so much as cyclical as constantly accrued. Indeed, the tendency to reach ever further into the past for original words and original rituals to encompass all time obsessed eighteenth-century scholars, as though a correct beginning ensured a correct end and true history found in the past implied the possibility and substantiation for their creation of good government in the present.

To pursue the analogy of this newly edited structure of sacrifice as metaphor for history, we note that the oldest portion of sacrifice is the inner core of the Three Oblations. It appears in early Han texts, around the beginning of the common era.[57] In the Tang *Kaiyuan li,* presented to the throne in 732, the resonating echo-like portions are fully elaborated (in figure 15, from segment 8, "Phoenix Carriage Leaves Palace," to its "echo" segment 25, "Returning," which ends the sacrifice).[58]

What the Qing editors adumbrated further was the preparatory portion of the rite. They emphasized looking and ordering, activities that resonated with editing methods of the time. Editors of the *Library* privileged texts on *li* with a special category, *zhengshu* or Books on Governance. This privileging was grounded in the perception that writing about ritual mediated the categories of timeless classic and time-bound history because such texts made possible the reactualization of the sages' past *words* in present *ceremonial*. They inserted the eye that read the text into the performance itself, privileging it in a new fashion. It is not odd that Qing scholars, with their obsession about editing the classics as Way to the *dao,* should have enshrined the terminology of this sacred activity in the objects and actions of sacrifice itself. In other words, in the rules of bibliographic classification and their defense we find an admission of *li*'s role as text/performance.

4

WRITING THE RITUALIST METAPHYSICS

Self and World

What runs through and connects [*guan*] learning: *li*. Thus the *dao* of the Sages is nothing other than *li*. . . . The Nature, reaching as it does the most secret, is seen [*jian*] by means of *li*. The Nature, reaching to the most subtle, is made manifest [*xian*] by means of *li*. Thus it is said "Nothing is more visible than what is secret, nothing more manifest than what is minute." LING TINGKAN, *Fuli*

Books on Governance carried the values of classical sagely standards into the *Library's* category of history. Commentaries on the Classics inverted this mediation, being each a sign of the times in which it was written. Thus, in the *Library,* every Classic came arrayed with a chronologically arranged train of the history of its interpretation. Choice and interpretation of commentary often carried immediate political significance to its writers, and modern scholars have rightly reread such exegetical debates for clues to factional battlelines.[1] But commentary can also reflect decisions that formed the values that underlay factional struggles and gave them meaning and effect.

I will examine the "Liyun" (*Li* Transforms through its Phases) chapter of the *Liji*, or the *Record of Rites,* one of the best and most systematic introductions to the metaphysics of *li*.[2] The *Record of Rites* was compiled in the first century B.C.E., during the Han dynasty. It is reputed to be records by the pupils of the seventy original disciples of Confucius.[3] Along with the *Zhouli* (Rites of Zhou) and the *Yili* (Ceremonial rites) it forms the *Lijing,* or *Classic of Rites.*

Two eighteenth-century editions of this Han classic will be consulted. The first is the imperially sanctioned Song Learning edition, the *Liji yishu* (*LJYS*), part of the *Qinding sanli yishu* (Imperial edition of the analysis of the meanings of the three rites), printed in 1748. It includes a wide range of commentary from the Han-Tang and especially the Song-Ming traditions (*ECCP* 236; *SKQSZM* 21/1:172). The second is the *Liji zhengyi* (*LJZY*) (Verification of meanings in the Record of Rites), as edited by Ruan Yuan (1764–1849) and others—a strictly Han Learning edition that presents only notes by Han dynasty scholar Zheng Xuan (127–200) and commentary by Tang dynasty Kong Yingda (574–648).[4]

The analysis that follows provides us with a vocabulary in which to discuss what I have called a "ritualist metaphysics" concerning the shape of the cosmos and humanity's place, and the uses of *li* within it. In addition, we will note how interpretation of the text changed between the Han-Tang version of commentaries favored by Ruan Yuan and the Song ones favored by those editing under imperial auspices. We will be concerned especially with the crucial areas of the knowability of the world and the formation of a subject appropriate to that knowing—with what, in Chinese terms, made a sage. Their choice of commentary will throw some light on the ironic position occupied by the most radical evidential Han Learning scholars vis-à-vis this metaphysics.

The chapter of the classic itself, "*Li* Transforms through Its Phases," falls roughly into three parts. First, *li* is situated within human time and social discourse; then, humankind and its *li* are placed in the context of a larger cosmos; finally, these two themes are woven together. The chapter as a whole is constructed so that each of its sections, while explicating its own main theme, includes references to the others. The narrative does not proceed in a linear fashion but introduces a succession of images that interrelate in a part/whole fashion. I will turn to the evidential Han Learning edition of the *Liji zhengyi* first.

The Dispersal of Being in Han-Tang Cosmology

"*Li* Transforms through Its Phases" begins with the image of the sighing Confucius. He feels sad to live in a corrupt and decadent time when rites are a necessary corrective for a society fallen from the "Great Harmony" (*datong*). The reader finds herself immediately inserted into a continuity the nature of whose past is discerned (negatively) from practices of the present. Foremost among these practices are *li*.

From Confucius's point of view, the *li* acted as the inaugural point between two past ages. During the Great Harmony, people lived in caves or nests, wore feathers and skins, and did not cook (i.e., did not use fire). When eating the flesh of animals, they even "drank the blood and swallowed the fur/feathers" (things that were pointedly removed in later sacrificial rites). This was the time before the Five Emperors and Three Sovereigns. After a time, sages (*sheng*) discovered fire; the uses of clay, metal, and weaving; and offerings to the dead.[5] During this time people had to make do with *li,* the simulacrum of the *dao* (*LJZY* 21/2:1416). When arguing over precedent and correct usage, later ritualists would often refer to a time of "origin" (*yuan*) or "beginning" (*shi*). It was to the period in the wake of the Great Harmony, the earliest period of cultural expertise, to which they referred, and not to a precultural golden age. As the text states: "In all things we follow this period" (*LJZY* 21/2:1413). There is no sense in this essay that time is reversible, that the Great Harmony can be recovered. It is possible, however, to go forward with the help of the practices of the *li* as the later great sage kings of Zhou (Kings Wen and Wu and the Duke of Zhou) had done.

From this chapter emerges first of all a picture of humanity's extraordinary place in the cosmos, a picture that seems to run counter to the cliché that the traditional Chinese universe was not anthropocentric. Han and Tang ritualists were indeed preoccupied with the human role, but in a way quite different from Western post-Renaissance glorification of humanity.

In China, since at least the Han period and arguably until the end of the nineteenth century, the world as natural and human was constituted systematically as a vast plane of resonating sets of perceptible correlations.[6] Some basic forms of correlative thought included correspondence between man and cosmos, between heaven and the imperium, and correspondence based upon the *Book of Changes* and numerological manipulation, especially upon the Five Phases (Henderson 1984: 1–22). Most scholars agree these theories reached a height of systematization with Dong Zhongshu (ca. 179–ca. 104 B.C.E.) and his theories of *ganying,* or resonance.[7]

In the essay "*Li* Transforms," two sorts of correspondence are featured: Five Phases and human-cosmic. Ritual performance heightens the efficacy of the already present correspondence. For instance, in their continuous transformation, the Five Phases of water, fire, wood, metal, and earth provided a model of order for diverse natural and human phenomena. Ted Kaptchuk calls them "five kinds of processes" and says they comprise a system of "correspondences and patterns that subsume events and things, especially in relationship to their dynamics. More specifically, each Phase is an emblem that denotes a category of related functions and qualities" (1983: 343, 344–57).

Joseph Needham charts a selection of twenty-nine sets of correlations, including seasons, cardinal directions, tastes, smells, numbers, musical notes, stars, weather, colors, and instruments. Also included are the five senses (*wu-guan:* eyes, tongue, mouth, nose, and ear) as well as the human psychophysical functions (*wushi:* demeanor, vision, thought, speech, hearing), parts of the body, affective states, and the viscera.[8] Different items appear correlated in different Five Phase tables, but we note especially that the human dissolves into related processes, and is correlated alongside the nonhuman world in this system. Human participation in ritual was precisely that: rather than acting as observer, the ritualist was stimulated by external signs, and he himself—his faculties, senses, responses, clothing, and actions—were systematically included in that very set of signs called forth by them.

Humanity had a role in cosmic process both necessary and assured. "*Li* Transforms" tells us that "the sage forms a triad with Heaven and Earth, stands side by side with spiritual beings in order to govern" (*LJZY* 22/2:1422). The process of conjoining Heaven and Earth is described in some detail:

Humankind is the power [*de*] of Heaven and Earth, the interaction of yin and yang, the union of embodied form and essential numina, and the most refined pneuma of the Five Phases.

Heaven holds yang and suspends the sun and stars. Earth holds yin and channels [it] into the mountains and rivers, broadcasts the Five Phases through the Four Seasons. [Its pneuma] combines and produces the moon, which waxes 15 days and wanes 15 days.

The movements of the Five Phases exhaust and displace each other. Throughout the Four Seasons and the twelve months, [the Five Phases] replace each other, in turn acting as fundamental. The Five Tones[9] give rise to the Six [yang] Pitches. When they are played on the twelve pipes they replace each other in taking the position of the first note.[10] The Five Flavors[11] [form] Six Combinations. In the Twelve Nourishments they alternate with each other as the main spice. The Five Colors[12] [appear in] the Six Patterns and on the twelve forms of clothing take turns as the main hue (*LJZY* 22/2:1423). Thus people are the heart/mind of Heaven and Earth, the limit of the Five Phases. They taste flavors, discriminate tones, wear colors, and are born.

When the sages fashioned rules they took Heaven and Earth as the basis; took yin and yang as the limits; took the Four Seasons as the handle to be grasped; took the sun and stars as a cord [for measuring?]; took the moon as a scale; took embodied form and essential numina as servants; took the Five Phases as materiality; took the righteousness of *li* as an instrument [*qi,* "means toward an end"]; took human feelings as the field for cultivation; took the four numinous ones as domestic animals. (*LJZY* 22/2:1424)

Displayed in ritual, according to this Han text, is the cosmos through its signs. Dissolved in this display, yet present as its heart/mind "centerer," were (usually male) human beings.

Recall the line from the chapter itself: "Man is the heart/mind of Heaven and Earth, the limit of the Five Phases." The commentary of Kong Yingda on this paragraph analyzes how such a relationship between humanity and cosmos was imagined as homology.

Heaven is far away, high above; beneath it, the Four Directions [*sifang*] with man living in the center [*zhongyang*]. In his movement and quiescence he responds to Heaven and Earth. Within Heaven and Earth there is man, as within man's chest there is his heart/ mind, whose movement and quiescence respond to the man. So when it is said "The heart/mind of Heaven and Earth," it is as Wang Xiao has put it: "the position of man between Heaven and Earth is like the heart among the Five Viscera. Man is by birth the most numinous of creatures. His heart is the most sagely of the Five Viscera." (*LJZY* 22/2:1424)

Because they were the microcosm par excellence, people could perceive differences in the cosmos and embody them in rituals; they could hear the harmony and give voice to it in music. Their role was both active and passive (this very duality conforming to model interaction of yin and yang) (Kong's commentary, *LJZY* 22/2:1423). Active as the facilitator of the ritual, which is the perfect model of resonance with the cosmos, the sacrificer submits himself to his own dissolution as part of its system of signs.

Any analysis of traditional Chinese culture ought not to begin in an a priori fashion with the Western idea of a unified observing consciousness. Another model altogether prevails: the concept of "centering" or *zhong* becomes most important for understanding consciousness as process, not essence. The Han commentator Zheng Xuan used the term "to center" this way: "*Li* is that by which to know men's heart/minds. It has effect as a centerer [*shi yu zhong,* that is, between the inner heart/mind and the outer countenance]" (*LJZY* 22/ 2:1422). This passage further speaks of *li* as the centerer of boundary sacrifices to Heaven and tumulous sacrifices to Earth. *Li* occurs between people. The metaphor, discussed in depth below, is "skein," or *ji,* which also means "to record or remember" (*LJZY* 21/2:1414).

We have discussed *zhong*'s (center, to center) dual status as noun and verb. In the above cases, I translated *zhong* in the verbal rather than the nominative sense. We should think of *zhong* as creating itself through the correct separation of upper and lower, the correct bounding of inner and outer. The double meaning of *zhong* as nominative and verbal perfectly indicates an act captured by a topographical metaphor, space constantly created and indicated through process. Humans were entrusted with the sacred task of centering because of their ability to "follow the mean." Sacrifice was one of the most complete attempts to display a processual substantialization of being emerging through action. Humanity's representative, the emperor, by virtue of his kingly status, participated in and sought to control the very process that substantialized him as a being.

Therefore, although ritualists were concerned with the human role in the cosmos, it is not quite correct to say that people "occupied" the center of the world, even conceptually. Rather, people "centered" it through their *li;* they facilitated its signification by giving it voice through music, pattern through writing, and order through *li.* Like a membrane or tympanum they mediated through total participation: immediate boundaries.

The location of subjectivity within a single, biological individual is a modern, Western phenomenon. The traditional Chinese ritualist sensibility did not limit and locate consciousness in such a way. Its propensity for organizing correlative effects resulted in what I call a "dispersal of being," in the division of the human and the nonhuman alike into sets of attributes. The importance accorded to *zhong,* whereby humanity constitutes the significant cosmos and gives its signs the ground upon which to signify by virtue of human mediation, dissolves a static idea of mind as substance into mind as process.

Within this cosmos of transforming resonances, it remained vital for people not so much to "join" nature (for this implies a separation) as constantly to illustrate and display that there was not and had never been a gap. But it was only possible to signify the absence of an absence with a presence, and this was perforce accomplished through the *materia* of signs, substantial artifacts, sounds, and movements.

For some Chinese thinkers, however, semiological, communicative practice itself intruded between men and the nonhuman cosmos. The philosophical Daoists (Laozi and Zhuangzi)[13] and their heirs in this matter, Chan Buddhists,[14] were harshly suspicious of words and struggled to circumvent their necessity. The

Daode jing (translated by Waley as "The Way and Its Power") does it by negating later in the text nearly everything it says at the beginning, as though indicating that, if words must appear, at least their signified meaning will be neutralized. Chan masters were famous for eliding words into silence, a silence then filled with gesture that performed the absence of words. This linguistically skeptical tradition profoundly influenced painters, poets, and calligraphers whose products were often constructed as similarly paradoxical "self-destructing" subversions of signification.[15]

From the Han dynasty onward, the ritualist tradition took another line altogether. That "experience be interpreted in linguistic terms," tantamount to an "insistence upon words," is by contrast a hallmark of the Confucian and neo-Confucian tradition, rather than Daoist or Chan Buddhist (Lynn 1975: 219). For "words" I would substitute the communicative practices that we have glossed as *wen*. These include calligraphy, painting, music, and *li* and were held to provide a living, dynamic connection to the hidden workings of the cosmos. I do not go as far as François Cheng in maintaining that the formal, ideographic character of the Chinese language provided "the single model active in the process of [*wen*-oriented activities'] constitution as systems" (François Cheng 1982:64).[16] Nevertheless, it is clear that the writers of the *Record of Rites* and the commentators Zheng Xuan of the Han and Kong Yingda of the Tang shared an idea of signification rather different from a modern European semiotic one. The notion of a dispersal of being along correlating planes of resonance implies a different theory of signification. Our own idea of signs that function as a denotative system, existing between an isolated all-knowing subject and his world, a medium to be manipulated at will to describe a world "out there," would have been foreign to the ritualist sensibility.[17]

Han-Tang commentary to "*Li* Transforms" presents an almost mechanical classification of things and ideas that provided a place for each in a schema, with only local and specific explanations for their interconnections. Dong Zhongshu may be considered the prime architect of this sort of "planar" thinking, according to which the world was broken down into attributes, then serialized, scrutinized, and compared. In this world, ritual was one mode of interconnection, perhaps by virtue of merely gathering the diversity of things into the spatial contiguity of one performance. This collection presented words as things among other things: one proceeds to read the interior from exterior signs and their relation should be immediately visible and apparent. The human being was likewise dissected into his attributes and displayed among the things of the world with which he would resonate.

The practice of text/performance in the construction and performance of Grand Sacrifice in the eighteenth century was supported by a version of the ritualist metaphysics outlined above. New elements were, however, added to the Han-Tang account presented here. The rise in the late Tang and early Song of a new philosophical synthesis produced new interpretations of *li,* crowding the menu of choices for eighteenth-century ritualists as they surveyed the tradition. We will examine these views by looking at other commentaries to the ritual classic as they appeared in the imperial edition of the *Record of Rites,* entitled *Liji yishu.*

Concentrating the Cosmos within the Self: Song-Ming Ritualists

In 1748, the *Imperial Edition of the Analysis of the Meanings of the Three Rites* (*Qinding sanli yishu*) was printed. Included were the *Rites of Zhou,* the *Ceremonial Rites,* each in forty-eight chapters, and the *Record of Rites* as the *Liji yishu* (Analysis of the meanings of the Record of Rites) in eighty-three chapters (*ECCP* 236; *SKQSZM* 21/1:172).

In 1778, about thirty years after its original editing, the entire *Qinding sanli yishu* was included in the *Library,* each of its three portions filed separately in its appropriate section under "Classics." As behooved people committed to Han Learning method, *Library* editors agreed that Han commentator "Zheng Xuan must be considered the specialist" (*SKQSZM* 21/1:179; Elman 1984: 65–66; Guy 1987: 155–56). Yet they still felt obliged to include the Cheng-Zhu, neo-Confucian commentators.

In fact, by so eagerly including Song commentators, the editors of the imperial edition of the *Record of Rites* under Fang Bao finally recouped all three stages of classical studies as Fan Wenlan has enumerated them: the Han-Tang, the Song, and the Qing (Fan Wenlan 1979b: 267–68). The inclusion and justification of neo-Confucian commentary by the editors of the *Library* throws into relief some rather flat clichés about eighteenth-century scholarship.

First it is an important indication of the error of a subsequent overemphasis placed upon the gap between Han and Song Learning.[18] Even more important, by discussing *li* in terms of such a broad range of commentary, eighteenth-century editors were creating a syncretic kinship between Han-Tang and Song sources that seems to contradict the currently popular interpretation that evidential scholars criticized "correlative thought."[19] While evidential scholars (whether they espoused Song or Han Learning) did attempt to break decisively with their past heritage, these same scholars were deeply involved in editing imperial ritual texts that were utterly embedded in that cosmology.

The editors felt that inclusion of neo-Confucian commentary would solve a problem of interpretation of the ritual classics. They thought the *Rites of Zhou* and the *Ceremonial Rites* dealt with the systematization of ritual (*lizhi*) while the *Record of Rites* (the book containing "*Li* Transforms") dealt with its meanings (*liyi*).[20] To study the systematization of *li,* one used evidential methods. But understanding the meanings of *li* required something more: study through *yili* "meanings and coherencies." For this, they turned to Song neo-Confucianists, whose "explanations often obtain [for readers] specifications of complexity and illuminatingly subtle meaning" (*SKQSZM* 21/1:179). In fact, there were other reasons why they felt at home with Song scholarship on ritual, reasons that did not require a "return to philosophy" on their parts. Song ritual study was not confined only to the conceptual. But precisely because the search for something "philosophical" (à la Europe) by post–May Fourth intellectuals placed the Song Cheng-Zhu school firmly in this secular realm, Song concrete studies of ritual texts have been neglected or downplayed since the turn of the century.

Thanks to Patricia Ebrey, we have a new and keener appreciation for how important texts on the performance of *li* became for Song scholars of the Cheng-Zhu school. Zhang Zai (1020–1077) was "credited by his contemporaries with leading a revival of ancient ancestral and funerary rites." He saw strict ritual performance as a means of self-cultivation (Ebrey 1991a: 51).[21] Zhu Xi later edited the *Jiali* (Family rituals), which Ebrey describes as a straightforward liturgy in five chapters betraying no interest in the meaning or intention of the performances.[22] It was a handbook of continuous interest and formed a major source for eighteenth-century ritual manuals like the *Comprehensive Rites* (Ebrey 1991a: 151).

Nonetheless, when we speak of the editing of the ritual classics themselves under Qianlong, we are in the world of commentary, and when these same men turned to interpreting and contextualizing *li* (and all the classics for that matter) they did so in light of their philosophical assumptions about *li* (coherence), *xin* (heart/mind), *xing* (nature), and *ren* (cohumanity). Song commentary on "*Li* Transforms" will illuminate the two most important aspects of the Cheng-Zhu ritualist metaphysics: the discourse on ontology centering upon coherence and the question of *ren* (cohumanity).[23]

The Song synthesis of traditional Confucianism with Buddhism and Daoism resulted in a school of thought quite different from that of the Han period, but it is an exaggeration to say, as even so eminent authority as Fan Wenlan does, that the two periods "were completely different" (1979a: 323). In fact, in basing their ethical critiques of Buddhism and Daoism in metaphysics, Song thinkers not only borrowed from the "enemy" (Graham 1978: xvi), they also reaffirmed and broadened Han cosmology as we have discussed it, still emphasizing human and cosmic correspondence through correlative resonance (Henderson 1984: 119). And this correlative resonance, so central to a ritualist metaphysics, underlay the logic of ritual performance in the eighteenth century whether or not the most advanced philosophy still found it compelling. Thus eighteenth-century classicists, bent upon retrieving rituals from the past, sought not only Han sources. They also appreciated later embellishments that reinforced and enriched Han ritual views. Their decision to include commentary from Han, Tang, and Song is not so peculiar if appreciated in light of an underlying ritualist logic.[24]

In the commentary to "*Li* Transforms," the Song neo-Confucian founders themselves are not quoted often. Zhang Zai (1020–1077) is quoted twelve times, Zhu Xi five times, and Master Cheng (Cheng Yi 1033–1107) only once, but in the commentary of later writers who follow the founders' teachings, we see an interpretation of ritualization developing parallel to that of the former Han-Tang periods.[25] This logic emphasizes macrocosmic/microcosmic manipulation and operates through the concept of coherence (*li*), which is thought to be shared by all things in the universe.

Zhu Xi, the ultimate synthesizer of Song neo-Confucianism, thought about the world constantly in terms of a shared universal principle of being. Things were no longer broken into their external attributes and serialized, but were instead treated as vehicles each of which must be understood as a singular, whole example of a shared, secret, universal essence: coherence. Each thing or event reproduces the Great Ultimate—and thus coherence—in its entirety.[26]

In this view, exteriority gives over to interiority and an emphasis upon ontology. Connections that were appreciated in the Han through difference and the resonance between the signs of attributes were replaced by the search for fundamental similitude in being. This new emphasis upon ontology overtook and subsumed process. Human beings were thought to be the pinnacle of the concentration of coherence, subjects who had "minds that are made for knowing," a world that was the duplicate of their own interior selves. In contrast to the model outlined above of an open pattern of the self laid beside and tuned to the rest of the cosmos, neo-Confucian moral metaphysics concentrated the cosmos within the self.

For example, the passage from "*Li* Transforms" with its division of the world into correlating sets formed the basis of our discussion of the "dispersal of being" as fundamental to Han-Tang ritualist metaphysics. Here, however, the first line of that passage in *"Li* Transforms": "Humanity possessed the power of Heaven and Earth, the interaction of yin and yang, the convergence of embodied form and essential numina, the most refined material force of the Five Phases . . ." immediately brings forth Zhang Zai's quite different discussion of the creation of man:

> The power of Heaven and Earth is such that they have endowed humanity as precious. The concentration of the material force of the Five Phases in order to create the most numinous being among all beings is its refinement. "Spirit" is a homonym for the word "to extend." "Ghost" is a homonym for the word "to return." All that creates "extends"; all that seeks the ending "returns." In the unity of embodied form, the interaction of yin and yang, the union of "ghostliness/returning" with "spiritual/extension," the material force of the Five Phases, the creation of things, all reach their perfection in man. (*LJYS* 125:85–86)

For Zhang Zai, humans were also most important creatures. But they were important because they embodied the process of creation that all creatures share. This interpretation provides a perfect example of Cheng-Zhu school emphasis upon humans participating wholly in cosmic process as they contained it in their very being.

Xu Shihui's commentary bases itself upon Zhu Xi's famous discussion of the *Diagram of the Great Ultimate* and further notes that humanity and Heaven share the universal principle of coherence:

> The Fundament of Heaven, soundless and odorless, is the pivot of true creative transformation,[27] the root of the concentration of all things. This is the concrete coherence of Heaven and Earth and the root of the creation of man is nothing but coherence. "It is active and produces yang; yang in its transformations unites with yin." "It is quiescent and produces yin; yin unites with yang." These are the movements of true coherence and the mechanism by which man is created. (*LJYS* 125:87)

Thus Heavenly correspondence also finds explanation in a language of micro/macrocosm given over to shared ontology. The passage in the original text of *"Li* Transforms" that first mentions the effect of Heaven-created correspondence reads:

> Governance is that which emanates from the Lord's body. Governance, therefore, must be rooted in Heaven's creation of correspondence [*xiao*] which sends down its decree

[*ming*]. When this decree descends to the soil, it is called "Correspondence of the Earth"; to the Ancestral Temple it is called "Correspondence of Humanity and Righteousness" [*renyi*]; when to the mountains and streams, it is called activity and work; when to the Five Sacrifices it is the systematization and institutionalization [of *li*].[28]

Jiang Junshi[29] provides classic Cheng-Zhu cosmology in his comments:

What Heaven, Earth, and the myriad things each have is coherence. In the chaotic beginning, Heaven was high and earth below; this was the taking form of material force, a division of coherence and form. Therefore the sages root themselves in Heavenly coherence and emanate order [by which affairs are] governed. (*LJYS* 125:75)

Fang Que's commentary to the same passage spells out exactly what is meant by *xiao*, or correspondence.

[Based upon] Prior Heaven and Later Earth, the upper and lower are ordered; based upon the Ancestral Temple, the respected and lowly are ordered; based upon mountains and streams, the inner and outer are ordered; based upon the Five Sacrifices, the large and small are ordered. (Ibid.)[30]

He painstakingly proceeds from a macrolevel to mark out categories on the microlevel, like inner and outer, upper and lower. These categories will be fundamental to the analysis of Grand Sacrifice to be undertaken later.

The above commentaries reinforce the Han-Tang idea of humanity as the link whose *li* render heavenly correspondences visible. The Qianlong editors themselves integrate the commentary on correspondence with the cosmological discussions by their final summarizing note that *xiao*, which we have translated, following Kong Yingda, as "correspondence," also means "distribution" (*sanbu*): "All the Coherences under Heaven are expressive of only one Heaven" (ibid.). Here "correspondence" as a process between different realms is substantialized as "distribution" of a thing called coherence, an indication of the shift of interest by Song neo-Confucians to questions of ontology (at least in the eyes of eighteenth-century editors).

The discourse of *li* was redefined by the Cheng-Zhu school as "not a body of ceremonies, but rather natural principles of coherence" that are "intangible. Personal effort should follow natural moral principles."[31] Human nature, itself another example of coherence, consists of "concrete principles, complete with humanity, righteousness, *li*, and wisdom" (Chan 1963: 614–15).[32]

The quest for coherence in all things was accompanied by a logical tendency to reduce process to substance. Its corollary in thinking about morality lay in the Cheng-Zhu emphasis upon *ren,* or cohumanity. Again and again the analysis of the Cheng-Zhu commentary of the chapter "*Li* Transforms" proceeds toward this reduction to a single term. For instance, instead of Tang commentator Kong Yingda's rich discussion of ritual as system of interilluminating signs, when the Five Phases are brought up, only one aspect is discussed: their extension as the Five Virtues. Then these are quickly reduced to one: *ren.*

The text of "*Li* Transforms" states: "Thus humanity is the heart/mind of Heaven and Earth; the limit of the Five Phases. He tastes flavors, discriminates tones, wears colors" (*LJYS* 125:95). Kong Yingda's straightforward macro-microcosmic explanation is of course included in the commentaries we are examining: "Heaven is above, Earth below: humanity lives at the center where its activity and quiescence resonates with [*ying*] Heaven and Earth. It is like a person's body having a heart/mind whose activity and quiescence resonates with the person" (*LJYS* 125:96). Because of this ability to resonate, human beings are able to clarify (*ming*) the Five Virtues (cohumanity, righteousness, propriety, wisdom, and trust) associated with the Five Phases and manifest (*zhu*) the flavors, sounds, and colors associated with them.

Fang Que's Song commentary on the same passage links the Five Virtues to the Five Phases but subtly shifts Kong's emphasis upon the more active role humanity plays. "The Five Phases flower as the Five Flavors whereby humanity nurtures taste; take effect as the Five Tones whereby it nurtures hearing; take form as the Five Colors, whereby it nurtures sight. After attaining these a human being is born" (ibid.). For Kong Yingda, the manifestations of the universe are possible because of humanity's position as "central" being, its capacity to act as the centering mediator. But in Fang Que's comment, attention is drawn to the Five Phases, which allow, through their various manifestations, the development of human senses. There is a discernible shift from emphasis upon active centering to passive substance, as what had been described as process now becomes constituent of humanity's very being.

Wu Cheng likewise emphasized humanity as the embodiment (and not the occasion of manifestation) of the Five Phases. His commentary mentions only their extension as the Five Virtues, leaving out all discussion of concrete, sensual activity (*LJYS* 125:97).

Another commentator reduces all of Kong's rich discussion of interilluminating signs to one: cohumanity or *ren,* as the shared substance is named. "The heart/mind of Heaven and Earth is *ren;* the fullest extension of *ren* is in people who have the form of the heart/mind of *ren.* Thus people are *ren. Ren* is the heart/mind of humanity, and that by which Heaven and Earth are seen" (*LJYS* 125:96). One virtue is substituted for all five, and is equated with humankind who is likewise a part substituted for (and then equated with) the whole of Heaven and Earth. The passage supplies an excellent example of the Cheng-Zhu school rhetoric of resemblance, which has its logical basis in the imputed shared substance of coherence.

In other words, while Han and Tang commentators stated directly that rituals were the means whereby human feelings or *qing* could be reached and any gap between interior and exterior fused, for Zhu Xi ritual leads us back, like everything else, to coherence. Ritual is associated with being and substance (coherence as *ti*) rather than action or function (*yong*). In other words, the old sense of *zhong* as created through process is reversed and process becomes trapped within being.[33] Thus, although micro-macrocosmic reasoning is used by both Han-Tang and Song ritualists, the logic informing such correspondence is fundamentally different; the emphasis shifts from shared process to shared ontology. Han-Tang centering was active; Song-Ming "centering" was passive.

The discourse upon ontology manifested itself in another way through the Cheng-Zhu commentaries chosen by eighteenth-century editors. In their approach to this Classic, the editors concentrated upon ontology and origin, both in explicating questions raised within the text (about the nature of man and his *li*) and concerning the origin and being of the text itself.

When the text takes up the series of Five Tones and Six Pitches played on the twelve pipes (*LJYS* 125:90), a highly technical discussion of music follows in the commentaries chosen by eighteenth-century editors. Discussing the Five Colors, the Six Patterns, and Twelve Types of Clothing, the Qianlong editors concentrated on intricate technical description, disagreeing with Fang Que's interpretation (accusing him of misreading the *Rites of Zhou*) (*LJYS* 125:95). By "technical" I mean that the editors betray their evidential scholarly bias by preferring throughout this section portions of commentary that treat questions of sources for information about music, clothes, and food rather than interpretation of the significance of the information.[34] Yet, I think the editors' commitment to Cheng-Zhu thinking can be seen manifesting itself at a much deeper level. The tendency to concentrate upon the text as an artifact-in-itself, to inquire into the grounds of its becoming (its sources) seems, in this light, to transpose the Cheng-Zhu emphasis upon being and substance into the text itself.

The editors of the imperially sponsored edition of the *Record of Rites*, men who espoused Song Learning while employing certain evidential techniques (such as concern for verifiable sources), approached the text more for itself and not as record-of-something-else. Thus they suppressed its nature as sign. They were interested in the history of the text, not in the text as historical record. Their substantialization of the text as a thing in itself privileged writing (and naturally, those who wrote, or commanded writing), and fueled text/performance as the writing of ritual and the ritualization of writing.

The Performing Body and the Clarifying Text: The Eighteenth Century

The ritualist metaphysics of the eighteenth century inherited an original Han tradition that had been reworked by Song scholars. It was quite different from anything ever developed in the modern West.

In the ritualist metaphysics as the eighteenth century inherited it, signs were always decipherable, although they may have functioned differently according to thinkers in different epochs. In Han texts they connected among difference of attributes; in Song texts they participated in the similitude of a unifying principle of coherence. But within both worlds, signs were given in the universe to be discovered and uncovered by human beings. Their readability and usability was always a matter for optimism for the prepared and sincere ritualist.

In the Han ritualist metaphysics, there was an optimism about the totality of order, available metonymically for consciousness through the things of the world via a kind of cross-referencing operation. For Han ritualists, consciousness was not considered innate and essential but something to be constantly recuperated and recreated. Song thinkers likewise believed in the possibility of total order, but for them it was accessible metaphorically through consciousness-as-coherence. Dai Zhen (1723–1777), the eighteenth century's greatest evidential philosopher, likewise never doubted language's ability to speak clearly of past sagely action.

The final goal of the classical learning is [the attainment of the understanding of] *dao*. To clarify *dao*, we need words [*zi*]. But words are formed on the basis of the study of meaning and language. From the study of language, we may then understand the true meaning of words [used in the classics]. From the understanding of the true meaning of these words, we may then comprehend the mind and will of the ancient sages.[35]

Dai believed that the *dao* had an internal ordering and pattern that was accessible to sages, that is, those who could study and retrieve the traces in texts of previous sages (Chung-ying Cheng 1986: 35–38, 51–53).

Dai Zhen culminated the evidential (Han Learning) critique of Song-dynasty thinking. That critique replaced a philosophy of coherence with one of *qi,* usually translated as "material force" or "energy." No longer were the things of the world and human nature thought to be merely imperfect vehicles of form for the perfect, substantialization of eternal process as coherence. Dai Zhen repeatedly objected to the Song bifurcation of coherence from *qi,* Nature from mind, the metaphysical from the physical (Ch'ien 1986: 274–76; Chan 1963: 709–11; Chung-ying Cheng 1986: 17–20). Eighteenth-century historian Zhang Xuecheng likewise maintained that the *dao* could not be separated from things, for if it was, then one would fail to see things whole (Nivison 1966: 241).

But even more important than their objection to the dualistic particulars of Song-Ming philosophy was the eighteenth-century thinkers' inheritance from the Song of deeper discursive rules governing the formation of subjectivity and language. Edward Ch'ien argues elegantly that, as traditional neo-Confucianists, the rebels against Zhu Xi (including Lu, Wang, and Dai) affirmed the person's intrinsic oneness as subject with things as object.[36]

Thus, in China, the person was never conceived of as an individual in our sense of the word. In Han-Tang texts people were opened to the universe, de-centered consciousness that centered the world of things. To Song thinkers, human consciousness (heart/mind) likewise embraced the external world but with a thoroughness never conceived of in China's pre-Song past. The Cheng-Zhu (and Lu-Wang) goal of melding the subjective and objective was quite different from the modern subject, constructed as distinct from and manipulative of an outside, objectified reality. In eighteenth-century China, it was upon the ground constituted by the ritualist metaphysics of the analogical sign and resonant subject that more pragmatic programs for ritual action in society were projected.

But what was new in the mid-Qing period? I think their profound interest in performance, in linking the performing body *to* a, and *through* a, clarifying text in a public space *between* people led them straight to Han-Tang commentary and its interest in *li* as "externality."

When "*Li* Transforms" itself introduces *li,* we are told *what li* accomplish, then we are told *how* they do so:

The *li* and ceremonials are the skeins [that promote *li yi wei ji*] through correctness, [the relation between] Lord and Minister [*yi zheng jun chen*]; through respect, [the relation between] father and son [*yi du fu zi*]; through admiration, [the relation between] brothers [*yi mu xiong di*]; through harmony, [the relation between] husband and wife [*yi he fu fu*]; through their creation, standards [*yi she zhi du*]; through fixity, the [boundaries of] fields and villages [*yi li tian li*]. (*LJZY* 21/2:1414)

Here we see *li* associated with concerns about order, both moral and social, but not upon the internal moral life of the person; rather *li* induce an undiscussed virtue through their organization of people into positions relative to others and in relation to the environment.

The chapter goes on to explain how *li* accomplished the goals outlined above. It states that the kings of Zhou employed *li* "to make known [*zhu*] righteousness; to realize [*kao*] sincerity in completion; to reveal [*zhu*] errors; to exemplify [*xing*] benevolence; to explain [*jiang*] courtesy; to show [*shi*] the constancy of the people" (ibid.).

These usages of *li* formed a body of practice two characteristics of which were particularly important for eighteenth-century ritualists. *Li* were located *between* people and they accomplished their goals by "bringing to light" (*zhu* in this instance is glossed by Han commentator Zheng Xuan as *ming*, to "clarify" or "bring to light"), or "showing" (*shi*) that which was hidden.

This notion of externality is further developed. According to the chapter, the six usages of *li* allowed projection "outside" the heart/mind (*xin*). It states that the "polar limits" of the heart/mind (*xin zhi duan*) are desire (for nourishment and sex) and distaste (for death and poverty). These desires and distastes should not "remain hidden in the heart/mind" (*ren cang qi xin*). Tang-dynasty Kong Yingda comments:

People are deep of heart/mind, impenetrable of countenance—if there is distance between the inner and outer [*nei/wai*]. A heart/mind that conceals desire and distaste is without embodied form [*xingti*]. One cannot know by virtue of regulation and measurement. . . . *Li* is that by which to know men's heart/minds. It has effect at the center [*zhong*]. The heart/mind, the countenance, must be visible externally [*jian yu wai*].[37]

According to "*Li* Transforms," *li* functions in the human world as interconnective: communication that is embodied in multiple visible ways. The first mention of *li* in the essay illustrates this nicely. In the line, "The *li* are the skeins that promote, through correctness, the relation between Lord and Minister," *ji* means "skein" but also means "to write" or "to chronicle."[38]

The "skein" may be taken as a perfect metaphor for the idea of the sign, but only if we concentrate upon language in its performative rather than representative capacity.[39] Metaphors of network and connection are common in discussion of *wen*-related matters: from *jing* and *wei*, literally "warp" and "woof," used to designate "Classical" and "Apocryphal" texts, this semantic domain stretches to include the *guanxi weng,* or "web of connections," that is one's social network.[40] The material reality of color, movement, sound, and mass that was organized by ancient Chinese within the system called *li* existed within an ensemble of similarly communicative practices. These included painting, poetry, calligraphy, and music, the practices of *wen.*[41]

A pair of essays by Ling Tingkan (1757–1809), a Han Learning scholar of some stature, provides an excellent example of a late-eighteenth-century pragmatic program for performance.[42]

Ling Tingkan Reactivates the Rites

Ling's essays, entitled "*Fuli (shang, zhong)*" or "Reactivating the Rites, Parts One and Two," reread the "Zhong Yong" chapter of the *Record of Rites* in order to retrieve it from overemphasizing the mind of the exemplary person (*junzi*).[43] Their value for our analysis lies in Ling's insertion of ritual action or *li* between the inner orientation of the opening statements of the "Zhong Yong" on the Nature (*xing*) and its later discussion of the *wulun* or "Five Bonds" that constitute human order.[44]

In his insistence on the necessity of concrete practice of ritual action for the extension (*da*) of the *dao,* Ling's theory emphasized *li*'s communicative properties, a theory close to the Han model examined above. His critique of the Song school of coherence is explicitly articulated at the end of the second essay:

Later Confucians [meaning Song thinkers] dismissed Confucius' words of reflection. They still sought elsewhere the so-called co-humanity, appropriate signification, *dao* and virtuous power [*ren, yi, dao, de*] but viewed ritual action as unnecessary. Moreover, in their time they took unitary coherence [*yili*] as the measure, so that there were few who did not lose their centrality when it came to their words or actions.[45]

Ling orients his notions of *li* to worldly action. Not surprisingly, the essays were collected in the pragmatic *Huangchao jingshi wenbian,* where they open the sections titled "Effecting Sociopolitical Order by Ritual Action."[46]

We will analyze "Reactivating the Rites, Part One," which is divided into three sections: the first discusses the Nature (*xing,* a person's endowment from Heaven at birth) as fundamental (*gu*); the second part, the extension (*da*) of this fundament in ritual action (*li*); and the third part, the relation between the fundamental and the extensive, that is, between the Nature and ritual action.

There is no split between Nature and culture introduced here, however, because both the Nature and ritual action are derived from *dao*.

From the Nature

The essay opens by stating that Heaven bestows upon people their Nature, which is good, and that this goodness can be reactivated through learning. It goes on to describe the Five Virtues that are simultaneously the outcome of perfect human relations and nascent in the Nature as a matter of course, as its *dao*. These include affection between father and son, bestowal of appropriate significance between lord and minister, the sexual differentiation that occurs between husband and wife, the order of precedence produced between elder and younger, and the trust of friends.

From this *dao* the sages shaped (*zhi*) *li* because they realized (*zhi*) its self-so-ness (*ran*). I translate *zhi* as "realize" and not "to know" or to "comprehend," which would imply a split between knower and known, consciousness and the world, that is foreign to the ritualist metaphysics. Ling is talking here about the "real"-ization, the making real, of the "self-so-ness" of the *dao*. *Li* as the "connecting thread" (*guan*) thus comprises the *dao* of the sages, existing to thread together past and present.

Create Extension

The second section of the essay explains the metaphysics of the creation of *li*. The ontology of one's Nature dictates the possibilities of realizing it. One's Nature gives rise to "emotion." Before its appearance the Nature is "centered," but emotion knocks it askew. At this point the author moves us from the (always present) fundament of being to its expression in time: in the first section the Five Virtues were contained within the Nature's being as part of its *dao*, and we were still in the realm of fundamental being.

In this second section, the virtues are "instantiated," or *dang*: to be in a particular time or place. They are instantiated through emotion, or *qing*, which must be "modulated" (*jie*, "rhythm, restraint, the divisions along a bamboo") through *li*.

Being affectionate, bestowing mutual significance, showing differentiation, following order of precedence, trustfulness, must use the emotions as a means of extending [the Nature]. Without *li* to modulate this activity, it would be excessive. Not extending properly, only by chance would it hit its mark. (Ling 1899: 54.1a)

The *dao* of human nature is tripartite: the Nature, emotion, and *li*. Realizing the instantiation through emotion of virtues present in the Nature, one extends virtue through the "pattern" (*wen,* pattern, decoration, civilization, and order) of *li*.

There is, ideally, no gap between the Nature, or fundamental being for the self, and its social extension through ritual. As though no separate self is imagined, only a self-already-in-relationship. The father, lord, husband, elder brother bears within that identity the hierarchical position of superiority toward son, minister, wife, or younger brother.[47]

This point has already been elaborated in the opening chapter on portraiture. Imperial rituals, whether the sacrificial unification of spirits and men, or the creation of the domain of the Son of Heaven as the incorporation of the lesser domains of peripheral lords, construct orders of differences that embody the proper positions of the people and things of the cosmos. These positions mutually constitute each other and the whole. I refer to this Chinese sort of hierarchy as a "logic of encompassment," and the mutual interpenetration of elements arranged with the logic of yin and yang elements provides the clearest example of this logic.[48] Hall and Ames's idea of part/whole relationship imagined as a hologram, or "field and focus," is useful as well. The self focuses part of a shifting field of relationships as a part that contains an adumbration of the whole (Hall and Ames 1987: 237–41).

Ling Tingkan carefully reminds us that *li* only "begins" in the ceremonies described but is not "encompassed" (*gai*) by them. The process of forming *li* is endless, never exhausted in one specific *wen.* Not an end in itself, finished and complete in one ceremony, but able to be inferred and enlarged (*tui*) so that no action (*xing*) lies outside it.

Relation between the Nature and Extension through Ritual
The third section discusses ritual as tool. Although the essay does not use the term *qi* (vessel, instrument, tool), it does give specific examples of tools and their uses. Both material and tools are needed to produce an artifact: the casting of metal produces knives; lumber plus compass and square equals axles. Ritual's relation to human Nature is the same as the tool to its material.

The three components of the being of the *dao* of humanity, the Nature, emotion, and ritual, are not related in some complementary way, nor in some linearly causal way, but exist in dialectically productive simultaneity. Emotion provides momentum, motive, and occasion for the Nature to realize itself through ritual. Ling reworks the line from the "Zhong Yong": "There is nothing more visible than what is secret, nothing more manifest that what is minute" (Tu 1976: 32–35). He says the Nature is made manifest and seen only through ritual, giving the reader an exteriorized point of view that is closer to the Han or pre-Han ritualist metaphysics than later Song concentration upon an ever-deepening interiorized subjectivity.

This third section then goes on to explain that *li* are held in common by rulers and ruled. Those above learn them and use them to teach those below, who also learn. So when the exemplary person learns the ceremonials of *li* in all their detail, then the virtues that were identified at the beginning of the essay as part of the being of people's Nature will come about spontaneously (*xuran,* "ordered in itself"; *panran,* "methodically by itself"; etc.). We are brought full circle and see that ritual elicits those responses from the Nature that the sage was able to perceive in the first place in *the already present social dyads of the Five Bonds.* These are indeed "self-so" responses for, in the Mencian tradition, the nature of humanity is fundamentally good. *Li* as simultaneously "learning" and "teaching" bridges the self and the world as it constitutes community.

In the realm of all beneath Heaven, there is not one person not circumscribed by *li,* not one event not dependent upon *li.* Therein lies order. How can one daily seek a return to one's Nature through *li,* and not realize the self? (Ling 1899: 54.1a)

In this essay, Ling provided an alternative to Song-Ming neo-Confucian practices of self-cultivation that were criticized in the Qing as too quietistic, too near Buddhist and Daoist practices. Ling believed that the self was made real and produced only within the ritual production of social life.

Ling presented a theory of performance, not a symbolic interpretation of ritual. For him, ritual did not stand *for* the *dao,* it partook of the being of the *dao* and extended it into visibility. (Hence my literal translation of the term *da* as "extension" rather than metaphorizing it into "expression.") The *dao* of ritual, or ritual as the *dao,* acted as *guan,* threading between people, making their social interconnection palpable through action.

The Chinese ritualist metaphysics posited that humanity was to perform the cosmos into being through ritual action and hence to perform society and self into the process. Therefore, a theory of language that emphasizes "reference," or language's role as separate, illusory "stand-in" for another reality, is inappropriate. Chinese ritualists were especially aware of the ambiguity of signs: their status as object *of* the world yet occupying a privileged and creative position within it. Music, language, and ritual action were connected as evocative communication, performative activities that directly constituted feelings and relationships through the process of attunement.[49]

The ritualizing body provided the site of this attunement as it disposed itself in the spaces of palace and altar. We can now turn to the extension of the texts of *li* into performance.

PART 3

Performance:

The Ritualizing

Body Inscribes

5

SACRIFICIAL SPACES

Contextualizing the City

Heterotopias . . . function in relation to all the space that remains. . . . Their role is to create a space that is other, another real space, as perfect, as meticulous, as well-arranged as ours is messy, ill-constructed and jumbled. This would be heterotopia, not of illusion, but of compensation.   MICHEL FOUCAULT, "Of Other Space"

In imperial China, people thought the world included Heaven as well as all that was beneath. The common phrase *tianxia* meant in popular usage "the world of mankind." Literally, however, it translates as "subcelestial," naming the world of people while using Heaven as its reference point. The phrase signifies the perceptible (*ming*) or earthly world by shifting our attention and naming the imperceptible, Heaven (*tian*) and, by extension, the unseen or *yu* world of spirits. The phrase in Chinese would seem, in fact, to indicate that the visible (*ming*) and invisible (*yu*) were conjoined in a single unity and to hint that Heaven was its most important component.

The throne took the cliché of *tianxia* seriously and cast itself as the most fitting director of Heavenly reference, arbiter of what that phrase would signify.

"Heaven and all beneath" was coterminous with the realm of the king. Imperial Grand Sacrifice was created to show most splendidly the unity of the realm as a perceptible reality. While these rituals constituted the cosmic cycle, they also became proof of the emperor's fitness to rule as the man who could intensify the "real" and show the unity of Heaven and Earth. The heterotopias of the throne's palace and altar complexes compensated for the everyday *in*visibility of this unity.

For all the awesome display of material wealth, the efficacy of the spectacle lay elsewhere than in kingly magnificence. Not all objects were present, after all. Indeed, the ensemble of things chosen implied the constitution of an order. This chapter considers and describes these orders in their architectural and textual forms. Sacrificial "spaces" were in fact also "places" in the special sense that Michel deCerteau uses those terms. According to deCerteau, a "place is the order in accord with which elements are distributed in relationships of coexistence" (1984: 117). A place becomes a space only when "it is actuated by the ensemble of movements deployed within it" (ibid.).[1]

Following deCerteau's formula, we might say that the palaces and altars of Beijing in their formal structure as buildings, platforms, gates, and walls formed a context for action. But if we understand them as part of the text/performance of imperial *li*, the situation becomes more complex. The royal portions of Beijing were the (relatively) enduring architectural complement of the recurrent ceremonial aspect of kingly ritual. Those ceremonies, in turn, actualized and made explicit the principles embodied in the architecture of the king. Hence, city and sacrifice cannot be explicated separately as "setting" and "action" but rather should be seen as products of the same ritual process, sensuous embodiments of sagely productive power. This ensemble of practices was imitated by gentry who renovated temples, mounted projects to restore ritual purity that began with research groups, and themselves performed sacrifices.[2]

The built city did stand as con-text, but quite literally provided the place for the production and storage of texts. DeCerteau notes that writing offers another sense of place. Handbooks like the *Comprehensive Rites* (*DQTL*) provided a combination of "map" and "tour" (deCerteau 1984: 118–22). This pair of terms repeats the relations of place and space within written texts themselves. The map displays its elements synchronically, all at once, while the tour facilitates a journey through and in relation to those elements. Just as I will show how the ritual city functioned as a moment in the process of kingly productive power, in similar fashion the texts of ritual manuals combined the map and tour into one neat package. Text signified performance and performance incorporated text, thus producing an appropriately embodied subject. I will first introduce the four Grand Sacrifices, then discuss in turn the ritual city and the place/space of some ritual texts.

Forms of Grand Sacrifice

The *Comprehensive Rites* manual is divided into the Five Rites.[3] The rites were classified according to their objective:

JILI "Auspicious Rites," which honor celestial ancestors (chaps. 1–17).

JIALI "Felicitous Rites," which take as their basis the way of the people (chaps. 18–40).

JUNLI "Military Rites," which show the great power of attack and victory (chaps. 41–44).

BINLI "Guest Rites," softening those who are far away (chaps. 45–46).

XIONGLI "Funerary Rites," which magnify the importance of the end (chaps. 47–52).

Two further chapters on clothing and retinues give a total of fifty-four, certainly not a long compilation by Qianlong standards.

There were three bureaus responsible for carrying out these rites:[4] The Bureau of Ceremonies' (*Yizhi qinglisi*) responsibilities included the Felicitous Rites of court assembly, enthronement, weddings, cappings, proffering of Veritable Records, edicts, the examination system; and Military Rites (Qianlong *DQHD* chaps. 20–35; *HDZL* 1763: chaps. 56–74). The Bureau of Sacrifice (*Siji qinglisi*) was responsible for all Auspicious Rites of sacrifice and all Funerary Rites. The Bureau of Hosting and Guesting (*Zhuko qinglisi*) took care of the enfeoffing of lords of the Outer Domains and received their periodic gifts of local products. A fourth, the Bureau of Provision (*Jingshan qinglisi*), provided the items used.

The work of the first three bureaus thus consisted of rites among members of the imperial domain (Felicitous and Military), between the imperial domain and the unseen world of spirits and ancestors (Auspicious and Funerary), and between the imperial domain and outside people (Guest). To put it more abstractly in eighteenth-century ritualist logic, the Bureau of Ceremonies supervised rites at the center (*zhong*), among the people of the Middle Kingdom; the Bureau of Sacrifice created and maintained relations between the higher (*shang*) and lower (*xia*) orders of Heaven and Earth; and the Bureau of Hosting and

16. Ceremonial order of Grand Sacrifice. Based on *DQTL 1756*.

PREPARATION -- FIVE DAYS

	HEAVEN	EARTH	ANCES-TORS	SOIL & GRAIN
-5 days	1 Viewing victims	Heaven*	Heaven*	Earth*
-3 days	2 Achieving seclusion	Heaven	Heaven	Earth
-2 days	3 Inspecting victim	Heaven	no	no
	4 Writing prayerboards	Heaven	Heaven	Earth
-1 day	5 Viewing killing of victims	Heaven	Heaven	Earth
	6 Standing spirit thrones, pitching tent, displaying victims' containers			
before dawn	7 Reviewing prayerboards	Heaven	Earth	Earth
dawn	8 Phoenix Carriage leaves palace			
	9 Viewing spirit places, altar places, victims' cotainers & Halls of Seclusion		no	no
night	10 Arranging and standing			
	11 Inspection of filled vessels			
	12 Differentiating places			

THE SACRIFICE -- A FEW HOURS

	HEAVEN	EARTH	ANCES-TORS	SOIL & GRAIN
That day (before dawn)	13 Inviting spirits to take places			
	14 Approaching the Order, washing, taking place			
	15 Welcoming the spirits			
	16 Presenting jade and silk		no•	no•
	17 Bringing forward flesh of victims		no	no
	18 Initial Oblation			
	19 Middle Oblation			
	20 Final Oblation			
	21 Receiving felicitous (liquor &) flesh, clearing dishes			
	22 Sending off the spirits		no	
	23 Watching burning/interring		no	
	24 Returning spirits thrones			
	25 Returning in Phoenix Carriage			no

Note: If nothing is marked in the space, it means the sacrifice has its own text on procedures.
- "Heaven" and "Earth": A note in such sections refers the reader back to the appropriate sacrifice for procedural details.
- "Presenting jade and silk" is combined with the Initial Oblation.

Guesting created and ordered boundaries between the inner (*nei*) imperial domain and the outer (*wai*) Lords.

In the *Assembled Canon,* under each ministry, ceremonies are arranged in three tiers: the Grand (*da*), Middling (*zhong*), and Miscellaneous (*xiao*). Only "Grand" rites were presided over by the emperor or his designated proxy (Qianlong *DQHD* chaps. 37–43; *HDZL* 1763: chaps. 76–81).

On the scheduled occasions of Grand Sacrifice, the most magnificent collection of people and things within the realm was assembled in service of the spirits. The syntagmatic (a term analogized from linguistics meaning "moving through time") sequence or ceremonial procedure of each sacrifice was the same (figure 16), and in their entirety they formed a larger sequence that took place in the course of one year. At the same time, certain paradigmatic elements within each ceremony differed, and these substitutions served to identify each sacrifice as particularly appropriate to its season (figure 17). Hence, each rite contained certain elements "selected" to differentiate it from the others. While Grand Sacrifices were identical along an "axis of combination," they differed along an "axis of selection." Their four altars survive today and are important tourist sites.

	HEAVEN	EARTH	ANCESTORS	SOIL & GRAIN
SEASON:	Winter	Summer	Spring/fall	same
CELEBRANT FACES:	North	South	North	South
VESSEL COLOR:	Blue	Yellow	Metal	Yellow
TYPE:	Yang	Yin	Yang	Yin

17. Types of Grand Sacrifice.

Heaven and Earth: Cosmology / Knowledge / Preparation

The Sacrifices to Heaven and Earth were a matched pair of ceremonies, one occurring at the Round Mound, south of the Forbidden City, the other at the Square Pool to the north.[5] These shapes reflected the traditional belief that the Heavens were round and the Earth square.[6] The round Altar of Heaven had three tiers and four flights of stairs giving access to it from each of the four cardinal directions (figure 18). The dimensions of the altar had been changed in response to an edict of 1749 from the emperor complaining that it was too

18. Three-tiered Altar of Heaven today. Photo by Angela Zito.

small. Architects were careful, however, to preserve at the emperor's behest relations in odd numbers, dimensions that were considered "heavenly," or yang. The number nine was itself a sign of emperorship, since it was considered a perfect and thus very powerful yang number (being 3 × 3).[7] The reconstructed altar thus featured multiples of odd numbers: the top and smallest terrace was nine *zhang* (each *zhang* equals ten Chinese feet), or 9 × 1; the middle terrace, fifteen *zhang*, or 3 × 5; and lower terrace, twenty-one *zhang*, or 3 × 7. Its balustrade panels total 360 to correspond to the 360 degrees of a "Heavenly circle." Between each terrace there were nine steps (Williams 1913: 26–27). The spirit tablets used in the Sacrifice to Heaven represented Heaven, various ancestors of the king, the sun, moon, stars, planets, and other heavenly phenomena like rain, thunder, and clouds.

The Temple of Earth, north of the city, was also enlarged when it was rebuilt in 1748 (Bouillard 1923: 55–57; *DQTL* 1756: chap. 2; *DQHD* chap. 38). It then consisted of a complex of two square walls surrounding a square altar of two terraces. All dimensions are in even, yin numbers. The deities represented by the spirit tablets included the earthly tutelary gods of seas, mountains, rivers, besides Earth itself, and of course the emperor's ancestors.

Just as they marked the space between them, the two sacrifices divided the year in two: at the winter solstice, when yin influence had maximized, the Sacrifice to Heaven was performed to boost the cosmos into its yang phase. At midsummer, at the summer solstice, the cosmos was again eased into its yin phase with the performance of the Sacrifice to Earth. This pair of Grand Sacrifices explicitly maintained the cosmic social order. Its tropes were resemblance, metaphor, and microcosm deployed as setting in space. In ceremonial procedures, we can associate Sacrifice to Heaven or Earth with the Period of Preparation, or *bei*. Thus was the knowledge of ritual past displayed as the power of the present monarch.

Ancestors: Filiality/Time/Movement

Contrasting with the open altars of Heaven and Earth was the closed building of the Tai Miao, or Ancestral Temple, situated within the imperial Inner City, to the southeast of the Forbidden City. Here the emperor sacrificed at every spring and autumn equinox, as well as on the new and full moons each month, thereby performing his filial obligations to his human forebears, the sources of one Chinese metaphor of rule, sonship. By contrast, in the Sacrifice to Heaven, the emperor acknowledged that his right to rule was bestowed by Heaven and that his domain rested within a larger, encompassing cosmic order. He mediated between the (social) part and (cosmic) whole as the "Son" of Heaven. As Qin Huitian puts it:

Of ritual action, none is more important than sacrifice. Of sacrifice, none is more important than that to Heaven. Heaven is the most perfect [*jun*] of deities; the Son of Heaven is the ruler [*zhu*] of humanity. Therefore, only the Son of Heaven sacrifices to Heaven once each year. (*WLTK* 1.1a/255)

Many scholars of Chinese imperial ritual have remarked that, since the Han dynasty, Sacrifice to Heaven had come to eclipse ancestral rites in importance. Certainly the relationship of the two cults was a constant source of tension for ritualists, who argued over their modes of performance in every major dynasty. Contention revolved around three interrelated problems: first, should Heaven and Earth be worshipped jointly in one ceremony or separately as they were in the eighteenth century; second, should this worship take place on open altars or in a temple; third, how many and which imperial ancestors should appear beside Heaven's spirit tablet as associative deities. At stake was the question of how literally the emperor's title of "Son of Heaven" was to be taken. How closely was this man to be identified with a deity, and more important, how closely was his family's right to rule to be identified with the Mandate of Heaven?

Worshipping Heaven inside a temple was thought by some to be a dangerous conflation of the *gong,* communal, and the *si* (or *jia*), familial. The first Ming emperor (Hongwu, r. 1368–1398) succeeded in building a temple for the joint sacrifice to Heaven and Earth, replacing open-air altar worship, only in the face of bitter opposition from his imperium (Ho Yun-yi 1976: 110–46). As with a previous controversy, when Song emperor Renzong (r. 1023–1063) began to worship Heaven in an enclosed hall, it was pointed out that this, in effect, made his status as "Son of Heaven" a little too concrete, turning the *gong* virtue of a communal Heaven to his own family's ends (Liu J. T. C. 1964: 45–49).

Which imperial ancestors were to be worshipped, and the manner of their honoring, could create just as much consternation and dissension. The most famous case of an emperor opposing the majority ritualist opinion about his own ancestors was the Great Ritual Controversy (*Dali yi*) of the Ming.[8] Carney Fisher rightly identifies the controversy as a question of inheritance versus adoption, as does Ann Waltner.

Shizong, the Jiajing emperor (r. 1521–1567), acceded to the throne upon the death of his childless first cousin. He wished to honor his natal parents, while most ritualists urged him to adopt into the main branch of the family, honor the father of the former emperor as a father, and treat his own father as an uncle (Fisher 1990: 54–69). These opposing ritualists argued from historical precedent that Shizong would be retrospectively including his father as an emperor when his father had never sat upon the throne. The emperor's faction argued that filiality had its origins in "human feeling," that carrying on the imperial succession did not entail abandoning one's own family (147–53). To understand the arguments we need to know something about the place of agnatic and filial descent in China.

Agnatic descent is inheritance by a nephew; filial descent is inheritance by a son. Both forms had long since been considered reasonable alternatives when it came to questions of succession.[9] But to inherit, nephews were adopted as "sons" by their uncles. Shizong was in fact an agnatic descendent who did not want to relinquish his ritual obligations to his natal family. In effect, he wanted to have two fathers.

Instead of becoming further entangled in the history of Chinese kinship formation, however, I would like to draw attention to how two ancient models for transmission of authority, the sage who is chosen and the heir who succeeds automatically, have influenced questions of succession. This reading will, I hope, give some insight into the conceptual repertoire within which people raised competing claims for succession.

Sarah Allan has analyzed a series of tales from Han and pre-Han China revolving around the moment when power was exchanged in the dynastic cycle.[10] The new heir to the throne, a person of high status who occupied the center of the kingdom (an "insider"), would often choose for his prime minister a man of low status, an outsider who had to be "discovered" by the king. I would maintain that the king and the minister taken together were fundamental aspects of kingship as a whole. Thus the principle of succession was contained within the prototype of this legend cycle: Yao's discovery of the worthy but unrelated Shun as his successor. In some sense, monarchy constantly "rediscovered" itself and reinvented itself by unifying and containing contradictory opposites—the process we have called "centering." The dilemma that Shizong's stubbornness on this issue presented for his imperium can be read through the ritual logic of Grand Sacrifice.

At the level of ritual institution, the distinction between choice and necessity in succession—to state the problem of the sage versus the heir in its most abstract terms—had been expressed through the competition between Sacrifice to Heaven and Sacrifice to Ancestors. We have noted that time after time the throne moved to elide the distinction between the two ceremonies and make the "choice" of Heaven's Mandate to rule disappear into the "necessity" of the dynastic family's own ancestral obligations through joint sacrifice. In effect, they tried to claim the Mandate forever by literalizing the metaphor "Son of Heaven." Of course, this tendency also allowed for the emperor to overload his own role, symbolically speaking, and combine within himself both sageliness and sonship, especially as these were measured by his commitment to the cultural constructions of *wen* and *xiao* filiality.

At the lower hierarchical level of family itself, the same contradiction appears, and the models of sagely choice of successor versus filial necessity might be roughly subsumed within kinship formation to agnatic (adoptive) and filial (birth) descent respectively. In Shizong's case, the problem of the conflicting demands of sonship by adoption or birth roused much heated discussion, since the categories had become infused and confused precisely because he was a king who should be, ideally, simultaneously sage and heir. Certainly by the Ming (Wechsler would argue by the Tang), imperial ancestors and Heaven had reached a kind of parity (Wechsler 1985: ix–x). The king was thought to rule more through sharing the virtuous power (*de*) of his forebears than through shared biological substance, and one self-perpetuating sign of that power was the Heavenly Mandate. Thus bringing the ancestors out on the altar of Heaven, or performing heavenly sacrifice in a temple, expressed Heaven's *choice* of this sage to inherit as its *son* at the same time that such sacrifices enacted the interpenetration of the visible and invisible portions of the king's realm.

In the Qing, the emperor and his ancestors were present on both Heaven and Earth altars, the human component of the triad of Heaven, Earth, and Man. Rites in the Ancestral Temple (Tai Miao) were devoted solely to the manifestation of filiality. However, the formal similarity of ancestral rites to rites for worshipping Heaven and Earth (see figures 16 and 17) collapsed the distinction of "sage" and "heir," strengthening the claim of the dynasty *qua* clan to rule China while proclaiming that perfect filiality is a prerequisite to sagehood. As we shall see, the power of the throne lay precisely in its ability to articulate (in the double sense of both "express" and "connect") the discourses of sagely *wen* and filiality. I will elaborate more fully on this important point in later chapters.

Through exchanges of food and wine, ancestral sacrifice linked people to their deified past. It also condensed the hierarchized subject positions of the Three Constancies and Five Bonds to the core dyad of father/son. The tropes of Ancestral Sacrifice were contiguity, metonym, and movement within the microcosmically resonant context of altars. We can associate it with the presentations, offerings, and oblations of the ceremonial order of Grand Sacrifice. Filial ceremony furnishes the oldest portions of rites of sacrifice—thus the temporality of slow conflation of heaven and ancestors is preserved in ceremonial form.

Soil and Grain: Hierarchy/Space/Articulation

Opposite the Ancestral Temple, to the southwest of the Forbidden City, was the Altar to Soil and Grain, site of the fourth Grand Sacrifice (Williams 1936: 41–47; *DQTL* 1756: 6.1a–21b). The altar was a raised square platform of tamped earth in five colors: white to the west, green to the east, black to the north, red to the south, and yellow in the center.

The cult was very old, older even than sacrifices to Heaven and Earth.[11] During the Zhou, underlords were enfeoffed by receiving a lump of the earth of the king's central altar of Soil and Grain of the appropriate color; they would then return home and found their own tumulus (Chavannes 1910: 442–43). Lester Bilsky dates the importance of Altars of Soil and Grain to the Eastern Zhou, when deities connected to the land of each underlord of the declining Zhou king were emphasized at the expense of the king's ancestral spirits (Bilsky 1975:

1 : 169–71). As a territorial cult, sacrifice to Soil and Grain distinguished outsiders from insiders. Ironically, what was once the sign of monarchical disintegration and local community distinction later became another mode of articulating the parts of the empire with its center (Creel 1964).

In the Qing period, millenia after the introduction of the *xian* administrative system under the Qin dynasty, sacrifice to Soil and Grain connected the emperor to his imperium in a relationship of whole/part. The ceremony was performed all over the empire in mid-spring and mid-fall: On the same day the emperor sacrificed on the imperial altar in Beijing, governors were doing so in the provinces, heads of prefectures in their chief cities, and magistrates in their county seats.[12]

While the ceremony was ordered the same for the entire empire, the assignment of ritual tasks varied. When the emperor or his delegate presided, they did not offer the three oblations. Instead, salaried and ranked members of the imperium did so. However, when a local official presided in the provinces, he himself offered the silk and wine cups because he too was salaried staff, unlike the emperor. His identification with the absent emperor remained ambiguous. He both presided *and* carried out lesser duties.

These distinctions point to peculiarities in the relationship between sacrificial and mundane authority, between the emperor and his imperium. In everyday administrative matters such as tax collection and adjudication, the district magistrate represented the emperor. He was a metaphorical equivalent and like any good metaphor existed in one domain linked through similarity to another (Boon 1972: 74–76). According to this logic, he should have been exactly equivalent in all aspects of governance, especially crucial sacrificial ones.

He was not. In the Sacrifice to Soil and Grain, the magistrate was encompassed by the emperor, a bit player in the rite taken as a whole physical expression of imperial authority. He was metonymically devalued: brought into the same domain, contiguous with the emperor while being displayed as an irrevocably different, and lesser, aspect of that domain. Built into the ritual was cognizance of the necessity of sharing some, but not all, of the emperor's sacrificial authority. Some things were performed by both the emperor and officials as celebrants in sacrifice (the incensing and offering of wine and meat of prosperity); other things, such as the Three Oblations, were not. Thus officials could play two roles, master and servant, in one rite, imitating the ultimate role of the emperor, who mastered the empire as servant of Heaven.

In the yearly cycle of Grand Sacrifice, a great deal was accomplished with an economy of means. Fundamentally identical rites of sacrifice performed at different times of the year (with minor changes in colors used to match the sacrificial objective) reiterated the terms in which the emperor (1) mediated Heaven and Earth with the social world by (2) enacting the role of perfectly filial son. Furthermore, (3) the dispersion of sites of sacrifice created a spatial hierarchy of ritual nodes of power in the walled cities of the empire. Before we analyze fully the ceremonial of the Sacrifice to Heaven, we will consider the city as artifact of kingly ritual process. Ceremony and building, like writing, was a method of embodying order in the cosmos and a valued extension of kingly authority.

The Ritual City

Grand Sacrifice took place within the capital city of the Chinese domain. From 1421 until the fall of the monarchy in 1911, that was the city of Beijing. The significance of very early Chinese cities as kingly ceremonial centers has been described in comparative terms by Paul Wheatley.[13] But no one has examined and explicated their design with reference to concrete ritual practices. The following highly selective summary of archaeological opinion on pre-Han urban forms will deepen our understanding of later imperial building as the result of *wen* activities.

The oldest ruins of cities in China were left by the Shang dynasty (1850–1100 B.C.E.) (K. C. Chang 1977: 218–56). These ruins form a "webbed" pattern, densest near the center of the site, sparser near its edges (K. C. Chang 1976: 48). Imagining the Shang domain as a horizontal plane, the royal palace-temple and its cemetery were in the center of the city (Wheatley 1971: 62). This urban complex, in turn, was the center of the larger web of cities scattered outward in all four directions. The king lived at the center of the center on structures built on platforms or mounds (K. C. Chang 1976: 68). From this literal height, the king and his family viewed the social order whose apex they occupied. People unconnected to the royal lineage lived below ground in pit houses a few meters in diameter (51).

By the end of the Eastern Zhou period (770–476 B.C.E.) the use of concentric walls further dramatized the hierarchy expressed by "webbing" under the Shang. Chang describes three contrasting areas of the city besides the central area where the king lived: the aristocracy lived within a small enclosure; industrial and commercial quarters were within a larger enclosure; while farm fields lay outside the city walls.[14] Walls within walls and courtyards within courtyards delimited the inner and the outer and gave architectural form to the hierarchical encompassment enacted in a ritual and social life whereby contrasting categories were marked out and mediated through the act of expressing them, bounding them ("centering"). Ming-Qing Beijing, known as the City of Three Circumferences (*sanzhong cheng*), also held the king at its center.

Very early the city displayed certain markers of the logic that was central to ritual and political life in China: the king "centered" the realm by creating a relation between two sets of relations. The kingly center was the nexus of inner/outer and upper/lower. Later architectural refinements of this design emphasized such points of intersection: gates through walls and stairs leading to platforms were important markers of ritual transition as well.

Another feature of early city design was the preference for wood, and the striking lack of stone. Material permanence was not important. Andrew Boyd hazards that early builders preferred "renewability," that the permanent features of the city were the planning and decorative principles, and that for the Chinese the concept of monumentality applied to the city as a whole (1962: 26).

For the Shang and Western Zhou, the city was the periodic manifestation of the royal lineage's wealth. But the building and rebuilding of the city also actuated again and again in the act of construction the cosmic principles of the city's design. Thus a new dynasty inevitably signaled the emergence of order from chaos by building projects. Later, the continuous "restoration" (*xiu*) of the architecture of one's forebears combined filial respect with sagely rescue of pattern from decay.[15]

After the consolidation of empire in 221 B.C.E., the emperor's city remained a sign of the king's productive power, which came from centering or mediating yin and yang forces of chaos and order. This power was cosmic in significance and material in its embodiment. In traditional China there could no more be a cosmic center without a king than a king without a city. The building of kingly cities was congruent with *li,* both practices by which emperors participated in and extended the order of the cosmos. If building was a form of ritual action, then the physical features of cities embodied the kingly process of cosmic harmonization. Four features equipped the city as a cosmic center:

First, the symbolism of a center was constructed as the nexus of inner/outer and upper/lower. In early Chinese cities, walls and platforms were used. In later cities, emphasis was placed as well upon gates through walls and stairs leading up to platforms. These areas of transition figured heavily in ceremonial texts. Second, the four cardinal directions were emphasized. Again and again the two sets of relations of north-south and east-west provided a grid upon which certain bipolarities were ordered by ceremonial process. Third, the parallelism of the heavenly macrocosm by an earthly microcosm placed the emperor in the proper position for "centering" the two. Fourth, numbers were often a means of ordering diverse things into the categories of yin and yang.

Ming-Qing Beijing

Frederick Mote once noted that China never had one city that dominated its civilization the way that Rome or Constantinople did theirs: "The idea that the city represents either a distinct style or, more important, a higher level of civilization than the countryside is a cliché of our Western cultural tradition" (1977: 101–2). The traditional city in China was not the dominant partner in an urban/rural split.[16] S. J. Tambiah's concept of the "galactic polity" better fits the Chinese imperial landscape (1985: 252–86). This model, developed to describe Southeast Asian kingdoms and employing the mandala as icon, codes in a composite fashion cosmological, topographical, and politico-economic features. Here power most concentrates in the center, with the king. It is not his monopoly, however, for local city centers tend to emulate the capital, so that Tambiah describes a planet surrounded by smaller satellites.[17] What we have is a hierarchy of places based upon an order of inclusion through difference expressed within a common social-ritual process.

The Manchus inherited the Ming complex of palaces and temples in Beijing (figure 19). In 1421, the Ming Yongle emperor (r. 1403–1424) removed the capital of the dynasty, which had been in Nanjing in the south, north to the site of the former Yuan capital, present-day Beijing (Farmer 1976; Xie 1980: 26).[18]

Beijing was planned as a series of circumferences. Originally these included, from the outside inward, the Inner City, or *neicheng,* 14.63 miles in circumference; the Imperial City, *huangcheng* (5.6 miles); and the Forbidden City, *zijincheng* (3.7 miles). Later, in 1552, the southern suburbs were partially enclosed with another wall. Plans had called for the entire city to be encompassed, but finances only allowed the enclosure of the Altar of Heaven (Hou Renzhi 1962: 103).

Within Beijing, the Forbidden City is also divided into outer and inner portions, Outer Audience (*waichao*) and Inner Court (*neiting*). In each area are three halls, or *dian,* the smallest in the middle. In the Outer Audience area, in the largest and southernmost hall called the Taiho dian, the emperor received Lords of the Outer Domains;[19] in the Inner Court were his private apartments (*RXJWK*

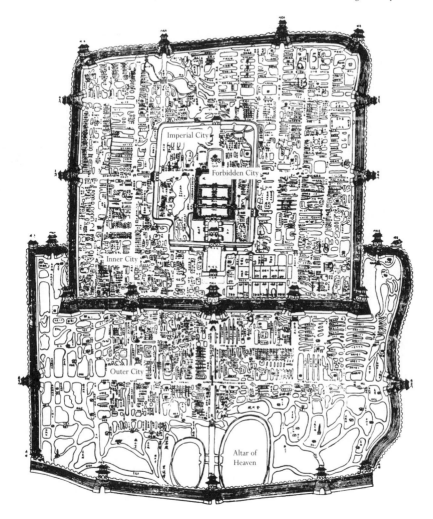

19. The walled city of Qing Beijing in the eighteenth century showing the outer and inner cities, as well as the imperial city and Forbidden City. From Sarah Pike Conger, *Letters from Peking* (1909).

13/1:179–83; 14/1:164–20, 269). In between, in a "gate" that is more like a building, the Qianqing men, he met with courtiers and ministers (*RXJWK* 13/1:176–77; *DQTL* 1756: chap. 19) (figure 20).

The Forbidden City seems to have been constructed to express a heavenly astral order (Xie Mincong 1980: 135; Meyer 1976: 46–52). Its name, *zijin-cheng*, literally translated as Purple Forbidden City, resonates with the polar region, the ruling house of the heavens, known as the Purple Occult Precinct (*ziwei yuan*). Certain gates within the city are named for stars in this region.[20]

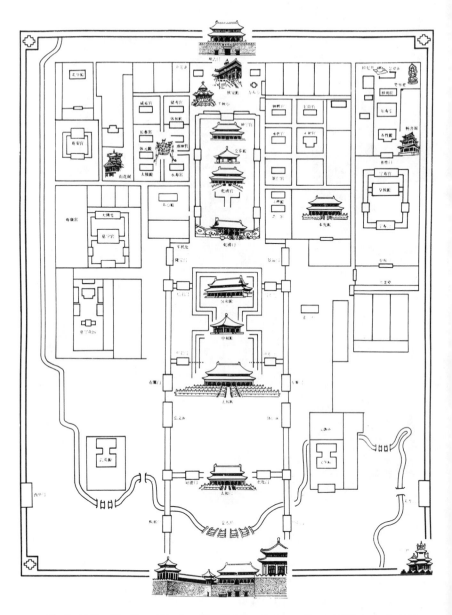

20. The Forbidden City. From *Zijin cheng dihou shenghuo 1644–1911* (Imperial life in the Forbidden City) (1981).

Buildings were also named in pairs that expressed yin-yang logic; for instance, the first character of the name of the southern building in the Inner Court, Qianqing gong, is the first, yang, "male" hexagram of the *Yijing*. It is matched by the first character of the name of the northernmost of the three Inner Court buildings, the Kunning gong, which is the second hexagram, the yin "female."

The most renovation, at the greatest expense, was carried out under the Qianlong emperor in the eighteenth century. Enlargements of the altars of Heaven and Earth were undertaken in 1749 and renovation of the front Three Halls of the Forbidden City was begun in 1765 (Xie Mincong 1980: 29; Ling Shun-sheng 1963: 40). Then, in 1774, the emperor decreed that a seventeenth-century history of Beijing, the *Rixia jiuwen* by Zhu Yizun (1629–1709),[21] be re-edited and supplemented.

Qianlong ordered editors to add chapters 9–28 on palaces under the present emperor. The editors begin that section with these general remarks:

Of old, those who established the realm first exalted the model of the Ancestral Temple and the Altar of Soil and Grain and respectfully founded the order of palaces and courts. Thus they imitated the stars as pivots, nurturing the kingdom as though it were encompassed in walls. Thus they displayed integrity and composure [*jing*] so as to diffuse the transformative power of Coherence and render permanent [*dian,* "canonical"] its superlative greatness.

The palaces handed down from previous generations are the carrying out of the wishes of deceased forebears, the entire building of the Inner and Outer Courts [*neichao, waichao*] an offering [*ju*] of repairs.[22] The way to the *Dao* lies in sensitivity to the proper time and it was necessary for the throne to order/instruct [*chi*] those in charge so that they could complete this enterprise of veneration.

A resplendent willingness to carry out our forefathers' vast plans creates a flourishing standard that will go down to posterity for ten thousand years. Today this carefully gathered record of the Domainal Dynastic Palaces and Halls in twenty chapters is laid before the original book's doorstep. Its editing being reliable, it will supplement original entries with information that will mutually validate them both. (*RXJWK* 9/1:127)

The editors describe the process of building, not architecture. When kings build they do a number of things reminiscent of the accomplishments of the cycle of Grand Sacrifice. First, they create an earthly analogue to heaven that "imitates the stars as pivots." They also preserve and extend the palaces of their forbears out of filiality, an "enterprise of veneration" that itself is an "offering" like a sacrifice. They "nurture the kingdom as though it were encompassed in

walls," a reference to the walled cities inhabited by the emperor's representatives. Finally, building renders "permanent," literally "canonical," the transformative power of Coherence. The word *dian* also refers to dynastic compilations of regulations such as the *Da Qing huidian* (*Assembled Canon*) in its various
editions.

How natural that the Qianlong emperor should further extend his "willingness to carry out the forefathers' vast plans" by commissioning their reinscrip-
tion in a new edition of the *Rixia jiuwen*. In these additional twenty chapters, the
rituals associated with each edifice are described, and then followed by lengthy
examples of imperial poetry written upon specific ritual occasions associated
with the buildings, and sometimes displayed there. Thus the interpenetration
of writing, ritual, and building was preserved, and presented.[23]

Walls and Gates: Inner and Outer

The imperial central city resembled other cities in emphasizing walls. Walled
cities, oriented by the four cardinal directions, were the primary form for central cities at provincial, prefectural, departmental, and county levels. Each of
these administrative centers housed the emperor's representative.

City walls did not so much separate town from country as instantiate the
creation of complementary inner and outer portions of a single totality, an ur-
ban-rural continuum. Mote discusses this continuum at persuasive length,
drawing upon sociological and economic factors (1977:101–6). The designation for the City God, *chenghuang,* which means "walls and moats," provides a
rich illustration of how this continuum was imagined.

Chenghuang came to designate not only "city" but also the particular tutelary
deity who was entrusted to mediate between the community and more powerful spirits (*shen*). But when a city served as a multiple administrative center, seat
of a prefecture as well as, for example, two counties, there would be several
City God temples in town, one for each area. The efficacy of the deity extended
beyond the walls, as did the jurisdiction of the resident governor or magistrate
who served as his earthly counterpart (Watt 1977: 354–55).

According to seventeenth-century encyclopedists, the words *cheng* and *huang*
are first seen in the *Yijing* (*Gujin tushu jicheng* 1964: 60.60). In the interpretation
of the hexagram *tai,* itself an image of "peace as heaven and Earth unite," the
"city walls will return to the moat" in times of disaster (*I-ching* 1967: 49–52).
In China, the earth for walls was dug out and the trenches formed moats beneath them. As the *Yijing* hints, the "emergence" of walls from moats illustrated
cosmogonic process. Like the Grand Primitivity, which divided into Heaven and

Earth, yang and yin, in this case also the One becomes Two. Flat earth simultaneously yields a mound (yang) and a moat that will be filled with water (both yin). According to Mote: "China's cities were but knots of the same material, of one piece with the net, denser in quality but not foreign bodies resting on it" (1977:105). The fact that cities were raised almost exclusively in lowlands and rarely made use of highlands or hills (Chang Sen-dou 1977: 83–84) suggests that flat plains and lowland valleys provided impressive settings for the display of wall-building, a dredging and wrinkling of the very earth from which the peasantry drew its sustenance. Thus, the purpose of walls was to aid the king in centering the domain. Their defensive function would be a natural outgrowth of this activity of domain maintenance.

In terms of the everyday life of the community as a whole, Mote's point about the lack of cleavage between town and countryside is well taken. However, Watt also reminds that there also existed a "Confucian tendency to define government as the 'civilization' of the countryside": "The less cultivated common people in the countryside were to provide food and labor in return for the order and virtue emanating from the humanizing nuclei" (1977: 356). In other words, walls were a boundary, but a permeable one. Walls and moats constituted a separation that effected a particular conjoining of the inner and outer. The initiative belonged to those within, those who controlled access between the inner and outer by control of the gates through the wall boundary.

The size and ornamentation of these massive gates far exceeded anything called for by their mundane function (Wheatley 1969: 17). Beijing, containing as it did the Son of Heaven, ultimate source of *wen,* pattern, order, "civilization," possessed the most impressive gates in the kingdom. The Outer City had ten, the Inner City eleven.[24] The Imperial City and the Forbidden City walls each had four, one facing in each direction. Within, the doorways to all buildings were named and often marked with imperial calligraphy on the lintels.

The largest gates in imperial Beijing acted as conduits of the north-south axis that passed through their portals. After entering Yongdingmen, south gate of the Outer City, one advanced through six more gates before entering the Forbidden City through Wumen, or "Meridian Gate." The distance between the two gates was three miles (Xie Mincong 1980: 117). The axial line of the city did not open up a vista that culminated in one important element (as, for example, at Versailles). Instead, the line of vision was guided through a succession of spaces in sequence (Boyd 1962: 73). The experience is one of controlled transition, not unimpeded forward movement.

How were these transitions embodied? What did a gate look like? First, they were higher than the walls around them, actually more like buildings through which a road passes than doors in a wall. Wumen, the largest of the Forbidden City gates, is surmounted by five pavilion-like roofed structures. Imperial gates are also approached through raised walkways, either stairs or arched bridges leading up to them.

Finally, the description of the emperor's processions provide other clues about the crucial role of the gate as mediating space. For instance, when the emperor processes to the Altar of Soil and Grain, he begins inside the Inner Court at Qianqing gate. There he surmounts a stepladder to his Ritual Chair (*liyu*) and is carried through the Outer Audience area, moving south. At the southernmost end of the Outer Court, at the Taiho gate, he dismounts and again via a stepladder remounts the Gold Palanquin. Then he is carried through the Wumen out of the Forbidden City and turns west to the altar complex (*DQTL* 1756: 7.4a).

In these processions, the transition between inner and outer, which took place along the ritual "horizontal," was marked by movement along the "vertical," between upper and lower as well. "Centering," or *zhong,* was accomplished at the moment between ascent and descent, within the portals of the gates. This was true not only for the emperor but for his servants on foot as well. Gates of buildings usually have a raised threshold, forcing walkers to step up and over, through space.[25] In this way, for the king's servants, each stage in the approach to the Audience Hall was a miniaturized version of the main event—assembly in the great forecourt of the Taiho dian, followed by movement up its three tiers of stairs.

Roofs, Pillars, and Platforms: Upper and Lower

Perhaps the most important element in the construction of the Chinese city as cosmic power, the wall, is curiously unnecessary as a structural component of its buildings. To understand this paradox, we must imagine how the city accomplished its unifying function, which was to aid the king in centering.

The buildings of Beijing's palace complex were composed of three parts: an earthen platform, the roof, and the pillars that supported it. The structure was traditionally thought to symbolize the now-familiar triad of Heaven (roof), Earth (platform), Humanity (pillar).[26] Its system of framing separated the elements of support and enclosure: Walls were structurally unnecessary and were used as moveable partitions that need not be present (Boyd 1962: 24). Interior space was not conceived as rooms forever enclosed but instead, in a way analogous to the interior of the embodied self being formed by layers of surfaces, was a flexible space. Rooms were divided with reference to pillars. This "space between" pillars was called *jian*.[27] It was the site of ceremonial action, and ritual handbooks prescribe ritual movement in reference to pillars, the markers of *jian*.

The pillars were made of single enormous tree trunks. Instead of a capital, these pillars support the roof with a cluster of cantilevered brackets that radiate, in principle, in the four cardinal directions (Pirazolli-t'Serstevens 1971: 88). When viewed from a distance, such buildings seem to be all high platform and sloping roof, two structural immensities held apart, and thus together, by the dwarfed pillars between, as though the burden of connecting Heaven and Earth were almost too much to bear.

The character that means pillar or column, pronounced *zhu*, is composed of two elements: the left side is the radical for wood while the right side, which supplies the character with its phonic elements, means "lord," "master," or "main." The word is quite important in *li*, where it designates the principal ritual actor, sometimes the sacrificer, *zhujizhe*, or the host, *zhuren*. Yet the analogy made between pillars and men in traditional architecture does not point directly to the emperor.

By the Han period, the character *zhu* was used to praise worthy officials as "Pillars of the Domain" in a rare instance of cross-cultural punning.[28] In the Taiho dian, during Grand Audience, the emperor was surrounded by his pillars. Some were lacquered in red and thirty feet high; others were quite a bit shorter and wore the robes of their offices. All assisted the emperor in his task of connecting Earth to Heaven, but only he was the *zhuren*. The emperor's power could be extended, but he himself was too necessary to ever be made redundant by perfect analogy. (See above on sacrifice to Soil and Grain.)

The structures of traditional Chinese building displayed the cosmic triad, thought of in Chinese ritual logic as vertical in relation: Heaven (upper), Humanity (centering), and Earth (lower). They thus had no need of walls that functioned in the ritual "horizontal" between the inner and outer. Or, thinking of it another way, the *absence* of a wall signified the ultimate permeability of the "innermost inner," just at the point when it was transformed by ritual as the manifestation of the conjoining of Heaven and Earth. This manifestation was crucial for Grand Audience when the Lords of the Outer Domains came bearing their credentials and local products to be included in the inner realm of the Son of Heaven.

Axiality

When the emperor held audience in the Taiho dian, he sat in the north and faced south. The southern attitude (*nanmianzhe*) had been associated with lordship in China even before the Han period.[29] The *Record of Rites* connects it to the lord's resonance with the yang principle, whose source lay in the south: "The ruler's turning [*xiang*] to the south has the significance of responding to yang. The minister facing [*mian*] north has the significance of responding to his lord" (*LJZY,* "Jiaotesheng," 25/2:1448). Thus, though the north is the *source* of yin (and therefore site of the Altar to Earth), it was the yang position for the human king when he faced south, source of yang. Then he acted as a concentrator of yang energy that, in turn, radiated upon his kingdom. Wherever the king stood and faced became an ever-shifting boundary between yin and yang.

The toponymy of the Forbidden City was taken from the disposition of the king's body as he faced south. "Front" and "rear" (*qian, hou*) meant in front and behind the king and designated south and north respectively. Usually these terms were used for palaces (*gong*) and halls (*dian*). "Right" and "left" (*you, zuo*) refer to the king's right and left hand, and were used especially for smaller side gates.

The north-south axis was most important in imperial sacrifice as well. If the king acted as the south-facing lord in audience, viewing his north-facing ministers, in sacrifice he reversed himself to face north toward the spirits (of the Ancestors, of Heaven, Earth or Soil and Grain). In thus taking up the position of servant himself, he embodied the complementary sides of hierarchy as befits one who ruled as *parent* of the people by virtue of being the *son* of Heaven.

East- and west-facing attitudes were not unimportant, however. In Guest Ritual, the host sat on the east, facing west, while the guest sat and faced opposite on the west. When it was necessary to rank lines of people, invariably the east was considered superior.

We can draw out a hierarchy of axiality: the north-south axis takes precedence over the east-west and, within each axis the south is superior to north, and east superior to west. Schematically it could look like this: $S > N > E > W$. According to this logic, a position in the southeast would be the most prestigious, precisely the location of the Altar of Heaven.

All four altars of Grand Sacrifice are placed according to the hierarchy of axiality. In figure 21, the two axes intersecting in the person of the emperor in Audience guide directional placement. Heaven and Earth altars were on a parallel north-south line that runs slightly east of the complexes for worship of Ancestors and Soil and Grain, thus indicating their superiority.

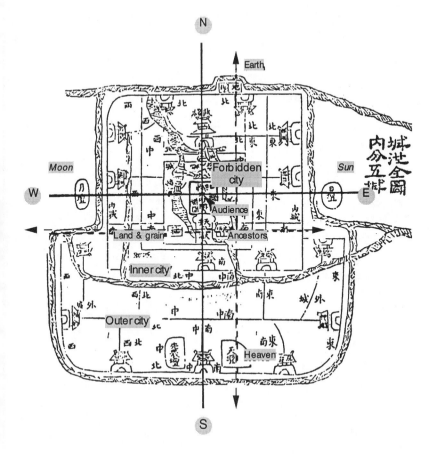

21. Placement of Altars of Grand Sacrifice in Beijing relative to directional axes (axes added). Map from Wu Changuan, *Zhenyuan shilue* (1788).

The Temple to the Ancestors and the Altar to Soil and Grain were, in turn, *slightly south* of the imperial east-west axis. Situated at each end of the imperial axis are altars to the Sun and Moon, outside the imperial city walls. Sun and Moon sacrifices head up the category of "Middle Sacrifices," inferior to Grand Sacrifices, a fact reflected in their relatively northerly placement along the east-west axis.

According to their axial hierarchy, these sacrifices should be ranked as follows: Heaven > Earth > Ancestral > Soil and Grain > Sun > Moon. Indeed, they are listed in that order in both the *Assembled Canon* and the *Comprehensive Rites*. This hierarchy was embodied as well in the form of the text of the *Compre-*

hensive Rites and influenced the process of its editing as part of sacrificial preparation.

Textual Space, Editing Choices, and Ritual Logic

The ritual manuals produced in the mid-eighteenth century "spatialized," as deCerteau would say, the place of the city we have just discussed; they narrated it into motion.[30] These texts created space in doubled fashion, as both "map" and "tour." DeCerteau describes how texts' "description oscillates between the terms of an alternative: either *seeing* (the knowledge of an order of places) or *going* (spatializing activities). Either it represents a *tableau* . . . or it organizes *movements*" (1984: 119). *The Comprehensive Rites of the Qing (Da Qing tongli,* or *DQTL*), it will be recalled from chapter 3 above, made its special contribution by narrating ceremonial to aid its performance in time. Its companion volume, the *Illustrations for the Assembled Canon of the Qing (Da Qing huidian tu* 1899, or *HDT*),[31] a collection of detailed diagrams, presents a kind of visualized synopsis of the ritual logic of Grand Sacrifice. Both texts prefigure by their internal arrangement the logic of the rites they contain, collapsing neatly any distinction between tour and map.

We will first examine the *Comprehensive Rites.* According to the preface ascribed to the emperor, the book would assist people in putting the *Assembled Canon* into practice. During its re-editing in the early 1820s for circulation among provincial officials, editors lamented that such a useful book had been kept in the palace, where few could see it. The following analysis is based on an 1883 reprint of that 1824 edition.

The original imperial preface calls the manual a detailed yet still comprehensible format for the Five Rites it contained. The Auspicious Rites section opens with the four Grand Sacrifices listed in the order of Heaven, Earth, Ancestral Temple, and Altar of Soil and Grain. Together, these four ceremonies formed a set that moved the emperor out of his palace in each of the cardinal directions around the capital: south to worship Heaven at the winter solstice, east to the Ancestral Temple in spring and autumn, and west to the Altar of Soil and Grain, again every spring and fall, in a year-long cycle.

The listing of the sacrifices in the text expressed their relative importance.[32] The first two sacrifices to Heaven and Earth were identical in ceremonial order and contain the full range of sections. The second two, Ancestral Sacrifice and Sacrifice to Soil and Grain, preserved this order but left out certain sections such as "Bringing Forward the Flesh of the Victims" or a separate presentation of jade and silk. At the level of ceremonial order, the north-south axis was listed first and more completely while the east-west axis followed like a reprise.

According to the ritual manual, the Sacrifice to Heaven was the "most complete and detailed" instance of sacrifice (*DQTL* 1756: 1.1a). The editors meant this literally and symbolically. In its textual treatment of the format of each section, the Sacrifice to Heaven was completely detailed. The second Earth sacrifice, although identical in order, referred the ritualist back to the Sacrifice to Heaven for format details when the action within the section was the same. In other words, although the two were identical in ceremonial order, a distinction was made at the level of format. One reason for this difference in format may have been that the Sacrifice to Heaven was performed at the winter solstice in order to tip the cosmos into yang at the moment when yin had reached its maximum influence. Listing Heaven first expresses the superiority of yang over yin, but not just by giving it pride of place. The structure of the text showed by its completeness that this "superiority" is a relation of encompassing > encompassed, that is, the distinction itself is encompassed by one of its terms, in this case by yang.

The same asymmetry obtained in the east-west axis. Ancestral Sacrifice, with its referrals to Heaven, was marked as yang. The Sacrifice to Soil and Grain was a yin rite, a subset of Earth's. It was so marked by the vessels used on its altar and its yellow color scheme. Its notes referred backward to the Earth Sacrifice, even though four times out of six we only encounter further referral to the Sacrifice to Heaven, as though to make this subordination clear.

We are left, it seems, with an encompassed asymmetry, as illustrated in figure 22. In the logic of yin-yang (more appropriately yang-yin), north-Earth is inferior to south-Heaven and west-Soil and Grain inferior to east-Ancestral. In the figure, the four sacrifices and their directions are arranged in staggered columns beneath their yin-yang designations along a scale of relative superiority in each pair.

Yet the north-south (Heaven-Earth) axis as a whole takes precedence over the east-west. In the figure, circles show how the paired asymmetries are placed into a whole-part relationship through two forms of editing: at the level of ceremonial order, north-south (Heaven-Earth) encompasses east-west; at the level of detail of format, the Sacrifice of Heaven encompasses all sacrifices, is indeed their recursive definition.

The order of Grand Sacrifice (S, N, E, W) shows a logic of hierarchical encompassment, the same hierarchy already noticed in the placement of the four

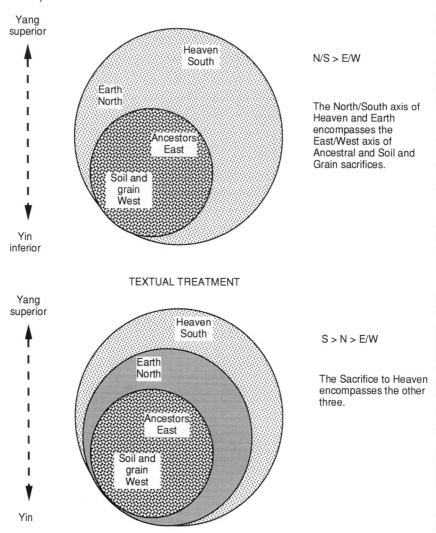

Yang
superior

↑
¦
¦
¦
¦
¦
¦
¦
¦
↓

Yin
inferior

Heaven
South

Earth
North

Ancestors
East

Soil and
grain
West

N/S > E/W

The North/South axis of
Heaven and Earth
encompasses the
East/West axis of
Ancestral and Soil and
Grain sacrifices.

TEXTUAL TREATMENT

Yang
superior

↑
¦
¦
¦
¦
¦
¦
¦
↓

Yin

Heaven
South

Earth
North

Ancestors
East

Soil and
grain
West

S > N > E/W

The Sacrifice to Heaven
encompasses the other
three.

22. Yang-yin asymmetry in the editing of the ceremonial order of the *DQTL*.

temple complexes of Grand Sacrifice along their appropriate axes. The text does
not "tell" us this but rather accomplishes it in and through its structure and
narrative sequence when all Grand Sacrifices are displayed as varying subsets of
the Southern Boundary Sacrifice to Heaven.[33]

This order of directions arranged hierarchically in turn provided a model
for arrangement of performance within each sacrifice. We can make reasonable
inferences about the relative importance of people at the sacrifice by drawing

upon the logic of axial directionality embodied in the order of the text. For instance, the emperor-celebrant, nobility, and participating members of the imperium face north or south toward the spirits, while assisting staff (from the Ministry of Rites, the Court of Grand Constancy, and so forth) face east or west.

To further demonstrate the ritual logic embodied in text, we may turn to the *Illustrations for the Assembled Canon of the Qing* (*Da Qing huidian tu* 1899). The *Illustrations for the Assembled Canon* included clothing, vessels, astronomical equipment, star charts, and earth maps. All information on ritual is arranged in the sequence of the sacrificial canon described above.

Under "Ritual Construction" (*Lizhi*), we find three diagrams, with explanatory texts, for each sacrifice. Preparing the altar, people, and things took up five of the six days recorded in the *Comprehensive Rites*. From these diagrams we learn how this preparation was organized spatially.

Figure 23 combines the three diagrams for the Sacrifice at the Altar of Soil and Grain.[34] Moving inward, we are presented with shrinking concentric areas. The accompanying texts make the overarching organization of contexts even clearer.

Within figure 23, Diagram One illustrates (and its text describes) the entire complex: the height and length of walls, tile colors, and the names of gates and buildings. Diagram Two situates itself visually within this context by illustrating a part of Diagram One (altar and wall) but describes in the text the places of tables and stands, and then the participants. We note that they are all standing directly on the altar. This diagram is called the "Order of Places" (*weici*). Diagram Three is an illustration of the places of vessels *upon* the tables and stands before one of the spirit tablets. It is called the "Standing of Arrangements" (*chenshe*).

The diagrams show a sequence of ever-narrowing encompassed spaces. Once again, reminding us of the Sacrifice to Heaven, expressed as first and most complete text, the sequence moves from largest, most encompassing to smaller, encompassed.

The temporal narrative of the *Comprehensive Rites* also used the four terms above—place (*wei*), order (*ci*), arrangement (*chen*), and stand (*she*)—in sequences that indicated movement from the encompassing to the encompassed. For example, before dawn on the day of a Grand Sacrifice, the emperor "Approaches the *order,* washes, then takes his *place* [*jiu ci guanxi jiu wei*]."[35] And in its descriptions of preparation of altars, first tables and stands were *stood* (*she*) upon the altar, then vessels were *arranged* (*chen*) upon them. Just as the "Order of Places" (*weici*) provides an encompassing context for "Standing of Arrange-

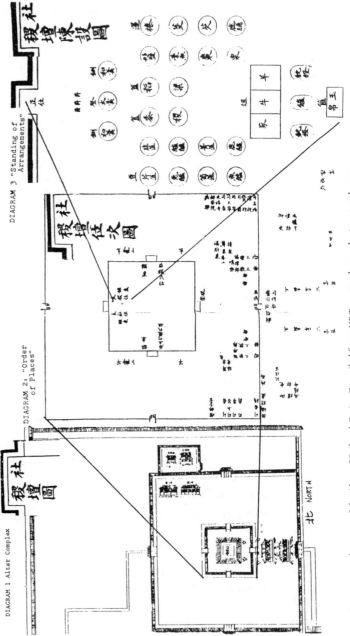

23. Construction diagrams of the Altar of Soil and Grain. Compiled from *HDT* 10.2a–3b, 10.5b–6a, 10.13b–14a.

ments" (*chenshe*)—Diagram Two to Diagram Three—so within each of these pairs, one is prior to and contextualizing of the other.

Once again this artifact of editing points us inward to an understanding of the rites themselves and will help us bridge into the next chapter on the Preparation phase of the ritual proper. The objects of this hierarchical placement were the participants and vessels used to hold food and drink offerings. In the narrative of the *Comprehensive Rites,* people seemed to have been isomorphic with vessels. During the preparation phase, both vessels in their storerooms and participants in the Hall of Seclusion were inspected. Attention was paid to their internal states: food went into vessels but participants fasted and were enjoined to concentrate upon emptying their heart/minds (*xin*). Exterior decoration was prescribed for both and took the form of patterns upon vessels and elaborate court dress for participants.

Yet in the *Illustrations,* both people and *stands* are prescribed for placement directly upon the altar (see figure 23, Diagram Two, part of the "Order of Places"). In other words, here participants are marked as isomorphic to the tables and stands that *hold* vessels. According to the logic of hierarchy embodied in the textual arrangement, participants were featured at both levels: they were simultaneously encompassed like vessels and encompassing like stands. As the offerers carried the jade cups of liquor to the spirits, were they at the same time container and thing contained?

These two short analyses give only a fleeting sense of the logic displayed by this text editing. They should be recapitulated on a more abstract level to give a clearer idea of precisely how the text as artifact of editing partook of the logic of Grand Sacrifice at the same time that it determined that logic.

On the evidence of the order of the four Grand Sacrifices in the *Comprehensive Rites,* we defined the yang-yin principle as organization of bipolarity such that one term contained the other as a necessary part of itself. This point cannot be overemphasized. At least in imperial sacrifice, the cliché relation of yang-yin as eternally oscillating and evenly supplementary poles was actually weighted and skewed to favor yang. In ritual practice the perfect symmetry of the logic so often described by Chinese metaphysicians and philosophers was constantly overloaded in certain of its terms. Thus an equipoised set of propositions was shifted to highlight, in this instance, the specificity of the power of the sacrificing king within the "orderly" hierarchy of interrelated parts and forces that are all equally essential for the total process.[36]

This logic of encompassed asymmetries organized other topographical metaphors in the sacrifice into related pairs that marked spaces and objects: south-north, east-west, the inside and outside of people or vessels, or the relation of the sovereign above and the people below. This sort of Chinese structuring is generally familiar. But the texts do not stop there. They arrange these pairs of bipolarities into relations. For instance, we have mentioned the descriptive hints in the period of preparation that point to the isomorphism of participants and vessels. Even more important than their substantive analogy was their relation to each other as mediated by their places within the whole of the rite, that is, the relation of their relations.

Hence the importance of the levels of encompassment is shown by the arrangement of contexts in the "Illustrations." By arranging pairs of bipolarities in relations of

encompassing   encompassed
Order of Places   Standing of Arrangements
weici   *chenshe*

the text created a possibility of dynamic ambiguity between levels. This ambiguity was resolved through action in performance as when, for instance, participants who carried up an offering seemed to be isomorphic with both vessels and stands.

Eventually, as I will show, the most important participant in Sacrifice was shown to be the emperor himself. An asymmetry interrupted the posited harmony of eternally oscillating poles, providing a possibility of movement within the rite, toward a statement of specificity: *Li* was not just about "order in the abstract"; through sacrifice it was constituted as a particular order with the emperor at its center. The logic is something like this: kingly sacrifice was necessary to continue the cosmic cycle. Such necessity seemed to presuppose a "king" who existed prior to the rites. Yet, within itself the rite produced the "King who is co-equal with Heaven," in Dong Zhongshu's phrase. It produced and placed him as cosmic constructor in a perfect redundance that ensured at one and the same time the renewal of the year and his own control. For the imperium, the constitution of the cosmos and king were simultaneous. The emperor mobilized a "body of yang power." As the focal, centering point for this powerful ritualization, the emperor also modeled correct yang-yin encompassment. Insofar as yang-yin was also used to explain/model gender distinction, this ritualization gave concrete content to a Chinese notion of masculinity.

The editing choices of the *Comprehensive Rites* and the *Illustrations* prefigured by their own configurations the Sacrifice: they partook of its logic at the same time that they fixed it. At this level of signifying practice and of the production of form, the relationship posited by the text/performance of Grand Sacrifice between the text and the rest of the action was one of interconnecting levels of structural homology. Text/performance therefore provided a model for the activity of contextualizing, a metaphor for wholeness and totality in general.

The combination of the structure and narrative sequence of the two texts provided a model for a hierarchy of encompassment: ranking elements in relation to an ever-shifting whole. In so doing, the metaphor for wholeness in general, at the level of ritual form itself, yields a very specifically chosen, carefully edited whole. Certain of its elements are definitely indicated as more important than others.

Furthermore, the act of writing itself was part of the described ceremonial procedure. Although the rite did not employ upon the altar the physical texts we have examined (insofar as I know), it did contain a sequence for the production of a text. Two days before the ceremony, prayerboards (*zhuban*) were written out. The day before, they were reviewed, and during the ceremony, incense was burned before them and they were offered and burned or buried like other offerings. Nothing else was completely produced, used, and destroyed within the six days narrated by the *Comprehensive Rites*. Text, the medium that indicated, described, and contained the rite, was at the same time contained by it.

Grand Sacrifice began in an exegesis and discussion of past ritual that culminated in texts that were both descriptive and prescriptive. Performance according to the texts was a re-presentation of the knowledge of past order coupled with the power of the emperor to command the objects and people needed to demonstrate its reality in the present Qing reign. Text and performance complemented one another, combining in an ever-changing whole. Only rituals according to the text were correct.[37] Yet the text as synopsis (a summarizing visualization) of the study of ritual was valid only when it also truly described and led to ritual performance that "accorded to circumstance."[38] Models of a Chinese polity that was eternally fixed in stagnant equilibrium can be dismissed. The constant effort to sight change, cite precedent, and re-site ritual practice bespeaks a sensibility that was fine-tuned to transformation.

In being so attuned, editors were acting according to the Chinese cosmological truism that the *dao* is never fixed but always in flux. Hence I would not want to reduce their realignment of elements that had been transformed into a "merely" rhetorical project of fixing change while transforming history into cosmology for their own purposes. For these men, history was a necessary part of cosmology, encompassed by its very laws. The ritualist metaphysics provided the vocabulary in which Qing emperors could explain how it came to be that they had replaced the Ming upon the throne.

Perfect rites in the present would reflect a perfect access to ritual past. Indeed, the editing of ritual texts displayed the process through which choices of language became a central element in ordering and re-presenting that past. Through such choices, the historical record could be subtly reordered by virtue of its linguistic presence and privilege upon the sacrificial altars of the imperium.

In text/performance, the emperor and his editors thought of themselves as being in the best positions to see the totality of *li*. This envisioned totality determined in advance each imperial act, and these acts in turn constituted the whole by re-presenting it in the prescribed manner. In pre-scribing (that is, writing in advance), the emperor shows his own rule to be prescribed.

Grand Sacrifice drew attention to the production of text as a privileged part of the world, creator of the contexts that contained it—much as the emperor constituted the cosmos that contained him as one of its most essential elements. We are at the heart of the question of discursive production. Within the imperium, Grand Sacrifice as text/performance posited a seamless fit between the emperor's word and action. The signifying practice of the editing of ritual texts imitated as it constituted the form of its signified, an extreme instance of the ritualist metaphysics' linguistic optimism discussed previously. Perhaps no more powerful bid for discursive domination can be made than the melding of signifier and signified. For it is in the gap between them that doubt, hesitation, and difference of interpretation reside.

The operations performed during the Period of Preparation alternated inspecting and judging with ordering and marking. In the Period of Preparation emerged the site of interface, of boundary between an order of intellect and knowledge (texts) and an order of practical effects (performance) that showed their inseparability and mutual necessity for the production of human meaning in the world. Here was enacted a practical cosmology.

6

COSMIC PREPARATION

Orders of Knowledge

On that day the king wore the robe covered with rising dragons as the emblem of heaven. He wore the cap with twelve pendants of jade pearls, the number of heaven. From the flag hung twelve pendants and it showed dragons and the sun and moon, imitating the heavens. Heaven hangs out its bright figures and the sages imitate them. This extra-mural sacrifice illustrates the way of heaven.   RECORD OF RITES, "Jiaotesheng"

In the Preparation phase of Grand Sacrifice, people, animals, things, and words were readied. Participants went into seclusion; victims were fed, washed, and slaughtered; vessels were filled with foods; prayers were written (see figure 16 in chapter 5). The "Jitong" chapter of the *Record of Rites* provides an extended discussion of the concept central to ritual preparation, *bei,* which means to "perfect" or "prepare." The term gives the sense that all potentiality for appropriate action has been gathered for possible release (*LJZY* 49/2:1602).

Auspiciousness is Perfect Preparation or *bei. Bei* designates all that is congruent [*shun*]. When nothing is inappropriate or incongruous, there is *bei.* Then we say that within, the self is full and without, all is in conformity with the *dao.* At their basis, the service of a loyal minister to his lord and that of a filial son to his family are one and the same.

Above, all is harmony with the spirits; without, all is in compliance with rulers and elders; within, there is filiality toward the family. Thus there is Perfect Preparation. Only the worthy can achieve this Perfect Preparation. If they do so, then they can sacrifice.

Therefore, the sacrifice of the worthy man focuses/intensifies [*zhi*] his integrity and faith, gathers his loyalty and composure. It is then offered through things and becomes the *dao* through ritual.

The language of alternation between inner and outer gives the impression that preparation was simultaneously internal and external, as though these spaces existed prior to sacrifice. We might think of this activity in another way, however. Preparation marked out, thus creating, relevant spaces and participants so as to produce a series of boundaries.

The goal of Perfect Preparation was to establish, through the process of centering, the conditions whereby the inner could assert superiority over the outer and the upper conjoin with the lower. Their actual conjuncture could only come about through sacrificial ceremonial, when the order was set in motion. But its prerequisite was Perfect Preparation. Thus, I would propose a new translation for the phrase in the "Jitong" chapter of the *Record of Rites* that has become the *locus classicus* for the idea that ritual originated within the essential nature of man. "Sacrifice is not a thing that comes from without; from centering it emerges and is born in the heart/mind [*zi zhong chu yu xin*]. The heart/mind being deeply moved, it offers upwards in ritual" (*LJZY* 49/2:1602).

Sacrifice, the process whereby the hidden internal and the mysterious external were both made visible as aesthetic pattern and thus accessible for ordering in the social world, originated neither from external constraints nor from inner necessity. It was instead the dialectical outcome of "centering." This work was accomplished in the material details of ritual performance. Such performance mediated the contradictions between the political and the familial, proving through its enactment that service to one's king and duty to one's parents did not collide and that the sage and the heir coincided. In imperial sacrifice, the emperor demonstrated the "reality" that things which seemed to be separate were, in fact, part of the same (that is, *his*) domain and purview.

Ordering Orders of Homology: Victims, People, and Vessels

The Period of Preparation accomplished three things. First, homologies were established between participants, victims, and vessels by subjecting all three to analogous operations of inspection and manipulation. These manipulations prepared all three as boundaries between an inner and outer field. Second, these perfectly prepared "centerers" were arranged upon the altars in relations of encompassing to encompassed or, put another way, relations of ever-increasing interiority that connoted a more universal inclusiveness.[1] Third, the emperor entered this process partway through as an actor whose movement through these orders began the transformation of spatial distribution into temporal direction. Thus the general model of sacrifice assembled through scholarship on the past was transformed into the specific sacrifice of the model filial sage king, the Qianlong emperor.

The language of the *Comprehensive Rites* ritual manual conflates the declarative and imperative moods so that description of canonical ritual practice was simultaneously an exhortation to repeat its actions in the present. The case could be made that all language functions simultaneously as descriptive and prescriptive; that is, in any written or verbal narration choices are made that exclude possibilities, presenting a version of past events that not only makes sense within the present context but attunes us toward a particular future as well. That this function was especially obvious in imperial ritual is not surprising; the emperor's rites were not an inversion or separation from everyday life but were most emphatically cast as an epitomizing and exemplary moment of existence whose effect through resonance would be matched in mundane relationships and actions all over the realm. This blurring of a language of declaration and exhortation to act elides a distinction between past and future in order to produce a perfect present order.

The sections of the Period of Preparation alternate Viewing and Inspecting, which privilege the eye and vision, with sections of actions that mobilize the rest of the body, such as Achieving Seclusion, or Writing. Each of the first twelve sections of the Grand Sacrifice to Heaven will be discussed within the framework just outlined, following exactly the ceremonial order of sections from figure 16. This chapter's headings come directly from the *Comprehensive Rites,* whose text will be paraphrased and followed by my commentary. Even though I will refer often to Han ritual classics in my exegesis, I do so upon cues from eighteenth-century texts like the *Five Rites* or the *Huangchao liqi tushi* (Illustrations of dynastic ritual paraphernalia, hereafter *Illustrations*).

The narrated account of Grand Sacrifice to Heaven begins with the "Viewing of Victims." These consisted of oxen, sheep, and pigs.[2]

Viewing Victims (*Shixing*) (*DQTL* 1756: 1.1b)

Five days before the ceremony, a prince of the royal blood (*qinwang*) is sent to the stables of the Altar of Heaven complex where he faces north to view the ox, sheep, and deer.[3] When all is finished, the Chief of the Stables kneels and calls out, "Things are as they should be [*ru*]." The inspectors then retire through the north gate.

We note that the inspectors face north while viewing the victims, just as they will face north when participating in the rite.

In the third year of the Qianlong reign (1738), two decades before the *Comprehensive Rites* was published, San Tai, in his position as president of the Ministry of Rites, submitted a routine memorial. Two months in advance of the winter solstice Sacrifice to Heaven, he requested that people be assigned to view the victims. Five days before the sacrifice, two princes of the blood, Yin Bi and Hong Zhou, were sent. A day before, San Tai and a *dailang* of the Ministry of Rites named Muhelin also went to inspect.[4] The performance of the rite, indeed various rites that were codified in the *Comprehensive Rites,* were carried out and recorded for decades before that manual was produced.[5]

Achieving Seclusion (*Zhizhai*) (*DQTL* 1756: 1.2a–2b)

Three days before the ceremony, at dawn, officials display a plaque announcing the Achieving of Seclusion and the figure of a bronze man. They are on a yellow table placed in a mediating gate between the inner court (where the emperor is achieving seclusion) and the outer audience parts of the Forbidden City.

They face the plaque south, and the bronze man west and the Director of the Court of Grand Constancy performs the rite of one kneeling and three prostrations. The plaque announces the exact date of the upcoming sacrifice to Heaven and enjoins all participants to "purify your heart/minds."

The plaque faces south in a position associated with rulership and so stands for the king. The bronze man[6] stands in the position, relative to the plaque, that courtiers will assume before the spirits at the sacrifice three days hence. The plaque acts as a metonym of the emperor while the bronze man is a metaphor of his servants. The plaque is placed in front of the main gate of the emperor's

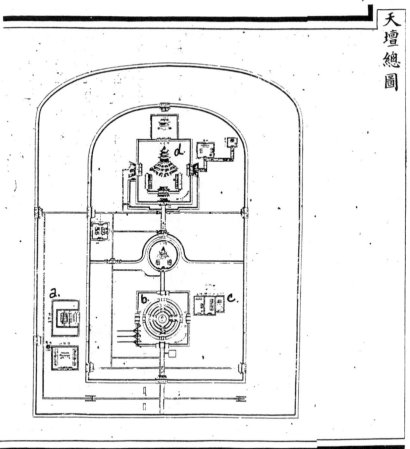

24. Layout of the Altar of Heaven complex. From *HDT* 1.1a–b.

palace chambers, where he will remain in seclusion for two nights before proceeding to the Altar complex to spend the final night. (See figure 24 for placement of Hall for Achieving Seclusion within the Altar of Heaven complex.) A
British observer later noted that at the same time, a table was placed bearing
the injunction to seclusion before the door of every yamen office in the Forbidden City (Williams 1913: 28).

What did "Achieving Seclusion" mean? At the simplest level, participants
were forbidden to eat meat or strong-smelling vegetables, drink wine, listen to
music, have sex, invite or be invited to a feast, or take part in mourning rites.
They were also forbidden to hear criminal cases (*HDZL* 1899: 415.1b; Williams
1936: 27). Speaking more abstractly, an edict from the Yongzheng emperor
(dated 1732) says:

The whole of each day of Achieving Seclusion requires concentration [*jianshu*] of the body and heart/mind; exhaustive [*jie*] integrity and achieved [*zhi*] composure that dare not relax. Thus the ability to serve solemnly leads to penetration of the brightness of the spirits. (*HDZL* 1899: 415.5a)

Achieved Seclusion was to be a period of concentration, gathering in and focusing of the will,[7] toward the end of increasing communication with the spirits. How do the concrete prohibitions fit with the emotional exhortations?

In the ritualist metaphysics model of consciousness discussed above, we noted that *li* provided an opportunity for human beings to illustrate that no gap existed between people and the *dao,* between mind and things, between the visible and invisible portions of the realm. Yin-yang and Five Phases cosmology provided a theory for this practice. Thus in the revived Han commentary, the sensual body was correlated alongside the acts and objects of ritual, dissolved among them.

Each prohibition during Achieving Seclusion involves a specific sense that will later be activated in sacrificial performance.[8] Taste, hearing, smell, and touch are all first disengaged from activities they will later participate in on the altar. But what about the eye, the organ that was so privileged by editors? The curious prohibition against legal cases suggests a suspension of the faculty of judgment, so important in the ritual process of Preparation as a whole, and may have had the effect of relegating the participants to the status of objects that were being prepared by others. A terminological link further highlights the intimate connection between scholarship, ritual, and governance: the word *an* means, variously, a "legal case," a "table used in sacrifice," and "to judge." In the latter usage, it appears constantly in the *Five Rites,* heading Qin Huitian's explanations about his own editing judgments: "Huitian decides . . . "[9]

As the participants were isolating and emptying their heart/minds, they wore either court costume or "auspicious costume."[10] Empty within from fasting and concentration of the will, they bear the decorations and patterns appropriate to their ranks in silk upon their skin.[11]

Inspection of Victims (*Shengxing*) (*DQTL* 1756: 1.3a)

Two days before the ceremony, the Head of the Ministry of Rites goes to the stables to inspect them. The ceremonial is the same as that of "Viewing the Victims."

The repetition of this section can be understood only as part of the larger structure of the ceremonial order as a whole, the grammar of the sacrifice, which was examined in chapter 3 (see figure 15). The inspection of live victims and the viewing of their slaughter alternated with inspections of participants and texts respectively. Furthermore, the first viewing is done by a prince or, on occasion, the emperor himself (*HDZL* 1899: 418.5a, Kangxi edict, 1675), the second and third by salaried members of the imperium (see note 4).

Writing of Prayerboards (*Shu zhuban*) (*DQTL* 1756: 1.3a)

The same day (two days before the ceremony) at first light, the Prayerboard (*zhuban*) is sent to the Grand Secretariat where a member inscribes upon it the words of the prayer.[12] It is then displayed, facing south, on a yellow table. A Grand Secretary goes before the table, stands facing north and writes in the imperial name. When this is finished, the member who wrote the prayer elevates it and returns it to the Hall of Purity, where it stays overnight.

As an example of the imperial word, the prayerboards faced south, as did the proclamation for Achieving Seclusion. We recall the special place that the texts of prayers occupied in the rite by virtue of being the only thing produced and destroyed wholly within the five days of Preparation.

Viewing the Killing of Victims (*Shi po xing*) (*DQTL* 1756: 1.3b–4a)

The day before the sacrifice, a pit six feet wide by six feet deep is dug east of the wall surrounding the Pavilion of the Slaying of Victims. An incense table stands outside the pavilion.

Seven officials from the Court of Imperial Repast, wearing court dress, the Court of Grand Constancy, the censorate, and the Ministry of Rites watch the slaying as the butcher takes the Phoenix Blade Knife and kills the victims. The hide (*mao*) and blood are placed in a *dou* container and buried.

The stripping of the victims' hide and the draining of their blood reduced them to the layer of boundary flesh between. They were empty inside and plain outside, unlike the participants, who wore their various prescribed silk robes.

Standing Spirit Thrones, Pitching Tents, Displaying Victims' Containers (*She shenzuo, gong wozhang, xingqi zhan*) (*DQTL* 1756: 1.4a–5a)

The day before the sacrifice, the altar is swept and a mat of hairy palm laid down.[13] On the first (top) terrace, he stands the Spirit Throne of Shangdi (Heaven), facing south. Thrones for the ancestors who have held the throne are stood to the east and west, facing each other.

On the second (middle) terrace, thrones are stood for the sun, moon, the stars of the dipper, five planets, twenty-eight solar mansions, all the stars of the sky, the Regents of Clouds, Rain, Wind, Thunder. All thrones are displayed under blue tents (figure 25). The emperor's yellow tent (Williams 1913: 29) is on the second terrace at the top of the southern stairs, facing north.

Meanwhile, offstage in the Spirit Kitchen, an archivist and erudites arrange the contents of various vessels (figure 26). In their proper order they display the vessels in the Spirit Storehouse (*shenku*).

At first glance, not much seems to tie the diverse preparatory activities of this section together. But in fact, all three are concerned with marking out the "container" space that will afterward be filled: thrones that will support spirit tablets; tents that will envelope the thrones and tablets, as well as the chief participant, the emperor;[14] and the containers for victims. The vessels for foods are then filled and displayed for inspection in the storehouse.

Shapes of vessels, the relationship of food and vessel (as container and thing contained, outer and inner), must be explored before we can understand the significance of the homology established between people and vessels.

In 1748 the Qianlong emperor sponsored research into ancient ritual paraphernalia, the fruits of which were finally printed as the *Huangchao liqi tushi* in 1766.[15] The edict that calls for the project stresses the need to return to the ancients (*qiangu*) for models in both food and vessels (*HDZL* 1899: 415.22b–23b, Qianlong edict dated 1747). Thus we have detailed line drawings in woodblock prints and descriptions for vessels, clothing, regalia, and musical instruments for every conceivable ceremonial occasion.[16] The vessels used on the Altar of Heaven are shown in figure 26. The editors' prefaces make explicit their intention in providing this compilation to assist the

sages of this dynasty to carry on in reciprocity with sages of the past, pattern things, cultivate clarity, and make perfection [*bei*] even greater, so there will be respect for Heaven and Ancestors, canons for the court, and punishments for the military. Never

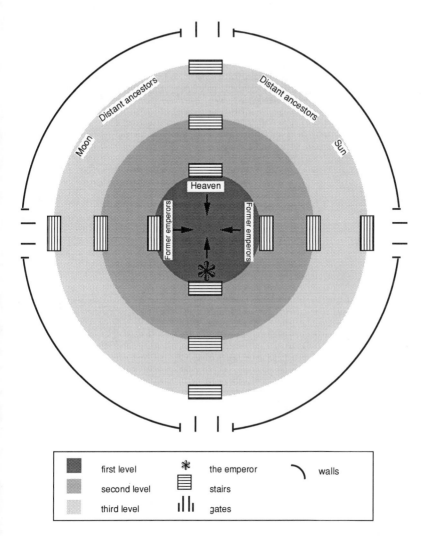

25. Placement of spirit tablets on the three-tiered Altar of Heaven.

inattentive, [our dynasty's sages] increase devotion among those who are responsible for exhibiting events, and preparing ceremonial. (*LQTS* first preface, 1b)

Qing scholars discovered that after the Shang, many vessels in the past had been made of clay or porcelain rather than bronze. While Qing ritualists preserved metal (or gilt) as the material for certain vessels used in the Ancestral Temple, for spirits worshipped on "altars" rather than in "halls" (that is, nonancestral spirits), porcelain was the order of the day (*LQTS* 2.1a–27b).[17] Careful

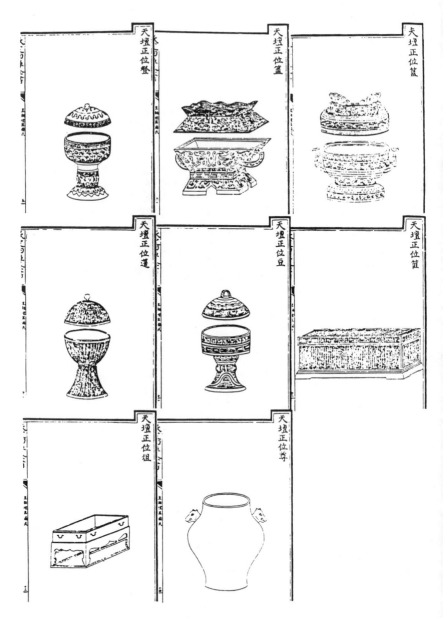

26. Vessels used on the Altar of Heaven. Starting top left: *deng, fu, gui, bian, dou, fei, zu, zun*. Compiled from *LQTS* 1.5a–14a.

readings by editors of the ritual classics like the *Zhouli, Record of Rites,* and *Yili,* the *Shuowen* dictionary, Han dynasty commentary, and even later ritual handbooks produced new, precise standards for the vessels.[18]

In porcelain, the vessels could be color-coded as an ensemble to indicate differences in their ceremonies. For instance, the *Illustrations* cites the *Shuowen's* entry on the *deng,* a single pedestal vase-like vessel with lid that held the "Grand Soup," as a "container made from pottery." It further cites Han commentator Zheng Xuan's advice that pottery vessels should be used at Altars of Heaven and Earth. The vessel used at the Altar of Heaven was blue, at the other Grand Sacrifices yellow.[19] The references to historical precedent seemed to carry weight *as precedent,* because only rarely did editors actually detail the past logical argument for a certain shape.

One vessel so treated, however, was the winecup called *jue* (figure 27). The winecups figured in the core ceremony of Grand Sacrifice, the Three Oblations offered by the emperor himself. On the Altar of Heaven, one type was made of azure jade and used for Shangdi, another in blue porcelain was used for other spirits on the altar (*LQTS* 1.3a–b, 1.16a–b). Entries for these two vessels call attention to shape as resemblance; in the case of the jade cup, the "Jiaotesheng" chapter of the *Record of Rites* is cited. There the jade cup is called a "simulacrum of the victims offered to Heaven and Earth" (*LQTS* 1.3b). In the case of the porcelain, the *Shuowen* is quoted saying that the *jue* is "a ritual vessel that resembles a small bird." Significantly, civil or *wen* members of the imperium wore bird emblems on their outer robes. The editors themselves note that old bronze *jue* had heads, tails, horns (*zhu*), and feet. These "horns" now functioned as ear-handles on the vessel (*LQTS* 1.16b).

Whether or not editors called attention to their symbolism, vessels were patterned with stars and "hanging clouds" on the lids. These decorations make sense only in their ritual context as homologies of human participants. Thus to our discussion of the resemblance between lids and hats we can now add the cosmic symbolism of stars and clouds that appear as decoration on both robes and vessels. (We will return to this point later.)

Reading Prayerboards; Reviewing Jade, Silk, and Incense
(*Yue zhuban yu bo xiang*) (*DQTL* 1756: 1.5b–7a)

Meanwhile, on this same day before the sacrifice, when so much is happening at the Altar of Heaven complex to the south, in the Forbidden City the emperor finally appears.

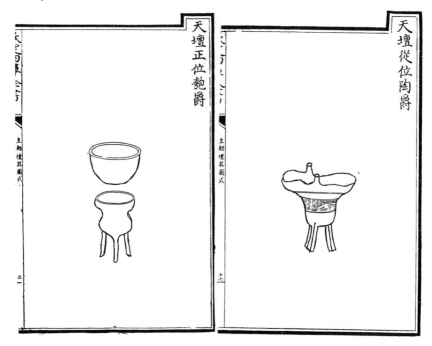

27. *Jue* winecups used on the Altar of Heaven. From *LQTS* 1.3a–b, 1.16a–b.

A yellow table is placed south of the throne in the main audience hall, Taiho dian. Repositories that resemble small closed palanquins are set up to the west for incense, prayerboards, jade, and silk.

The emperor arrives by carriage and stands facing these repositories while the items are carried in by procession and placed on the table. Their carriers perform the single kneeling and three prostrations. Then the emperor approaches, reads the prayers and performs the same bowing. After things are stored away, he repeats the bowing there. These repositories are carried out and the emperor returns to his palace. The plaque and bronze man are also moved to the Altar of Heaven, where the emperor will go next.

At this moment, with the reading and reviewing of prayerboards and other offerings, the emperor first appeared in the action of the rite. This small segment of the greater rite assembled the main actors (distinct from those who will participate the next day as spectators) in their roles as ushers, chanters, and offerers and functioned as a practice session for the Grand Sacrifice of the next day.

The emperor did not conduct the review from his throne, which remained empty throughout the whole proceeding. Rather, he took his place among his courtiers as they all faced north toward the offerings placed before the empty throne. In effect, the emperor offered incense to the writings of his own imperium, which had been produced at his order.[20]

The offerings singled out for inspection by the emperor inside the Forbidden City at this stage were jade, silk, and texts. Placed in bamboo basket vessels called *fei,* these offerings differed from the contents of the vessels that never left the boundary area of the Altar of Heaven complex (grain, vegetables, fruits, and meats). Their spatial separation not only reflected a distinction between food and nonfood offerings, it also called attention to their status as artificed objects versus agricultural products, a distinction further reinforced by their respective locations within the inner city walls and between the inner and outer walls. In this way, the city and its palace was associated with weaving, carving, and writing, while the periphery of the city was associated with farming and the raising of livestock.

However, nothing truly "wild" was represented here; the distinction was not a stark one of "culture" versus "nature." Instead, the difference lay between forms of social production that included agricultural as the necessary yet hierarchically inferior component of the encompassed asymmetry of urban/rural. Thus we must refine Frederick Mote's useful insight that Chinese cities were continuous, co-equal partners with the countryside to point out that the city was rather the site of centering, ritually and socially encompassing the vast, yet hierarchically inferior farmland surrounding it.

The Phoenix Carriage Leaves the Palace (*Jinyu chu gong*)
(*DQTL* 1756: 1.7b–13a)

After the Review of Prayerboards, the head of the palace Gendarmerie gives the order to clean and clear of people the route from the Qianqing gate to the Altar's gate. The Grand Cortege (*dajia boluo*) is arranged. The cortege is immense and filled with banners, pennants, fans and standards, guards, officials and musicians, horses and even elephants (see figure 28).

Those officials not participating in the sacrifice are ordered to gather to the east and west of the Wumen gate of the Forbidden City to view the emperor's departure.

The emperor in dragon robes over regular dress travels in two different carriages,

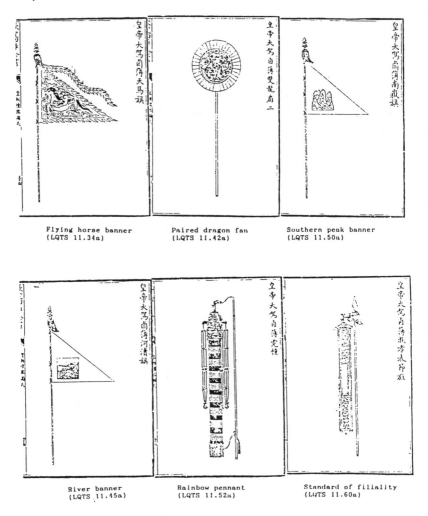

Flying horse banner
(LQTS 11.34a)

Paired dragon fan
(LQTS 11.42a)

Southern peak banner
(LQTS 11.50a)

River banner
(LQTS 11.45a)

Rainbow pennant
(LQTS 11.52a)

Standard of filiality
(LQTS 11.60a)

28. Objects carried in the cortege. From *LQTS* 11.34a–11.60a.

which he mounts and dismounts using portable stairs. Changing at the outer gate of the Forbidden City, he hastens in procession to the Altar of Heaven to continue his achievement of Seclusion.[21]

The cortege itself was, by all accounts, an extraordinary sight. Documentary paintings in color allow us to appreciate the gigantic scale of these undertakings that were the mark of not only Grand Sacrifices but imperial weddings and comings and goings of all kinds (see figure 29).[22] Pictures of each item in the *Illustra-*

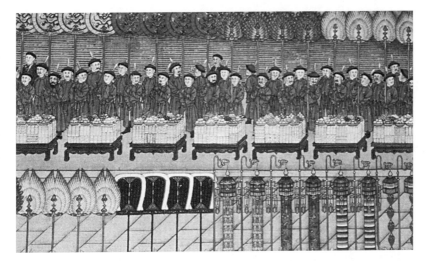

29. Detail of painting of objects for the cortege, painted during the Jiaqing reign, 1796–1820. From *Zijin cheng dihou shenghuo* (Imperial life in the Forbidden City), 109.

tions were listed in the order of their appearance in the *Comprehensive Rites*. Besides the officials mentioned above, each portion of the cortege was accompanied by as many as ninety soldiers. My estimation of the number of people involved just in the marching, not counting the rest of the spectators on their knees outside the Forbidden City, is about thirty-five hundred.

Interesting from the point of view of homology are the banners. These triangular flags carried various pictures. Signs for the secondary deities on the Altar of Heaven including clouds, wind, thunder and rain, various constellations, the sun and moon; the eight hexagrams of the *Yijing;* the Five Elements; the five sacred mountains and four seas; a zoo of mythological creatures and birds carried in the hands of the bearers presented a peripatetic microcosm.

Reviewing Spirit Places, Altar Places, Victims' Containers, and the Hall of Seclusion (*Shi shenwei tanwei xingqi zhaisu*) (*DQTL* 1756: 1.13a–14b)

The emperor rides to the southern boundary area [Altar of Heaven] and enters the complex through the west door. He proceeds on foot, with retinue, to visit various sites of preparation including the storehouse of the spirit tablets of Heaven and the Ancestors. He offers incense before the tablet of Great Heaven, and then to his predecessors on the throne. He performs the "Three Kneelings and Nine Prostrations."[23] The emperor then goes outside and north to the first terrace of the Round Mound to respectfully view the (empty) spirit thrones. He is then conducted out the left (east) gate of the inner wall to the Spirit Storehouse, where he views the *bian* and *dou* vessels. Other officials are sent simultaneously to view the victims.

The emperor emerges from the inner wall at the west gate and is carried to the portal of the Hall of Seclusion where he retires till morning. A vigilant guard is kept through the night.

On this day before the sacrifice, the emperor himself is the chief reviewer and inspector, examining the handiwork of his officials. These reviews and inspections were taken very seriously, underscoring the importance of the Period of Preparation for the rite as a whole.[24] Whether it was participants or things that came under the gaze of reviewers, they are treated in edicts discussing the details of the surveillance in remarkably similar terms. For instance, in 1686 the Kangxi emperor mentioned that names of participants were collected by archivists of the Ministry of Rites, who also saw to it that participants carried out their fasts while the Court of Grand Constancy inspected the contents of vessels (*HDZL* 1899: 412.3b–c).

Another inscribed surface appears in this section—the spirit tablets to August Heaven, the ancestors, and the associated deities. The tablets were eight inches wide by two and one-half feet high. They were finely carved wood on top and bottom, smooth in between and enclosed in ornate and gilded cases, which then were stood upon the pedestal "thrones" (Happer 1879: 31–32). The relation between ancestral tablets and face is one that must claim our attention.[25]

Ancestral tablets were called *shenzhu,* literally "spirit masters." What probably began as three-dimensional phallic symbols of fecundity eventually became flat surfaces with holes for the "face" and still later tablets upon which were carved or written the name of the deceased (Lin Shun-sheng 1966) (and by extension, the cosmic deities like Heaven and Earth, who are also worshipped in sacrifice). Later rituals of placing the last dot on a character seem to reenact this development; Laufer describes a southern rite that gave human form to the wood by dotting it with "eyes" and "ears" (1965: 445–50). Buddhist, Taoist, and local religious practice of statue consecration also dot the pupils of the deity last.

Girardot interprets the custom of "fixing" the tablet with a proper ancestral status through the dotting of the "eye" as the recuperation of the potentially dangerous world of the dead for the civilized order of the living (1988: 263). The written tablet presented the visible sign of access to the invisible world of the spirits. Hence, the literal designation "spirit master" for the tablet makes sense, especially the use of the word *zhu* (master).

In modern Chinese usage, *zhu* appears in the binome *zhuguan,* used to translate the notion of "subject" or "subjective." It has two parts: *zhu* meaning "ruling" or "main" and *guan* meaning "to observe."[26] As noted above, the *zhuren* was the main sacrificer or the banquet host. In Chinese medicine, *zhu* designates the central point of the internal energy spheres that make up the body. These are not organs but rather points of centrality that organize a radiating field around themselves.

In China, the person splits after death. Its bones return to earth in the grave, while its pneuma is captured in the tablets that return to the ancestral hall to reside in words on a surface.[27] That name is both iconic and symbolic; a signal to worship and a symbol of transformation after death to ancestorhood. It represents the transformation of the individual accomplished through the agency of collective practice, an instantiation of individual subject as subject of the collectivity.[28] Anthropologist Emily Martin (Ahern) points out that in the Taiwanese community she studied, ancestral tablets functioned in a dual fashion, as a boundary of the lineage. They faced outward as sign of lineage solidarity while inwardly they served to differentiate the members of the body of the lineage (Ahern 1973: 116). As we shall see later, the emperor is identified with the ancestral tablets. As he faced the *shenzhu* of heaven and his ancestors in the role of *zhuren* in sacrifice, he likewise became the centering site for the creative bounding of and grounding of contradiction.

Until this point in the Period of Preparation, only the tables (*an*) and spirit thrones (*zuo*) have been "stood" (*shen*) upon the altar. All vessels, participants, and tablets are secluded in their various halls, awaiting placement.

Arranging of Standings (*Chenshe*) (*DQTL* 1756: 1.14b–1.15a)

The night before, the Court of Grand Constancy sends representatives to light the lanterns and place the filled vessels upon the altar before each of the Spirit Thrones on the first two terraces. The contents included wine, grain, cooked meats, pickled and boiled vegetables. Rather than list everything here, figure 30 represents the offerings and ves-

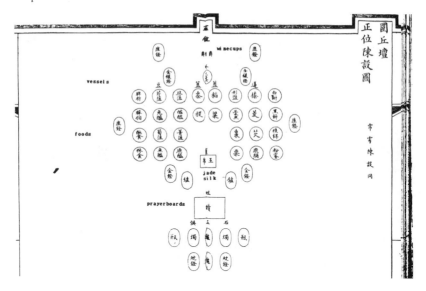

30. Offerings to Heaven. From *HDT* 2.4b–5a.

sels before the tablet to Heaven. This arrangement is repeated, with a few omissions, before each deity's tablets. Then the musical instruments are laid out.

People eating food connect the inner body and the outer world by consuming that which lies outside themselves. Food reacts within the body to produce effects. In traditional China the entire body, its physical form and energetic fields including the psyche, was kept balanced by eating foods thought to nourish yin or yang tendencies, as need arose (Kaptchuk 1983: 131–32). Thus, in China, as in most societies, eating and exchanging food was (and is) not only a socially significant act (Wolf 1974: 176–77). It was also thought to be constitutive of the individual physical body's ability to resonate correctly with its cosmicized milieu. According to the *Record of Rites,* ritual had its origin in social life with food.[29] Food is a favored object today for "gift exchange" or the formation of *guanxi* connections, precisely because it is so literally suited for incorporation into the receiver's substance.[30]

Anthropologists have also emphasized the cognitive aspects of cuisine as a code that exemplifies basic cultural presuppositions about culture and nature, order and disorder, and so forth. In this case, food becomes the bearer of an edibly concrete logic so like the animals that Lévi-Strauss (1975) describes as not only good to eat but also "good to think."

Grand Sacrificial food offerings in their vessels provide insight into problems of social relations as these are mediated through principles of categorization. First we will discuss how food offerings in their vessels marked, as they sought to resolve, the contradiction between ancestors and cosmic deities appearing on the same altar. Later we will explore how vessels and their contents were an important element in resolving (ritual) knowledge into practice while constructing Grand Sacrifice as the foremost site of significant interface between such oppositions. Both of these objectives were accomplished through the "culinary code" of sacrifice. This code lay in the set of related contrasts made up of differences among foods (inner contents), differences among vessels (outer pattern), and the relations between these two orders of contrasts. These contrasts operated through the yang-yin principle, the organization of bipolarity such that one term contains the other as a necessary part of itself.

Arthur Wolf (1974) points out that in Taiwanese communities, offerings to ancestors take the form of a meal, while offerings to the gods (deities) do not, the former implying equal status while the latter indicate gods' superiority to men or ancestors. What happens when both appear on the same altar, as they do in the Grand Sacrifice to Heaven?

In Grand Sacrifice, an intimate ancestral relationship was extended to both deities and ancestors, while at the same time a distinction was maintained between sacrifices to heaven and to the ancestors. The coincidence between Heaven and Ancestors was shown through similar food offerings in both sacrifices. These contents dictated the types of vessels used to hold them, but certain elements of vessel design also reflected differences between Heaven and the Ancestors.

Yinshi, the word for "food," is a binome composed of *yin,* "drink," and *shi,* "food." As K. C. Chang points out, within the distinction of "drink-food," the word for food contains a dichotomy between grain and *cai,* or dishes of meat and vegetables eaten in smaller quantities to accompany grains. The same term *shi* refers both to the whole and one of its parts, so Chang diagrams their relationship as a hierarchy (figure 31)[31] (1976: 134).

The simplest meal consisted of grain and water.[32] Drinking nourishes yang, thus it is yin in substance; eating nourishes yin and is yang in substance.[33] Chang suggests that the third category, the subcategory of "food" called "dishes," should perhaps be associated with fire. Since grain is also always cooked in sacrifice, a more important distinction may lie in the fact that dishes combine foods with water into soups, stews, minces, and preserves. They are yin and yang, and our diagram should be redrawn to look like figure 32.[34]

Certain vessels were associated with certain foods in Han and pre-Han texts.

31. Hierarchical relations of food and drink.

32. Combinations of food and drink.

Chang concludes from archaeological evidence that bronze vessels were used for grain foods and drinks made from grain. *Bian* baskets and *dou* pots for meat or "dishes" were made of pottery or wood. Eighteenth-century ritualists preserved the match between vessel type and contents by producing porcelains that preserved the shape and decorative patterns of Shang bronze serving vessels. Thus the formerly bronze *gui* and *fu,* although now made in porcelain, were still used for early rice and sorghum, and two kinds of millet respectively.

However, rather than marking encompassing yang-yin distinctions within one sacrifice, the difference between metal and porcelain was used at another level, to mark distinctions between *types* of sacrifice. We have just seen how *gui* and *fu* used on altars for cosmic deities like Heaven and Earth were made of porcelain. But in the Ancestral Temple, metal *gui* and *fu* were employed. In an edict dated 1747, this difference of materials was duly noted and connected to a range of distinctions. Bronze vessels were linked through their "patterning," or *wen,* to ancestors and yang, while porcelain vessels were linked through their "plainness" to cosmic deities and yin (*HDZL* 1899: 415.22b–25b).

Thus the same set of vessels bore two messages: through similar contents, it was shown that all sacrifices were the same, that ancestors *are* gods. At the same time sacrifices (and thus gods and ancestors) were declared different through different vessel shapes. With great economy, a disjuncture was established between the inner and the outer portions of vessels—taking advantage of its "bounding" function—which then became the bearer of a paradox of similarity and difference. It helped smuggle in presentably the uncomfortable hubris of the claim that the king's ancestors were, in fact, like gods—almost.

Inspection of Filled Vessels (*Sheng zheng*) (*DQTL* 1756: 16.a–b)

After the "Arranging of the Standings" is complete, an official from the Ministry of Rites leads an erudite of the Court of Grand Constancy to inspect the jade, silk, and filled vessels. The contents of each *bian, dou, deng,* and *zu* should be laid out in correct order before the deities and ancestors. They then inspect the second terrace.

In the eighteenth century, there was a concerted effort to reproduce on the Qianlong altars the same foods listed in the ancient classic, the *Zhouli.*[35]

In Grand Sacrifice, dishes that were yin-yang combinations (soups, stews, minces, and preserves) dominated the offerings. We can hypothesize that the power of these offerings did lay in their "mixed" nature, which made them especially efficacious as mediators between the heavenly yang world of spirits and the earthly yin world of people. As the "Jiaotesheng" chapter of the *Record of Rites* says: "In the *bian* and *dou* put the products of water and land. Do not use unusual spices or think that having many is the point. Thus can you connect [*jiao*] with pure brightness" (*LJZY* 25/2:1446).

These mixed categories required preparation, the artifice of the cook. It is hardly surprising they predominated in a ritual that so emphasized "Perfect Preparation." Of twenty-nine foods arranged before each deity on the Altar of Heaven, twenty-one were "dishes" of some sort. Four were plain cooked grains placed in the *fu* and *gui.* The remaining four present an interesting anomaly: they were offered whole, raw, and unartificed in any way. These consist of shaped salt, filberts, water chestnuts, and a plant like a water lily, all placed in *bian,* to the deity's left. The offerings that appeared on the altars thus present a hierarchy of bipolarities based upon the degree to which they have been "worked upon" and that can be diagrammed, as in figure 33.

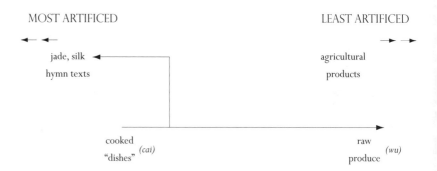

33. Offerings arranged from most to least artificed.

Yet in recipes for sacrificial foods published in the 1870s, even the most "raw" items carried certain stipulations. The shaped salt had to be pure white and chosen to look like a "tiger-leopard" mountain, so that it should be a simulacrum for a "product."[36] The filberts, water chestnuts, and "water lily" were chosen carefully for their perfection and color and stacked round side down, point up to imitate the shape of the *bian* basket (*Wenmiao shangding yuebei kao* 1:18a). Although these items were not physically cut or cooked, they nonetheless hardly arrived at the altar in a wild state because they were so carefully chosen for their value as markers of resemblance. In the case of the salt, the cryptic injunction that it should "stand as 'product' or *wu*" is comprehensible only in terms of the contrast between, at one end, crafted objects like silk, jade, and paper (representing the activities of weaving, carving, and writing) and, at the other end, raw, unworked "products" like the salt.

Just as the distinction discussed earlier between "crafted/urban" and "agricultural/rural" could not be simply restated as culture versus nature, neither is the distinction between cooked and raw so reducible. We once again have an encompassed asymmetry between different forms of social production. The previous distinction of carving, weaving, and writing (activities producing *wen*) contrasted with farming and husbandry (harvesting of *wu*). The similar distinction within forms of food offerings lay between, on the one hand, those that require knowledge *and* craft—to choose the correct ingredients and cook them—and, on the other hand, those that required only the power to discriminate.[37] Cooking was hierarchically superior to simply exercising correct judgment.[38] The cooked offerings at the Sacrifice to Heaven that combined yang-yin characteristics mediated the *wen* skills of the kingly city and the *wu* productivity of the countryside. The diagram redrawn looks like figure 34.

34. Mediation of city and country by Altar of Heaven.

As Spence has noted, food was important at the imperial level during the Qing in sacrifices, at banquets and, in that age of obsessive documentation, also in compilation and codification.[39] Types of banquets for people were as carefully graded and regulated as the offerings at altars.[40] Thus food was both a medium of exchange (among people and between humans and spirits), and the object of precise, discriminating scholarship, rather like *li* itself. The function of food as a marker of social distinctions made it desirable as object of knowledge. After describing the placement and clothing of participants, I will discuss the implications for a theory of ritual knowledge that this marking of ever-finer distinctions had.

Differentiating Places (*Bianwei*) (*DQTL* 1756: 1.17a–19a)

The *Comprehensive Rites* posits two categories of participants: those who "celebrate the rite" (*xingli*) and those who "direct events" (*zhishi*). The emperor acts as the chief celebrant. He, along with the representatives of the imperial line, the titled nobility, and the civil and military officials who participated, follow the instructions of the directors. The latter included members of the institutions responsible for preparing Grand Sacrifice: the Ministry of Rites, the Court of

Grand Constancy, the Court of Banqueting, and the various guards. Their places are identified in the text through reference to their actions (figure 35).

Differentiate the places of the celebrants who will carry out the ceremony: On the first (topmost) terrace (where tablets for Heaven and former emperors will appear) are placed the Prayer Reciter, the Receiver of Felicitous Flesh, and the emperor when he worships (figure 35, a–c).

On the second terrace (where tablets for early ancestors and lesser celestial deities will appear under tents) place the emperor's yellow tent at the top of the southern stairs (*wujie,* "meridian" or central stairs; figure 35, d).

On the third terrace, princes and dukes line up at the foot of eastern and western stairs, in order of descending rank gauged by closeness to the center. On either side of the "Spirit Way" (*shendao,* which passes through the "meridian stairs") stand princes or dukes who will present the associate offerings (figure 35, e–f).

Outside the square wall, the participating civil and military officials line up in rows of five, in descending order of rank from the center (figure 35, g).

Differentiate the places of the directors of the rite: on the first terrace the emperor's place is flanked by a Prompter and a Mat Holder. Behind the tables holding the offerings of jade, silk, incense, winecups, and prayers are the officials responsible for handling these objects. Two representatives of the Ministry of Rites are on hand, as are a Censor and a director of Music (figure 35, 1–13).

On the second terrace are another Prompter and Mat Mover (figure 35, 16–17).

On the third terrace are Ushers from the Court of Grand Constancy, and a number of officials who will lead the princes and dukes in the ceremony (figure 35, 18–20).

Inside the square wall, but below the terraces, place four Recorders, the musicians, and dancers. Place officials to assist with the burning of offerings near the furnace in the southeast corner (figure 35, 21–24).

Outside the square wall, place eight officials among the participating officials to lead them in ceremony (figure 35, 25).

The distinction between ritual "celebrants" and those who "directed" the rite was crucial. The deployment of the small group of people who were the "celebrants" becomes highly significant when read in conjunction with the placement of spirit tablets and the shape of the altar complex. There were six zones of relative interiority, from the three terraces, outward through the round and then square walls, a depiction of "round" heaven within "square" earth. The break between the (upper) raised terraces and the (lower) flat ground almost, but not quite, coincides with the Heaven/Earth distinction. In figure 36 these zones are listed, along with the spirits and people placed upon them.

This emplotment of people and spirits was a complex enactment of the cos-

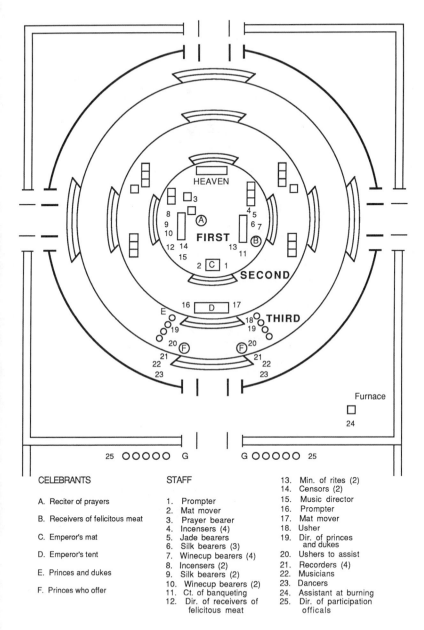

HEAVEN

FIRST

SECOND

THIRD

Furnace
24

CELEBRANTS	STAFF	13. Min. of rites (2)
		14. Censors (2)
A. Reciter of prayers	1. Prompter	15. Music director
	2. Mat mover	16. Prompter
B. Receivers of felicitous meat	3. Prayer bearer	17. Mat mover
	4. Incensers (4)	18. Usher
C. Emperor's mat	5. Jade bearers	19. Dir. of princes and dukes
	6. Silk bearers (3)	
D. Emperor's tent	7. Winecup bearers (4)	20. Ushers to assist
	8. Incensers (2)	21. Recorders (4)
E. Princes and dukes	9. Silk bearers (2)	22. Musicians
	10. Winecup bearers (2)	23. Dancers
F. Princes who offer	11. Ct. of banqueting	24. Assistant at burning
	12. Dir. of receivers of felicitous meat	25. Dir. of participation officials

35. Placement of participants for Grand Sacrifice to Heaven on the three-tiered altar.

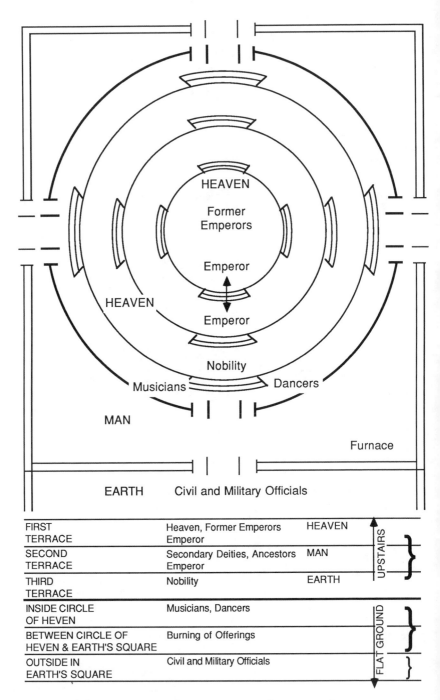

FIRST TERRACE	Heaven, Former Emperors Emperor	HEAVEN	
SECOND TERRACE	Secondary Deities, Ancestors Emperor	MAN	UPSTAIRS
THIRD TERRACE	Nobility	EARTH	
INSIDE CIRCLE OF HEVEN	Musicians, Dancers		
BETWEEN CIRCLE OF HEVEN & EARTH'S SQUARE	Burning of Offerings		FLAT GROUND
OUTSIDE IN EARTH'S SQUARE	Civil and Military Officials		

36. Zones of relative interiority related to "upper" and "lower" on the Altar of Heaven.

mic triad of Heaven, Earth, and Humanity. However, it was skewed before the ceremony began in order to overidentify certain elements of the imperium with Heaven, even as they mediated Heaven and Earth. No designated "celebrants" other than the emperor himself, except titled nobility and relatives by descent or adoption to the imperial house, appeared on the raised round terraces of the "Heavenly" altar. In other words, it was inhabited by "sons." Between the raised round altar and the outer square wall was an intermediate zone of no celebrants at all, only officials involved with directing the mechanics of performance. Finally, outside the square wall, earthbound, were the officials of the imperium who participated as "celebrants" in the sacrifice by virtue of their success in the examination system (modern day "sages").

Within the heavenly zone on the altar, however, the emperor was also singled out as special: he occupied a tent like the spirit tablets, while no other celebrants even appeared on the second terrace. If the three terraces repeated the same triad structure of Heaven above, Earth below, and humankind between, clearly the emperor occupied the "upper and central" position. As he moved during the performance between the topmost terrace, inhabited by Heaven and tablets of dead emperors, and the second terrace of associated ancestors and deities, it became clear that his "centering" was made even more powerful by an overidentification with the upper or superior element (see figure 36).

Let us turn from the iconic value had by the emplotment of people and tablets within the altar spaces to participants themselves. Clothing indicated the progressively more precise homology being established between people and vessels. In the *Illustrations,* clothing for all ranks of nobility and officials and their wives was specified in drawings and text in precisely the same terms as those for vessels cited above. The illustrations are similarly placed in relation to the text, and the format of information is the same as well. (See figure 12 in chapter 1 for a composite from the *Illustrations.*)

In Grand Sacrifice participants all wore court costumes (*chaofu*) that were identical in cut, but differentiated according to pattern and color (Vollmer 1977: 31–16). The emperor's was bright yellow, the heir apparent's apricot, and the imperial sons golden yellow. Everyone else, the nobility and the officials, wore blue silk *chaofu.*

The Qianlong emperor revived the use of the Twelve (cosmic) Emblems on his own robes. His bright yellow *chaofu* served for audience ceremonies, sacrifices to Earth and the ancestral temple, where the color was deemed appropriate. But for other sacrifices, the same garment was reproduced in different colors, according to the same code that applied for vessels. On the Altar of Heaven, the emperor wore *chaofu* in a shade of sky blue different from that of his officials' regular dark blue court costume; at the sacrifice to the sun, he wore red; and at the sacrifice to the moon, he wore bluish-white.[41] Although all participants shared in the process of preparation that analogized them to vessels, the emperor was singled out to carry through the homology to its logical end and, dressed in colors that actually matched the vessels, he was marked as the most perfect vessel of all.

The *chaofu* of nobility and officials also signified differences between the imperium and the people, and among its members. Prescriptions in the *Illustrations* extended from the emperor to *shengyuan,* those who had passed the qualifying tests for the examinations that would lead to official positions within the imperium.[42] That the examinations were a *rite de passage* upward and inward toward the center of imperial power is amply illustrated in the eighteenth-century satirical novel *The Scholars.* Clothing furnished an important marker of distinction between the common people and those who would eventually participate in imperial sacrificial ritual and the other important duties of governing the realm.

While members of the imperium shared similarly designed *chaofu,* differences among them were indicated at a further level of exteriority. Position in one of nine ranks, and membership in the civil or the military side of the imperium, was indicated by insignia attached front and back, to outer, wide-sleeved coats.[43] Military officials wore a series of mythical four-legged beasts; *wen* officials wore birds.[44]

Clothing marked difference among people: between scholars and those who had not passed examinations, between *wen* and military officials, between the emperor and his imperium. Yet during preparation in Achieving Seclusion, all participants were directly enjoined, no matter what their rank, to submit to inspection, fast, and prepare their heart/minds in composure and integrity. We noted how this "Perfect Preparation" was expected to result in filiality within the heart/mind (*LJZY* 49/2:1602). Thus people were simultaneously similar and different.

We noted above that vessels were similarly encoded, split between inner contents and outer form. Inner contents signified similarity between sacrifices while vessels' outer forms encoded differences, especially between sacrifices to cosmic deities and those to human ancestors. As vessels' material substances encoded the boundary between deities and ancestors, participants' positions encoded the boundary between sages, men who advanced to power through scholarly merit (in this case, the staff of prompters and other officials), and sons who inherited power (the nobility who celebrated the sacrifice).

From the perspective of exterior sacrificial costume, sages and sons were marked as different. However, as differently garbed members of the imperium achieved seclusion, it was proven that men were alike in their filiality even though on the outside they might differ. From the perspective of interior preparation, filiality embraced both the relation of lord/minister and father/son. Sages were sons. The relation of vessels to people began as the relation of the following sets of contrasts:

VESSELS	outer / decoration / different	deities ≠ ancestors
	inner / foods / same	deities = ancestors
PEOPLE	outer / clothing / different	sages ≠ sons
	inner / heart-mind / same	sages = sons

During sacrifice, these contrasts were resolved in favor of similarity, staged as "interiority" through the overdetermining actions of eating and drinking. The third term of the most important of the homologies that structured the period of preparation was the victim. We recall that the victim was drained of blood and shaved of hair. The *Record of Rites* remarks that[45]

the taking of the hair and blood announces [*gao*] that [the victim] is/has been "secretly, implicitly whole" [*youchuan*]. Announcing this implicit wholeness constitutes giving value to the way of purity. Blood sacrifice increases *qi* or vital force. Sacrificing the lungs, kidneys, and heart values the organs that control *qi* [*qizhu*]. (*LJZY* 26/2:1457)

The inner and outer portions of victims were removed the better to represent pure boundary, and the eating of their flesh was a crucial act in sacrifice as centering.

Recapitulation of Themes

Everything discussed so far was classified as "Preparation." The Period of Preparation of Grand Sacrifice intensified everyday life. None of the objects that appeared on the altar were rare or bizarre, but each was the best of its kind. The attendants likewise represented a rearrangement of everyday official life, constituted from different departments into an ensemble of directors that existed only in the ritual context. The Period of Preparation also produced an order that was then self-consciously encountered in the alternation of segments of "looking" (viewing, inspecting, reading) and "ordering" (exhibiting, arranging, and writing). These alternating activities yielded an order of homologies for further ritual manipulation, even as they provided a metamodel for the processes of gaining and producing knowledge.

This model, based within the ritualist metaphysics of resonant consciousness and linguistic optimism, carried ritualists beyond language to action of the body: fasting, cooking, killing; and the rest of the gestures to come: bowing, kneeling, singing, and dancing. It thus situated reading and writing as *productive activities* with the special power of calling into being other kinds of human productivity. Intellection was not sufficient in and of itself, however. If writing about ritual had sufficed, by the eighteenth century surely enough words had been accumulated to render further (bodily) performance unnecessary. We will return to this model for knowing, but we turn now to review homologies created during the Period of Preparation.

Orders of homology were established especially among victims, people, and vessels. A logic of resemblance through imitation (*fa, xiang*), contiguity (*chen*) and correspondence (*ying*) underlay these orders. From the intricate textual discussions and precise provisions for foods, clothing, vessels, the abstraction of the bipolarity of inner and outer materialized. In other words, to show clearly the possibilities for "centering," distinctions first had to be made (hence terminology like *bianwei,* or "Differentiation of Places"). Vessels divided into outer forms and inner contents; people into inner heart/minds and outer costumed role. But with victims' transformation into pure boundary, drained of blood and shaven smooth, we understand that the point of this division was to provide occasion for the display of unification, "centering" on the part of celebrants. By bringing inner and outer into coincidence, sacrifice would manifest, by extension, the unity of high and low: fathers and sons, lords and their servants.

Other boundary surfaces were produced and honored: prayerboards and ancestral tablets were both sites where texts useful for penetrating into the unseen portion of the realm materialized. All these signifying objects importantly made explicit the implicit contradictions in social life between person and collective, sages and heirs, fathers and sons.[46]

The differentiation of inner and outer calls attention to the acts of "discrimination" (*bian*), "proportioning" (*chen*), and "inspection" (*cha, sheng*). The "Liqi" (Ritual Vessel) chapter of the *Record of Rites*[47] stresses that the value of the things, people, and actions of ritual never lies in their essential identity, but is a matter of their relation to each other, which is termed *chen,* "proportion." Confucius is quoted:

Ritual usages must be carefully inspected [*sheng*]. Rituals differ; they are relative. This is called "proportion." (*LJZY* 23/2:1433)

Tang commentator Kong Yingda adds:

Since the *li* are various, differences are discernible. If they were not discernible, there would be no way to know the Way of Ritual. The differences among *li* can be found through inspection and lay in such things as tallness, shortness, largeness, smallness, pattern and plainness. (*LJZY* 23/2:1434)

The text then goes on to discuss various distinctions of Zhou-Han ritual.

The ancient sages thus gave honor to what was internal, and sought pleasure in what was external, found a mark of distinction in paucity, and one of what was admirable in multitude; therefore in the ceremonial usages instituted by the ancient kings we should look neither for multitude nor for paucity, but for the due relative proportion. (*LJZY*, translation from Legge 1885: 1:402)

This radically relational notion of knowledge has other implications, which we take up by returning to the opening statement of the "Ritual Vessel" chapter:

Ritual vessels [are] the Grand Preparation; Grand Preparation is the heightening of the fullness [*sheng*] of the power of exemplary virtue. (*LJZY* 23/2:1433)

and its commentary by Kong Yingda:

"the Grand Preparation" means that the body has become a vessel and thus can perfect itself sufficiently to fill up with the power of exemplary virtue.

The word *sheng* means both "to fill" and "to be full." Action and result are collapsed into a single verb. The word *zhi* in *zhizhai,* "Achieving Seclusion," also incorporates the result of its action into itself. The various terms used to describe "looking" in the Period of Preparation in both the *Record of Rites* and the self-consciously archaic *Comprehensive Rites* are similarly "performative" as when, in English, the pronouncements "I promise" or "I do" conflate act and result. So "observing" (*guan*) was also perception for ritualists. To look was to know. And conversely, the act of looking and the looker were consistently included as part of the grounds of knowledge. Since "*Li* is the utmost of all things" (*LJZY* 24/

2:1440), ritual knowledge was a privileged domain. As Kong Yingda comments upon that phrase:

Intelligent discrimination is "dividing and differentiating." Saying this, if one wishes to look and intelligently discriminate the ten thousand things, one must first possess within [oneself] the clarity of knowledge that comes through examination. If the heart/mind within is not clarified, then one cannot "divide and differentiate" externality. (*LJZY* 24/2:1440)

Thus, in the ritualizations of *li,* words were things (for example, envoys' credentials in Grand Audience, prayerboards in Grand Sacrifice, imperial edicts) and they also had the power to bring other things into being (to fullness, or to perception). The word was not a representation of the world but an operator *within* it. Late Tang and early Song philosophers were organizing a Confucian revival, as were early proponents of *kaozheng* in the late sixteenth century. Qing dynasty *kaozheng* scholars likewise reinvested in the ritualist metaphysics through an emphasis upon careful specification of things and actions through language.[48]

By the eighteenth century, past discussions about correct ritual knowledge had been taken up as integral aspects of the performance of rites themselves. In this commitment they were closer to Song dynasty antiquarian scholars than perhaps even they appreciated.[49] For ritualists under the Qianlong emperor, re-presenting sacrifice likewise entailed re-presenting theories of knowledge embedded in and enacted as ritual practice.

7

FILIAL CEREMONY

Centering

When a filial son sacrifices, he is anxious that nothing be left undone. When the time approaches, none of the things used can be left unprepared. Then, his center empty, he can carry it out. . . . The filial son moves as though holding jade or elevating a full vessel.   RECORD OF RITES, "Jiyi"

Worship of Heaven and Earth was explicitly likened to services of parents, which were always performed jointly for the mother and father. Before the Qing period, such arguments were the basis for the first joint ceremonies to the two deities, and evidential scholars took those arguments into account.

When Qin Huitian reviewed these discussions in the *Five Rites,* however, he came out in favor of separate sacrifice, the current imperial form (*WLTK* 1a–8a/255–69).[1] We may suspect sycophancy, but his discussions were based on the evidential intention of investigating the Classics for precedent for joint sacrifice. Qin concluded there were none. This did not prevent him, however, from pursuing in lengthy citations the question of the analogy between father and mother and Heaven and Earth deities from the point of view of ritual duty. He quotes a much-admired Song man of letters, Luo Mi:

The master said, "Serving [*shi*] fathers is filiality; serving Heaven is clarity [*ming*]. Serving mothers is filiality; serving Earth is bright display [*cha*]." The serving of Heaven and Earth by the exemplary person [*jun*] is exactly like the serving of parents by filial sons. If one knows how to serve parents, one will know how to serve Heaven and Earth. (*WLTK* 1.5a/263)

Eighteenth-century ritualists wondered how to connect filiality to parents with sacrifice to Heaven and Earth in the absence of classical precedent. The cycle of Grand Sacrifice as a whole form provided an answer in practice, if not in discussion. An important element in the power of the cycle was the way a single ceremonial order connoted themes associated with all four sacrifices. In the Period of Preparation, an order predicated upon the triad of Heaven, Earth, and Humanity was created; in the actions that followed, the main celebrant performed an ancestral sacrifice. The celebrants and spirits were assembled, music and dancing accompanied the offerings being made, and then men, deities, and ancestors dispersed. Thus the model of cosmic order produced by ritualists when they sacrificed to Heaven or Earth contributed to the maintenance of the ideology of filiality in ceremonial performance.

In the Period of Preparation, attention was called to the interiors and exteriors of vessels, victims, and people in order to construct them as boundary makers. In the gestures and actions of the ceremony that followed, these boundaries were further shown to be not division, but rather the possibility of a mediation that allowed difference to exist while controlling the conditions of its existence in terms of a higher principle. In concrete terms, during preparation, participants were likened to vessels and victims in ways that bore explicitly upon filiality.

In particular, we noted that during the Period of Preparation an ambiguity was preserved on the relationship of sagehood and sonship. Participants' differences within the imperium were marked by their (outer) clothing, especially whether they were salary-drawing members who gained their status through the exam system ("sages" of merit) or were members of the imperial clan, present by birthright ("sons" through inheritance). Yet, all participants were expected to prepare fully, and in the same fashion, during the Period of Seclusion: in their inner heart/minds, all men, sages or sons, were capable of filiality. Filiality denoted the cosmicized virtue of achieving a perfect harmony of position within the complex human hierarchy organized in bipolar dyads (see chapter 1). Filiality not only fell upon all Chinese human beings as a moral duty, it provided a ground for the civilizing of human beings at all.² It was a discourse that raised to the level of valued virtue the harnessing of the cosmos to human ends.

As the Grand Sacrifice shifted into the actual ceremonial movements discussed in this chapter, the taken-for-granted cosmos of correlative resonance brought to perception and ordered in the concrete details of Preparation was subtly organized through the vectors of performing bodies. In the ceremony, the emperor's body was singled out for homology with the spirits, and for actions that transited boundaries between upper and lower, confounded container and thing contained, and openly showed him as the perfect mediator, the One Man who encompassed and included the very distinctions that made up his realm.

In chapter 3 I called attention to the "grammar" of Grand Sacrifice. As the ceremony went into motion, the simple alternating of "looking" and "ordering" during the Period of Preparation (see figure 15) gave way to a series of recursive segments each of which was "answered" by its opposite. The beginning of this recursive figure was signaled by the emperor's emergence from his palace; its end by his return (figure 15, segments 8–25). In between, the spirits were invited, then sent off (figure 15, segments 13–15); the emperor approached the altar and then walked away (figure 15, segments 14–23), and so forth. This ceremonial symmetry modeled a perfect reciprocity between ancestors and gods above, as initiators, and people below, as those who completed the connection of Heaven and Earth. However, it also inscribed a structure of encompassment, as each pair of actions was included in a wider set, providing a "nest" of contexts. The specific production of the emperor's powerful position was accomplished through this careful attention to context.

The work of Preparation was not innocent; it was predicated upon the eventual display of the emperor as the perfect body of yang power. Yet, on the other hand, its purpose in producing the king could never be fully appreciated until an actual emperor *performed* the ritual. In this way, the dialectical reciprocity of historical and cosmic knowledge with bodily performance took on life in the emperor's body. We are reminded of Ling Tingkan's theorization of *li* as performance in chapter 4 above. The perfection of filiality was an achieved state, even if the original capacity (and context) existed in advance.

To facilitate discussion, I divided the text of the *Comprehensive Rites* into the categories of Assembly, Offerings, and Dispersal. Each segment of the rite once again uses the designation found in the *Comprehensive Rites*. They will be summarized and discussed in the order in which they occur.

Assembly

Inviting the Spirits (Qing shenwei) (DQTL 1756: 1.19a–20b)

At dawn, after offering incense and performing the single ketou before them,[3] bearers fetch the prayerboards from their storehouse in the Altar of Heaven complex to place them on the altar.

A group from the Ministry of Rites enters the Spirit Tablet Storehouse, performs the full ketou,[4] and offers incense, inviting the spirits of Heaven and ancestors to descend. They emerge, place the tablets in repositories, and perform the single ketou. They deposit the repositories at the foot of the Meridian Stairs (in the center) and carry the tablets up: Heaven's and the former emperors' to the top terrace, distant ancestors to the middle terrace.

Approaching the Order, Washing, Taking Places (Jiu ci guan xi jiu wei) (DQTL 1756: 1.20b–22b)

The Director of the Court of Grand Constancy goes to the Hall of Seclusion, and "memorializes," inviting the emperor to the Altar to perform the ceremonies.

The emperor, in sacrificial robes, mounts the Ritual Palanquin, and exits. The curtained Jade Palanquin waits outside the gate and he is invited to mount it. The Hall of Seclusion bell is rung and the emperor proceeds to the altar with a small cortege.

At the outer square wall he stops and dismounts. He is led to his dressing tent, where he waits as everyone else gets ready.

The Director of the Court of Grand Constancy intones,[5] "The Spirits have taken their places and the ritual can begin." The emperor emerges from his tent and washes his hands.

Its bearer unrolls the prayer mat in the emperor's place of worship in the small tent at the head of the stairs on the second terrace. The emperor's worship marking board (*baipai*) marks his place.[6]

The emperor enters the outer square wall through the east door of the south gate, walks up the central stairs, and takes his place facing north.

The men who will present offerings to associate deities are led in the west door of the south gate to take their places. The nobility are led in and then the *wen* and military officials. All face north. Musicians and dancers take their places.[7]

The emperor and the spirit tablets were treated similarly. Both were invited out of their spaces of separation and seclusion. Both proceeded to the altar, carried on the shoulders of bearers, in enclosed vehicles. Both paused outside the square wall, at the crucial point of transition between earthly and heavenly realms. There were limits to this similarity, however. The emperor did not enter the altar through the central gate, which was reserved for the spirit tablets.

The clearest manifestation of the emperor's status as connector between gods and men lay in the *baipai,* the marking board that preceded him in all his actions. The ancestral tablets memorialized the spirits' presence, present and past, functioning as a surface that rendered their presence visible. A distinction was made in the rite between the spirits' tablets and the *shen* themselves, who were invited to descend into the tablets. The emperor was treated both like a spirit who *has* a tablet—represented by the *baipai*—and like a tablet itself in the way that his very body and its gestures were an important site of interface between men and gods.

The other "celebrants who offered to associate deities had wooden boards of rank [*pinji muban*] placed where each performed his ceremony" (*HDZL* 1899: 416.14a–b).[8] These other celebrants had markers but were not transported and treated like tablets. They were suited to celebrate sacrifice, both as future ancestors in the flesh and by virtue of their positions in the imperium, but in the emperor we once again note the "category confusion" that denotes his singularity as the chief centerer. When he was present, the other celebrants acted on the altars as his extensions. The emperor was constituted across differences, encompassing them within himself, while his actions were the most complete examples of things that others could do only partially.

Everyone assembled on the altar. The nobility and the emperor occupied the literally higher heavenly position up on the Round Mound, separated from the official component of the imperium situated below and outside the square wall. Movement of tablets and participants upward, onto the altar, signaled a shift in motif from inner/outer to upper and lower oppositions. Of course, those whose ritual expertise was necessary likewise gained a place upon the Round Mound; ritual knowledge had its rewards.

The Offerings

Burning offerings in the southeastern furnace signaled both the beginning of the sacrifice proper, and its end (figure 15, segment 15). The bullocks were burned to welcome the spirits whose presence would be marked by music played in each segment until they inspired the rest of the offerings from a final massive fire in the furnace and departed. The crucial segments of the ceremony were the Three Oblations; they did not produce a later echo, but instead provided an asymmetrical context for the emperor's own overidentification with Heaven.

This triple segment in the center skewed the neat structure of the rite in favor of the yang superior element, which in this case rested in the spirits.

Welcoming the Spirits (Yingshen) (DQTL 1756: 1.22b–1.24a)

The Invoker (*dianyi*) intones: "The service to welcome Heaven with a whole burnt offering begins." While a bullock burns in the furnace to the southeast of the Round Altar, bearers take up incense.

The Conductor strikes up the first music of the ceremony, the Suite of Original Peace. The incense bearers move forward to Heaven's tablet. The emperor's *baipai* is taken up.

The Invoker invites the emperor to ascend to the highest terrace. He is conducted forward and the Invoker leads him to Heaven's tablet. The incense bearer kneels. The Invoker memorializes: "Kneel." The emperor kneels. The Invoker memorializes: "Offer incense." The emperor does so three times, repeating the sequence at each of the shrines to Former Emperors. The Invoker memorializes: "Retire." The emperor is conducted back to the second terrace, where his *baipai* tablet is replaced. The Invoker memorializes: "Perform the Full Prostration" and the emperor performs it. The Invoker intones: "All perform the Full Prostration" and all celebrants do so.

The music stops.

The presentation of incense to welcome the spirits provided the model for the action in upcoming segments. An invoker called out instructions that were then followed by the emperor with further assistance from various attendants. People did nothing unless explicitly told to. Thus, the rite was narrated as it was performed. This redundancy drew attention to the relationship between the form of the ceremony as both words and acts.

The close fit between word and act was literally embodied in ceremony, by bodies moving in space. The text, spoken aloud by the invoker, required kneeling, even by the emperor. The discourse of the ritual manual, delivered aloud by a minor member of the imperium,[9] posited an anonymous subject that insisted upon predication—the rite itself as embodiment of past sagely practice—thus eliding its character as imperial production.

There was no room for spontaneous innovation once the rite was under way. All considerations of appropriateness had been taken before this point: in the deliberateness of Preparation, particularly as the text was being fixed.[10] Thus editing emerges as a powerful moment (and moment of power) in ritual production for it fixed the forms that the entire imperium was bound to enact. No matter what status differences were manifested within the rite, the necessity for seriousness and adherence to form fell upon all alike.[11] From this projection of a larger cosmic whole, to which it was itself subject, the throne derived its power of subjection.

In these segments the first full prostration was performed (known as the "kowtow" in Western sources). Participants knelt, then stretched themselves fully three times upon the ground, repeating the sequence three times. In the full prostration, the body moved through three positions: On a vertical axis, standing (upper) and kneeling (center), and finally, on a horizontal axis, flat upon the ground (lower). Offerings were passed from hand to hand and then elevated, and prayers read in the kneeling, or "centered," body position. Although partial prostrations punctuated the rite often, the full nine prostrations occurred only three times: to welcome the spirits, to mark the emperor's reception of wine and meat (figure 15, segment 21), and to send off the spirits (figure 15, segment 22).

The prostration, or *ketou,* was an important mark of submission to authority in China. In everyday life, children ketoued to parents as a mark of respect. In audience, when the emperor "faced south" as the ruler of his realm, his imperium and foreign envoys prostrated themselves before him.[12] In Grand Sacrifice to Heaven and his ancestors, the emperor reversed this practice and lay himself flat upon the earth in respect, demonstrating that all servants had their masters and that power lay in occupying the centered "pivot" position that combined both roles.

The emperor centered in another way: in each following segment, the emperor went back and forth, up the central stairs from the second terrace to make offerings in the upper space. If the three terraces are to be considered a stack of upper/center/lower, as we have suggested, climbing the stairs moved the emperor from the central to upper. That this rise was then quickly followed by a drop to the knees only reinforces its centering power. Conversely, when kneeling in the ultimate "centering" position, offering to Heaven, the imperial body was still upright, sharing the vertical axis with the superior, standing position.

Presenting Jade and Silk (Dian yu bo) (DQTL 1756: 1.24a–25a)
The Invoker intones: "The jade and silk," and these offerings are made the same way while the Luminous Peace hymn is played.

The emperor is led up from the second terrace, kneels upon request, places (*dian*) the offerings which are handed to him into the *fei* basket. He first places before Heaven, then to the Former Emperors. He returns to his place on the second terrace. (There is no prostration.)

The music stops.

Proffering the Flesh (Jin zu) (DQTL 1756: 1.25a–26b)

The *zu* trenchers are in place; bearers of the *geng* soup ascend the center stairs to the top terrace. They pour the broth on the victims three times and retire. The music begins, this time the Unified Peace suite.

The emperor ascends to the first terrace and offers the trenchers of bullocks in the same fashion. After he returns to his place, the music stops.

In its discussion of music in sacrifice to Heaven, the *Five Rites* ruminates upon which tones should fill the position of the *santong,* the "Three Connectors" Heaven, Earth, and Humanity. In the Han, when such questions were taken up with great seriousness, it was proposed that the first three tones of the twelve generated from the basic pitch-pipe should be designated as the triad. Qin does not argue with this cosmically significant musical classification; on the contrary, he pursues closely past discussion on how to fill it (*WLTK* 5.12a/431).

As Qin points out, the essay on music collected in the *Record of Rites* says, "Music creates similarity and unity; *li* creates difference and separation." Music in eighteenth-century Grand Sacrifice seems to fulfill this injunction. After elaborate distinctions and homologies had been established during the Period of Preparation, music signaled (in each of segments 15 through 23, figure 15) "centering" proper, the encompassing of those carefully produced distinctions into a new order.

In pre-Han times, music was not only an image for universal order (Nakeseko 1957: 147; DeWoskin 1982: 86–87), it was also the strongest proof of the resonance that connected human heart/minds with the things of the world. Music, the ordering of sound, was not thought to be innate, but to arise as resonance upon external stimulation (*LJZY* 37/2:1527; DeWoskin 1982: 97). The essay on music says:

All tones are produced from the human heart/mind when feelings are aroused toward centering. They are sounded and when these sounds acquire patterning, they are called tones. . . . Music comes from the center. *Li* is created in the exterior. When music emerges from centering then there is stillness; when *li* is created in the exterior then there is active patterning. (*LJZY* 37/2:1527)

DeWoskin captures the sense of music as conducive to centering when he describes the lute, or *qin:*

Without the touch of the performer's fingers the *qin* is either a silent comforter or left to resonate on its own to the sound around. The instrument mediates with the outside world not only in the expressive or emotive act, from within to without, but in the receptive act or responsive act, from without to within. (1982: 142)

But music not only mediated inner/outer states; in ritual it was considered particularly well-suited to conjoin upper and lower opposition as well. The *Record of Rites* explains:

Harmonizing [inner] feelings and [external] deportment and face is the undertaking of both music and *li*. When *li* are established, then the valuable and base are differentiated; when music is patterned, then the upper and lower are harmonized. (*LJZY* 37/2:1529)

This conjoining refers without doubt to superiors and inferiors in society. Of the Son of Heaven's control of music, the essay says:

If music extends [fully] like this, then the affection between father and son will be harmonized, the order between elder and younger will be clarified, all within the four seas will be composed. If the Son of Heaven does this, then *li* will be truly practiced. (*LJZY* 37/2:1329)[13]

Music in Qing Grand Sacrifice was fixed in the first year of the dynasty. The number of hymns played in each sacrifice was correlated with a cosmically appropriate number: nine for Heaven, eight for Earth, six at the Ancestral Temple, and seven for the Altar of Soil and Grain (*HDZL* 1899: 415.17b–18a).[14]

The lyrics were included in the *Comprehensive Rites*. These hymns were so dense with allusion as to be practically semaphores of the Classics. But the themes pursued aloud on the sacrificial altar are immediately apparent: for instance, at the Sacrifice at the Altar of Soil and Grain, people chanted about the power of yin, agriculture, throngs of spirits, fertility, and social order (*DQTL* 1756: 6.1a–9a). The hymn lyrics for each sacrifice contain appropriate references. All, however, likewise narrate the ceremony itself, referring to vessels, wine, oblations, foods, descriptions of the altars, and so forth. Once again participants were reminded that the meaning their bodies inscribed in space was prescribed in text, in advance.

In the presentation of the jade and silk and the proffering of the trencher, the most artificed of offerings are grouped together with the only cooking done upon the altar (when the broth is poured over the flesh of the victims). The word that has been translated as "proffer" (*jin*) turns up again later in a different context. Here, the offerings are proffered to the spirits; later they will be proffered to the emperor.

Initial Oblation, Reading the Prayer (Chu xian du zhu) (DQTL 1756: 1.26b–28b)
The Invoker intones: "The initial oblation." Bearers remove the hoods from the *zun* storage jars and ladle out the wine, filling the *jue* winecups. The winecup bearers then wait by the various spirits' tablets.

The Long Life Suite begins. The military dancers move with spears and battle-axes.

The emperor is again led up the first terrace to Heaven's tablet. The cup bearer kneels. The Invoker memorializes: "Kneel" and the emperor kneels. The cup bearer proffers (*jin*) the *jue* and the emperor receives (*shou*) it. He carefully offers it by placing (*dian*) it within its stand (*dian zhong*). He rises. Then he is conducted to the prayer table where he kneels. All kneel.

The music pauses.

The Prayer Reciter reads aloud the prayer. When finished, he stands before the tablet of Heaven, kneels and places the prayerboard in the *fei* basket containing the jade and silk. He performs the single ketou.

The music begins again and the emperor leads the company in performing the single ketou.

The emperor then offers *jue* cups before each of the tablets of the Former Emperors. Those who present offerings to associate deities on the second terrace now (in a compressed reprise of the first terrace offerings sequence) offer incense, silk, and winecups. After everyone has returned to his place, the music stops. The military dancers retire; the *wen* dancers enter.

The Middle and Final Oblations (Ya dong xian) (DQTL 1756: 1.29a–b; 1.29b–30a)
The Invoker intones: "The Middle Oblation." The cup bearers come forward and wait. The musicians strike up the Excellent Peace Suite. The emperor offers winecups only to the ancestral shrines on the east. The *wen* dancers move with their wands and plumes.

After the emperor retreats to his place on the second terrace, the music stops.

The Invoker intones: "The Final Oblation." The sequence is repeated to the west, to the sound of the Perpetual Peace Suite, and *wen* dancing.

The Three Oblations should be treated as an entirety: the dancing marked this series of three as a kind of subrite within the larger figure. Here the homology between person and vessel was finalized, and this inner/outer consonance combined with an identification of the "upper" through offering to heaven.

The winecups had a special affinity with people: we have noted how their shape was likened to birds, the insignia worn by *wen* officials under the Manchus. Winecups were called *jue,* a word that, when combined with *wei,* "position," meant official rank. [15] The winecups were the only vessels to stand empty during the Period of Preparation and the ceremony, like participants who fasted and bore only their composure within. Finally the winecups were filled on the altar, not by pouring but by ladling instead. This ladling action immersed one vessel (ladle) into the contents of a larger one (*zun*), changing that "inner" liquid into its outer surrounding. Thus the wine was a thing simultaneously inner to the *zun* storage jar and "outer" to the ladle, a blending of both states. This wine was offered in the Three Oblations, and as the site of the broaching of inner and outer, it was the source of powerful transformations.[16] As such, it resonated with the human body of boundary surfaces described in chapter 1, the body of yang power.

As countless Confucians have said for as many years, it was one's personal intentions, one's inner feelings, that counted more than outer formalities in the performances of ritual. Yet these feelings had to be expressed, communicated, and *externalized*. Paradoxically, the wine was transformed back into purely "inner" contents as it was ladled *out* and transferred to the *jue* winecups, filling them. By this time, participants were ideally also filled: with awe, integrity, and respect, and ready for the single offering to Heaven alone, unaccompanied by any offerings to associate (ancestral) deities. The prayer that followed immediately was very telling. It reads:

Heir, the Son of Heaven, [emperor's own name] dares announce to August Heaven, Emperor Above: The winter solstice is here, the time when the six types of material energy [*qi*] commingle as in the beginning. We respectfully carry out canonical ritual, carefully leading ministers with jade, silk, animal victims, seclusion, and the fullness of offerings[17] perfected [*bei*]. This burnt ancestral offering is sacrificed to the Emperor Above; it is raised to our Great Ancestor [the dynastic founder], who Mounted Heaven, the Broad Mover, Sagely Virtuous Exemplar, Spiritual Mover, Founder of the Written Record, Occupier of the Pivot, One who is *Ren* and Filial, [possessor of] Vast Military Prowess, Utmost in Elegance, Imperial Peace, Broad *Wen*, Fixed Strength, Exalted August Emperor [and so on]. (*DQTL* 1756: 1.27b–28a)

Equally long lists of the attributes of the other four emperors who had occupied the throne before the Qianlong emperor were intoned. By this time in the ceremony, a listing of the best in kingly (that is, human) virtues does not seem inappropriate; on the contrary, inner virtue was externalized, made accessible through the text of the prayer. These virtues combined the *wen* qualities of the king as creator with his military qualities of destroyer, his filiality with his sagely merit, all characteristics of the ideal king. In some sense, these paeans to imperial goodness adumbrated the internal history of the sacrifice to Heaven in the

Qing dynasty. The prayer memorialized the successful negotiation of the contra-diction of sages and heirs, collapsing the distinctions of filial sonship and merito-rious inheritance of power by the ambiguous opening of the prayer. *Si tianzi,* "Heir, the Son of Heaven," employed both the word *si,* used to designate an heir by adoption, and *zi,* the word for biological son.

The military dancers with their axes and shields appeared in the First Obla-tion. The *wen* dancers, with their wands and plumes, performed in the Middle and Final Oblations. This "dancing" (*wu*—perhaps better translated as "postur-ing"), considered as the bodily, spatial analogue to the music that would draw all heart/minds together, was carefully prescribed.

Two different provincial handbooks produced in the mid-nineteenth century illustrate in detail the positions (figures 37 and 38). Both handbooks provide the lyrics for the hymns, annotated for instruments, and following that, illustrations of the positions of the dancers.[18] They are shown swaying and bending, bowing and turning, waving their axes or plumes in stately fashion. A different posture accompanies *each word* of the lyrics, and these words appear above each illustra-tion. In the overlapping of word, picture, and action, these texts on dancing epitomized text/performance. They reflected and created a culmination of sorts in fitting actions to words, in prescribing in advance what would be done on the altars.

Receiving Felicitous Liquor and Meat, Removing the Viands (Shou fu zu che zhuan)
(DQTL 1756: 1.30a–31a)

In this especially intricate example of the interaction between ritual "directors" and "celebrants," the action was, as usual, narrated and then choreographed carefully.

The Invoker intones: "Bestow the Felicitous Liquor and Meat." The Director of the Court of Banqueting elevates (*gongju*) the meat before the tablet of Heaven.

Celebrants are called to their places for "eating and drinking." The emperor is con-ducted to the first terrace flanked right by two directors of the Court of Banqueting (who handle the food) and on the left by two *shiwei* guards.[19]

All are called to kneel and drink. The officials on the right proffer (*jin*)[20] the wine. The emperor receives it [on his knees], reverently elevates it, and passes it to the offi-cials on the left. This is repeated for the meat. Upon being invited, only the emperor performs the single ketou. He is led back to his place where he leads the company in performing the full ketou. Music (the Splendid Suite) is played as the viands are cleared and the jade is removed. The music stops.

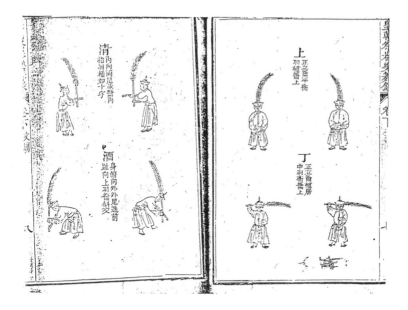

37. *Wen* dancers. From the ritual handbook *Huangchao liqi yuewu lu* 2:7b–8a.

38. Detail of painting of Sacrifice to the First Farmer showing positions of musicians (closest to altar), dancers (behind them), and the mass of officials (farthest from the altar). Handscroll; color on silk; 61.8 cm × 467.8 cm. Palace Museum, Beijing. From *Zijin cheng dihou shenghuo* (Imperial life in the Forbidden City), 110.

The close connection forged by the emperor with the spirits through offerings was confirmed as he received and then offered the felicitous liquor and meat. Until this time only the spirits received anything. We note also that the emperor knelt (itself a "centering" position) between representatives of his *wen* and military officials, their mediating center. But according to the *Comprehensive Rites,* the emperor did not eat or drink during the ceremony. In these rites, power was actualized in the giving rather than receiving.

The *Record of Rites* states that the disposition of sacrificial leftovers (eating) was least important (Legge 1885: 2:242–44). The offerings were "left over" after the spirits had arrived and "inspired" their essence. Human participants ate the material leavings, and the distinction between men and spirits was preserved. Identification lay in the acts of Oblation. The presentation of the *jue* winecup especially, with its close homology to the prepared human participant, was a bestowal of the self that created a relationship of debt with the spirits.

As the emperor accepted wine and meat like a spirit but refused to eat them like a man, he enacted the dual nature of his rule, not quite a god and not yet an ancestor but more than a man, both sage and heir. The second full set of Three Kneelings and Nine Prostrations signaled the climactic nature of the moment.[21]

Sending Off the Spirits (Song shen) (DQTL 1756: 1.31b–32a)
The Invoker intones: "Send off the Spirits." The Bright Peace Suite starts up and, as it plays, the Invoker memorializes, "Prostrate yourselves." The emperor leads the company in performing the full ketou.

Watching the Burning of Offerings (Wang liao) (DQTL 1756: 1.32a–33a)
The Invoker memorializes: "Take the Prayerboard, silk, and dishes to the furnace." The various bearers kneel before each tablet, perform the single ketou, and take the things away. As they pass the emperor, he turns in place to face them, making room. They go to the furnace.

The Invoker intones: "Watch the burning." The musicians play the Great Peace Suite.

The emperor emerges from the inner round wall via the east door in the south gate. He watches the burning of the prayer, silk, incense, and wine. The officials who make offerings to the associate deities emerge from the eastern and western gates to watch.

The Invoker "memorializes": "The ritual is complete (*li cheng*)." The emperor is led respectfully back into his dressing tent (outside the square wall).

The spirits were sent off with a full prostration, as they were welcomed. The ending rewound the beginning of the offering segments in reverse. After the prostrations came the burning of the rest of the offerings. The emperor and all celebrants were now standing in the mediating zone between round heaven and square earth, where the dancers and musicians performed. For the special celebrants, and especially for those many officials who never mounted the Round Mound to Heaven, or even set foot inside its round walls, the moment of watching the billowing smoke rising from the furnace was an important and final act of "looking," the last act that anyone performed upon command before the invoker announced the completion of the rite. This ceremonial mobilization of ocular participation harks back to the importance of the eye as the privileged organ in the editing moment of text/performance.

The Dispersal

Returning the Spirit [Tablets] to Their Places (Shen wei huan yu) (DQTL 1756: 1.33a)
The rite of Grand Sacrifice being complete, officials ascend the altar and perform the single ketou before each tablet. They remove them from their thrones and bring them down to be placed in their Dragon Repositories.

The tablets are carried to the August Arched Space, where the president of the Ministry of Rites proffers incense just as when he welcomed them.

Returning in the Phoenix Carriage (Hui jin) (DQTL 1756: 1.33b)
The emperor changes clothes in the tent and mounts his Ritual Palanquin to the west of the sacred way.

Outside the altar complex, the imperial cortege awaits. Musicians play the Suite of Spiritual Protection.[22]

The procession approaches Meridian Gate. The officials who did not participate in the rite are lined up to welcome the emperor. The bell is rung. The assembled officials follow the emperor into the Forbidden City and halt south of the Gold Water Bridge while he enters his palace. Then they retire.

Officials from the Court of Grand Constancy take down the plaque announcing seclusion and the bronze man.

The final two segments took place after the rite was finished but were still included in the handbook. They further unwind the structure built up from the emperor's emergence from the palace. The fact that the contexts took as their outermost limits his emergence and return points once again to the emperor's unique role in producing the rite that produced him as king.

Sacrifice and Filiality

In the close connection between sacrifice and filiality, we can see important ramifications of possibilities for the hegemony of *li* in social consciousness. The best method of concretizing *li* in practice was thought to lie in sacrifice. And *li* were thought to have originated in the veneration of ancestors. Funerary ritual, and the commemorative sacrifices to the dead that followed, displayed formal continuities across economic and status divisions in society.[23] The imperial role in providing models for rituals of kin particularity that could be generalized outward can hardly be minimized. For the imperium, the cult of ancestor veneration underlay ideas of history itself. In employing armies of scholars to research the details of past ritual usages, the imperium transformed the socially particularized past of each dynastic "family" into a general imperial history.[24]

In this section, however, we will investigate the relationship of the logic of centering in sacrifice to the cult of filiality in a more personal sense. Filiality itself provided a way to live the paradox of identity and difference that lay at the heart of Chinese social life as it was transmitted across generational boundaries. Here *li* can be seen most clearly as hegemonic, as generative of the very grounds of normality, refracted into its own narrower ideology.

When he discussed ancestral sacrifice in the eighteenth century, Qin Huitian still often referred to the three chapters of the Han period *Record of Rites* that dealt with "Categories of Sacrifice," "Meaning of Sacrifice," and give an "Account of Sacrifice."[25] We will briefly explore how sacrifice and filiality were related in these classics thought so important by this major commentator.

In chapter 23 of the *Record of Rites,* we are told that people sacrifice because they differ from other creatures, being cognizant of their own deaths (*LJZY* 46/ 2:1590; Legge 1885: 2:203). They do not disappear when they die but live on as *gui,* or ghosts. The king and his titled nobility were the only ones to have temples and altars with which to rescue their ancestors with rites. The common people (*shuren*) were left in their ghostly state. It was only later that access through ancestor worship to the invisible realm became available to all.[26]

Although sacrifice was created to mark distinctions between groups of people, we have noted in this analysis that its effectiveness was achieved through various processes of identification and mediation. Chapter 24 of the *Record of Rites* (*juan* 47 of *LJZY*) speaks in the idiom of kinship, which after all is a set of elaborations and strategies for constructing similarity. The discourse on kinship in China was not limited to the relations of living people, but extended to embrace and coerce the dead from the past. Similarly, insofar as sacrifice was the central ceremony of *li* in general, the incorporeal world was incorporated, and the definition of "human" expanded through *li*.

The correct sentiments of filiality received their fullest expression in sacrifice even as they were objectified in it. The important oblations, music, and dancing are explained in the *Record of Rites* as "external representations" designed to amplify the (internal) purpose of the superior man (*LJZY* 49/2:1603; Legge 1885: 2:242).

The *Record of Rites* explains in detail how a son should feel toward his deceased parents, retaining such a memory of them that "as he gave full play to his love they seemed to live again and to his reverence they seemed to stand before him."

The superior man, while his parents are alive reverently nourishes them; and when they are dead he reverently sacrifices to them. His chief thought is how, to the end of life, not to disgrace them. (*LJZY* 47/2:1592; Legge 1885: 2:211)

Even his own body must be returned to them as their legacy:

Of all that heaven produces and earth nourishes there is none so great as humanity. His parents gave birth to his person all complete, and to return it to them all complete may be called filial duty. (*LJZY* 48/2:1599; Legge 1885: 2:229)

In short, the entirety of chapter 24 is a description of how a close identification with one's parents in life should be continued even at great effort after death.

The vocabulary of filiality was extended to describe many social relationships. Disloyalty to rulers, insincerity with friends, and cowardice in battle were all stigmatized as unfiliality (*LJZY* 47/2:1594). A good government was a matter of the correct treatment of the virtuous, the noble and the old, the ageing and the young: the last three analogized from the family (*LJZY* 24.19b). In fact, "one who is filial approximates to be king" (*LJZY* 47/2:1594; Legge 1885: 2:217). In the political hierarchy as well as the familial, one was supposed to identify closely with the person directly superior:

Whatever good was possessed by the Son of Heaven he yielded as the virtue of Heaven; whatever good was possessed by a feudal lord he ascribed to the Son of Heaven; whatever good was possessed by the minister or Great Officer he attributed to the Prince of his state; whatever good was possessed by an officer or common man, he assigned its basis to his parents and the preservation of it to his elders. (*LJZY* 48/2:1600–1601; Legge 1885: 2:233)

In the constant upward displacement of individual actors' responsibility, the final word, so to speak, lay in Heaven, in the invisible. Here rested the objective existence of filiality, and ultimate repository of its authentication as human agency disappeared. The constant concern with the invisible becomes, in the Chinese case, not just worship or beseeching, but ironically a matter of constituting and maintaining as well. Such was humanity's place in the cosmos, necessary to the very existence and maintenance of Heaven and Earth through the performance of their rituals. Sacrifice had to generate the steps toward the invisible realm that was the objectification of filiality, and the displacement of its own agency. It then, of course, had to loop back again to reappropriate this objectification through sacrifice to ensure the continuance of cosmic (and everyday) life and, crucially, its rule.

It is a moot point whether the invisible realm would be better described in native terms as composed of entities that act of their own volition when invested with such responsibility, or in sociological ones such as the "collective representations" of an empire of filial sons. Both designations point to the necessity of reappropriating the power (which we can gloss as *ling*) invested there. Steven Sangren (1987b) has written extensively on the ideological implications of *ling* as mystification of a community's agency. I agree with his insights but feel we should move beyond his more purely Marxist notion of ideological displacement to concentrate upon this process's positive contribution to an ongoing sense of selfhood and ruling hegemony. In the empowerment of sons we see how this hegemony operated and glimpse its gendered dynamics.

In the *Record of Rites,* the two key themes in ancestral sacrifice were the placement of the participants, particularly the "personator," and eating and drinking. The personator (*shi,* literally meaning "corpse") was a living man who became the ancestor for the ceremony:

According to the rule in sacrifice, a grandson acts as the representative of his grandfather. Though employed to act the part of the personator, yet he was the son of the sacrificer. When his father, with his face to the north served him, he made clear how it was the way of a son to serve his father. (*LJZY* 45/2:1605; Legge 1885: 2:246)

The paradoxical position of the emperor, who was both master of the empire and Heaven's servant, was outlined above in our discussion of Grand Sacrifice to Heaven. In ancestor veneration that pivotal position was recast in terms of kinship. How can a man be, at the same time, both father and son? To put it another way, how can that which is different and separate (the self) yet constitute the only link of continuity between two others (the son and grandfather)?

The system of kin similarity envisioned through impersonation of grandfathers was not just a simple stack of separate persons (in the words of James Joyce, "Every man his own father") but a matter of interlocking sets; every man his own grandfather, so to speak. Such identity of alternate generations was expressed in the *zhaomu* order of name tablets in the ancestral temple. Starting the count from a single ancestor, second-generation tablets were placed to the left (*zhao*), the third to the right (*mu*), the fourth to the left, and so on.[27]

The eating and drinking described in the *Record of Rites* further marked and created this differentiation, as they did in later imperial sacrifices. "Leftovers" of the sacrifice were consumed in sequence: after the personator-as-ancestor had eaten and departed, groups ate according to their rank. As the eating proceeded down through the ranks, there were more people consuming less (*LJZY* 49/2:1605). Ancestral sacrifice, as presented in the *Record of Rites* and still performed in the eighteenth century, shared a basic principle: it literally enacted traditional Chinese hierarchy. The whole, symbolized by a single ancestor eating all the food, preceded and contained an infinitely divisible number of parts. In everyday court life, an imperial meal recapitulated this incorporation of hierarchy through food (see chapter 1).

It is a Chinese ritualist cliché that "*li* creates distinctions and music creates harmony." It is a cliché of another sort that one must have difference in order to have anything to unite. Sacrifice also marked distinctions in the nonhuman world:

They sacrificed to the sun on the altar, to the moon in the hollow to mark the brightness of one and the gloom of the other and to show the difference of the upper and lower. . . . The sun comes forth from the east, the moon appears in the west. . . . when the one ends the other begins in regularity thus producing the harmony of all under the sky. (*LJZY* 47/2:1594; Legge 1885: 2:219)

We have seen how difference was created in sacrifice through the generational triad of grandfather/father/son. In terms of the categories familiar to us from our lengthy analysis of Grand Sacrifice, the homologies are:

upper	grandfather	spirits	heaven
center	father	sacrificer	humanity
lower	son	participants	earth

Yet identification had to occur simultaneously with differentiation if sacrifice was to fulfill its role as central and best expression of filiality, because close identification with ancestors constituted *xiao*.

With great economy, the ritual provided for this close father/son identification by an inversion of son/personator/subject and father/sacrificer/ruler:

> The ruler went to meet the victim, but not to meet the personator to avoid transgressing certain taboos. While the personator was outside the gate of the temple, he was regarded only as a subject; inside the temple he had the full character of a ruler. While the ruler was outside the temple gate he was the ruler; when he entered the gate, he had the full character of a subject or son. (*LJZY* 49/2:1605; Legge 1885: 2:245–46)

The ruler/sacrificer is here associated with the victim, as pointed out in the analysis above. Is this role reversal a temporary renunciation of the ruler/sacrificer's authority? It is tempting to see it as an example of the ritual inversion of authority that Victor Turner so aptly describes as a social and psychological necessity.[28] Yet can we be sure that ritual is in all cases a tension-relieving reversal of everyday life rather than its intensification? Can it not be rather that ritual tells us how the relativity of power is possible at all? That underlying the ethos of *xiao* (the superiority of fathers) is the superiority of sons?

Although fathers were structural necessities both biologically and ritually as passive receivers of filial actions, it was in the role of son/sacrificer that (ritual) power resided. In his role as son of the father, a man was entitled to embody the grandfather/spirits. It was by becoming, in turn, the son of his own son that the father/sacrificer could "penetrate" (*tong*) the invisible through sacrifice. In sacrifice sons were grandfathers and fathers were sons, in other words, potential ancestors. Such an identification with the invisible world of ancestral spirits shot one "forward into the past." A son did not so much mean eternity as he enacted its presence within time, continuity within constant change. In the end everyone had to become a son, even sages, because only as a son did one have access to the possibility of the filial action that was enacted in the sacrificial mediation of centering. Here lie the completed implications of the emperor as a body of yang power: as the perfect son he was the object of emulative desire. Insofar as yang was associated with masculinity, *this* was one thing that masculinity meant: the tremendous power to stand as the *zhuren* in sacrifice—to be a son.

It would be mistaken to relegate filiality to a negative role of ideological mystification. Filiality was powerful *because* it was positive, active in its bestowal of authority upon fathers by sons, and also because it had the potential for creating identification. A son was the perfect embodiment of social and physical continuity. It was to sons that authority passed while remaining in the same place: with the ancestors in the invisible portion of the realm. Sons (members of the imperium and subjects) simultaneously validated both this authority and their holding of it by being its creators and nourishers in sacrifice.

Filiality has traditionally held great explanatory power when applied to any relation of superior/inferior. I have tried to show that this is so because its main ritual, sacrifice, created a "center" that separated higher from lower while allowing the close identification of that center with the superior or higher position. By roughly the Ming period onward, this particular mode of ritualization was generally applied as a means of positioning the self vis-à-vis a cosmic whole. Sacrifice as an organized activity gave concrete existence to filiality within the larger construction of the cosmos as horizon of human agency. If the imperium generated its most complete form in Grand Sacrifice, it must be remembered that the hegemonic power of *li* lay in its *generalizability* to all men who were, after all, every one born a son. In the homologies between sons, emperors, and magistrates, filial sacrifice and imperial participation in ritual, the oft-assumed parallel between the Chinese family and the large domain was socially enacted and culturally constituted.[29]

By connecting the cult of filiality to the logic of sacrifice, we understand something of the personal and psychological fitness of the complex ritual practices outlined in this study. In the cult of filiality and its enactment in sacrifice, we find one nexus for the simultaneous social production of the individual and the collective, a more technical way of stating our paradox of people needing to construct themselves as different (that is, a separate self) and yet the same (part of a collective). This construction was accomplished dialectically: the objectification of social relations as "ancestors" or "cosmic deities" was reappropriated through centering in sacrifice. That centering was prescribed in the *Record of Rites* as intensely embodied activity:

The sacrifice of the filial son can be realized/comprehended [*zhi*]: He takes his place, his reverence conveyed by his bent body; he comes forward, his reverence conveyed by a look of pleasure; he proffers, his reverence conveyed by an expression of desire; he returns to his place as if awaiting fate itself. . . . A filial son moves as though carrying jade or holding a full vessel in two hands. (*LJZY* 47/2:1594)

The disposition of the son's vertical body when still, of his style of movement in the horizontal plane, of the play of emotion upon the signifying surface of his face, all conveyed and created successful sacrificial sincerity. This microtopography of the son-in-motion condenses into the performing body the larger movements we have traced in Grand Sacrifice to Heaven. The collapse of container and thing-contained is illustrated again by the injunction to move the filial self as though acting as a vehicle for the material signs of filiality: jades and vessels.

The centering of a world of gods and humans through the person of the emperor or his magistrates, who both governed and submitted to governance, simultaneously controlled the inferior, honored the superior, and gave paradoxical place to the son/magistrate/human, whose enactment of *li* created the present out of the past.

8

THE POLITICS OF BOUNDARY

Inscription and Incorporation

We commonly consider inscription to be the privileged form for the transmission of a society's memories. . . . Yet it would be misleading to underestimate the mnemonic importance and persistence of what is incorporated. . . . Every group will entrust to bodily automatisms the values and categories which they are most anxious to conserve.   PAUL CONNERTON, *How Societies Remember*

In the introduction I outlined four frames within which to understand Grand Sacrifice. Reviewing them will allow us to bring into focus how Grand Sacrifice created certain boundaries, logical and social. First and most literally, within the form of ceremonial action, the bounding of altar space, the classifying of food, the alternation of looking with arranging, and finally the movement of people in performance brought into being certain psychosomatic dispositions. Second, the boundary between the throne and its literati ritual managers was articulated in the discourses upon appropriate rulership signified in the ritual form: would it be sages who wrote and edited or sons who performed ceremony? What about the form in which the boundary between past and present sagely practice was made visible in the current imperial reign? Third, what implications did the rise of ritualist preoccupations have on the boundary between imperium and commoners and the hegemony thereby created? Fourth and finally, what is illuminated by concentrating upon distinctions between Chinese and European theorizing about social life? I would like to work backwards, beginning with the last problem of comparison.

Not Descartes's Body: Comparison

By the eighteenth century, the self-conscious efforts of evidential scholars were bent upon reactivating past *li* as extension of the good governance of the sages. This ritualist metaphysics operated at the most fundamental level to organize concepts of the relation of the human world to the extrahuman cosmos, the self to other selves, and language as performance and communication. Within this metaphysics history mediated society's relation to the *dao,* a source of power for those who articulated its changes. The most rewarded and desired sense of subjectivity accrued to those who could "center" contradiction and difference.

By the Qianlong era, the editor's gaze crossed and penetrated (*tong*) the plane of signs within which such subjects centered. Metaphors of penetration and the opening of a surface resonate with the distant founding myth of Hundun, emperor of Chaos and of the Center.

The Emperor of the South Sea was called Shu; the Emperor of the North Sea was called Hu, and the Emperor of the Center was called Hundun [Chaos]. Shu and Hu from time to time came together for a meeting in the territory of Hundun, and Hundun treated them very generously. Shu and Hu discussed how they could repay his kindness. "All men," they said, "have seven openings so they can see, hear, eat and breathe. But Hundun alone does not. Let's try boring him some!" Every day they bored another hole, and on the seventh day Hundun died. (Chuang Tzu 1964: 95)

Hundun's perfect surface was opened, thus inaugurating human order.[1] Hundun's violation, the perforation of his sur-face, provided the possibility of the signifying surfaces of social life. Equally important, in this founding myth, becoming a person required an *interruption* of internal unity and coherence; an opening out to the world rather than its systematic distancing into a separate objectivized reality.

In late imperial China, we do not find what Hannah Arendt (1958) calls the Archimedian point, occupied by a subject alone with only God or reason, separated from the dense web of the life of the world by the lies of language and doomed to endless symbolic interpretation.

Arendt's subject was constructed within the discourses of modern, Western, disembodied Cartesian unitary consciousness that has found social expression in the ideology of possessive individualism. The ritualist metaphysics of eighteenth-century China implies a history of subjectivity and its expressions, of the self and the world, that reads differently from the tale of the triumph of the individual as a social goal or of human rationality in the mastery of nature. Another model altogether prevailed in the eighteenth-century Chinese ritualist metaphysics: the concept of "centering," or *zhong,* is most important for understanding consciousness imagined as process, not simply essence. Here instead we find a centering of the world and the self by persons living upon their boundary. In the self-centering paradigm, claims to interiority make sense only in connection to the world. Critical Marxist and poststructuralist studies on the "subject" that have criticized the notion of a unified, isolated self are thus most helpful in understanding the eighteenth-century ritual problematic of centering selves.

A concern with the subject and subject positions has replaced Mind, consciousness, and individual as an analytic category for exploring notions of the self (Judith Farquhar 1994). Why? Focusing on "subjectivity" instead of "individual" takes into account that people's selves are processual and that they change over a lifetime of experiences; that one person can occupy many "subject positions" within multiple discourses (female, woman, daughter, wife, reader, intellectual, consumer, etc.); and that these dynamics are constructed within an ensemble of social relations. This subject is not the same as a living individual; rather, as sociologist Stuart Hall reminds us,

It is the category, the position where the subject—the I of ideological statements—is constituted. Ideological discourses themselves constitute us into subjects for discourse. (1985: 1020)

Thus, attention to how ideologically motivated cultural formations tend to form specific selves *for* themselves, people who find themselves "at home" in those forms, provides a promising starting point for cross-cultural comparison. We must grant that human "selves" are not substantialized unities that everywhere and in every epoch interact according to the same set of universal laws dependent upon some eternally available idea of "human nature."

It is more important than ever that analysts come to terms with historical and social difference in a way that can take its measure without simply lapsing into exoticization. Analyzing processes of "subjectification" that occur within material milieux of bodily constraint and movement, of language use and of the disposition of built space, can be very helpful. I would further propose that *control* of the *terms and practices* that "subjectify" (practices that, first, placed embodied selves in mutually hierarchized positions and, second, provided them with a sense of identity so that they could "recognize" themselves as an appropriate father, son, subject, daughter, friend) was itself a source of social power in eighteenth-century China. *Li* were considered both as moral/political and extrahuman/cosmological, extending the *dao* visibly into the world. Humanity's role was to activate that *dao* to the best of its ability, and therefore those people better positioned to carry out this cosmic injunction (literate males) were ipso facto placed to identify and enforce versions and visions of social value. To some readers, this may seem to be a needlessly roundabout restatement of clichés about how Chinese culture ruled itself. But its worth lies in its specificity—allowing us to map more precisely the embodied practices through which such social arrangements were carried out.

Li were intimately connected to the body: Boodberg has pointed out that the characters for ritual (*li*) and body (*ti*) are the only two to share the right-hand element meaning "the ritual vase." Boodberg is undoubtedly correct in his presumption of what the two concepts share: a sense of organic form. The body *is* an organism and the *li* are "organic" in the sense of always being present in being, in their "self-so" (*ziran*) participation in the *dao*.[2] But the interpretation of the two characters need not be so abstract. The explicit homology of the body and ritual vessels was crucial to sacrifice. Analyzing this homology showed us how the body itself was imagined so as to provide the incorporated anchor for inscriptional activities. Within *li,* the body itself provided both sign and site for signification.

As a sign, the activities of bodies provide metaphors for the rest of the world. Indeed, the human body has functioned generally, and continues to function, as a powerful organizing metaphor for nature, society, and self in many social contexts all over the world. But the theorization of this function will have a history specific to its cultural context. One must draw a distinction between metaphorization *from* body to another domain such as society or nature (body as sign) and the situation of the lived body itself as a location for various practices (body as site), performances, and disciplines that shape and subjectify the self. (Of course, body metaphors are themselves powerful organizers of such practices.)

In Grand Sacrifice each participant's own body was not a closed container-thing but rather, like the altar spaces, a complex concatenation of evermore intimate boundaries. The body was an ensemble of focused fields whose shifting edges and surfaces provided the sites for articulation between inner and outer. If the self could contain and develop an interiority, it was because it could differentiate and bound. What is often interpreted in Chinese philosophical texts as the privileging of interiority, an inner self, can be better understood as valuable proof of boundary creation and control for which the body was necessary. Thus the "centering" action of the self through the body paradoxically takes place at its edges, on its surfaces, and through its senses, which act as gates to the outside world. Concentrating upon the body as boundary maker focuses us firmly in the realm of culturally constructive practices like dress and gesture. We overcome the metaphysical discourses of secret, hidden interiority as the "inside" is exposed as created in relation to the "outside" by the boundary itself.[3] The pertinent questions become: How are these boundaries created and by whom?

Imperial Grand Sacrifice presents us with a model of ritualized bodiliness and subjectivity coming into being through what Roger Ames calls "process ontology" (Hall and Ames 1987). People do not consist of divinely endowed or biologically fixed human nature. Instead they are exemplars of dynamically contingent positions both in space and in social hierarchy. In the terms developed here, they are boundary makers and breakers. There is no boundary unless there is the possibility of its transgression; for "centering" to occur, boundaries must be reestablished and reproduced. This notion has profound implications for the construction of gender, for in such a shifting cosmos, how could it be fixed? Here Tani Barlow's discussion of yin/yang and gender is very illuminating.

The forces yin/yang are many things: logical relationships (up/down, in/out, husband/ wife), practical forces, "designations for polar aspects of effect," and in a social sense, powers inscribing hierarchy. . . . What appears as "gender" are yin/yang differentiated positions: not two anatomical "sexes," but a profusion of relational, bound and unequal dyads, each signifying difference and positioning difference analogically. (1994: 135, 136)[4]

We have seen how useful yang-yin logics were in organizing the encompassing assymmetries of Grand Sacrifice. I would like to highlight three aspects of yang-yin that I consider to be especially important for boundary creation within *li* in social life: their polarity, their relative positionality, and their tendency to accomplish relations of unequal encompassment.

Their "polarity" differs from post-Cartesian "duality" such as mind/body, spirit/matter (to name some of the great ones). Yang and yin mutually transform into each other: as night into day, extreme heat into a cooling phase, the waxing moon into a moon that wanes, as what goes up coming down. When understood as interimplicated in this manner in philosophical writing and later interpretation, each term seems equally powerful. Thus the version of polar reciprocity that has retained a remarkably tenacious hold on the imagination is one of equality. Of course, in the ritual and social workings of the relationships explained/created within yang-yin logics, this is never truly so.

The yang tendency to encompass yin privileges in material ways aspects of human life associated with yang, such as masculinity. Even if these aspects were privileged for other social reasons to do with production of economic value, the enactment of that privilege *as outcome of yang association* acts to cosmicize and fix the privilege. The sexual endowment of human beings, yang masculinity and yin femininity, resisted any easy reciprocal transformation from yang to yin *at the social level.* As Charlotte Furth (1988) has shown, however, physiologically there were thought to exist gray areas of confusion and ambiguity. Instead of biology grounding gender, we find gender referenced within the logic of *li,* the social performance of appropriate boundary.

That brings us to their positional and relative relationship: Something can be yin only in relation to something that is yang—and everything in the cosmos is thought to be so positioned, including people in the Five Bonds. The father whose sons obey him do so because he has given them the example of his own filial obedience. They are yin to him as he is yin to his own father. (The filial food chain tops out with Heaven.) No one is ever completely in charge here. It *is* possible to imagine women occupying yang positions: every mother did so by virtue of her parenting. And everyone moved up the chain with age. There are very special examples of women occupying positions endowed with the yang power of initiation rather than the yin power of completion[5] such as the culturally frightening precedents of Empress Wu Zetian of the Tang, who was ritually an emperor, Empress Ci Xi, Jiang Qing. There were also the endless tales of cross-dressing women taking the examinations or performing deeds of filial valor (Barlow 1994). Thus, as Barlow has concluded, gender essence cannot be fixed as yin, for biological women could occupy the yang position. Conversely, biological essence was not a final determining explanation for domination.

Finally, as I have shown for Grand Sacrificial form, and as Steve Sangren has shown for the worship of the goddesses Ma Tsu and Kuan-yin, yang always somehow "encompasses" yin. They are not equi-poised equals: Sangren notes that yang is constantly associated with "order," yin with "disorder" (Sangren 1987b: 65). Furthermore, by virtue of the boundary between the two being itself a culturally ordered construction, order contains disorder. So studies that exalt the "feminine" yin principle remain abstract and in fact can mask real gender inequity.

Yin-yang logics of mutually transforming polarity, relative position, and encompassing inequality created the fluid boundaries so necessary to centering within the discourse of *li*. The primary constructive metaphor for bodies in imperial ritual practice was vessels as boundary makers. The positions of embodied power it constructed were ruler/subject, father/son, positions usually—as Barlow reminds us—*but not always* occupied by biological males (Barlow 1994). The vessel metaphor of Grand Sacrifice organized only two of the Five Bonds—but the most powerful two. What people occupying these positions centered into a controllable whole were texts and performances. Thus I have called their embodied position the body of yang power: the power of encompassment.

Those interpellated into the positions of wife, daughter, younger—usually *but not always* the biologically female—were obviously disadvantaged under inscriptions that privileged the yang body of boundary-making and encompassment. People who did not "center" faced exclusion from the twin authority of both writing and ritualization.

There are important implications for gendering in specifying closely how the body of yang power was produced. One vexing problem in studying gender in imperial China has been the marked absence just outlined of a foundational discourse of biological essence upon which gender inequity has been based.[6] Much feminist critical historiography has deconstructed the roots of Euro-American women's oppression in biologism, which in this case can be treated as a Big Ideological Mystification. Deprived of this "resource" for theorizing, where does the feminist historian of China turn?

Foucault's work on the microprocesses of "discipline" seems one promising avenue.[7] For Foucault "discipline" does not act upon an already previously present embodied subjectivity (the way Biology intrudes upon innocent women's bodies and appropriates them from outside) but rather brings it into being through practices as varied as schooling, medicine, and judicial punishment. Foucault's body exists in a field of power relations that "have an immediate hold upon it; they invest it, mark it, train it, torture it, force it to carry out tasks, to perform ceremonies, to emit signs" (1979: 25). Foucault does not reify power as something that conquers from without, seeing it rather as that which produces from within, generating and conjoining the simultaneous effects of both individual body/subjects and the social body (1982). A salient feature of Foucault's project has been to include theorizing as *one practice among the many* that constitute such powerfully constitutive discursive forms.

There are at least three reasons why such an analytic project seems especially helpful in understanding *li*. First, Foucault is relentless in his rejection of post-Cartesian objectivisms that would separate minds from bodies, ideas from institutions. Foucault stands as a nondialectician because he does not entertain the foundational epistemological splits upon which dialectical reasoning is founded—especially subject/object.

The problem for Chinese living within *li* differed from our own metaphysical difficulty of closing gaps: between nature and culture, self and other, subject and object, person and God, meaning and performance. On the contrary, they set about making distinctions in a cosmos that threatened to bind itself too closely together, to collapse into an ungovernable homogeneity. Boundaries had to be made, but within the rules of this cosmic frame, they then had to be deployed toward an understanding of unity that contains difference (= hierarchy). Foucault's vision of an ever-shifting terrain of micropowers promises a better language in which to speak of the Chinese universe of dynamic contingency. For him, power is not simply wielded from above, but rather circulates through the social body's various sites of productivity (institutions, subject positions, linguistic practices). At the same time, his language of "power" allows us to consider still problems of hegemony and dominance and to avoid lapsing into imputation of Chinese utopian difference to our own oppressive reifications. The second and third uses to which he can be put will be discussed below.

Imperial Hegemony and Literati Culture

The second and third frames from the introduction call for exploring the boundaries between throne and literati, imperium and commoners. Because these relations interpenetrate, I will first discuss them together by reviewing a second reason I think Foucault's approach to power in social life is useful in understanding *li*. He is devoted to the social "body"—the personal body is produced through social practices and, conversely, through those practices social life ramifies. In a world governed by the common sense of possessive individualism, the difficulties of capturing and conveying a sense of how thoroughly everyday life in imperial China was saturated by micropractices of sociality cannot be overstated. When Chinese sociality *is* imagined by analysts, there has been a tendency to exoticize it negatively, seeing the Chinese as those "groupie" Others, heirs to a long-standing tradition of totalitarianism. How to convey a sense of hierarchy, a form of social organization we imagine is long dead among ourselves, that preserves possibilities of resistance within itself?

This specifically Chinese sort of hierarchy operated according to a logic of the encompassment of asymmetries we have just outlined in yang-yin thinking. In such a social formation, power lay in "centering," creating boundaries that displayed difference as mutually and connected portions of a greater whole. Dorothy Ko has noted that from the seventeenth century "Confucian reformers sought to cure the world by restoring hierarchies and boundaries" (1992: 16). The "centering" position of the body of yang power (most perfectly exemplified by the emperor) was ideologically charged as the most desirable subject position, the "initiator."

The imperial body, in both the personal sense of the emperor and of his imperium, came to life in ritualizations like Grand Sacrifice that provided the intersection of filiality (*xiao*) and text (*wen*), two potent forms of social power. The discourse upon filiality (*xiao*) through ancestor worship obsessed about incorporation and its repetition through time by means of performing rituals within an embodied lifetime. Among the complex discourses of *wen,* I have emphasized the retrieval of history through the editing of inscriptions. The throne conjoined these two authoritative discourses as two forms of value, filiality and literacy. Thus studying a ritualization like Grand Sacrifice allowed me to explore how the circulation of meaning (in writing and ritual) and the production of persons (in the form of filial sons) coincided at the imperial level to produce a powerfully productive/coercive formation. The throne articulated this boundary between inscription and incorporation, between text and performance, not only seeking to control access and expression but also, and perhaps more powerfully, providing a persuasive model for their appropriate conjunction.

In ceremonial, the two-dimensional orders of signification in text were embodied by three-dimensional bodies; perimeters of self were extended as boundaries were transited, and the inner/outer and high/low were centered. When the subject who centered was the Chinese emperor himself, the generalized production of self and society within the ritualist metaphysics produced instead a particular hegemony: the imperium.

In the concept of hegemony we find a powerful tool for understanding the process whereby the humanly constructed world becomes a "natural" horizon for meaningful action and the contingent and historical transform into the preordained and eternal. When we begin to account in this radical way for the *production* of meaning that underlies action for specific actors rather than merely describing how rituals functioned to integrate in terms of abstract categories such as "order" or "harmony," we find ourselves poised "between" levels of society already reified in sociological categories of "Big" and "Little" traditions, or "popular" and "elite." Here extremely important points of discursive commonality and difference appear, shared across sociological and regional divides.

Imperial Grand Sacrifice, as text/performance, articulated a specific relation of hegemony between the gentry/literati class and common people within itself (like a hinge). For the literati, the imperium consecrated the claim of successful examination candidates to be *the* representers/inscribers of culture in general as they wrote the emperor's rites. The cultural categories they inscribed were enacted in every home performance of sacrificial rituals of ancestor worship. In performance, the emperor's altars displayed the categories of social arrangement on a microlevel: The inner/outer, the high/low, and the "center" remain residual ways that Chinese people still arrange their social terrain.[8] Thus the imperial center can be seen as one factor enabling the hegemony of the gentry/literati, the mediating third party that made it possible, rather than simply as wielder of the direct power of force, either military or economic.

Power was not predicated upon a state-versus-civil-society model wherein a sovereign subject (king/state) oppresses a passive object (people/society). Power was instead generated through a series of macrocosmic/microcosmic resemblances, through the authority to exemplify for the totality an ideal cosmosocial order. The king claimed the authority to instantiate the perfect part and thus to enable the existence of the perfect whole. He could accomplish this only with the assistance of his official imperium, and the literati/gentry class in general.[9]

It is the *cons*tructed nature of this hegemony that interests me rather than its "structure" because *cons*truction, with its implication of reciprocity and interaction, better connotes social life as discursive space. Within this space, thoughtful and material life occur as mutually implicated moments of a totality (Laclau and Mouffe 1987). This approach to the analysis of social life opens a field upon which people not only contend for already available resources, symbolic or material, but rather simultaneously construct what they seek to appropriate.

Grand Sacrifice as text/performance highlights an underlying unity that existed between writing and ceremonial performance in the eighteenth century

and served to further enhance the role of the *wenren,* or "person of letters."
Historian Evelyn Rawski states:

> The *wenren* model had existed in earlier dynasties, but its importance increased in late
> Ming, and it became highly relevant for the men born under the Ming who lived as
> adults under the Manchus. . . . The thwarted political ambitions of many in this genera-
> tion were deflected toward the sphere of culture. (1985: 13)

The split that Rawski implies between "culture" and "politics" was one that was
enfolded and neutralized by imperial ritualism and the discourses of *wen,* the
cosmic text-pattern that was available for those who could distinguish it and
materialize it in writing, painting, building, and ritual.[10] Thus this study has
described how productions that modernity deems "aesthetic" in fact endowed
their creators with a kind of moral authority in traditional China. The question
acquires sharp specificity in the eighteenth century, a time of rising literacy beyond traditional "elite" circles, and a period when scholarship was, in economic
terms, freeing itself from reliance upon the king as its sole patron.[11] Yet, paradoxically, these same elites were able to flexibly turn their service in putting on
the king's rites to local political advantage in a time of social flux.

Changes in economy, society, and philosophy fueled a rise in literacy and a
desire for education on the part of more people than ever before. By late Qing,
there were enough schools to teach one-third to one-half the male population
to read.[12] But simultaneously and ironically, by the eighteenth century there was
such fierce competition in the examinations that many of the most famous scholars of the day either never received a degree or never served in imperial posts
once they finally succeeded at the examination (Ho Ping-ti 1962: 147–48; Miyazaki 1981: 117–18). Indeed, Elman and Mann have proposed that it was the
narrowing of this institutional venue for personal advancement that contributed
to the alternative lifestyles and intellectual aims of many scholars (Elman 1984:
6; Susan Mann Jones 1975). The examination system's failure to expand opportunity to keep even with population growth meant a progressive breakdown in
the imaginative link proposed between hard-working individuals and the imperium with its Horatio Alger–like ideology of success. Scholars turned to other
means of claiming prestige. With their mission of refurbishing the present and
rescuing it from past error as they "plumbed" texts, ritualists, whether actually
employed by the throne or not, construed their position as a privileged one.
From there, editors could transform the "flatness" of the present through a new
sensitivity to the dimension of time as history.

If the rise of literacy posed what might be construed as a contradiction between the people and their rulers, the weakening of the examination system's hold upon intellectual aspiration posed a contradiction among the rulers themselves. The claim that sagehood lay in scholarship and not necessarily in government service thus may have seemed to solve both contradictions at once: literati maintained their status and authority to rule as *wenren* (one still had to be arguably even *more* literate to claim sagehood) while compensating for a growing distance from the monarchy, a heretofore important component of elite local prestige. But in fact, this presumption that the route to sagehood lay in scholarly production created more contradictions than it solved, both between literati and monarchy and between literati and the masses.

To begin with the literati and the throne: Forging a direct link between scholarship and sagehood could have implied the empowerment of scholars as writers and editors for themselves, or at least for their local or agnatic interests (the same thing?), rather than as writers in service of the king.[13] Although it may be argued that such a separation between the production of meaning and its writers on the one hand, and the monarchy on the other, did develop in the nineteenth century, buttressed by a resurgence of anti-Manchu feeling, in the eighteenth century the *kaozheng* community had not yet reached such a point of disillusionment. It seems to have been the case that if scholars could not in fact perform as members of the imperium, they still flocked to participate in it by producing texts on the ritual protocols of its re-creation. They maintained a deep writerly interest in *li*. But because of *li*'s fundamental role in constructing and maintaining self and society, and its close relation to sagely action, the throne remained as deeply committed to its discourse. I think scholars' dedication to *li* compromised the possibility of true collective autonomy from the interests of the throne.

To turn to literati and commoners: At the same time, linking scholarship and sagehood paradoxically opened a different possibility for liberation. Connecting sagehood to literacy in an era of rising educational and reading opportunities was hardly the way to insure that the lower orders would remain in their places, content to be led by "other" sages above them. If the late Ming call upon textual authority resulted in a reassertion of the power of *wen* for the few in the short run, the evidential mastery of text presaged enormous possibilities for the many who would eventually learn to read.

Once evidential method is seen as a mode of articulating an ongoing traditional discourse on sagehood with the problem of nouveau literacy, new possibilities for interpretation arise. At the very least, the eighteenth century can no longer by seen as the "graveyard of the promising intellectual trends toward a modern sensibility," in Quinton Priest's fine, ironic formulation (1986: 27). Instead, it can be argued that by that time the roots of a modern sensibility (precisely, a Chinese modern sensibility) about education, intellection, the self, and the state had been laid.[14]

Re-membering the Past: Throne and Literati

The discourses of *wen,* whether concerning writing, painting, building, or ritual performance, continuously elaborated an interlocking set of practices designed to situate subjectivity at the mediating center, capable of elaborating distinctions. The examination system was only the most obvious institutionalization of *wen.* This study has shown, I hope, that participation in text/performance through rituals of sacrifice lay at the heart of the imperial effort to produce and control both meaning and the subjects who would interpret that meaning. The real audience for these text/performances was the literati themselves.

Of course, this effort was doomed to only partial success. Even as they participated in the emperor's editing projects, and as they concocted their own, evidential ritualists formulated new rules for constituting textuality that, in a historical sense, robbed language of its heretofore ideal usefulness in providing cosmic resonance and control. As they worked within the ritualist metaphysics, they simultaneously undermined it. This process began in the late Ming and culminated in the late Qing.

By the mid-eighteenth century, the ideal "resonant" relationship of words (signs) and things (signified) had begun crumbling at two levels: within scholarship itself and in the relationship of scholars to their work. Within scholarship, philological studies proved again and again that texts were internally inconsistent and mutually contradictory, especially in describing the chronological sequence of past events. The promise of resonance and control was withdrawn at the level of individual event in the text by the declaration that many classics were forgeries. A "transparency" of language that should have allowed the sagely person to "correct the names" (*zhengming*) and bring language and its referents into perfect alignment darkened into opacity.

These new readings did not, however (and contrary to the triumphalist interpretations of various twentieth-century scholars), lead directly to liberation from tradition into modern science. On the contrary, among ritualists, this newfound suspicion that texts were wrong about specific *event* resulted in the expense of enormous effort to recover *structure*. They studied institutions (*zhidu*) of the past through philological analysis and then sought to reproduce them in the present through ritual practice. Disappointment and dis-ease with reading, with textual description of past reality, pushed ritualists to a final attempt at re-institutionalizing a revived ritualist metaphysics in physical performance. Anxiety at failed inscription drove them to incorporate new inscriptions through *li* in ritualization. But this effort to continue the suppression of difference at the level of sign and signified generated tremendous tension expressed socially by obsession with control of textuality.

Foucault's self-reflexive inclusion of theorization itself as constitutive of power/knowledge helps to make sense of this intricate dance (the long-promised third area in which his approach is useful). The "ritualizations" that occasioned and molded subjectivities in terms of action within space were only one part of *li*. Thus, *li* was not "ritual" in the way we usually think of ritual—a simple bodily performance—rather it contained "ritualization" à la Bourdieu's habitus as one of its most volatile and valuable areas of discursive construction and domination. *Li* as discourse sought to encompass and control all such potent activity from how to dress, build a house, eat, and entertain guests to how to venerate ancestors. It did so by claiming the right to award classificatory power to certain positions and practices. Literati consecrated their abilities according to the discursive rules of *li* itself by "ritualizing" their own writing and record-keeping—calligraphy, editing and studying, the myriad ways the imperium employed texts as ritual artifacts. By subjecting themselves to the same micro-ritualizing disciplines arranged in spatio-temporal logics homologous to other ceremonial, their own agency disappeared in their labor to make the emperor visible.

Meanwhile, the old promise of resonance, and thus control of language, and thus of action, was not to be permanently restored at the level of collective institutionalization either. The relationship of scholars to textuality had shifted too far. By the end of the eighteenth century, it was careful scholarship that gave the right to pronounce upon ritual power and not ritual power that bestowed the right to scholarly authority. In other words, having made visible the ritual past, they returned it inexorably and finally to history, destroying the necessary fore-gotten roots of the ritualized body in the present. There was no way to reverse this inversion—and appeals to sacred imperial *li* would not, eventually, save the authority of the monarchy or, arguably, themselves as its perceived appendage.

In his essay "The Teaching of the Rites," written in 1788, Zhang Xuecheng

describes the double bind of the literati ritualist very well: "In ritual the temporal context is paramount. . . . You should honor the institutions of the rulers
of your own time."[15] Eighteenth-century scholars surely honored the institutions
of their time. They won a possibility of intellectual independence from the
throne through their new appreciation of achieving sageliness through editing
and philology. However, their enthusiastic interest in kingly *li* embedded in the
founding moment of this consciousness the seeds of a profound connection to
the nascent state. Modern intellectuals are surely heirs to this complex set of
contradictions. Their twentieth-century vicissitudes bear witness to the difficulties they have faced in articulating boundaries between the state and themselves as a class.

Motivated by the Palpably "Invisible": Form in Sacrifice

Text and performance of Grand Sacrifice shared not only common themes but
also common logics and organization whereby they presented those themes for
practice. The logic of encompassment whereby things were included in an order
of hierarchy was the most salient aspect. Texts were edited to formally emblem-
atize this process, which would then be concretized in three-dimensional people
and things on the altars.

Here we find the final and most intimate framework within which boundaries
were inscribed and controlled: upon the bodies of participants. In the Period of
Preparation, the spatial polarity of inner and outer was mobilized. People, vessels, and victims were defined as homologous because of their position in this
hierarchy, and then their nature as boundaries, sites of cosmic signification, was
manifested through attention to their inner and outer states.

In the performance of the ceremony in its phase of movement, the hierarchy
of people and things was organized through the polarity of upper and lower as
they moved up and down on the stairs of the tiered altar. The imperial act of
"centering" oppositions that had been heretofore materialized as inner/outer
and upper/lower involved overidentification with the superior, upper element.
In the case of sacrifice, this meant the ancestors, Heaven and the emperor himself. The uneven valuation of the interior over the exterior and of the high over
the low was thus enacted in rites of sacrifice. Its bodily gestures, its chosen
objects, were felt as always already appropriate ("forgotten" in the sense of
"fore-gotten"), and thus merely "discovered" and never admitted as wholly "invented." The imperial pinnacle of the complex *li* of filiality connected a sense

of perfectly integrating the simplest categories of bodily orientation, inner/outer and upper/lower, to the most far-reaching of cosmic truths and, of course, the grandest of ruling ambitions.

For eighteenth-century Chinese ritualists, human intervention in cosmic process depended upon an ability to provide the site for knowledge to emerge as ordered pattern from chaos. Various discourses of painting, ritual, and medicine shared this underlying "principle of thirdness" and conceived of the site of emergent knowledge as an ever-shifting, humanly created boundary. Their metaphors for this site were two-dimensional, those of the surface, (*mian,* in its social sense of "face"), the woven web (*jing,* the classics), the network (*mo,* arteries and veins of calligraphy and body energetics), or the vessel (*qi,* center of sacrifice).

Thus in eighteenth-century China, boundaries and interfaces were highly charged, highly significant, and uniquely human creations. These interfaces were always dynamic, enacted, and controlled in transgression and transit. In this episteme of boundary and surface, agency and subjecthood belonged to those who could discern the cosmic patterns of *wen,* in other words, those who were both literate *and* capable of performing *li,* those mobilizing the (masculinist) body of yang power. As a means of further understanding this masculinist position, I would like to return briefly to issues of gender.[16]

Here we might examine the ritualizations within *li* of spatial seclusion practiced upon the bodies of women as distinctions performed into being upon the flesh of those most often occupying the yin position of completer.[17] But we must do so remembering Foucault's (1982) important point that power can never be reduced to mere coercion, and that in fact freedom of some sort is one of the preconditions and supports of power.[18]

Feet broken and wrapped in ten feet of white silk reiterated more intimately in skin and bone a boundary already visible as walls. Women performed these rituals of bodily boundary discipline upon their daughters so that they might successfully marry and bear sons.[19] Women sacrificed themselves *for* their sons, who would themselves become centerers in performing ancestral sacrificial ritualizations. A feminine gesture of bounding performed by a yang mother upon a yin daughter is in turn eventually encompassed by the daughter's son's text/performance. His act of encompassment is more complete. How is this concretely so in terms of Grand Sacrifice? Is another sort of boundary being maintained between production and circulation?

The throne sought control in Grand Sacrifice over both the production of persons and the circulation of meaning in the discourses of *wen* and *xiao* as text/performance. In its performance aspect, the imperium enacted the production of *xiao* (filiality) in the imperial round of ritual, especially sacrifice. But it also sought to extend its modeling of *xiao* through formal textual specification of homologous ancestral veneration practices for the bodies of loyal subjects throughout the realm in the intimacy of domestic space. Furthermore, in its sanction of the circulation of authoritative handbooks, it encouraged emulation of the throne in the act of script production as well.

We might then be tempted to take a pessimistic view of women as doubly negated. Rarely literate, they could only approximate the fulfillment of filial duty due to their own ancestors, whom they left behind to join another family. Yet they were necessary to this particular discursive production in dauntingly material ways. They wove the silk upon which men wrote and bore the sons who venerated their husbands. These disciplined relinquishments of mobility, of participation in circulation, insured and justified the control of their pro-duced value. But it is important to note that "discipline" has a very Foucauldian ring. In this case it also denotes a kind of participation, a learning of a skill and the knowledge of a position—the skill of being feminine, of embodying a cer-tain and necessarily absolutely (if shifting) different place within the whole. In-deed, recent discussion of women's poetry in the late Qing shows that despite efforts to allocate writing to yang maleness, women continued their literary production (Robertson 1992: 64; Mann 1991: 56).

The circumstances under which they did so were, however, very telling in terms of the logic of *li* and ritualization I am proposing. Their participation in adult sociality, and thus *li,* first of all meant endless performance in the intricate round of the disciplined female life of footbinding, marriage, childbearing, and domestic labor. By confining yin-positioned women physically into demarcated gendered walled spaces, men created an encompassing totality of yang = male = whole, and reserved praxis for themselves, assuming that women would ideally only enact the scripts they prepared. And it was true that women rarely participated in the expressive practices of writing, building, and ceremonial that constituted *wen,* cosmic text-pattern. Thus they rarely achieved the centering of a praxis that combined text and performance in the terms laid out in Grand Sacrifice.

When women did write poetry, according to Maureen Robertson, they often did so in voices that internalized the masculine position (1992: 68). In other words, taking up the yang position often entailed speaking in a masculine voice.

Conversely, when men wrote from the yin position, they ventriloquized a woman's voice, producing a voyeuristic subject of "passive, narcissistic women, [and] romanticized suffering" (69). Thus, in writing poetry, gendered reversibility of voice was quite common. Yet encompassment of yin-positioned women deprived of the opportunity to "center" continued, perhaps aided and abetted by the masculine "theft" of their voice, another form of encompassment.

Robertson points out that pre-seventeenth-century women who left literary legacies were "all courtesans, entertainers, Daoist women, people living outside the family context," where their writings could circulate. "The social circulation of these women was analogous to the free circulation of their writings; both were transgressive and were equated with sexual promiscuity" (73). Later, women developed a literary culture "almost entirely within the domestic setting" (101). Women could write provided they remained bound to home and family, reinscribing the boundary between production of persons (*xiao*) and circulation of meaning (*wen*). In other words, either they *or* their writing circulated, *never both*. Foucault's nuanced treatment of the complex interplay of bodily performances and the classificatory practices that seek to shape them should prove very useful in sorting out these very complicated issues of gender and power.

Granting *li* its full sophistication means thinking of it as a discourse that sought not only to model perfect praxis but also to designate which subject positions would be excluded from the possibility of full participation. We watch our "object," Chinese social experience as recorded in artifacts and texts, dissolve into complex, reflexively constructed processes. As cultural historians we may have to approach categories like "gender" in a wholly new fashion. The reflexively constructed processes of social life that form the object of cultural history must be accounted for upon two levels: as description of that life (the positivist level) and as the thoughtful and material processes that generated such description (the discursive level). Folded within the "facts" of social life are the myriad local theorizations that guided their production. Overlooking this component of our "object" truly robs its creators of *their* subjectivity and allows the construction of an exclusive history wherein we produce theory and our informants produce data. (We think, they act; we observe in the audience taking notes while they ritualize.) Such "objectivizing" methods subject *li* and its practitioners to an encompassment analogous to the way the body of yang power sought to relegate those in yin positions to endless performance, necessary to the project but never quite as perfect as our thinking selves.

The Chinese politics of surface and boundary remains to be written, but it will surely look different from our politics of subject/object—perhaps an algebra of positions rather than a geometry of solids. We have had a glimpse of its profound connective power, extensible from imperially sponsored, "high" cultural activities like painting and editing, through sacrifice ritual, to "low" everyday social interaction. But we still do not know its rules of exclusion, its negativities, the ways in which it coerced people in their everyday life.

Notes

Prologue

1. I saw three of these volumes: one each for QL 21 and 22, and one for QL 59.10–62.11). No one at the archive could say if they were missing or simply never recorded for each year (*Neige gexiang dangbo dengji* 155/4–16.5: no. 1819 for QL 59.10–62.11; no. 1898 for QL 22; no. 1905 for QL 21). My tutor, Zhu Jiajin, tells me they were recorded.

2. See Wang Yunying 1985: 114 for an illustration of this cap.

3. Chinese recognition of what a modern Marxist would call the dialectical workings of thinking and doing have been noticed before and arguably provided a resource for rendering plausible and meaningful the twentieth-century institutionalization of state Marxism.

Introduction

1. The word "imperium" is defined as "imperial sovereignty or empire" and does not usually refer to people. However, as I hope to make clear in this study, participation in the various phases of imperial ritual was designed to cast officials as a portion of the imperial whole, a living extension of imperial power. This study, therefore, approaches that power from a different angle than the one implicit in studies of Chinese "bureaucracy," acknowledging that issues of sovereignty for traditional empires differed from those for the modern nation state. Use of the anachronistic term "bureaucracy" to refer to non-Western imperial formations posits an unsuitable model of behavior based upon

the categories of nineteenth-century social scientific rationality. See Tambiah 1985: 252–86; Inden 1992; and S. H. Rudolf's idea of "ritual sovereignty" (1987: 731–46).

2. I use the word "sacrifice" to translate *jisi.* In ritual matters English lacks the lexical fineness of Chinese. While certain elements of the ceremony recall sacrifice as it has appeared in anthropological description (see especially Henri Hubert and Marcel Mauss, *Sacrifice* [1964]), the fit is not perfect. In their analysis, they generalized the Judaic sacrificial model to the Vedic to show fundamentally disparate realms occasionally connecting, but Chinese imperial rituals manifest a link between people and spirits or ancestors thought to be always there, merely invisible in daily life.

The character *ji* consists of two hands above a graph whose early meaning was "omen" and whose later usages center upon ideas of showing, manifesting, and displaying. The etymology of the character *si* is unknown (Karlgren 1957: 255). The two were linked as the compound *jisi* in reference to "all sacrifices, major and minor" by Eastern Zhou times (Bilsky 1975: 1:25).

Bilsky sidesteps the issue of meaning, calling everything he discusses "sacrifice" in English while providing careful analyses of the changing usages of various terms throughout the Han and pre-Han periods (1:233–39). I too use the term "sacrifice" here although perhaps "display" would be a translation less burdened by misplaced analogy.

3. The main source for the study is the ritual manual *Da Qing tongli* (Complete rites of the Qing) (chief compiler Lai Bao; commissioned by the Qianlong emperor in the first year of his reign, 1736; completed in 1756: 50 *juan*). A second edition was commissioned in 1819 (chief compiler Mukodengo). It gained four *juan,* one in the first section, *jili* (auspicious rites), and three in the second section, *jiali* (felicitous rites). This edition was completed in 1824. I use three editions here: a reprint of the 1756, 50-*juan* original, contained in the *SKQSWYG* vol. 655; an 1824 woodblock edition of the 1824 re-editing; and an 1883 woodblock reprint of that 1824 edition. For a complete discussion of the texts involved in the study, see chapter 6 below.

4. See Bell 1992 for an extended discussion of "ritualization" not as the enactment of preexisting beliefs but as the provision of a setting that allows for the enforcement of certain social relations and cognitive possibilities while excluding others.

5. In his work on imperial ritual in the Tang, Harold Wechsler notes in passing, "Patterns of communication themselves represent a type of ritual." On discussion of ritual precedent, he says, "The litany of argumentation itself became fixed, forming an integral and indispensable part of the ritual process." He did not pursue the question, however (Wechsler 1985: 264, 131).

6. I will return to this fascinating and highly speculative point in my conclusion rather in the spirit of Philip Kuhn's oblique remarks connecting political style and bureaucratic management under the Qianlong emperor to bitter factionalism in twentieth-century politics (1990: 232).

7. Because of its scope, this aspect of the problem will have to stand as a constant referent to be held in mind. I hope in another book to explore the problem of filiality

in a popular context. In the meantime, readers can consult the important contributions on precisely these issues made by Ebrey (1991a; 1991b) and Chow (1994).

8. See Ebrey's extensive work on *Chu Hsi's Family Rituals* (1991b), which she translated and then contextualized in *Confucianism and Family Rituals in Imperial China: A Social History of Writing about Rites* (1991a). She notes that the *Comprehensive Rites* (*DQTL*), the Qianlong imperial manual for the performance of the five rites, was regularly referred to by Ren Rohai in his 1842 *Sili congyi* (Following what is appropriate in the four rituals). Ren would have left out information for actually performing the imperial rites of sacrifice, while basing the household forms upon the imperial model (Ebrey 1991b: 197, n. 40).

9. See Judovitz 1988, Reiss 1982, and Barker 1984 for historical discussions of the problem in Europe. See Mitchell 1991 and Hevia 1995a, 1995b for application of this "doubt" in cross-cultural historical study.

10. This preoccupation with form grows out of my encounter with structuralism, especially a reading in Marx that emphasizes his own interest in "forms," e.g., the "money form" or the "commodity form" (Johnson 1986: 44). Thus I deeply agree with Richard Johnson's defense of the study of form with which I opened this introduction.

11. For an introduction to the problem of subjectification and subject positionality in China, see the introduction in Zito and Barlow 1994.

12. As Barlow has put it, a protocol is "neither a mere code nor a map, nor a 'role.' It rests on a shifting foundation, the cosmic activity of yin and yang, yet it provides advice and counsel on achieving naturalized, normative, gendered relational subjects" (1994: 261).

Chapter 1

1. In pointing to "problems of authenticity," Vinograd touches upon an important general eighteenth-century cultural motif. But the throne also undoubtedly found these portraits to be positively productive.

2. The Frankfurt school of neo-Marxists reopened the discussion of the relation of base to superstructure in the face of mass society and increasing commodification. See Jay 1973 for an introduction. Italy produced Marxists like Labriola (1980), who retheorized "materialism" as inclusive of cultural production, and Gramsci (1992), whose theory of hegemony became extremely influential in British cultural studies.

3. On signification, Henriques et al. say: "The use of the term 'signification,' and what Kristeva has called 'signifying practices,' attempts to go beyond the language-thought dualism and the linguistic concept of language. . . . [It] is not that words determine but that those practices which constitute our everyday lives are produced and reproduced as an integral part of the production of signs and signifying systems" (1984: 99).

4. Foucault's work presents a genealogy of the "modern" and European subject. He mentions the European monarchical past in both *Discipline and Punish* and *The Order of*

Things, but utterly neglects discussion of Europe's colonizing projects and contacts with other peoples. Some may wish to read his arguments about power/knowledge only as historical description of their time and place—in France, monarchy disappears and modernity begins. Although the relationship of monarchy to modernity differs in China, I feel that some of Foucault's micromethod is useful.

5. For example, Foucault's project on bio-power provides a genealogy of how modern European discourses of power and control coalesced around the body itself, coercing it within definitions and concrete practices that bind by virtue of their very invisibility. Supposedly grown out of the "natural" order of things, Foucault delineates how the discourses upon discipline and sex have themselves helped produce the order of things modern (Dreyfus and Rabinow 1982: 111–14, passim).

6. In their seminal book, Corrigan and Sayer write of such an approach to those who rule: "Their political power lies rather in the routine regulative functioning of state forms themselves, in their day-to-day enforcing, as much as by what they are as in any particular policies they carry out, of a particular social order as 'normality,' the boundaries of the possible" (1989: 203).

7. On the emperor's ego, see Jonathan Spence, who calls him "a man who has been praised too much and has thought too little . . . who has played to the gallery in public life, mistaken grandeur for substance, sought confirmation and support for even routine actions" (1990: 101).

8. At the risk of being accused of intrusive matchmaking where neither party would even wish to be invited to the wedding, I think that a critical Marxist language of reification can be fruitfully married to Foucault's idea of the discursive object if we distinguish levels of its analysis. Foucault operated at the level of critical social analysis, criticizing the usual Marxist assumption that discourse and the "real" were ontologically separable (the notion of "false consciousness"). But at the level of the everyday, a discursive object acquires for those who live with it the status of "thing."

9. Williams 1977: 109–11. As originally theorized by Antonio Gramsci, "hegemony" arguably preserves a keener sense of resistance and difference than Foucault's "power/ knowledge."

10. For discussion of the Manchu conquest, see Wakeman 1985. Gertrude Roth Li reminds us that the concept of "Manchu-Chinese equality was part of the Manchu's concept of the *doro* or *gurun-i doro,* the guiding principles for ruling the country, and written into the Khan's laws" (1975: 137). The concept shaped the early examinations for the imperial service, which began in 1629 and were open to all. But "discussions on the matter of recruitment of officials after 1632 are couched entirely in Chinese terms" (146). By 1638 the examinations were closed to slaves. On a predominance in preconquest Manchu life of "oral tradition," shamanic ritual, and clan customs, see Crossley 1987: 761 and note 11.

I recognize that this contrast between hierarchy and egalitarianism can only be taken as relative, as naming a difference between Han sedentary and steppe nomadic peoples that they themselves construed in multiple ways. It could also be argued that the mystique of nomadic egalitarianism is a projection of Western desire. For a fascinating continuation of this trope, see Deleuze and Guattari 1987, the essay entitled "Treatise on Nomadology: The War Machine."

11. Mark Elliott notes that the axis of division to emerge after 1644 was that of center and periphery, especially in the relations between the capital and provincial Manchu banner garrisons, and between intramural and frontier areas (1993: 32).

12. Anderson 1983: 25–26. In *K'ang-hsi and the Consolidation of Qing Rule, 1661–1684,* Lawrence Kessler provides the contrasting and prevailing view of Manchu state-building by referring to Weber's theory of "rationalization of rule." Nurhaci's charismatic rule developed into a feudal confederacy of Manchu and Mongol tribes, and this in turn became a more centralized and feudal state, finally ending up as a "bureaucratically managed state along traditional Chinese Imperial lines" (1971: 6). Here the Manchus are thought to recapitulate a general model for world development that owes as much to Marx as it does to Weber. A representative Chinese Marxist view of the question is found in Zheng Tianting 1980b.

13. On the banner system, see especially Meng Sen 1980; Wakeman 1985: 1: 53–55, 200–201; Hsu 1970: 22; Farquhar 1971: 13–15; Crossley 1990; and of course Elliott 1993.

14. See Farquhar 1978: 33; Snellgrove and Richardson 1980: 184; Wakeman 1985: 203; Hevia 1993; Zito 1995.

15. Farquhar 1968: 199; Arthur W. Hummel, *Eminent Chinese of the Ch'ing Period* (1975: 596, hereafter cited as *ECCP*).

16. Two Western scholars lay out the Manchu-Mongol contest over this story. According to Bawden, this detail is "a Manchu tradition legitimating its succession to the inheritance of Ghenghis Khan. Mongol popular tradition denies the seal ever came into the possession of the Manchus at all. The relics of Ghenghis which Ligdan had carried off were returned to Ordos" (1989: 47).

Elliott (1993: 4), however, states that the imperial seal of Chingghis (*sic*) was presented to Hong Taiji by the widow of Ligdan. He cites a Chinese source (Tie and Wang 1987).

17. Wakeman 1975: 78; Kessler 1971: 8; for instance, the nature of senior *beile* Amin's opposition—wanting his own fief, wanting booty, refusing orders—indicates that he felt that Hung Taiji was just one of the four senior *beile* and should rule with them collectively. He did not want to be Khan himself but attacked the notion of empire (Roth Li 1975: 44–50).

18. Farquhar 1971: 19. Zheng Tianting notes the differences between the funerals of Nurhaci and Hung Taiji (1980a: 73). Roth Li points out that Nurhaci unwittingly laid "the institutional ground for an autocratic emperor and not collective leadership through such measures as sumptuary laws and the even division of booty" (1975: 54–55).

19. Kessler 1971: 9–10. Some scholars have referred to this shift toward hierarchy as "bureaucratization"; see ibid.; Pei Huang 1974: 168–84. Wakeman calls it a change from feudal to patrimonial power (1975: 78). The use of the term "bureaucratic" for the Qing period strikes me as anachronistic. It skews our sense of the epoch and calls forth all sorts of misplaced analogies to an implied rationality that is firstly modern and secondly west European in its cultural imperatives.

20. Nurhaci and Hung Taiji were both assiduous in cultivating Chinese defectors. Among the more famous advisers in the *wen* aspect of kingship (as opposed to the *wu* or military men who joined the Manchu armies) were: Fan Wenchong (1597–1666), a native of the Mukden region who surrendered in 1618 and advised Hung Taiji on the shadow government founded at Mukden (*ECCP* 231); Ning Wanwo (d. 1665) another native of Liaodong, served in the Literary Office and fixed the rules for rank and costume for the Six Ministries (*ECCP* 592; Xiao 1963: 1:226). Ironically, the most important adviser to Hung Taiji on "sinification" (or *hanhua*) was a Manchu, Sahaliyen (d. 1636). Although he started as a soldier, in 1631 he returned to Shenjing, the capital, were he was in charge of the Ministry of Rites for the five years until his death (Zheng Tianting 1980a: 65; *ECCP* 631).

21. Elliott has an interesting reading of this move: "The physical elevation of Hung Taiji for the first time during councils with other princes (his brothers) appropriately symbolized the elevation of the Manchu state in politically equal terms with the Ming" (1993: 4–5).

22. See Crossley 1990b; Elliott 1993. See also Zuo Buqing 1989: 32–37; Zeng Jiabao 1990.

23. Elliott points out that "in all Inner Asian regimes participation in the army was universal or nearly so, and not restricted to a certain military class, so that the military organization of the conquering people included all members of society. The banners thus embraced all Manchus; not just soldiers but men, women and children together" (1993: 9). It is the universality of the martial ideal for all Manchus I wish to emphasize: as Elliott notes, the Manchu *doro* or Way (a loan word from Chinese used after Qianlong's reign) consisted in precisely these aspects: shooting with bow and arrow; riding; living a frugal life; speaking Manchu.

24. This broader definition seems closer to past glosses upon the word, as in, for instance, the line from the "Xue er" chapter of the *Lunyu* (Analects): "When they have any energy to spare after the performance of moral duties, they should use it to study *wen*" (*Lunyu* 1:6). Both the Han commentator Zheng Xuan (127–200) and Song philosopher Zhu Xi (1130–1200) define *wen* as the "Arts of the Dao, rites or *li,* music, archery, chariot-driving, writing, and mathematics" (Chan 1963: 20).

25. In his study of the Qianlong reign, Harold Kahn admits that he did not attempt to calculate the amount of time allotted to "sacerdotal or ritual responsibility as over against administrative and political tasks," but suggests that it was "not inconsiderable." One must agree with his conclusion that a more precise work schedule of the emperor

needs to be made if "the true temper of the emperorship is to be more accurately gauged" but regret his easy splitting of the religious and the political (Kahn 1971: 216–17).

26. Food exchange and consumption is basic to the offerings of Auspicious sacrificial rites, and to the banquet, audience, and wedding rites in the Felicitous category. Military rites incorporated sacrifices to Heaven, Earth, the Ancestors, and the Altar of Soil and Grain (*DQTL* 1756: 40.1b). In Guest rituals tea was drunk, and banquets were supervised by the Court of Banqueting, *Guanglu si* (*DQTL* 1756: 43.2a). Internal references send us back to Auspicious banqueting forms (*DQTL* 1756: 43.3a) and the official who is hosting the guests is called a *zhuke siguan* (*DQTL* 1756: 43.6b). Finally Funeral rites features sacrificial offerings of food (*DQTL* 1756: 45.9b).

27. Wang Shuqing 1983: 61. The British ambassador sent to China in 1793–1794, Lord Macartney, records in his journal that "the emperor sent to us a variety of refreshments, all of which, as coming from his table, the etiquette of the Court required us to partake of, although we had dined but a short time before" (Cranmer-Byng 1963: 140). Likewise, John Bell's journal of the earlier Russian embassy of 1719–1722, at the end of Qianlong's grandfather's reign, records that they were presented with confections and a "large piece of excellent mutton. The Officer acquainted the ambassador that these provisions were brought from the emperor's own table; and therefore hoped he would eat of them. This circumstance was accounted a singular mark of favor" (1991: 129).

28. This theological logic could be called upon to criticize the inegalitarian failures of the merely human social institutions of the church. For the important and messy implications of this possibility of equality, see Bynum 1991 on the medieval women's ecstatic Eucharistic practices that challenged the male hierarchy of the church.

29. On polarity, see Hall and Ames 1987. Graham notes that yang-yin relations were not thought to function in the same way as the post-Cartesian dualistic binaries so constantly criticised by Derridean philosophy and deconstructed by postmodern literary critics. Since Graham's subtle argument depends upon his interpretation of Derrida, we can hardly do it justice here. But Graham notes that in pointing out Western philosophy's fascination for Being and Presence over Non-being and Absence, Derrida has sought to "reverse" this suppression by calling attention to its under-term. Graham thinks that such a strategy never works for yin-yang reversal, which moves logically to one extreme, only to rebound back through to the opposite pole, "smashing the dichotomy"—we might call it "centering" them (1990: 227–29). Graham's overall point, which ought to be stressed, is that the window of opportunity for a break into transcendence introduced with the Mohists in the classical period passed with the Han cosmological synthesis, as humanity re-embedded itself into a welcoming and powerful cosmos (1989: 313–19). The polar logic of this cosmos never split into binaries that would open up the possibility of a metaphysics of transcendence.

30. The quote is from *Record of Rites*, "Li Transforms," *Liji zhengyi* 22/2:1422. Por-

kert uses the image of the pivot to enrich our understanding of "centering" in terms of yin and yang: "The pivot is prerequisite to any turning movement yet does not participate in this movement. The pivot may therefore be conceived as a motionless center or as an organ that controls movement." Here, yin and yang are tripartite, not simply bipartite, imagined sharing a third term (Porkert 1974: 36–37).

31. For an excellent example of "centering" in philosophical terms, see Tu Weiming 1976. In his work on guest ritual, James Hevia has developed a model of action that focuses upon "centering" in a manner more closely related to Tu's interpretation of it as a "middle way" than to my own model of boundary-making and mediation (Hevia 1995b: passim).

32. Portions of this section have appeared as "Silk and Skin: Significant Boundaries" in Zito and Barlow 1994: 103–30.

33. For the effect upon China of the European depression of the 1620s, see Wakeman 1986: 1–26 and Atwell 1986: 223–44.

34. Details of Skinner's well-developed model of economic macroregions can be found in his "Regional Urbanization in Nineteenth-Century China" (1977: 211–49).

35. See Rawski 1985: 6–10 for a summary of her position that replacement of "direct controls over individuals by the indirect controls of the market" resulted in profound social change. Mark Elvin (1973: especially chaps. 15–16) describes the same process as culminating in the eighteenth century. See also Kuhn 1990: 30–48. Naquin and Rawski (1987) likewise use the extension of a market economy as a cornerstone of their book *Chinese Society in the Eighteenth Century.* Anthropologists, however, have continued against the automatic assumption that money "behaves" the same way in all cultural circumstances (Parry and Bloch 1989). And if we appreciate Marx's insight into money as a reified marker of specific social relations, it follows that we must understand those specific social relations in order to analyze the role of money.

36. See Berling 1985: 188–218 and Sakai 1970: 331–68 on ledger books for moral demerits. See also Brokaw 1991.

37. In this essay Cahill does not mention a possible influence through Buddhist iconographic traditions of depicting a deity's attributes. Later these attributes come to stand for the deity.

38. I am thinking of Jehol, where the realm was reproduced in miniature, including a small Potala after Lhasa's.

39. Francis Barker's extraordinary essay contrasting Jacobean conventions of representation and the body with the "disembodied Cartesian body" becomes directly relevant when he discusses the Jacobean king: "The figure of the king guarantees, as locus and source of power and as master signifier, a network of subsidiary relations which constitute the real practice and intelligibility of the lives of subjects. . . . The body of the king is the body that encompasses all mundane bodies within its build. . . . the social plenum *is* the body of the king, and membership in this plenum is the deep struc-

tural form in the secular realm. . . . this sovereignty achieves its domination . . . across an articulated but single ground" (1984: 31).

40. Hay 1983b: 89. Porkert calls *qi* "configurational energy" (1974: 167) and lists thirty-two kinds (167–76).

41. Bryson 1983: 89, 92. Bryson's work also provides an excellent summary of the emergence in European painting of the "optical theorization of the body" that reduces and simplifies the material, muscular body, continuous with physical reality. "This [new] body of perception is monocular, a single eye removed from the rest of the body and suspended in diagrammatic space." This "Cartesian self" is the implicit contrast to the construction of subject and sign I am proposing for eighteenth-century China.

42. There is a version even earlier than Ni Zan's: I saw a slide in the Cornell Knight Slide Collection of an anonymous Song painting held in the Taipei Palace Museum Collection. Thus Qianlong was also imitating Ni Zan's *own* gesture to the past. The Ni Zan painting is reproduced in *Zhongguo zongdai minghua ji* 1965: 220. It also appears in Cahill 1982: 117. According to its seals, this painting was held by the Qianlong emperor. An even earlier version, minus the screen is by Qiu Ying in *Lidai renwu hua xuanji* 1959: no. 52.

43. Under the Qing, the situation was more complex because Beijing had two walls. The emperor lived in the inner city; the peasants outside the walls of the outer city. The altar was between the two areas, within the walls of the outer city, where Chinese members of the imperium and merchants lived.

44. See John Hay (1994) for his important essay on the role of clothing and its relation to the body.

45. Even the title of the *Huangchao liqi tushi* (Illustrations of dynastic ritual paraphernalia) reflects this homology of people in clothing and vessels. The word *qi* has usually been translated "vessel," but the volumes include clothing, carriages, and musical instruments besides.

46. Philip Kuhn shared this information with the Columbia Seminar on Modern China, New York, October 1984.

47. "*Li* provided the moments for sets of social and cosmological categories that were usually distinct to connect. It did so by identifying them in terms of higher-level principles that provided their transcendental ground. . . . Cults [like the City God] are modes of extending the reach of human agency, of garnering *ling,* the power inherent in the cosmic landscape for human purposes. The availability of such power depended upon 'centering' the cosmos, that is, mediating its contradictions" (Zito 1987: 349–50).

48. Girardot defines "face" as generically Confucian, that is, "the traditional Chinese ethical system that affirmed the importance of becoming fully human through social interaction." According to Girardot, Daoists rejected this idea of "face," seeking instead the "no-face" condition of Emperor Hundun of the Zhuangzi tale (1988: 259). Girardot

is correct in warning against an overly simplified distinction between Confucian and Daoist "face," and we must note instead that the concept of surface/boundary is crucial in both Daoist and Confucian thinking.

49. This double layer of face once again is uncannily described by Barker, speaking within the pre-Cartesian, Jacobean context: "The world achieves its depth not in the figure of interiority by which the concealed inside is of another quality from what is external, but by a *doubling of the surface*. . . . It functions to extend time rather than to excavate a hidden level of reality" (Barker 1984: 28–29; emphasis in original).

50. Ricoeur argues for a "positive" concept of ideology, saying that imagining ideology only as a distortion underestimates its true role in society and gives thinkers the illusion that they can stand outside its influence (1978a: 44–59).

Chapter 2

1. The argument that follows was first published in *positions: east asia cultures critique* 1, no. 2 (Fall 1993): 321–48.

2. I borrow this term from Catherine Bell's important study, *Ritual Theory, Ritual Practice* (1992).

3. For symbolic anthropologists like Clifford Geertz and especially David Schneider (students of Parsons), "culture" was conveyed by material and publicly accessible symbols (Geertz 1977). While this admirable emphasis upon the external finally saved American anthropology from earlier attempts to "get inside" informants' heads, it also harbored idealist tendencies best summed up by Geertz's much-discussed formulation that "culture is like a text" (1977: 30–33). And, we are left to assume, actors are like readers. What Geertzians have notoriously neglected is the "writing" aspect of culture as text: how the system is produced within social life. Structuralism's sins of reification are more widely known: denial of an intentional subject, neglect of history (Ortner 1984: 137–38).

4. Victor Turner (1969) stresses that symbols produce social transformations, and do not merely offer a representation to be "read." As Edward L. Schiefflin puts it:

Performance does not construct a symbolic reality in the manner of presenting an argument, description, or commentary. Rather, it does so by socially constructing a situation in which the participants experience symbolic meanings as part of the process of what they are already doing. (1985: 709)

For Stanley Tambiah, a performative theory of ritual serves most importantly to draw attention to a ritual's power to constitute a social reality, rather than merely mystify another, prior "real world" of "brute facts" (1985a: 155).

5. One of the most influential American texts is Wing-tsit Chan's *A Sourcebook in Chinese Philosophy* (1963: 14–15). See also Chan, "Introduction: The Humanistic Chi-

nese Mind," in Moore 1969: 1–10; Jochim 1986: 34. In China, Feng Youlan discusses *li* as external constraints (1959: 337–39).

6. Patricia Ebrey has noted the paucity of studies that actually explore the meaning of ceremonies (1991a: 5). See also note 8 below for institutional histories of *li*. Pamela Crossley seems to be calling for a belated return to this older functionalist reading of ritual when she discusses the "emperorship" as "an ensemble of instruments playing a dynamic role" that "itself can be interpreted as an organism" (1992: 1471).

7. I have always felt that twentieth-century writers on China missed Weber's point. He studied China out of a wish to sacralize a modern social phenomenon, which he called "bureaucracy," by drawing attention to social organizational forms in traditional society (which, as we have seen, were classified as "nonrational" in nineteenth-century typologies) that resembled it. His work on China and India was conceived as proof of his hypothesis in *The Protestant Ethic* that certain values were necessary to the rise of capitalism. China scholars have inverted his insight and relentlessly searched for the utilitarian and pragmatic ends of imperial institutions, never connecting these to the expressive *forms* that defined and carried through more limited goals such as social control or legitimacy.

8. For instance, for the Han, see Bielenstein 1979: 3–300. For the Sui, see Wright 1957: 71–104. For the Tang, see Wechsler 1985; McMullen 1987: 181–236. For the Song, see Liu 1964. For the Ming, see Ho Yun-yi 1976; Fisher 1990.

9. The bibliography on kingship is vast: those anthropological studies that have emphasized kingship as both a center for organizing specific societies and the challenge these differences bring to European discourse on and about monarchy include Valeri 1985; Sahlins 1985; and Inden 1990. For an extensive bibliography that centers on Africa, see Feeley-Harnick 1985.

10. Paul Rabinow states that "Unlike Aristotle, Descartes' conception of knowing rests on having correct representations in an internal space, the mind" (1986).

11. On separating the body from the mind, see essays in *Giving the Body its Due* (Sheets-Johnstone 1992), especially "The Bodily Nature of the Self or What Descartes Should Have Conceded Princess Elizabeth of Bohemia" by Albert Johnstone (16–47), and "The Human Body as Historical Body and Cultural Symptom" by Robert Romanshyn (159–79). On separating the actor from the world, see Bourdieu 1977; Bell 1992.

12. Space does not permit me to recapitulate debates over the relationship between *li* and "popular religion." Elsewhere I have discussed how homologies in ceremonial form link imperial sacrificial *li* and veneration of the City God (Zito 1987). For overviews and new approaches to the problem of elite/popular, see Bell 1989; DeBernardi 1992. See also Sangren 1984.

13. Ebrey 1991a: 188–219 and Chow 1994: 71–128 amply document the Qing obsession with the production of ritual knowledge at the local level.

14. Marxist critics of a Foucauldian approach feel that in encompassing such

breaches in order, a discursive approach stifles the possibility of change. I disagree—surely bringing resistance and opposition into the analytic frame allows us to understand precisely *how* change works, as an element of the humanly wrought social order. Thus we are free of relying upon factors beyond the reach of human planning, external catalysts that, ultimately, are metaphysical entities with magical effects (for example, "class struggle" or "the withering away of the state").

15. See papers from the panel on "Culture, State, and Person in the Making of Emperorship," Association of Asian Studies annual meetings, Washington, D.C., April 1995.

16. The recent collection *Imperial Rulership and Cultural Change in Traditional China* footnotes its definition of "culture" to the Random House Dictionary: "The sum total of ways of living built up by a group of human beings and transmitted from one generation to the next" (Brandauer and Huang, eds., 1994: xviii). Although the editor thinks that they operated with such a broad anthropological definition, it is clear from his introduction, and from the essays, that most writers had a much more constricted view of "culture" as not economic, not social, not psychological, etc.

17. On kinship positionality, see Barlow 1989: 12–15; Barlow 1994. See also Hamilton 1984.

18. In Wu Jingzi's mid-eighteenth-century novel *Rulin waishi* (The scholars), a veritable catalogue of bogus ceremonies, correct knowledge, frivolous displays clash to produce a lively picture of life within the discourses of *li*.

19. Ernst Kantorowicz's classic *The King's Two Bodies* opened the problem for institutional historians. A. M. Hocart's important *Kings and Councillors: An Essay in the Comparative Anatomy of Human Society* preceded it by two decades, bridging Europe and India in seeking a taxonomy of state "forms" in early monarchy. See also a number of useful essays in M. Feher, ed., *Zone: Fragments for a History of the Human Body*.

20. Even the early editions of Frazer's *The Golden Bough,* first published in 1890, explicitly linked the problem of the Divine King and his "death" in all societies to the question "Why did Jesus Christ have to be crucified to assure his followers of eternal salvation?" (Feeley-Harnick 1985: 273–75). Louis Marin (1988) discusses at great length the last gasp of so explicit an analogue between Christ crucified and Louis XIV.

21. A great deal more can be said on this fascinating transformation. Kantorowicz showed that the Tudor conception of the "King's two bodies," his body natural and body politic, was an example of the intertwined practices of medieval theologians, jurists, and political philosophers, who slowly untangled monarchy from religion. He sees this trend culminating in Dante (1957: 451–95). Roy Strong's (1973) discussion of Renaissance royal festivals and entertainments in courts all over Europe details how elements of religious pageantry were recontextualized in the service of new ideas of human-centered universal monarchy.

22. Louis Marin on the power of representation under Louis provides an excellent analysis of the origins of the modern power-effects of the media (1988: especially 3–15).

23. For a good discussion of the implications of the Mandate of Heaven and emperorship, see Wechsler 1985: 12–13.

24. Sarah Allan (1981) has produced excellent structural analyses of the variations of the legends on this theme. See also Ann Waltner's short discussion of the issue in relation to adoption (1990: 12).

25. That *wen* as "civilizing" should contain in this case the other two, as well as a miniature example of itself, presents a perfect example of the logic of hierarchy I have tried to show above: part-for-whole substitution.

26. Shenyang was established as the capital in 1625. Hung Taiji, however, was not unambivalent about the new Chinese model. He continued to recall the Jin dynasty of his Jurched forbears. In the same year, on December 9, Hung Taiji, now known as the Emperor Taizong in the record, exhorted his assembled kinsmen and officials to read the basic annals of the Jin and not abandon tribal customs (Wakeman 1985: 73, 207–8).

27. *Qingshi gao* (Draft History of the Qing 1976: 82.57/2486; 83.58/2503; hereafter cited as *QSG*); Xiao Yishan 1963: 1:175. Even so seemingly straightforward a compilation as this employs certain rhetorical strategies. Very often, the subject of a sentence is unstated as it is here. I supplied "the emperor," because in fact he is ultimately responsible for such actions. But it should be made clear that it does not appear in the text. We have an active sentence without a subject, difficult to translate into the English transitive mood. But putting the sentence into the passive (". . . the ground was measured . . .") in no way reflects the activity of "measuring, establishing, sacrificing, and changing." The Chinese text deliberately leaves out an active, human subject and thus empties that space of initiative, allowing for a displacement of earthly effort into a vague feeling of cosmic inevitability, a shifting of agency.

28. *QSG* 83.58/2516–17. During the Western Zhou period, the *sheji* altars of soil and grain were taken as the symbol of the polity. Each king sacrificed at the altar of soil of his own realm, itself defined as all that could be seen from that tumulus. A conquering king would cover the altars of his vanquished enemy, depriving them of the sustenance of positive/celestial yang forces (Tjan Tjo Som 1952: 384).

29. Kessler 1971: 12. Roth Li points out that each of these formalizations of central governance may have been connected to the Khan's problems with the senior *beile,* especially Amin in 1629, Mangulttai in 1630, and Daisan in 1635 (1975: 128–29).

30. See *DQTL* 1756: chap. 45. The term *gong* is usually translated as "tribute." For a redefining of the word as "precious things," see James Hevia's critique of the tribute system model in his "Guest Ritual and Interdomainal Relations in the Late Qing" (1986: 23–60; see also Hevia 1995b).

31. Another example of part-for-whole capturing of the whole Han-style hierarchy.

Chapter 3

1. Hereafter *Five Rites;* in references, *WLTK*.

2. Hereafter the *Library.*

3. Kai-wing Chow's recent study of "ritualism" in late imperial China presents a sophisticated version of this argument founded, I think, upon a conception of ritual as formulaic authoritarianism that ultimately stultifies morally responsible individual initiative and growth (1994: 211).

4. According to Susan Mann (Jones) it presented "a scholarly climate dominated by a few leading theorists and defined by the activities of the majority of employed scholars, all of whom engaged in some kind of textual research" (1975: 36).

5. Liang Qichao (1959: 47) influenced Hu Shih in perpetuating this thesis. For one example of what I feel is Hu Shih's misreading of evidential scholarship, see "The Scientific Spirit and Method in Chinese Philosophy" (1967). On the *Siku chuanshu* and literary censorship, see below.

6. Priest 1986: 27. Eighteenth-century painting has been judged to range from overly orthodox to work obsessed with inauthenticity and imposture (Vinograd 1992: 125–26). After the free-ranging fun in erotica of the seventeenth century, the heavy hand of imperial censorship turned eighteenth-century writing staid and formal (McMahon 1987: introd.). In short, nothing went culturally (read, morally) right in a time of supposed oppression and collaboration.

7. In 1995 the Institute for Qing Studies at People's University held a conference on the eighteenth century in China and the world. See Luo Ming 1986: 164 for a comparison of China and Europe at that time.

8. The pioneering work of Guy and Elman was tremendously helpful in formulating my own research on *Kaozheng* scholarship.

9. He has pointed out that the Song Cheng-Zhu school conceived of the dao in three aspects: its substance or being (*ti*); its function or action (*yong*); and the scriptural tradition or *wen* (Yu 1975: 118; 1977: 19–20). Through many shifts and starts over eight hundred years, it was finally the last aspect, the scriptural tradition, that became paramount in the eighteenth century as method for communing with the *dao* (Yu 1975: 123; 1970: 19–41).

10. Patricia Ebrey notes the spread of family sacrificial ritual from the Song onward through the editing and reprinting of Zhu Xi's famous *Jiali* (Family rituals) (1991a: 150–51). The early Qing saw a revival of interest in physical performance of *li,* according to Kai-wing Chow (1994: 38). See below for further discussion of this latter point.

11. Shaw 1983: 62. Xiao Yishan credits the Qianlong reign with ninety-four titles, some of them containing hundreds of volumes (1963: 2:32). See also Guy 1987: 323.

12. See Shaw 1983: 63 for the establishment of the Office for Publication of the Three Comprehensive Encyclopedias during the Qianlong period. Here an imperially edited project emended and continued the original (three) "*Santong,*" producing the fa-

mous (nine) "*Jiutong*" set of encyclopedias and encompassing what had been formerly classed as "privately edited" books. See Li Zongtong 1984: 129.

13. Guy makes the case that this role, while not altogether new, was elaborated far more intensively in the eighteenth century than ever before (1980: 35). Nivison also points out that Zhang Xuecheng felt that the state was the ally of the true historian; it preserved books, kept documents, and acted as a curb on incorrect writings (1966: 243). (Nivison's references to the state could be reread in our terms as "domain" or "imperium.")

14. See Benjamin Elman's pathbreaking work on this community. I agree completely with his thesis that, with the rise in number of degree holders in the eighteenth century, "holding a degree seldom guaranteed an official career. Scholarship, in many cases, filled a career vacuum that had not existed to this extent earlier" (1984: 96).

15. The term *li* is usually translated "Principle." In using "coherence," I follow Willard Peterson (1988), who argues most persuasively for this translation. He points out that pre-Han usages of *li* can be rendered "pattern" or "order," but that the semantic field of the term shifted by late Tang (14). Nonetheless, his choice of "coherence," which he defines as "the quality or characteristic of sticking together" nicely preserves a continuity with the pre-Han sense (14). At the same time, "coherence" expresses far better that cosmic immanence so crucial to understanding the ritualist metaphysics and does not trap us in transcendent terminology.

16. Guy 1980: 228–29, quoting Qian Daxin, "Xiaoxue kanxun," in *Qianyantang wenji* 24:15a. Guy's translation.

17. Derrida (1976) wishes to take up writing as notation of all sorts, freed from its enthrallment to speech. See especially chap. 1, "The End of Writing and the Beginning of the Book."

18. Robert Joseph Mahoney (1986) provides evidence in his thesis that the two wings of Song neo-Confucianism, the Cheng-Zhu School of Coherence, and the Lu-Wang School of Mind, did indeed differ on the forms that communication, learning, and education should take.

19. Elman states: "Agreement on the centrality of *li* became a cardinal point that united Han learning scholars throughout the Qing dynasty. Their emphasis on decorum and institutions was a direct reaction against what they considered the neo-Confucian misuse of *li* [coherence] for abstract and speculative studies (1984: 116). See also Ebrey 1991a; Chow 1994.

20. Yan Yuan, *Sishu zhengwu* (Correction of errors in the Four Books) 1.2b, in *Yanli congshu* I/47. Quoted in Elman 1980: 107.

21. His *Zhouguan bianfei* (Demonstrations that the Rituals of Zhou are inauthentic) concluded it was not the work of the Duke of Zhou (Elman 1984: 116).

22. Guy 1987: 46. On the influence of Hui Dong on Yangzhou scholarship, see Elman 1984: 123.

23. *Guochao xianzheng shilue* (Short summaries of worthies of the dynasty), woodblock edition, n.d., 17.27b.

24. Guy 1984: 34–37. I here amend his translations.

25. On imperial book collecting projects, see Guy 1984: 10–16.

26. Later nineteenth-century sacrificial handbooks were in fact based on the *Comprehensive Rites* and the *Assembled Canons*. For an interesting example of one edited in the wake of the Taiping Rebellion, see Xu Yangda 1871.

27. Under history we will consult the *Da Qing tongli* (Comprehensive Rites of the Qing), chief compiler Lai Bao, commissioned in Qianlong 1, 1736, completed in 1756, 50 *juan*. This edition is collected in the *SKQS,* and reprinted in *SKQS* Zhenben series eight, vols. 125–29. A second edition was commissioned in 1819, chief compiler Mukodengo. It gained four *juan,* one in "Auspicious Rites" and three in "Felicitous Rites," and was completed in 1824. I also use an 1883 woodblock reprint of the 1824 re-editing. Under "history" I will also consult the *Huangchao liqi tushi,* in the *SKQS* Zhenben series six, vols. 122–29 (hereafter cited as *LQTS*). Finally, also the *Da Qing huidian,* Qianlong edition, 1763; Guangxu edition 1899 (hereafter cited as *HD*); *Da Qing huidian zeli,* Qianlong edition, 1763; Guangxu edition, 1899 (hereafter cited as *HDZL*).

28. Under classics we will consult in detail the *Liji zhengyi* (Verification of meanings in the Record of Rites) (hereafter cited as *LJZY*), edited by Ruan Yuan (1764–1849), and the *Liji yishu* (Analysis of the meanings of the Record of Rites) volume of the *Qinding sanli yishu* (Imperial edition of the analysis of the meanings of the three rites), printed in 1748 in eighty-three chapters (hereafter cited as *LJYS*), in *SKQSWYG* 124–23. I have here used the 1984 photo reprint of the Wenyigo edition, a complete copy of the first edition of the *Library* produced in 1782 for storage in the Wenyigo, a building built for this purpose in the Forbidden City. It contains 79,931 chapters. Under classics we will also examine the *Wuli tongkao* (Comprehensive investigation of the Five Rites), edited by Qin Huitian (1761).

29. Mote (1987) has pointed out the pitfalls of relying only upon *Library* editions of texts; an incomplete understanding of their editing process prevents modern scholars from knowing if and how originals were changed. But since my point was to discover how ritual was conceptualized in relation to the imperium, the categories employed within the *Library* itself became a source.

30. This system was first used when Xun Zhu and Zheng Hua catalogued the Imperial collection of the Jin dynasty (265–313). Their fourfold division replaced an older system of seven (or six) categories that had come down from the earliest known bibliography compiled by Liu Xiang and his son Liu Xin by order of emperor Han Chengdi in 25 B.C.E. That now-lost essay on principles of classification included the classics and works on epigraphy and phonology, philosophy, poetry, military strategy and calculating arts, and medicine and health. There was, however, no separate category for history. Annals of kings, as well as material on ritual, were filed under classics. See Wei Yingqi 1944: 17–19.

31. Within the very category of "classics," the editors embedded the treatises on the methodologies that would, like a series of time bombs, blow apart the category itself. Scholars were thoroughly investigating certain texts, using the methods outlined in the *xiaoxue* subsection. Some of their work was quietly included in the *Library*. See *SKQSZM* 1/1:101 for Yan Ruoju's work. Hu Wei's *Yitu mingbian* (Clarifying critique of the Diagram of the Changes), proving the cosmograms of *Changes* to be of Daoist provenance, was not included.

32. "In this category the government seemed to be calling attention to its own scholarly efforts: seventeen of fifty-five titles were Qing government sponsored compilations. Another four were recovered from the Ming Dynasty *Yongle dadian* (under imperial auspices)" (Guy 1987: 233).

33. Guy 1980: 231, 233. Judging from an overview of the texts, this may be so. However, from the headnote for the category *zhengshu*, one gathers that it was scholars who picked up the idea from examining private bibliographies. Unfortunately, these bibliographies are not identified. *SKQSZM* 82/1:693.

34. These consist, to name a few of the better known, of Du Yu's (735–812) *Tongdian* (Comprehensive Canon), 200 chapters; Ma Duanlin's (ca. 1370) *Wenxian tongkao* (Comprehensive investigations of writings), 348 chapters; the *Ming huidian* (Assembled canon of the Ming), completed 1497, and of course, various editions of the *Assembled Canon of the Qing.*

35. The modern historiographer Li Zongtong combines "canons" and "institutions" into one category when he remarks that "What people in the past called the 'canonical emblems and institutional standards' (*dianzhang zhidu*) can be summed up as *li*, or rites" (1984: 149).

36. In these meditations I have consulted Wei Yingqi 1944: passim; Li Zongtong 1984: 1–13, 27–35, 149–53; and Jin Yubi 1962: 116–20.

37. A later writer, Jiang Xun (1763–1820), posited that the *Assembled Canon* was to the *Rites of Zhou* as the *Comprehensive Rites* was to the *Ceremonial Rites* (*Yili*). Unfortunately, this analogy does little to clarify their conceptual relationship because the question of which was the more fundamental (*ben*) text, the *Rites of Zhou* or the *Ceremonial Rites*, had vexed scholars since the Tang (Jiang Xun, n.d., although internal evidence suggests early twentieth century).

38. They include the Tang dynasty *Da Tang kaiyuan li* (Rituals of the Kaiyuan reign period), 150 chapters, produced between 726 and 732; the Song dynasty *Zhengho wuli xinyi* (A new explanation of the Five Rites in the Zhengho period), 220 chapters, produced between 1111 and 1120; the *Da Jin jili* (Collected rites of the Jin Dynasty), 40 chapters, dating between 1128 and 1234; and the *Ming jili* (Collected rites of the Ming), 53 chapters, dated 1369. This last is the exception to the rule I am inducing—it is arranged topically, like a *huidian*. However, the fact that Qing editors skipped it as an explicit example and turned to the *Kaiyuanli*, with its narrative structure, would seem to confirm my point.

39. *DQTL* 1756: *fanlie,* point 6. The *Da Tang Kaiyuan li* provided a self-consciously chosen model for the *Comprehensive Rites* precisely because it preserved a narration of each rite "according to its self-so order" (*ge jiu ziran cixu*) (*DQTL* 1756: *fanlie,* point 3).

40. *DQTL* 1824: Original *fanlie,* point 6. For the shapes and sizes of vessels, carriages, clothing, etc., users are referred to *LQTS.*

41. A notion comparable to the elusive one I am trying to develop here comes from Evan Eisenberg. In his book *The Recording Angel: Explorations in Phonography,* he says: "A record is a sculpted block of time . . . carved from another time and place. . . . But a record of music does not record historical time. It records musical time which, though it exists in historical time, is not of it." Quoted in Hamilton 1987: 97.

42. For general discussion of Zhang's declaration that "the Six Classics are all histories," see Cang 1984: 101–30 and Nivison 1966: 202–203.

43. Quoted in Elman 1984: 31, his translation.

44. The quoted terms are from Elman 1984: 6, although he is reticent about drawing such direct connections between new methods of scholarship and a European-style scientific revolution. John Henderson (1984), however, is more willing to arrive at this dubious conclusion. See especially his section on "Progress of Science" (165–68).

45. Although Zhang's unusual and unpopular articulation of his positions may have made him seem eccentric, in thinking of the classics and histories as fundamentally the same, he is a true child of his age.

46. Nivison quotes Zhang Xuecheng on the classics: "The principles of Heaven and Man, nature and fate, are all contained in the Classics. *The Classics are not the words of any one man, and yet the basic principles in them always form a single whole* (1966: 161; emphasis added).

47. Zhang Xuecheng, writing in 1789, objected to the privatization of the *dao* of the classics by early Confucianists (Zhang 1985: "On the Dao" 10–12). See also Nivison 1966: 151.

48. Taken from a question he asked as examiner in Hunan in 1767 and quoted in Elman 1984: 72.

49. Nivison notes, "It had been rather traditional in Chinese historiography to regard words (edicts, memorials, literary pieces) and events (the actions of rulers or deeds of great men) as antithetical to one another" (1966: 224).

50. I follow Nivison's discussion of how classics were thought to indicate the *dao* of the "ought" (*dangran*), the moral imperative of principle that existed as a standard of value outside of history (Nivison 1966: 141–42).

51. As Robert Murphy sums it up, in social life "activity is sequential in time, continuous, and nonrepetitive; norms are timeless, discontinuous, repetitive, and one-dimensional. Norm and activity seldom meet, and there must always be strain between them. And the nature of man and his existence commonly convert the strain into discontinuity and contradiction" (1971: 242).

52. *Wuli tongkao* prefaces 1a–b/1–2; emphasis added. Lu Wenchao (1717–1796),

respected collator and evidential scholar, produced the definitive edition of the *Yili* in 1795 (*ECCP* 549–50). Lu Wenchao's preface also appears in his *Baojing tang wenji* (Collected writings from the Hall of Preservation of the Classics) 8.20a–21b/123–24.

53. On the importance of ritual in scholarship of the eighteenth century, see Elman 1984: 116; Guy 1987: 43–45; Zhang Shunwei 1962.

54. In her discussion of the publishing of women's writing, Dorothy Ko draws attention to this passion for making visible: "Visibility was the essence of the urban print culture and the monetary economy that sustained it. . . . The age of visual representation demanded that hidden words be exposed and novelties be projected in an exaggerated fashion" (Ko 1994: 65).

55. Both Elman and Henderson emphasize the rationalizing urge of evidential scholarship, and certainly the possibility of its contribution to social and intellectual shifts in the nineteenth and even the twentieth century (Elman 1984: 254–56; Henderson 1984: 230–39).

56. I must thank James Hevia for drawing my attention to this echo-like effect in Chicago in 1984.

57. See the "Jifa," chapter 49 of the *Record of Rites, LJZY* 49/2:1607.

58. *Da Tang kaiyuan li,* in *SKQSWYG* 646:19–896. For Sacrifice to Heaven, see *Da Tang Kaiyuan li* 4, *SKQSWYG* 646:67–77. There are only seven segments noted in the ritual text: they are Achieving Seclusion, Arranging and Standing, Inspection of Victims, Presenting of Jade and Silk, Proffering of Ripe and Cooked Foods, Returning to the Palace. The section "Proffering of Ripe and Cooked Foods" includes the Three Oblations, which received more marked attention in the Qing.

Chapter 4

1. Carney Fisher attacks the problem of the "Great Ritual Controversy" in the Ming, the struggle between the emperor and the majority of the imperial bureaucracy over posthumous designations and ceremonies for the royal family, by first delineating the Han and Song precedents in classics and commentaries (1990: 10–92, 230–45). Harold Wechsler contextualizes the foundation of Tang imperial ritual in terms of the differing significances that commentaries by two Han scholars, Zheng Xuan and Wang Su, had for the men of Tang (1985: 37–54).

2. I base my translation of the chapter title on a gloss by Ren Ming upon the word *yun,* often translated as "phase," as in the Five Phase (*wuxing*) theory. The idea is that the subcelestial realm will follow these phases and govern itself. *Yun* also carries a connotation of "transformation" and can be used as either a verb or noun, so that we could say "*Li* Transforms (other things)" or "The Transformations of *Li*" (Ren 1982: 23). This same chapter, with its mention of the *datong* or the utopian Great Harmony, was the inspiration for Kang Youwei's *Datong shu,* which in turn influenced Mao Zedong's ideal of the commune. For an explanation of the *Datong shu,* see Liang Qichao 1959; Wakeman 1973: 115–36.

3. The first entry in the *Library's General Catalogue* for the "Record of Rites" section is the *Liji zhengyi*. Its colophon quotes the history of the editing of the *Record of Rites* from the "Manuscript Essay" of the *Suishu*: "At the beginning of the Han, Prince Hexian found 131 chapters by Confucius's disciples and presented them at court. Later, Liu Xiang (died 9 B.C.E.) was collating and found those chapters and others totalling 214. The Elder Dai De reduced them to 85 in the *Da Dai Liji*. Dai Sheng further reduced this to 46 in the *Xiao Dai Liji*. Later Ma Rong (79–166) added three more for a total of 49" (*SKQSZM* 63/1:168).

4. All translations are my own unless stated otherwise, but readers can find an English translation of the chapter in Legge 1885: 2:364–93.

5. The Five Emperors include Zhuan Xu, who separated Heaven and Earth; Huang Di, who was traditionally thought of as the progenitor of the Chinese people; Di Ku; and Di Yao and Di Shun, who established the model of choosing the royal heir according to merit. The Three Sovereigns traditionally include Fu Xi, domesticator of animals and beginner of domestic life; Zhu Rong, inventor of fire; and Shen Nong, inventor of agriculture (Chang 1983: 2–3).

6. In this usage I follow John Henderson, who says "correlative thought . . . draws systematic correspondence among aspects of various orders of reality or realms of the cosmos such as the human body, the body politic, and heavenly bodies (1984: 1). I do not wish to imply that "correlative thought" was substantively singular and timeless. It was more a style of thinking that allowed for many possibilities and positions within itself, depending upon the circumstances of the thinker.

7. Dong Zhongshu has been described as the heir to the fusion of the theories of the Yin Yang Five Phases School with Mencian thought. The greatest New Text scholar of his day, he interpreted the classics of his time in light of these theories of correlation. Zheng Xuan incorporated much of Dong's work in his own sweeping commentary (Fan Wenlan 1979a: 307).

8. See Needham 1978: 1:154–55 for a table of selected correlations. For an explanation of Five Phases theory, see Needham 1954: 2:243–68; Porkert 1974: 43–54.

9. The five tones are *gong, shang, jiao, zhi,* and *yu.* See DeWoskin 1982: 43–45.

10. The six yang pitches were produced on the six upper pipes. There were also six lower pipes for a total of twelve (DeWoskin 1982: 46).

11. The five flavors are sour, bitter, salt, sweet, and pungent.

12. These are azure, scarlet, yellow, white, and black.

13. There has been controversy over whether a person named Laozi ever existed. In the 1920s and 1930s there was general agreement on a date between the third and fourth centuries B.C.E. (Chan 1963: 138). Zhuangzi lived ca. 399–295 B.C.E.

14. The rise of Chan has been dated by historians from the reign of Song emperor Hongren, 601–674, although tradition dates the sect's origin to Bodhidharma (fl. 460–534) (Chan 1963: 425–26).

15. See Ch'ien 1986: 241 on the linguistic skepticism of a Song neo-Confucianist whose syncretism embraced Chan and Taoist thought.

16. Henderson seems to be following a similar line of reasoning when he writes on the emergence of parallel prose in the Han: "It seems that the linguistic parallelism of the argument itself constitutes an implicit proof of the proposition. For inasmuch as the basic structure of the cosmos is symmetrical, a cosmological proposition which can be stated in a symmetrical or parallel fashion has a strong claim to truth, insofar as the structure of language corresponds with the structure of reality" (1984: 44).

17. Observations by Hall and Ames would seem to bear out my theory (1987: 292–94).

18. Chow (1994) likewise feels their difference has been overstated.

19. Henderson makes the interesting and fairly convincing case that Qing scholars mounted a significant critique of "correlative thought" (1984: chap. 5). Since he eschewed exploring the social implications of his analysis, he left unanswered the nagging question of why such a far-ranging critique confined itself only to the realm of the intellectual. Elman does a more thorough job of connecting bookish with other social concerns, dealing better with the material world in which those scholars lived and which they studied (Elman 1984: especially chaps. 3–4). But neither takes up the contradiction of why those same critics were so often involved in editing ritual texts deeply embedded in a correlative ritualist metaphysics.

20. In his edition of the *Record of Rites,* Sun Xidan (who received his *jinshi* degree in 1778) says that *zhidu* includes palaces, halls, carriages, flags, clothing, etc., that is, the physical materia of ritual (Sun Xidan 1868: 48).

21. As a social historian, Ebrey links this popularity of ritual text to the restructuring of kinship and thus ancestral ritual in the Song (1991a: 45–102).

22. This is the reading by Ebrey (1991a: 104–9). For an alternative that pays much closer attention to both form and meaning in Song theorists' work on wedding ritual, see de Pee 1996.

23. My defense of translating *ren* as "cohumanity" is both philosophical and philological: philosophically, *ren* always implies the presence of others in one's own life; without these others as recipients of "benevolence" or "love," the virtue would be impossible. Philologically, the form of the character, a person and the number "two" suggests such an interpretation. For a finely honed discussion of *ren,* see Hall and Ames 1987: 110–25. They note that *ren* is a "process which entails both deference to others and an authored excellence of one's own" (122).

24. Without a thorough familiarity with the complete works of the forty-six commentators quoted in the course of presenting the text of the chapter "*Li* Transforms through its phases," it is pointless to discuss them in a way that attributes motive (such as "Chen Hao thought . . ."). Because the forty-six commentators are presented in decontextualized fragments, and because our interests are in the Qing, we must look at

the whole chapter as a selection and rearrangement by eighteenth-century editors to represent their own interpretations of the text. Thus we can glimpse a distillation of reflections of the thinking of the editors of the *Liji yishu* as they quote from later neo-Confucian writers.

25. Besides Zheng and Kong, the next most commonly cited writer is Fang Que of the Northern Song, who received his *jinshi* degree between 1120 and 1126. He wrote the *Liji jishuo* (Collected explanations of the Record of Rites), a text much favored by Zhu Xi. For his biography, see *Song-Yuan xue an* (Scholarly biographies of the Song and Yuan periods) 98/19b. Fang is quoted thirty times.

Chen Xiangdao is quoted twenty-three times. Also a Northern Song scholar, he received his *jinshi* degree in 1067. One of the most eminent scholars of the period, he was highly respected and produced a text called *Lishu* (The book on rites). The *Lishu* was 150 chapters long and was complimented by Pi Xirui for "connecting comprehensively the classical tradition" (Pi Xirui 1961: 257). For Chen's biography, see Franke 1976.

Wu Cheng (1249–1333), who wrote the *Liji zuanyan* (Collected explanations of the Record of Rites), is also quoted twenty-three times. Wu followed the Cheng-Zhu school tradition of separating the "Zhong Yong" and "Da Xue" chapters into their own volumes. His text was included in the *Library,* where the editors commented on the care taken in its editing (*SKQSZM* 21/1:169–70).

Chen Hao's *Liji jishuo* (Collected sayings on the Record of Rites), finished in 1322, was the imperially favored edition of the classic during the Ming. In most of his work, Chen compared neo-Confucian and Han commentary, but in this one he deliberately relied upon the Han. He is quoted twenty-one times. This work is also included in the *Library* (*SKQSZM* 21/1:170). Finally, Xu Shihui, who received his *jinshi* degree between 1522 and 1566, is the Ming author of the *Liji jizhu* (Collected annotations on the Record of Rites), and quoted twenty-two times.

26. For instance, Zhang Zai said, "The sage identifies his character with that of Heaven and Earth" (Chan 1963: 497) and "there is no distinction between the Way of Heaven as being great and the nature of man as being small" (507). It was in the Cheng brothers that the neo-Confucian doctrine of man and the universe forming one body took root (524). Cheng Hao said, "To [the man of humanity] there is nothing that is not himself" (530). And "Man and Heaven and Earth are one thing" (539).

27. For Zhu's commentary, see Li Guangdi, *Xingli jingyi* (Essential meanings in nature and principle) (Woodblock edition: 1717; reprint ed. undated woodblock), 1:3a.

28. *LJYS* 125:74; Legge 1885: 1:376. Note that this is not commentary, but the original text.

29. Appears sixteen times in the chapter.

30. See note 25 above for Fang Que.

31. Here Zhu Xi is quoting Cheng Hao (Chu Hsi 1967: 128).

32. I would replace Chan's "principle" with "coherence" and "humanity" with "cohumanity."

33. I have always thought that Song landscape painting served as an excellent metaphor for this reversal: narrative scrolls are combined into one hanging two-dimensional space, and time is captured.

34. Elman says of the later *Library,* "The overriding concern of the editors was the proper use of sources and principles of verification" (1984: 65).

35. Cheng Chung-ying 1971: 52, quoting Dai Zhen 1924: 2:35–36.

36. Ch'ien notes that these thinkers did not have the "egocentric rationalism of Descartes" to contend with in their philosophic past. The problem was not, he says, "to establish a continuity between man as subject and things as objects through experience as an epistemological principle. Rather it was articulating a monistic theory of man so that experience would be assured of an ontologically unitary foundation in man's being and be able to function as an existentially self-transcending activity to effect the Neoconfucian mystical vision of man forming one body with Heaven, earth, and the myriad things." We can restate Ch'ien's terms by noting that the problem for these thinkers lay in resolving issues about human nature, not the nature of the world (Ch'ien 1986: 270).

37. *LJZY* 22/2:1422. "Polar limits" conveys the idea of a pair of opposites that interpenetrate and comprehend all the between; Kong Yingda likens them to the ends of a rope.

38. An important elaboration of the idea of "skein" was carried on over the usage *yiguan* in the *Analects (Lunyu* 4:15; 15:2). Wing-tsit Chan translates this as "one thread." He summarizes interpretations from the Han to the Qing: from the Han-Tang idea of "one body of doctrine," through Song notions of "one mind" to Qing interpretations of *yiguan* as "action or affairs" (Chan 1963: 27). We note that all schools shared an idea of *yiguan* as a connector, a means whereby knowing was facilitated. Their differences depend upon how they envisaged the knowing subject and what is to be known. Han-Tang scholars emphasized an externally available system of doctrine; Zhu Xi a unifying coherence of all principles; and Dai Zhen, the activity of self-cultivation and study. (For a perceptive analysis of the problem in similar terms, see Ch'ien 1986: 254.) On Dai Zhen see Chan 1963: 721.

39. Indeed, for Volosinov, pioneering Marxist theorist of language, signs have an objective existence "between" people, and it is by the "chain" of their signs that a community is held together. "The existence of the sign is nothing but the materialization of [that] communication" (Volosinov 1973: 13).

40. This semantic domain has begun to generate the study it deserves: see Mayfair Yang 1994.

41. Hay 1983a: 84. Zong Baihua points out that the special difficulty in studying the arts of traditional China lies in the fact that, while each does have a system of principles, they also "encompass" each other (*huxiang baohan*) (1981: 26).

42. Ling Tingkan was born in Huizhou. In 1779 he went to Yangzhou, where he

worked in a bureau censoring dramatic works, meeting Ruan Yuan there in 1781. In 1782 Ling went to Beijing, where he became acquainted with Shao Jinhan and Wang Niansun. He became a *jinshi* in 1790 and served in provincial educational posts. Ling was an authority on the *Record of Rites,* and his *Lijing shili* (Explanatory examples from the ritual classics) was preserved by Ruan after his death (*ECCP* 514–15). Chow discusses Ling (1994: 191–202).

43. The "Zhong Yong" was important for the Cheng-Zhu school, especially as guide to a program of self-cultivation. Tu Weiming's discussion of "Zhong Yong" gives an excellent summary of this inner oriented interpretation. See his *Centrality and Commonality* (1976). For *junzi* I follow the translation suggested by Hall and Ames (1987: 188).

44. The Five Bonds were (in this hierarchical order): father/son, ruler/minister, husband/wife, older/younger siblings, friend/friend (see chapter 1).

45. Ling's essays are collected in He Changling 1899: 54.1a–2b. This excerpt appears on 54.2b.

46. The *Jingshi wenbian* is a collection of 2,010 essays and excerpts from memorials, reports, etc. by more than six hundred writers of the Qing intended as a guide to government (Teng and Biggerstaff 1971).

47. In her important analysis of the person and the art of *guanxi* in modern China, Mayfair Mei-hui Yang states "Chinese culture presents a frequent lack of clear-cut boundaries between self and other, as one Western-educated Chinese scholar has noted: 'In Chinese culture, the dyadic relationship where there is a me inside of you and there is a you inside of me is something that approximates a cultural law. It can be played out with many possibilities" (1989: 39), quoting Sun Longji 1983: 137.

48. I first articulated this perspective in Zito 1984.

49. The concept of the "performative" was elaborated by J. L. Austin (1962).

Chapter 5

1. DeCerteau reverses the usual sense of these terms: As Jonathan Z. Smith points out, it was Kant who first proposed that "It is . . . solely from a human standpoint that we can speak of space" (quoted in Smith 1987:27). He further quotes geographer Yifu Tuan that "space is more abstract than place." Perhaps deCerteau wishes to bring both space and place into the purview of the humanly constructed and thus disrupt the Kantian distinction between nature and culture.

2. Local temple building increased dramatically after the fourteenth century, and gazetteers from the Ming and Qing periods are replete with references to temple renovation. These often quote stelae engraved with memorial narratives of the projects. For example, see *Shuntian fuzhi* (1886: juan 6). The heart of the novel *Rulin waishi* is the tale of how a small group of gentry men revived sacrifice at their local Confucian temple. See Wu Jingzi 1981: 125–92.

3. The two characters of the term *wuli,* or Five Rites, first appeared paired in the

Book of Documents. The entire series is first listed and elaborated in the *Rites of Zhou,* in the "Da zongbo" chapter.

4. Ho Yun-yi 1976: 216–18, appendix C, on the historical development of the Ministry of Rites and functioning bureaus.

5. Descriptions of the Altar of Heaven and its ceremonies include Williams 1913: 11–45; Blodgett 1899: 58–69; Meech 1916: 112–17; Happer 1879: 23–47; Bouillard 1922a: 1421–1443; 1922b: 1679–1716; 1923: 53–67; *DQTL* 1756: chap. 1; *DQHD* chap. 37.

6. Chan 1963: 281. John S. Major identifies this as the *gaitian* model wherein the Earth is defined by solstitial and equinoctal points projected onto the celestial equator while the heavens are domed, parallel, and defined by the circle of the celestial equator (1984: 133).

7. On the association of the number nine with emperorship, see Zhang Xixin 1981: 26.

8. Waltner 1990: 1–4, 144. Carney Fisher supports his discussion of the famous Ming case with interesting and useful reviews of precedents in the Han and Song (1990: 1–46).

9. On the shift from agnatic to filial descent after the Shang and subsequent developments in the Han, see Fisher 1990: 246–63. On Song neo-Confucian modifications in kinship practices, see Ebrey 1986, 1984. Kai-wing Chow has discussed the impact upon later classical scholarship of sixteenth- and seventeenth-century efforts to resurrect Zhou ancestral rites and the *zongfa,* or "core-line" system, in order to rebuild lineages at the local level (1994: 110–28, 130).

10. This discussion is based on Allan's important article "The Identities of Taigong Wang in Zhou and Han Literature" (1973). I restate her rich analysis in terms useful to my own concerns.

11. The God of Grain, Hou Ji, was honored as the founder of the Zhou royal house. See *Shijing,* number 245. For a discussion of his legend as mythic transformation between cults of nature and cults of ancestors, see Granet 1975: 90–96.

12. The information from this point forward on Soil and Grain sacrifice has appeared in Zito 1987.

13. Wheatley 1971. It is not my intention to cover the same ground that has been glossed by comparativists. (The metaphor is floor-waxing; all those patterns preserved forever under a shiny surface treatment.) Although Wheatley's book provides an accessible overview of Chinese archaeological studies, it does have some problems. Wheatley (1969) considers his project a corrective for a "Europocentrism," which he says deflects the attention of urbanologists from the traditional and non-European city. Toward that end he has studied the most ignored aspect of these cities, the "cosmo-magical symbolism" that informed their design (1971: 9). He gathers more than enough data to convince his reader that here indeed is a phenomenon that does not yield well to explanations based on common sense. Yet his conclusion disappoints:

But the primary interest of the social scientist lies less in the symbolism itself than in the nature
of the city of which it constitutes a functional and organic part. (1969: 21)

He seems to have translated the particularly Euro-Christian categorical split between
the sacred/nonrational and profane/rational into new terms: the symbolic and the
functional. The lack of a method that grants symbols a full material existence as the
mediators through which society reproduces itself deflects Wheatley's project away
from analysis toward description.

14. Chang 1977: 348–49. Walls themselves became so identified with cities that
the two are called the same thing: *cheng.*

15. Even today the government of the People's Republic participates in this traditional notion of preservation that emphasizes the metaphysical whole of a building
rather than its material parts. As long as these are faithfully reproduced *in situ,* guide-
books and local people will inevitably report that the building is "original."

16. Such a development would seem to me to herald the threshold of modernity in
China. When it began in China is a subject of debate that I cannot enter into here, but
even if the process was under way in the eighteenth century, older models of the use of
space were very much in evidence. It is those processes, and their intimate connection
to kingly ritual, that concern me here.

17. Tambiah points out a fundamental duality underlying the constitution of the
relations between the center and its provinces: "On the one hand there is a faithful
reproduction on a reduced scale of the center in its outlying components; on the other,
the satellites pose the constant threat of fission and incorporation in another sphere of
influence" (1985a: 261).

18. An estimated one hundred thousand craftsmen and about one million laborers
were employed on the fourteen-year project. Materials arrived from every corner of
the empire, especially wood from the southern tropical forests of Yunnan and Guizhou.
One account tells of the transport of a stone from Suzhou, south of Shanghai: "The
large stones for the slanting ramps for the Three Halls were each 33 feet long, 10 feet
wide and 43 feet thick. They were sent to the capital using 20,000 handlers. It took
208 days at a cost of over 10,000 ounces of silver from the local officials and people"
(Xie Mincong 1980: 25).

19. The *Rixia jiuwen kao* by Zhu Yizun (1785: 11/1:150–51). Originally printed by
Zhu in 42 chapters in 1688, with additions by his son, Zhu Kuntian (1652–1699); the
Qianlong revision in 160 chapters was printed ca. 1785. See also *DQTL* 1756: chap. 17.

20. The Southern gate Duanmen for instance (Xie Mincong 1980: 135).

21. Zhu served officially and was also a well-known classicist. His bibliography, the
Jingyi kao (Study of the meanings of the classics) was printed posthumously by Lu Jianzeng in 1755 (*ECCP* 182–85).

22. The word is *shanqi,* to mend, copy, write out, or repair. Note right side of *shan*
also means "to perfect."

23. For Ancestral Temple poems, see *RXJWK* 9/1:132–35. For poems written on ritual performances at the Meridian Gate (grants of amnesty, promulgation of edicts), see *RXJWK* 10/1:142–46. For poems inspired by audiences held in the Taiho dian, see *RXJWK* 11/1:151–53. For poems on studying the classics in the Wenhua dian, see *RXJWK* 12/1:159–64. This form is repeated for every building discussed.

24. Three on each side and two on the north, where the center gate was missing, to prevent yin influence from sweeping down the main north/south axis.

25. The popular belief that high thresholds trip ghosts may be an inversion of the ritual function I describe here, which places the human in the position of cosmic mediator.

26. Marcel Granet says, "Deux éléments dans les constructions Chinoises sont fondamentaux. L'édifice, en lui-même, importe moins que la terrasse qui le supporte et que la toîture qui le couvre" (1968: 209).

27. In modern Mandarin, the measure word for "housespaces" is still *jian* and has been nominalized into meaning "room." For instance, Mao Qiling's (1623–1716) discussion of "Jisuo" (Sacrificial space) refers to the layout of houses in terms of *jian*. See his n.d., 1.2a–16a.

28. In the *Hanshu,* "Biography of Yongguang," Yong guang is so praised.

29. *Lunyu* 15.4. Here Confucius discusses how the sage king Wu did nothing in order to govern but sit facing south and receive his officials in audience.

30. Portions of this section appeared in Zito 1984.

31. This very late (1899) and perforce definitive edition drew upon past editions of the *Canon* and a Qianlong period pictorial *Illustrations of Dynastic Ritual Paraphernalia (Huangchao Liqi Tushi* 1766).

32. When discussing the form of the rite I will use terms in the following manner: "Ceremonial Order" refers to the sequence of heading of sections in the sacrifice, for instance "Viewing the Victims" followed by "Achieving Seclusion," etc. (see figure 16). "Format" refers to the description of the action within each section. "Elements" are items or actions that make up the sections. When "Format" changes, it is because "elements" differ or are left out. Hence the description refers to the *ceremonial order* of *sections,* each of whose *format* contains varying *elements.* Formally we might write it thus—Ceremonial order : sections :: format : elements.

33. Thus proving at the level of editing form the often repeated observation that Sacrifice to Heaven became the most prominent imperial ritual by the Tang period.

34. These diagrams were chosen for reproduction here because of their manageable size. Those for other Grand Sacrifices are arranged the same way. The three diagrams come respectively from the *HDT Illustrations for the Assembled Canon* 10.2a–3b; 10.5b–6a; 10.13b–14a.

35. *DQTL* 1756: 1.22b. The word *ci* also denotes the tents that stand *she* upon the altar. "Order" is not a mistranslation, however. I have merely used one of its senses to make my point. Actually, since the tents (sometimes referred to as *wo*) are pitched first

and *contain,* variously, spirit thrones and tablets, participants and vessels, they are a substantialization of the abstraction *ci* meaning an encompassing order.

36. Kang 1974: 198. Thus I prefer "encompassed asymmetries" to Andrew Plaks' use of "encompassed complementarities" (Plaks 1977: 309–52).

37. People were present at each of the four Grand Sacrifices to record the proceeding, especially any errors. On the altar were the Censorate's Chief Imperial Archivist of the Left and an Assistant Chief Imperial Archivist. Off the altar were four recorders from the Hanlin Academy (*DQTL* 1756: 1.18a, 2.14a, 3.8b–9a, 6.4a–b). For a brief mention of the Censorate's role in rituals, see Zhang Deyi 1981: 117.

38. In 1818, more than sixty years after its compilation, the emperor ordered that the *Comprehensive Rites* be taken out of storage and reprinted for general distribution. A censor thereupon pointed out that in the intervening years, "as people did what was suitable to the occasion, everything from the various canons of Court Sacrifice to the Regulations for Examinations has changed and no longer completely tallies with the original book" (*DQTL* 1756: first page of the "Flow of Memorials Preface").

Chapter 6

1. For inner/outer in Taiwan folk religion, see Feuchtwang 1974: 105–29. For Sacrifice to Heaven in the Ming, see Ho Yun-yi 1979: 147–85.

2. For Grand Sacrifice, all three types were used. For Middling rank sacrifice, the pig was omitted (Qianlong *DQHD* 1763: 76.1.a, 82.1a). Since each spirit received the full complement, in Qianlong's time twenty of each animal would have been needed. E. T. Williams mentions that "fourteen bullocks" and a "large number of sheep and pigs" were used for the Sacrifice to Heaven (1913: 28).

3. The ox, sheep, and pig were roasted whole, but the deer was minced and added to other dishes. Thus while it required inspection, it is not treated as one of the emblems of Grand Sacrifice (*DQTL* 1756: 1.5a).

4. *Neigetiben:like* 68/2–66 (QL 3/10/28). The information about who actually served in these roles was appended to the original request (a standard format), and dated QL 12/7 and 12/10 respectively. Yun Bi was one of the Kang Xi emperor's sons, thus Qianlong's uncle. Hong Zhou (1712–1770) was the Yongzhen emperor's fifth son, one of Qianlong's brothers.

5. See similar memorial from San Tai on viewing the victims for the Altar for Good Harvest, located within the Tiantan (Altar of Heaven) complex. *Neigetiben:like* 68/2–66 (QL 3/12/20).

6. The bronze man was invented by Ming Taizu (r. 1368–1398) to stand as a constant reminder of vigilant fasting. Ho Yun-yi 1979: 174.

7. The *Five Rites'* longest entry on the subject of Achieving Seclusion comes from the "Jiaotesheng" chapter of the *Record of Rites.* Here the sacrificer is urged not "dissipate his will" (*sanzhi*) (*WLTK* 3.10a/351).

8. Although on the face of it, the procedures for seclusion seem similar to mourn-

ing, nonetheless Auspicious and Funerary Rites were mutually exclusive categories. The required retirement from official posts while mourning for parents may have its origin in this ritual taboo. If manifesting the unity of the visible and invisible realms was crucial for governance, those unable to mediate through sacrifice clearly could not govern. Or, as Susan Naquin has suggested to me, the prohibition may reflect the ultimate primacy of family over domainal ritual obligation. Evelyn Rawski, however, notes that at the imperial level every effort was made to privilege domainal obligations (1988: 250–53).

9. *WLTK* 1.2b/258; 1.10a/273; 3.3a/337; passim. See *WLTK* First Head Chapter 1b, for Fang Guancheng's "opinion."

10. An edict dated Jiaqing 1802 details what various ranks of participants should wear while fasting, highlighting the importance of clothing (*HDZL* 1899: 415.28a–b).

11. A memorial by Zhang Yunsui, governor of Guizhou, discusses the precedents for how many days people should abstain for each level of sacrifice. He laments that the unclarity of the rules for abstinence at the local and provincial level lead to abuses (*Gongzhong nei zheng: Liyi* 340/4–56, QL 5/9/28).

12. The color of these boards was fixed in the *Assembled Canon:* on the Altar of Heaven, "clear blue" paper with vermilion ink was used. For Earth, the paper was yellow, the ink "yellow-black." For the Ancestral Temple and the Altar of Soil and Grain, "pure white" paper and "yellow-black" ink (*HDZL* 1899: 415.19b).

13. Meech describes seeing "a coarse kind of matting made of the black hairy outer covering of the palm woven roughly into long strips which are laid parallel to each other and cover the whole altar floor" (1916: 114).

14. See chapter 5, note 35, for a discussion of the tent as a substantialization of the notion of "order" designated by the term *ci*.

15. *Huangchao liqi tushi* 1759: comp. Yunda, reprinted in the Siku quanshu zhen ben collection, series six, vols. 122–29 (hereafter *LQTS*).

16. An original manuscript version of the *LQTS* exists in the Palace Museum in Beijing. Curator Zhu Jiajin told me it is an oversized folio in ink and water-color. Unfortunately, I was unable to examine this edition.

17. Vessels in the Confucian Temple followed the Ancestral Temple patterns, reinforcing the important ritual distinction between formerly human ancestors and cosmic deities.

18. Surviving vessels held at the Palace Museum in Beijing dating from the reign of the Yongzheng emperor forward match the descriptions in the *Illustrations* exactly. This suggests that eighteenth-century ritualists took very seriously the scholarship done on ancient rites and did their best to reproduce the exegesis in material form.

19. *LQTS* 1.5a–5b, 1.28a; at the Altar to the Sun, it was red, 1.48a–b; at the Altar to the Moon, it was white, 1.60a–b.

20. The Qianlong emperor was sensitive to this aspect of the review. In an edict dated 1751 he proposed that the Repository for Prayerboards be moved over behind the incense on the left (east) so that he would not be burning incense into empty space.

Apparently this procedure was eventually rejected by editors because the *DQTL* places the Repository for Prayerboards to the west, with the other offerings (*HDZL* 1899: 415.22a). (I have found no record of debate on the matter.)

21. Under the name of San Tai, a palace memorial summarizes the historical precedents for types of palanquins used in imperial processions and outlines the routes through the Forbidden City that he recommended the emperor should take to the Altar of Heaven. *Gongzhong neizheng: Liyi* 340/4–56 (QL 7/12/17).

22. Two paintings picture in color every detail of the cortege, its order and regalia. Dating from the Jiaqing reign (1796–1820) is "Huangdi faji buoluo tu" (Protocol in Imperial Procession), held in the Palace Museum, Beijing. (I viewed this scroll at the Palace Museum in September 1992.) Portions may be seen in Xu Bihai 1983: 25 and *Zijincheng dihou shenghuo* 1981: 14. The other painting, "Guangxu dahun tu" (Illustration of the Guangxu emperor's wedding), also held by the Palace Museum, Beijing, shows various aspects of procession and ceremonial. (At the Palace Museum in Beijing, I also viewed four panels of this painting, which is extraordinarily detailed.) See figure 29 for a detail of the painting.

23. This complete prostration is performed by the emperor before the spirit tablets in Grand Sacrifice and by his courtiers before him.

24. One recurring violation was ritualists' not reporting to their offices for seclusion, but instead "secluding" themselves at home. In the first year of his reign (1736) the Qianlong emperor decreed that all should report to the yamen (*HDZL* 1899: 415.6a–b). In 1743, it was pointed out that out-of-town officials should fast in the dormitories of their respective liaison offices; princes and dukes were allowed to fast the first two days at home, the last in a dormitory outside the altar. Officials had to fast in their yamen the first two days, then join the princes and dukes (*HDZL* 1899: 415.6b–7a). An edict of 1749 makes it clear that the reason people are to gather together under official auspices is precisely so they can be easily kept under surveillance (*HDZL* 1899: 415.8a–9b).

25. Girardot has discussed the relationship between "face" and ancestral tablets most insightfully (1988: 262–64). A great deal remains to be systematically explored in the extensive ethnographic literature on Chinese funerary practices and their relation to the ritual I work upon in this study.

26. See chapter 5 for a discussion of the relationship between *zhu* as "ruler" and *zhu* as "wooden pillar."

27. As architect of the Vietnam memorial (a series of stelae engraved with the names of all the war dead), Maya Lin says, "The name is one of the most magical ways to bring back a person" (*New York Times*, July 30, 1988, p. 7).

28. I am grateful to John Calagione for clarifying discussion on this point.

29. "*Li zhi chu shi zhu yinshi,*" "Liyun" (*LJZY* 21/2:1415).

30. "Incorporation, then, represents a tactical incursion into the recipient's personal space where he or she can be manipulated from within" (Mayfair Yang 1989: 25).

31. The following discussion is indebted to him.

32. Chang quotes the *Lunyu,* the *Record of Rites,* and the *Mencius* to support his assertion (1976: 135). An ironic anecdote from the mid-eighteenth-century novel, *The Scholars,* might further clarify: When the good-hearted, poor tutor Zhou Jin is visited by the greedy, successful scholar, Wang Hui, Wang sits down to an enormous meal of wine, rice, chicken, duck, and pork, while Zhou sits by with his own meager repast of water, rice, and a little cabbage. Jonathan Spence quotes this passage as an example of how "you were what you ate." We note that Zhou Jin's minimal meal only admitted of a little cabbage on the side of the main elements of grain and water (Spence 1977: 271).

33. From the "Jiaotesheng" chapter (*LJZY* 25/2:1447). Eating and drinking are listed as but one method for nourishing the two cosmic principles. Music is also employed, so that there is music while drinking and none with food.

34. After this analysis was completed, I came upon Girardot's excellent discussion of wonton soup. Although he emphasizes the "chaotic" nature of soup as it contrasts with separate "orders" of yin and yang, I am in complete agreement with his conclusion that soups and stews are markers of ritual occasions. See Girardot 1988: 29–38, especially the diagram on p. 35.

35. Qin Huitian provides the *locus classicus* when discussing the contents of the *bian* and *dou* in his ritual encyclopedia on the *Five Rites,* and we find that the *Comprehensive Rites* follows the *Zhouli* almost exactly (*WLTK* 3.14a–b/359–60). Did imperial sacrifice bear a relationship to everyday eating habits? Conventional categories for food in eighteenth-century local gazetteers show that food from most of them was offered in sacrifice. But the will to archaicize—thus emphasizing the difference in social status of those who ate the old foods—is also shown in the marked absence of any of the new world crops that fed the seventeenth-and eighteenth-century population explosion. Maize, potatoes, and peanuts certainly never appeared on the emperor's altars (Spence 1977: 261, 263).

36. "*Ji wei wu xiang,*" *Wenmiao shangding yuebei kao* 1870: 1.18b–19a.

37. In his recipe book, poet and *bon vivant* Yuan Mei (1716–1798) says that one must first understand a food's natural properties (*xiantian*). The search for ideal ingredients meant that credit for a fine banquet must be divided two ways: 60 percent to the cook and 40 percent to the shopper (Spence 1977: 272).

38. As Yuan Mei's cook put it: "If one has the art, then a piece of celery or salted cabbage can be made into a marvelous delicacy, whereas if one has not the art, not all the greatest delicacies and rarities of land, sea or sky are of any avail" (quoted in Spence 1977: 292).

39. Spence mentions volumes collected in the *Library* (see *SKQSZM* 116/1:1000); the exhaustive treatment in the Qianlong encyclopedia the *Huangchao santong;* and the massive amounts of information found in the early-eighteenth-century encyclopedia, the *Gujin tushu jicheng* (Spence 1977: 284).

40. Spence quotes the *Guanglusi shili* (Examples from the Court of Banqueting),

1839: there were six grades of banquets for Manchus, five grades for Chinese (1977: 282–84). See also above, chapter 1.

41. *LQTS* 4.8a–13a. For photos of surviving sacrificial robes, and other imperial *chaofu,* see *Zijincheng dihou shenghuo* 1981: 66–68.

42. *LQTS* 5.127a–129b. Miyazaki describes the ceremony of acceptance of this degree during the Qing by "licentiates" (as he translates *shengyuan*). They first wore their "uniforms" of dark blue robes, bordered in black, and the "sparrow" cap, to the examination director's residence, where he presented them with the cap ornament appropriate to their new status (Miyazaki 1981: 30). "Proffered scholars" or *jinshi,* successful candidates at the most advanced level, received clothing from the emperor.

43. See Schuyler Cammann's classic treatment of these insignia in "The Development of the Mandarin Square" (1944–1945: 71–130).

44. Cammann quotes Qing official Zhou Xun's explanation for this split: birds denoted literary elegance; animals fierce courage (1944–1945: 76). The association of *wen* officials with an upper realm of Heaven or the sky was commonplace: In the novel *The Scholars,* they were compared to stars (Wu Jingzi 1981: 31).

45. Legge's translation fits our analysis of the inner and outer constitution of boundary even better. He says, "Examining of hair and taking of blood announces that the victim is complete within and without" (1885: 2:444–45).

46. As Lévi-Strauss puts it: "The effectiveness of symbols would consist precisely in this 'inductive' property by which formally homologous structures, built out of different materials at different levels of life—organic processes, unconscious mind, rational thought—are related to one another" (1963: 201).

47. Qin Huitian quotes extensively from both this chapter and the "Border Victim" chapter of the *Record of Rites* in his general discussion of vessels and their uses (*WLTK* 3.9a–18b/349–68).

48. The tantalizing question then arises: What connection could this idea of language have had with Indian notions of words and things, which had, by the Song, been assimilated in China via Buddhism?

49. The artist Li Gonglin (ca. 1042–1093) writes of the ritual vessels in his collection: "The sages made vessels and adorned them with forms to record the Way and to pass down admonitions. They lodged in the use of vessels subtleties that otherwise could not have been transmitted and passed on to these later men. This enabled extensively learned scholars to seek forms through vessels and then to seek meanings through forms" (Harrist 1995: 242, quoting the *Zhoushi* of Zhai Qinian). I am grateful to Christian de Pee for pointing out this source to me.

Chapter 7

1. For Qin's conclusions on the debate, see 1.6b/266.

2. I am currently working on a project that will investigate these aspects of filiality in everyday life.

3. "*Yigui sankou*"—literally "one kneeling and three knockings"—consisted of kneeling once and knocking the head on the ground from that position three times.

4. "*Sangui jiukou*"—literally the "three kneelings and nine knockings." This consisted of kneeling and prostrating three times, repeated three times.

5. Orders given by the staff are indicated in the text by two different verbs: "intone" (*zan*) is used when the entire company is addressed, everyone except the emperor is addressed, or the spirits are addressed. "Memorialize" (*zou*) is employed for orders to the emperor. "Memorializing" was the most common form of report from an inferior to a superior in the imperium. It was usually written.

6. Every time the emperor moves, this tablet precedes him around the altar.

7. Celebrants all face north; the attending staff, dancers, and musicians face east or west.

8. This memorial from the first year of Qianlong's reign (1736) discusses how the Department of Ceremonial shall stand these boards before the celebrants appear on the altar. The celebrants use *ban,* while the emperor's marker is called a *pai.* No mention is made of markers for any of the other participants in the *Comprehensive Rites.* From this I conclude that they were not moved when the celebrants did, and thus did not enter into the action.

9. The invokers and ushers were ranked at "superior seven" (Brunnert and Hagelstrom 1912: 57).

10. Recommendations were made after ceremonies, based upon impressions that participants had during the rite. In a memorial dated 1749, the Court of Grand Constancy pointed out that the inspection of the vessels carried out by the Ministry of Rites along with censors was inappropriate and that their Court should henceforth be included. The emperor agreed (*HDZL* 1899: 416.7b).

11. An order dated 1741 states that "laughing and giggling among the celebrants or staff shall be noted, whether they are of the imperial house, of the nobility or great ministers" (*HDZL* 1899: 416.14b).

12. James Hevia has written extensively and elegantly upon the implications of the ketou in cross-cultural contexts (1994: 181–200 and 1995a).

13. The first five tones are also correlated with social life in the following fashion: 1 = the lord, 2 = the minister, 3 = the people, 4 = events, 5 = things (*LJZY* 37/2: 1528).

14. Nine as an odd, yang number and eight as an even, yin number are obviously appropriate, but the other two are mysterious anomalies. I have found no discussion on the subject.

15. We read in an eyewitness account by the brother of the last emperor that when he was young, he could not wear court costume (*chaofu*) on ritual occasions because he had no *juewei.* Lacking the rank and clothes, younger men, of course, could only secretly watch rituals at court and not participate (Pu Gui 1982: 118–23).

16. The ladle may seem like a lowly item, but in shape it resembled the *ruyi,* a

curved scepter associated with maleness and rulership. It was also an eating utensil. But without knowing more details about relative usage of spoons and chopsticks in everyday life, it is difficult to make a direct inference about eating and breaching the boundary of inside and outside.

17. The word *pin* is used in ritual texts to refer to the foodstuffs and the ranks of participants, another gloss on the similarity of the "inner" states of people and vessels.

18. See *Zhongsi hebian* (1854) and *Huangchao jiqi yuewu lu* (n.d.). The handbooks were produced during the Restoration undertaken in the wake of the devastation wrought by the Taiping Kingdom.

19. The *Shiwei chu* controlled the affairs of the three Superior Banners. Since directors of the Court of Banqueting were ranked as "Superior Three," probably these representatives were too, since such guards range from Superior Three to Inferior Five in rank (Mayers 1897: 9).

20. The same term is used for proffering the trenchers to the spirits.

21. The sacrificial meat and the felicitous liquor were parcelled out after the ceremony. This was also the case after the Manchu royal family's personal sacrifices that took place in the Kunning Palace within the Forbidden City, where daily the meat that had been placed before the spirits was bestowed upon members of the court (Wang Peihuan 1993: 119–20).

In QL 40, for example, after the sacrifice on the Altar of Soil and Grain, the Court of Banqueting officials De Cheng and Yao Hai were ordered to bestow bottles of sacrificial liquor on behalf of the emperor upon concubines of the third rank, the imperial sons and daughters, the inner princes and members of the Grand Council. Amounts were specified (*Gongzhong gexiang dangbo dengji* no. 5215, dated QL 40/1).

22. This suite was not included in the sacrificial hymns proper, which number nine, plus this last number.

23. See especially Watson and Rawski 1988. The conclusions of the editors support my contention. Watson says, "If anything is central to the creation and maintenance of a unified Chinese culture, it is the standardization of ritual" (3). Rawski notes that "Chinese culture in the late imperial period (sixteenth to nineteenth centuries) had achieved important commonalities in belief that cut across the boundaries of regions and social strata" (22).

24. And in personal scholarship, scholars like Qin Huitian stressed the importance of mining the Dynastic Histories for detail on *li,* expanding beyond the treatises to annals and biographies. He argued that genre convention dictates the form of a history's parts: "What is seen in biographies will be left out of treatises. Use one, lose one. As they say 'For every one thing cited, 10,000 will be left out' " (*WLTK* fanlie 2a).

25. *WLTK* (88.1a–62b), on ancestral sacrifice for various references to the *Record of Rites.*

26. The *Jiali* (Family rituals), attributed to Zhu Xi, was written to illustrate the immutable principles of *li* within every family. See Ebrey 1991a, 1991b.

27. See K. C. Chang's analysis of alternating rule between pairs of Shang lineages. The ruler/sacrificer not only combined the roles of father and son, he also embodied the unity of two lineages (1976: 84–85).

28. In his seminal work, *The Ritual Process* (1969), Turner emphasizes the value of rituals that invert and thus subvert the everyday social hierarchy, creating a feeling of "communitas," or radical egalitarianism.

29. Emily Martin (Ahern) is startled when informants describe their relations with gods as most like that between parents and children instead of being comparable to subject and bureaucrat. Their resort to filiality as an explanation is a perfect example of the hegemonic process I have tried to describe (1981: 99).

Chapter 8

1. On the penetration of Hundun as the triumph of cultural/historical order over natural/asocial chaos, see Girardot (1988: 77–112). Max Kaltenmark refers to the untimely zeal of Hu and Shu in wishing to interrupt Hundun's unity by giving it sense organs as the "Founding King's original Sin" (Kaltenmark 1969: 101).

2. Boodberg 1953, quoted in Hall and Ames 1987: 87.

3. One *locus classicus* for work on boundary-making is Douglas 1966. Judith Butler (1990) has recently applied Douglas to gender, emphasizing in a manner analogous to my own the liberatory possibilities of moving from metaphysics of gender essence to the cultural construction of gender as performance.

4. Gender operating as subset of the correlative logic of yin/yang is laid out nicely by Song philosopher Cheng Yi: "Yang occupies five and resides on the outside; yin occupies two and stays on the inside; thus male and female attain their correct place. The way of honored and lowly, inner and outer correctly corresponds to the great meaning of Heaven and Earth, yin and yang" (cited by Dorothy Ko in the context of discussing gender in the eighteenth century [1992: 15]).

5. See Hevia 1989 for use of "initiation" and "completion" in the context of guest ritual.

6. Charlotte Furth (1988) has produced the first body of work exploring traditional medical texts' work on women. As I read them, the essays provoke the suspicion that the neat Enlightenment split between culture and nature within whose crevice natural sciences like biology have flourished was, in the Chinese case, a very messy and constantly transforming boundary. Judith Farquhar's (1994) ethnographic and historical work on Chinese medicine draws more explicit attention to "transforming resonance" as an underlying cosmology that destabilizes any fixed biological essence for bodies.

7. My discussion of Foucault draws upon Bell 1991 and essays in *Feminism and Foucault: Reflections on Resistance* (Diamond and Quinby 1988), especially Sandra Lee Bartky's "Foucault, Femininity and the Modernization of Patriarchal Power."

8. On the residual in social formations, see Williams 1977: chap. 7.

9. Chow is particularly eloquent and persuasive on the importance of the throne to securing local gentry hegemony (1994: 3–6).

10. Willard Peterson likewise points to a seventeenth-century preoccupation with "literature, books, calligraphy and painting, collecting and appreciating as other men might put . . . into moral philosophy or politics" (1979: 32).

11. On literacy in the Qing, see Rawski 1979.

12. See Rawski 1979: 21–41, 140, for the precise figures of 30 to 45 percent of men and from 2 to 10 percent of women.

13. The point can be made that a new eighteenth-century relation to the textual authority of the sages bypassed the imperium in China in the way that Reformation protestants sought to bypass the Roman Catholic Church in appropriating the word of God directly in the Bible.

14. Elman 1984: 256 points to continuity in scholarly discourse between evidential exact scholarship and twentieth-century Chinese work on oracle bones. The continuities I am speculating upon are of a deeper and more elusive nature, and have to do with establishing certain hegemonic modes of formation of subjectivity and knowledge.

15. Nivison 1966: 167. I have modified his translation of Zhang Xuecheng 1985: 1.7.

16. I am currently working on how, in the eighteenth century, *xiao* functioned in various domains (domestic/familial, ritual, classical commentarial) to organize gender distinction in service of, or in resistance to, the wider state ideological project of identification with the imperial center's model of a masculinist body of yang power.

17. The issue of separate women's spheres in China provides one theme taken up by writers in an excellent special issue of *Late Imperial China* on poetry and women's culture. For instance, Marie Bruneau contrasts the late imperial Chinese circumstances with those in Europe, pointing out the irony of a strict separation that seems to have protected women's writing from the extremes of anxiety felt by European men who faced women more often on their own "public" terrain (1992: 162).

18. Dorothy Ko is especially eager to make the case that gender distinction in China differs so profoundly from that of Europe that seclusion provided positive opportunities for women to develop a true "separate sphere" (1992: 14 and passim). We will later discuss "discipline" and "mastery" as important (and satisfying) aspects of the operation of micropowers.

19. Ko has discovered women's erotic poetry extolling bound feet (1992: 11).

Glossary of Chinese Characters

an	案	chenshe	陳設
		chi	飭
bai pai	拜牌	chu xian du zhu	初獻讀祝
ban	版	chuandai	穿戴
bei	備		
beijiao fangze dasi	北郊方澤大祀	da (extend)	達
bian	籩	da (grand)	大
bianwei	辨位	da jia lubu	大駕鹵簿
biaowen	表文	da li yi	大禮議
binli	賓禮	daguan	大觀
Bishu shanzhuang	避暑山庄	dang	當
bishu yuan	秘書院	dangran	當然
		dao	道
cai	菜	daoxue	道學
cha	察	Dasi	大祀
chanming	闡明	datong	大同
chaofu	朝服	de	德
cheng (integrity)	誠	deng	登
cheng		dian (canonical)	典
(proportioning)	稱	dian (halls)	殿
chenghuang	城隍	dian yu bo	奠玉帛

dian zhong	墊中	hui luan	回鑾
dianli	典禮	Huidian	會典
dianyi	典儀	huxiang baohan	互相包含
dianzhang zhidu	典章制度		
dou	豆	ji (collection)	集
		ji (skein, record)	紀
fa	法	ji (trace)	跡
faming	發明	ji wei wu xiang	即為物象
fan	飯	jia	家
fei	篚	jiali	嘉禮
feng	風	jian (polluted)	奸
fu	簠	jian (room-space)	間
		jian (see)	見
gai	蓋	jian yu wai	見於外
gai tian	蓋天	jiangxue	講學
ge jiu ziran cixu	各就自然次序	jianshu	檢束
geng	羹	jianzong tiaoguan	兼綜條貫
gong (collective)	公	jiao (connect)	交
gong (palace, first		jiao (extra-mural)	郊
musical tone)	宮	jiao (third musical	
gong (precious		tone)	角
things)	貢	jie (exhaustive)	竭
gong wozhang	供幄張	jie (modulate)	節
gongju	供舉	jiemu zhi xianhou	節目之先後
gu	固	jili	吉禮
guan (connect)	貫	jin zu	進俎
guan (examine)	觀	jing (classic)	經
Guanglu si	光祿寺	jing (composure)	敬
guanxi	關係	Jingshan qinglisi	精膳清史司
gui	簋	jinqxue	經學
guoshi yuan	國史院	jinshi	進士
gushi	故事	jisi	祭祀
		jiu ci guanxi jiu wei	就次盥洗就位
Hongwen yuan	宏文院	jizhuan	紀傳
hou	後	ju	舉
Huangchao	皇朝	jue	爵
Huangcheng	皇城	juewei	爵位

jun	峻	neicheng	內城
junli	軍禮	neiting	內廷
junzi	君子	Neiwufu	內務府
kan	看	pai	牌
kao	考	pan	蟠
kaozheng	考證	panran	判然
keju	科舉	pin	品
		pinji muban	品級木板
li (coherence)	理	polian	剖臉
li (ritual)	禮	puxue	樸學
li cheng	禮成		
li yi wei ji	禮義爲記	qi (energetic force)	氣
li zhi chu shi		qi (vessel)	器
zhu yinshi	禮之初始諸飲食	qian	前
lian	臉	qiangu	前古
liang	良	Qianqing gong	乾清宮
libu	禮部	Qijuji	起居記
liyi	禮義	Qinding	欽定
liyu	禮輿	qing	情
Liyun	禮運	qing shenwei	請神位
lizhi	禮制	qinwang	親王
longpao	龍袍	qizhu	氣主
luanyu chu gong	鑾輿出宮	qun	群
mao	毛	ran	然
mian	面	ren	仁
mianzi	面子	ren cang qi xin	人藏其心
ming (mandate)	命	renyi	仁義
ming (visible)	明	ru	如
mingbai	明百	ruyi	如意
mingwu	明物		
mo	脈	sanbu	散佈
		sancai	三才
nanjiao yuanqiu dasi	南郊圓丘大祀	sangui jiukou	三跪九叩
nanmianzhe	南面者	santong	三統
nei	內	sanxian	三獻

sanzhi	散志	shiwei chu	侍衛處
sanzhong cheng	三重城	shixue	實學
shan	膳	shou	受
shang (second musical tone)	商	shou fuzuo che zhuan	受福胙徹饌
shang (upper)	上	shu zhuban	書祝版
shangdi	上帝	shun	順
shanqi	繕葺	Si Tianzi	嗣天子
shanshui	山水	sifang	四方
she	設	siji qinglisi	祠祭清吏司
she shen zuo	設神座	siku	四庫
sheji	社稷	song shen	送神
shen	神		
shendao	神道	tai miao	太廟
sheng (fullness)	盛	ti	體
sheng (inspect)	省	tianxia	天下
sheng (sage)	聖	tiao	條
sheng zi	省齋	tong	通
shengsheng	省牲	tongkao	通考
shengyuan	生員	tongxue	同學
shenku	神庫	tui	推
shenwei huan yu	神位還御		
shenzhu	神主	wai	外
shi (event, serve)	事	waichao	外朝
shi (history)	史	wang liao	望燎
shi (inspect)	視	wei	緯
shi (inspect)	眂	weici	位次
shi (manifest)	示	wen	文
shi (show)	施	wenda	問答
shi po sheng	眂剖牲	wenren	文人
shi shenwei tanwei shengqi zhaisu	眂神位壇位牲器齋宿	wenzhi	文治
		wenzi yuanyu	文字怨獄
shi yu zhong	事於中	wo	喔
shi'er zhang	十二章	wu (dance)	舞
shiji	事蹟	wu (military)	武
shimo	始末	wu (product)	物
shisheng	眂牲	wuguan	五觀
shiwei	侍衛	wujie	午階

wujing zongyi	五經總義	yi mu xiongdi	以睦兄弟
wuli	五禮	yi she zhidu	以設制度
wulun	五倫	yichao zhi qushi	一朝之故事
		yigui sankou	一跪三叩
xia	下	yili	義理
xian (appear)	顯	ying	應
xian (manifest)	現	yingshen	迎神
xiang (simulacrum)	象	yinshi	飲食
xiang (turning)	向	yizheng jun chen	以正君臣
xiantian	先天	yizhi qinglisi	儀制清吏司
xiao (filiality)	孝	yong	用
xiao (imitate)	效	you (dark)	幽
xiaoxue	小學	you (right)	右
xin	心	youquan	幽全
xin zhi duan	心之端	yu	羽
xing (model)	型	yuan	原
xing (the Nature)	性	yucha shanfang	御茶膳房
xing (to perform)	行	yue	閱
xingli	行禮	yue zhuban yu	
xingli yijie	行禮儀節	bo xiang	閱祝版玉帛香
xinglixue	性理學	yulu	語錄
xingti	形體		
xiongli	凶禮	zan	贊
xiu	修	zhan sheng qi	展牲器
xiudao	修道	zhang (emblem)	彰
xiumiao	修廟	zhang (measure)	丈
xiuwen	修文	zhaomu	昭穆
xiuxing	修行	zhen	朕
xuran	序然	zhengming	正名
		zhengshu	正書
ya dong xian	亞多獻	zhi (fourth	
yan (examine)	驗	musical tone)	徵
yan (spoken words)	言	zhi (intensify)	致
yi (ceremonial)	義	zhi (realize)	知
yi (doubt)	疑	zhidu	制度
yi du fu zi	以篤父子	zhishi	執事
yi he fufu	以和夫婦	zhizhai	致齊
yi li tian li	以立田里	zhong	中

zhongyang	中央	zijincheng	紫禁城
zhu (master)	主	ziran	自然
zhu (pillar)	柱	Ziwang	子王
zhu (reveal)	著	zixiu	自修
zhuban	祝版	zizheng yuan	子徵垣
zhuguan	主觀	zongfa	宗法
zhujizhe	主祭者	zongmiao sishi	
zhuke qinglisi	主客清吏司	daxiang	宗廟祀時大饗
zhuke siguan	主客司官	zou	奏
zhuren	主人	zu	俎
zi (son)	子	zun	尊
zi (word)	字	zuo (left)	左
zi zhong chu yu xin	自中出於心	zuo (throne)	座

References

Ahern, Emily Martin. 1981. *Chinese Ritual and Politics.* Cambridge: University of Cambridge Press.

——. 1973. *The Cult of the Dead in a Chinese Village.* Stanford: Stanford University Press.

Allan, Sarah. 1981. *The Heir and the Sage.* Asian Libraries Series no. 24. San Francisco: Chinese Materials Center.

——. 1973. "The Identities of Taigong Wang in Zhou and Han Literature." *Monumenta Serica* 30:57–99.

Alpers, Svetlana. 1983. *The Art of Describing: Dutch Painting in the Seventeenth Century.* Chicago: University of Chicago Press.

Anderson, Benedict. 1983. *Imagined Communities.* London: Verso Editions.

Arendt, Hannah. 1958. *The Human Condition.* Chicago: University of Chicago Press.

Aries, Philippe. 1976. *Western Attitudes toward Death: From the Middle Ages to the Present.* Translated by Patricia Ranum. Baltimore: Johns Hopkins University Press.

——. 1962. *Centuries of Childhood.* Translated by Robert Baldick. New York: Pantheon.

Asad, Talal. 1993. *Genealogies of Religion: Discipline and Reasons of Power in Christianity and Islam.* Baltimore: Johns Hopkins University Press.

——. 1979. "Anthropology and the Analysis of Ideology." *Man* 14, no. 4 (December): 607–27.

Atwell, William S. 1986. "The 'Seventeenth Century Crisis' in China and Japan." *Journal of Asian Studies* 45, no. 2 (February): 223–44.

Austin, J. L. 1962. *How to Do Things with Words.* Cambridge: Harvard University Press.

Balazs, Etienne. 1964. "China as a Permanently Bureaucratic Society." In *Chinese Civilization and Bureaucracy.* New Haven: Yale University Press.

Barker, Francis. 1984. *The Tremulous Private Body.* New York: Methuen.

Barlow, Tani E. 1994. "Theorizing Woman: Funu, Guojia, Jiating." In Zito and Barlow 1994.

Barnett, Steve, and Martin Silverman. 1979. *Ideology and Everyday Life: Anthropology, Neo-Marxist Thought and the Problem of Ideology and the Social Whole.* Ann Arbor: University of Michigan.

Bawden, Charles R. 1968. *The Modern History of Mongolia.* London: Weidenfeld and Nicholson.

Bell, Catherine. 1992. *Ritual Theory, Ritual Practice.* New York: Oxford University Press.

———. 1989. "Religion and Chinese Culture: Toward an Assesment of Popular Religion." *History of Religions* 29, no. 1 (August): 35–57.

Berger, Peter, and Thomas Luckmann. 1966. *The Social Construction of Reality: A Treatise in the Sociology of Knowledge.* Garden City, N.Y.: Doubleday.

Berling, Judith. 1985. "Religion and Popular Culture: The Management of Moral Capital in *The Romance of the Three Teachings.*" In Johnson, Rawski, and Nathan 1985: 188–218.

Bielenstein, Hans. 1979. "The Restoration of the Han Dynasty." 4th special issue on The Government. *Bulletin of the Museum for Far Eastern Antiquities* 51:3–300.

Bilsky, Lester. 1975. *The State Religion of China.* Vol. 1. Taipei: Chinese Association for Folklore.

Blodgett, Henry. 1899. "The Worship of Heaven and Earth." *Journal of American Oriental Society* 20, no. 1 (January–July).

Boodberg, Peter. 1953. "The Semasiology of Some Primary Confucian Concepts." *Philosophy East and West* 2:317–32.

Boon, James. 1972. *From Symbolism to Structuralism.* New York: Harper Torchbooks.

Bordo, Susan. 1988. *The Flight to Objectivity: Essays in Cartensianism.* Albany: State University of New York Press.

Bouillard, G. 1922a. "La Temple du Ciel." *La China* 27 (1 Oct.): 1421–43.

———. 1922b. "La Temple du Ciel." *La China* 28 (15 Oct.): 1679–1716.

———. 1923. "La Temple du Terre." *La China* 34 (January–March): 53–67.

Bourdieu, Pierre. 1977. *Outline of a Theory of Practice.* Translated by Richard Nice. Cambridge: Cambridge University Press.

Boyd, Andrew. 1962. *Chinese Architecture and Town Planning.* Chicago: University of Chicago Press.

Brandauer, Frederick P., and Chun-Chieh Huang, eds. 1994. *Imperial Rulership and Cultural Change in Traditional China.* Seattle: University of Washington Press.

Brokaw, Cynthia. 1991. *The Ledgers of Merit and Demerit: Social Change and Moral Order in Late Imperial China.* Princeton: Princeton University Press.

Bruneau, Marie Florine. 1992. "Learned and Literary Women in Late Imperial China and Early Modern Europe." *Late Imperial China* 13, no. 1 (June): 156–72.

Brunnert, H. S., and V. Hagelstrom. 1912. *Present Day Political Organization in China.* Translated by A. Beltchenko and E. E. Moran. Shanghai: Kelly and Walsh.

Bryson, Norman. 1983. *Vision and Painting: The Logic of the Gaze.* New Haven: Yale University Press.

Burke, Kenneth. 1969. *A Grammar of Motives.* Berkeley: University of California Press.

Butler, Judith. 1990. *Gender Trouble: Feminism and the Subversion of Identity.* New York: Routledge.

Bynum, Caroline. 1991. *Holy Feast, Holy Fast: The Religious Significance of Food to Medieval Women.* Berkeley: University of California Press.

Cahill, James. 1982. *The Compelling Image: Nature and Style in Seventeenth-Century Chinese Painting.* Cambridge: Harvard University Press.

Cameron, Averil. 1987. "The Construction of Court Ritual: The Byzantine Book of Ceremonies." In Cannadine and Price 1987.

Cammann, Schuyler. 1952. *China's Dragon Robes.* New York: Ronald Press.

———. 1944–45. "The Development of the Mandarin Square." *Harvard Journal of Asian Studies* 8:71–130, plus plates.

Cannadine, David, and Simon Price, eds. 1987. *Rituals of Royalty, Power and Ceremonial in Traditional Societies.* New York: Cambridge University Press.

Cang Xueliang. 1984. *Zhang Xuecheng he "Wenshi tongyi"* (Zhang Xuecheng and "The Comprehensive Discussions of the History of Cosmic Pattern"). Beijing: Zhonghua shuju.

Cao Zongru. 1936. "Zongguan neiwu fu kaolue" (A study of the Imperial Household Department). In *Wenxian luji* (Collected essays), n.p.

Chan Wing-tsit. 1963. *A Source Book in Chinese Philosophy.* Princeton: Princeton University Press.

Chang Chun-shu. 1974. "Emperorship in 18th Century China." *Journal of the Institute of Chinese Studies of the Chinese University of Hong Kong* 7, no. 2:26–42.

Chang, K. C. 1983. *Art, Myth and Ritual: The Path to Political Authority in Ancient China.* Cambridge: Harvard University Press.

———. 1977. *The Archaeology of Ancient China.* 3d ed. New Haven: Yale University Press.

———. 1976. *Early Chinese Civilization: Anthropological Perspectives.* Cambridge: Harvard University Press.

Chang Pide. *Zhongguo muluxue jiangyi* (Lectures on Chinese bibliography). Taipei: Commercial Press, 1973.

Chang Sen-dou. 1977. "The Morphology of Walled Capitals." In Skinner 1977b.

Chavannes, Edouard. 1910. "Le dieu du sol." In *Le T'ai Chan.* Paris: E. Leroux.

Cheng, François. 1982. *Chinese Poetic Writing.* Translated by D. Riggs. Bloomington: Indiana University Press.

Cheng, Chung-ying. 1986. "The Concept of Face and Its Confucian Roots." *Journal of Chinese Philosophy* 13, no. 3 (September): 329–48.

————. 1971. *Tai Chen's Inquiry into Goodness*. Honolulu: East-West Center Press.

Ch'ien, Edward. 1986. *Chiao Hung and the Restructuring of Neo- Confucianism in the Late Ming*. New York: Columbia University Press.

Chow, Kai-wing. 1994. *The Rise of Confucian Ritualism in Late Imperial China: Ethics, Classics and Lineage Discourse*. Stanford: Stanford University Press.

Chu Hsi. 1967. *Reflections on Things at Hand: The Neo-Confucian Anthology*. Translated by W. T. Chan. New York: Columbia University Press.

Chuang Tzu. *Basic Writings*. 1964. Translated by Burton Watson. New York: Columbia University Press.

Cohen, Myron. 1990. "Lineage Organization in North China." *Journal of Asian Studies* 49, no. 3:509–34.

Cohn, Bernard. 1981. "Anthropology and History in the 1980s." *Journal of Interdisciplinary History* 12, no. 2 (Autumn): 227–52.

Cohn, Bernard, and Nicholas B. Dirks. "Beyond the Fringe: The Nation State, Colonialism, and the Technologies of Power." Paper presented at the Mellon Symposium in Historical Anthropology, September 1986.

Conger, Sarah Pike. 1909. *Letters from Peking*. Chicago: A. C. McClurg and Co.

Connerton, Paul. 1989. *How Societies Remember*. Cambridge: Cambridge University Press.

Corrigan, Philip, and Derek Sayer. 1989. *The Great Arch: English State Formation as Cultural Revolution*. London: Basil Blackwell.

Cranmer-Byng, J. M., ed. 1963. *An Embassy to China: Being the Journal Kept by Lord Macartney during His Embassy to the Emperor Ch'ien-Lung*. London: Longmans, Green.

Creel, Herlee. 1964. "The Beginnings of Bureaucracy in China." *Journal of Asian Studies* 23, no. 2 (February): 45–74.

Crossley, Pamela Kyle. 1992. "The Rulerships of China." *American Historical Review* (December): 1468–83.

————. 1990a. "Thinking about Ethnicity in Early Modern China." *Late Imperial China* 11, no. 1 (June): 1–35.

————. 1990b. *Orphan Warriors: Three Manchu Generations and the End of the Qing World*. Princeton: Princeton University Press.

————. 1987. *"Manzhou yuanliu kao* and the Formalization of the Manchu Heritage." *Journal of Asian Studies* 46, no. 4 (November): 761–90.

————. 1985. "An Introduction to the Qing Foundation Myth." *Late Imperial China* 6, no. 2 (December): 1–36.

Da Qing Gaozong qunhuang de shilu (Veritable records of the Qianlong reign). Reprint ed. Taipei.

Dai Zhen. 1924. *Dai Dongyuande jiwen* (Collection of essays of Dai Dongyuan). Part 2. Peking.

DCJMBP. Dkon-mchog-'jigs-med-dban-po II (1728–1791). "Rje bla ma srid zhi'i gtsug rgyan pan chen tham cad mkhyen pa blo bzang dpal ldan ye she dpal bzang po'i zhal snga nas kyi rnam par thar pa nyi ma'i od zer zhes bya ba'i smad cha" (The latter part of the biography, called "Rays of the sun," of the foremost lama, the crown ornament of Samsara and Nirvana, the omniscient panchen, the glorious and good Losang Belden Yeshe]. In *The Collected Works of Dkon-mchog-'jigs-med-dban-po II, the Second 'Jam dbang bzad of Bla brangfa bkra sis shis'khyil*. New Delhi: Ngawang Gelek Demo, 1971. Translated by Nima Dorje with Angela Zito and Elizabeth Benard.

DeBernardi, Jean. 1992. "Space and Time in Chinese Religious Culture." *History of Religions* 31, no. 3 (February): 247–68.

DeCerteau, Michel. 1984. *The Practice of Everyday Life*. Berkeley: University of California Press.

Deleuze, Gilles, and Felix Guattari. 1987. *A Thousand Plateaus: Capitalism and Schizophrenia*. Translated by Brian Massumi. St. Paul: University of Minnesota Press.

de Pee, Christian. 1996. "Can Wrongs Make a Rite? 'Ritual' and 'Custom' in the Writing of Weddings in Eleventh through Thirteenth Century China." Paper presented at the Workshop on New Directions in the Study of Chinese Women 1000–1800, Leiden, Sept. 11–14.

Derrida, Jacques. 1976. *Of Grammatology*. Translated by Gayatri Chakravorty Spivak. Baltimore: Johns Hopkins University Press.

DeWoskin, Kenneth. 1982. *A Song for One or Two: Music and the Concept of Art in Early China*. Michigan Papers in Chinese Studies no. 42. Ann Arbor: University of Michigan Press.

Diamond, Lee, and Irene Quinby, eds. 1988. *Feminism and Foucault: Reflections on Resistance*. Boston: Northeastern University Press.

Dirlik, Arif. 1978. *Revolution and History: The Origins of Marxist Historiography in China, 1919–1937*. Berkeley: University of California Press.

Douglas, Mary. 1966. *Purity and Danger*. London: Ark Paperbacks.

DQHD. Da Qing huidian (Assembled Canon of the Qing). 1899. Guangxu ed.

DQHD. Da Qing huidian (Assembled Canon of the Qing). 1763. Qianlong ed.

DQTL. Da Qing tongli (Comprehensive rites of the Qing). 1756. Compiled by Lai Bao. Beijing: Qianlong ed. Reprinted in the *SKQSWYG*, vol. 655. Cited in traditional *juan* and page number.

DQTL. Da Qing tongli (Comprehensive rites of the Qing). 1824. Edited by Mu-ko-teng-o. Woodblock ed.

Dreyfus, Hubert, and Paul Rabinow. 1982. *Michel Foucault: Beyond Structuralism and Hermeneutics*. Chicago: University of Chicago Press.

Duby, George, ed. 1987. *A History of Private Life v.II: From Feudal Europe to the Renaissance*. Cambridge: Belknap Press.

———. 1976. *The Three Orders: The Imagining of Feudal Society* Chicago: University of Chicago Press.

Dumont, Louis. 1980. *Homo Hierarchicus.* Chicago: University of Chicago Press.

Durkheim, Emile. 1933. *The Division of Labor in Society.* Translated by George Simpson. New York: Free Press.

―――. 1915. *The Elementary Forms of the Religious Life.* Translated by J. W. Swain. London: Allen Unwin.

Ebrey, Patricia. 1991a. *Confucianism and Family Rituals in Imperial China: A Social History of Writing about Rites.* Princeton: Princeton University Press.

―――. 1991b. *Chu Hsi's Family Rituals.* Princeton: Princeton University Press.

―――. 1986. "The Early Stages in the Development of Descent Group Organization." In Ebrey and Watson 1986.

―――. 1984. "Conception of the Family in the Song Dynasty." *Journal of Asian Studies* 43, no. 2:219–45.

Ebrey, Patricia, and James Watson, eds. 1986. *Kinship Organization in Late Imperial China, 1000–1940.* Berkeley: University of California Press.

ECCP. Emminent Chinese of the Ch'ing Period. By Arthur W. Hummel. 1943. Washington, D.C.: Government Printing Office, 1943; reprint ed., Taiwan: Shengwen, 1975.

Elias, Norbert. 1978. *The Civilizing Process.* Translated by Edmund Jephcott. New York: Unzen Books.

Elliott, Mark. 1993. "Resident Aliens: The Manchu Experience in China, 1644–1760." Ph.D. diss., University of California, Berkeley.

Elman, Benjamin. 1984. *From Philosophy to Philology: Intellectual and Social Aspects of Change in Late Imperial China.* Cambridge: Harvard University Press.

―――. 1980. "The Unravelling of Neo-Confucianism: The Lower Yangtze Academic Community in Late Imperial China." Ph.D. diss., University of Pennsylvania.

Elvin, Mark. 1973. *The Pattern of the Chinese Past.* Stanford: Stanford University Press.

Eno, Robert. 1990. *The Confucian Creation of Heaven: Philosophy and the Defense of Ritual Mastery.* Albany: State University of New York Press.

Fairbank, John K. 1970. *Ch'ing Documents: An Introductory Syllabus.* Cambridge: Harvard University Press.

Fan Wenlan. 1979a. "Jingxue jiangyenlu "[Lectures in Classical Studies]. In Fan Wenlan 1979c.

―――. 1979b. "Zhongguo jingxueshi de yenbian" (Shifts in the history of classical studies in China). In Fan Wenlan 1979c.

―――. 1979c. *Fan Wenlan lishi lunwen xuanji* (A selection of Fan Wenlan's essays on history). Peking: Zhongguo shehui kexue chubanshe.

―――. 1959. *Zhongguo lishi jianbian* (Simplified version of a comprehensive history of China). Reprint ed., Beijing: Renmin chubanshe, 1965.

Farmer, Edward. 1976. *Early Ming Government: The Evolution of Dual Capitals.* Cambridge: Harvard University Press.

Farquhar, David M. 1978. "Emperor as Bodhisattva in the Governance of the Ch'ing Empire." *Harvard Journal of Asian Studies* 38:5–34.

————. 1971. "Mongolian vs. Chinese Elements in the Early Manchu State." *Ch'ing-shih wen-t'i* (June): 11–23.

————. 1968. "The Origins of the Manchus' Mongolian Policy." In *The Chinese World Order,* edited by John K. Fairbank. Cambridge: Harvard University Press.

Farquhar, Judith B. 1994. "Multiplicity, Point of View and Responsibility in Traditional Chinese Healing." In Zito and Barlow 1994: 78–101.

Farquhar, Judith B., and James Hevia. 1993. "Culture and Post-war Historiography of Modern China." *positions: east asia cultures critique* 1, no. 2:486–525.

Feeley-Harnick, Gillian. 1985. "Issues in Divine Kingship." *Annual Review of Anthropology* 14:273–313.

Feher, Michael, ed. 1989. *Fragments for a History of the Human Body.* Zone nos. 3–5. Cambridge, Mass.: Zone Books.

Feng Youlan. 1959. *Zhongguo sixiang shi* (A history of Chinese thought). Taiwan: Commercial Press.

Feuchtwang, Stephan. 1977. "School Temple and City God." In Skinner 1977b 256–302.

————. 1974. "Domestic and Communal Worship in Taiwan." In *Religion and Ritual in Chinese Society,* edited by Arthur Wolf, 105–29. Stanford: Stanford University Press.

Feuerwerker, Albert. 1976. *State and Society in Eighteenth Century China: The Ch'ing Empire in Its Glory.* Michigan Papers in Chinese Studies no. 27. Ann Arbor: University of Michigan Center for Chinese Studies.

Fisher, Carney. 1990. *The Chosen One: Succession and Adoption in the Court of Ming Shizong.* Sydney and Boston: Allen and Unwin.

Foucault, Michel. 1986. "Of Other Spaces." *Diacritics* 16:22–27.

————. 1982. "The Subject and Power." In Dreyfus and Rabinow 1982: 208–26.

————. 1979. *Discipline and Punish: The Birth of the Prison.* Translated by Alan Sheridan. New York: Vintage Books.

————. 1978. "History of Systems of Thought." In *Language, Counter-memory and Practice,* edited by Donald Bouchard, 199–204. Ithaca, N.Y.: Cornell University Press.

————. 1972. *The Archaeology of Knowledge.* Translated by A. M. S. Smith. New York: Harper Torchbooks.

Franke, Herbert. 1976. *Sung Biographies.* Weisbaden: Franz Steiner.

Freedman, Maurice. 1974. "On the Sociological Study of Chinese Religion." In *Religion and Ritual in Chinese Society,* edited by Arthur Wolf, 19–42. Stanford: Stanford University Press.

Furth, Charlotte. 1988. "Androgynous Males and Deficient Females: Biology and Gender Boundaries in 16th and 17th c. China." *Late Imperial China* 9, no. 2 (December): 1–32.

Gao Hongming. 1995. *Chanzu shih* (A history of footbinding). Shanghai: Wenyi chubanshe.

Gao Jin, comp. 1771. *Nanshun shengdian* (Splendid canon of southern journeys). Wood-block ed. Preface dated 1771. Also included in the *SKQSWYG* as vols. 1:13, 2:18, 3:9, 4:9.

Geertz, Clifford. 1980. *Negara: The Theatre State in Nineteenth-Century Bali*. Princeton: Princeton University Press.

———. 1977. *Local Knowledge*. New York: Basic Books.

Girardot, Norman. 1988. *Myth and Meaning in Early Taoism: The Theme of Chaos (Hundun)*. Berkeley: University of California Press.

Goldberg, Stephen. n.d. "Figures of Identity." Unpublished manuscript.

Goodrich, L. Carrington. 1966. *The Literary Inquisition of Ch'ien-lung*. Baltimore: American Council of Learned Societies Studies of China and Related Societies, 1935; reprint ed., New York: Paragon.

Goody, Jack. 1987. *The Interface between the Written and the Oral*. Cambridge: Cambridge University Press.

Graham, A. C. 1990. *Disputers of the Tao: Philosophical Argument in Ancient China*. LaSalle, Ill.: Open Court.

———. 1978. *Two Chinese Philosophers*. Original ed., 1958; reprint ed., London: Lun Humphries.

Gramsci, Antonio. 1992. *Prison Notebooks*. New York: Columbia University Press.

Granet, Marcel. 1975. *The Religion of the Chinese People*. Translated by Maurice Freed-man. New York: Harper and Row.

———. 1968. *La pensée Chinoise*. Paris: Editions Albin Michel.

Grimes, R. L. 1976. *Symbol and Conquest, Public Ritual and Drama in Santa Fe, New Mexico*. Ithaca: Cornell University Press.

Guochao xianzheng shilue (Short summaries of worthies of the dynasty). N.d. Wood-block ed.

Guoli Taiwan daxue jiaoshiyuan zhuzuo mulu (Index to the writings of the faculty of the National Taiwan University). 1975. Taipei: Taiwan National University Library.

Guy, R. Kent. 1987. *The Emperor's Four Treasuries: Scholars and the State in the Late Ch'ien-lung Era*. Cambridge: Harvard University Press.

———. 1980. "The Scholar and the State in Late Imperial China: The Politics of the Ssu-k'u ch'uan-shu Project." Ph.D. diss., Harvard University.

Hall, David, and Roger Ames. 1987. *Thinking through Confucius*. Albany: State University of New York Press.

Hall, Stuart. 1985. "Signification, Representation, Ideology: Althusser and Post-Structuralist Debates." *Critical Studies in Mass Communication* 2, no. 2 (June): 91–114.

Hamilton, David. 1987. "Canning Time." *The Nation,* Aug. 1–8, 97.

Hamilton, Gary. 1984. "Patriarchialism in Imperial China and Western Europe, a Revision of Weber's Sociology of Domination." *Theory and Society* 13, no. 3 (May): 393–425.

Hansen, Chad. 1983. *Language and Logic in Ancient China.* Ann Arbor: University of Michigan Press.

Happer, A. P. 1879. "A Visit to Peking." *The Chinese Recorder* 10, no. 1: 23–47.

Harrist, Robert E., Jr. 1995. "The Artist as Antiquarian: Li Gonglin and His Study of Early Chinese Art." *Artibus Asiae* 55, nos. 3–4:237–80.

Hay, John. 1994. "The Body Invisible in Chinese Art?" In Zito and Barlow 1994.

———. 1985. "Poetic Space: Ch'ien Hsuan and the Association of Painting and Poetry." Paper delivered at the symposium Words and Images: Chinese Poetry, Calligraphy and Painting, Metropolitan Museum of Art, New York, May.

———. 1983a. "Arterial Art" *Stone Lion Review* 11:70–84.

———. 1983b. "The Human Body as Microcosmic Source for Macrocosmic Values in Calligraphy." In *Theories of the Arts in China,* ed. Susan Bush and Christian Murck. Princeton: Princeton University Press.

HDT. Da Qing huidian tu (Illustrations for the Assembled Canon of the Qing). 1899.

HDZL. Da Qing huidian zeli (Examples attached to the Assembled Canon). 1899. Guangxu ed.

HDZL. Da Qing huidian zeli (Examples attached to the Assembled Canon). 1763. Qianlong ed.

He Changling, ed. 1899. *Huangchao jingshi wenbian* (Collected writings on statecraft in our time). Shanghai: Zhongxi shuju.

Hearn, Maxwell. 1980. "Qing Imperial Portraiture." In *Portraiture.* Vol. 6 of *International Symposium on Art Historical Studies.* Kyoto: Society for International Art Historical Studies.

Henderson, John. 1984. *The Development and Decline of Chinese Cosmology.* New York: Columbia University Press.

Henriques, Julian, et al. 1984. *Changing the Subject: Psychology, Social Regulation and Subjectivity.* New York: Atheneum.

Hevia, James. 1995a. "The Scandal of Inequality: Koutou as Signifier." *positions: east asian cultures critique* 3, no. 1:97–118.

———. 1995b. *Cherishing Men from Afar: Qing Guest Ritual and the Macartney Embassy of 1793.* Durham: Duke University Press.

———. 1994. "Sovereignty and Subject: Constituting Relations of Power in Qing Guest Ritual." In Zito and Barlow 1994: 181–200.

———. 1993. "Lamas, Emperors, and Rituals: Political Implications in Qing Imperial Ceremonies." *Journal of the International Association of Buddhist Studies* 16, no. 2 (Winter): 243–78.

———. 1989. "A Multitude of Lords: Qing Court Ritual and the Macartney Embassy of 1793." *Late Imperial China* 10, no. 2:72–105.

Ho Ping-ti. 1962. *The Ladder of Success in Late Imperial China.* New York: Columbia University.

Ho Yun-yi. 1976. "The Organization and Functions of the Ministry of Rites in the Early Ming Period (1368–1398)." Ph.D. diss., University of Minnesota.

Hocart, A. M. 1970. *Kings and Councillors: An Essay in the Comparative Anatomy of Human Society.* Chicago: University of Chicago Press.

Hou Renzhi. 1962. *Lishi shangde Beijing* (Beijing in history). Beijing: Zhongguo qingnian chubanshe.

Hou Wailu et al. 1963. *Zhonggguo sixiang tongshi* (A comprehensive history of Chinese thought). Beijing: Renming chubanshe.

Hsiao Kung-chuan. 1960. *Rural Control in Imperial China.* Seattle: University of Washington Press.

Hsu, Emmanuel. 1970. *The Rise of Modern China.* New York: Oxford University Press.

Hu Hsien Chin. 1944. "The Chinese Concept of Face." *American Anthropologist* 46: 45–64.

Hu Rulei. 1979. *Zhongguo fengjian shehui xingtai yenjiu* (Researches in the form of Chinese feudal society). Beijing: Sanlian shudian.

Hu Shih. 1967. "The Scientific Spirit and Method in Chinese Philosophy." In *The Chinese Mind,* edited by C. A. Moore. Honolulu: University of Hawaii Press.

Huang Pei. 1974. *Autocracy at Work: A Study of the Yung Cheng Period, 1723–1735.* Bloomington: University of Indiana Press.

Hubert, Henri, and Marcel Mauss. 1964. *Sacrifice.* Translated by W. D. Hall. Chicago: University of Chicago Press.

Hunt, Lynn. 1986. "French History in the Last Twenty Years: The Rise and Fall of the Annales Paradigm." *Journal of Contemporary History* 21:209–24.

Hunt, Lynn, ed. 1989. *The New Cultural History.* Berkeley: University of California Press.

Hutton, Patrick H. 1989. "The History of Mentalities: The New Map of Cultural History." *History and Theory* 20:237–59.

Hymes, Dell. 1972. *Re-Inventing Anthropology.* New York: Pantheon.

I-ching. 1967. Translated by Richard Wilhem. Princeton: Princeton University Press.

Inden, Ronald. 1992. *Imagining Ancient India.* London: Basil Blackwell.

Jay, Martin. 1973. *The Dialectical Imagination: A History of the Frankfurt School and the Institute of Social Research: 1923–50.* Boston: Little, Brown.

Jiang Tingxi, ed. 1964. *Gujin tushu jicheng* (Synthesis of illustrations and books past and present). Reprint of woodblock ed. Taipei.

Jiang Xun. N.d. *Da Qing huidian yaoyi* (Selected discussion on the Assembled Canon).

Jin Yubi . 1962. *Zhongguo Shixue shi* (History of Chinese Historiography). Beijing: Zhonghua shuju.

Johnson, David, Evelyn Rawski, and Andrew Nathan, eds. 1985. *Popular Culture in Late Imperial China.* California: University of California Press.

Johnson, Richard. 1986. "What Is Cultural Studies Anyway?" *Social Text* 16:38–80.

Johnson, Samuel. 1878. *Oriental Religions and Their Relation to Universal Religion: China.* Boston: Houghton and Osgood.

Judovitz, Dalia. 1988. *Subjectivity and Representation in Descartes: The Origins of Modernity.* Cambridge: Cambridge University Press.

Kahn, Harold. 1985. "A Matter of Taste: The Monumental and the Exotic in the Qianlong Reign." In *The Elegant Brush: Chinese Painting under the Qianlong Emperor, 1735–1795,* edited by Ju-hsi Chou and C. Brown, 188–302. Phoenix: Phoenix Art Museum.

———. 1971. *Monarchy in the Emperor's Eye: Image and Reality in the Ch'ien-lung Reign.* Cambridge: Harvard University Press.

———. 1967. "The Politics of Filiality: Justification for Imperial Action in Eighteenth Century China." *Journal of Asian Studies* 26, no. 2 (February): 197–203.

Kaltenmark, Max. 1969. *Lao Tzu and Taoism.* Translated by Roger Greaves. Stanford: Stanford University Press.

Kamachi, Noriko, John K. Fairbank, and Chuzo Ichiko. 1975. *Japanese Studies of Modern China since 1953.* Cambridge: Harvard University Press.

Kang, Shin-pyo. 1974. "The Structural Principle of the Chinese World View." In *The Unconscious in Culture,* edited by Ino Rossi. New York: E. P. Dutton.

Kantorowicz, E. H. 1957. *The King's Two Bodies: A Study in Medieval Political Theology.* Princeton: Princeton University Press.

Kaptchuk, Ted J. 1983. *The Web that Has No Weaver: Understanding Chinese Medicine.* New York: Congden and Weed.

Karlgren, Bernard. 1966. *Grammatica Serica.* Taipei: Chengwen Reprints.

Keightley, David. 1978. "The Religious Commitment: Shang Theology and the Genesis of Chinese Political Culture." *History of Religions* 17:211–25.

Kessler, Lawrence. 1971. *K'ang-hsi and the Consolidation of Qing Rule, 1661–1684.* Chicago: University of Chicago Press.

Ko, Dorothy. 1994. *Teachers of the Inner Chambers: Women and Culture in Seventeenth Century China.* Stanford: Stanford University Press.

———. 1992. "Pursuing Talent and Virtue: Education and Women's Culture in Seventeenth and Eighteenth Century China." *Late Imperial China* 13, no. 1 (June): 9–40.

Kuhn, Philip. 1990. *Soulstealers: The Chinese Sorcery Scare of 1768.* Cambridge: Harvard University Press.

———. 1987. "Political Crime and Bureaucratic Monarchy." *Late Imperial China* 8, no. 1 (June): 80–104.

———. 1970. *Rebellion and Its Enemies in Late Imperial China: Militarization and Social Structure.* Cambridge: Harvard University Press.

Labriola, Antonio. 1980. *Socialism and Philosophy.* St. Louis: Telos Press.

Laclau, Ernesto, and Chantal Mouffe. 1987. "Post Marxism without Apologies." *New Left Review* 166 (November–December): 79–106.

Latour, Bruno. 1993. *We Have Never Been Modern.* Cambridge: Harvard University Press.

Laufer, Berthold. 1965. "The Development of Ancestral Images in China." In *Reader in Comparative Religion,* edited by William Lessa and Evon Vogt. New York: Harper and Row.

Legge, James, trans. 1885. *Li-chi, Book of Rites.* Oxford: Oxford University Press. Reprint ed., Hyde Park, N.Y.: University Books, 1967.

LeGoff, Jacques. 1971. "Is Politics Still the Backbone of History?" In *Historical Studies Today,* edited by F. Gilbert and S. Grauber. New York: W. W. Norton.

Leung Man Kam. 1977. "Juan Yuan (1764–849): The Life, Works, and Career of a Chinese Scholar Bureaucrat." Ph.D. diss., University of Hawaii.

Lévi-Strauss, Claude. 1975. *The Raw and the Cooked.* Translated by J. and D. Weightman. New York: Harper and Row.

————. 1963. "The Effectiveness of Symbols." In *Structural Anthropology,* translated by C. Jacobsen and B. Schoepf. New York: Basic Books.

Li Guangdi. 1717. *Xingli jingyi* (Essential meanings in nature and principle). Woodblock ed.; reprint ed., n.d. woodblock.

Li Guoliang. 1988. "Bishu shanzuang yushan zatan" (Tidbits on Imperial meals in the Bishu shanzhuang). *Gugong bowuyuan yuankan* no. 1:83–85.

Lidai renwu hua xuanji (A selection of portraits through the ages). 1959. Shanghai: Xinhua shudian.

Li Sheng. 1979. *Zhongguo liyue* (Chinese rites and music). Taiwan: Sansan shufang.

Li Zongtong. 1984. *Zhongguo shixue shi* (A history of Chinese historiography). Beijing: Youyi chuban she.

Liang Qichao. 1959. *Intellectual Trends in the Qing Period.* Translated by Immanuel Hsu. Cambridge: Harvard University Press.

Lin Shun-sheng. 1966. "Ancestral Tablet and Genital Symbolism in Ancient China." *Bulletin of the Institute of Ethnology, Academia Sinica* 21–22:81–96.

————. 1963. "Beiping de fengshan wenhua" (Sacred enclosures and stepped pyramid platforms of Beiping). *Bulletin of the Institute of Ethnography of the Academia Sinica* 16:83–100.

Ling Tingkan. 1899. "Fuli" (Reactivating *li*). In *Huangchao jingshi wenbian* (Collected writings on statecraft in our time), edited by He Changling, 54.1–54.2b. Shanghai: Zhongxi shuju.

Liu, J. T. C. 1964. "Fengshan wenhua yu Songdai mingtang jitian" (The Fengshan complex and sacrificing to Heaven in the Hall of Enlightenment during the Song period). *Bulletin of the Institute of Ethnology, Academia Sinica* 18:45–58.

LJYS. Qinding Liji yishu (Imperial edition of the analysis of meanings in the Record of Rites). 1983. In the *SKQSWYG,* cited by volume and page numbers in the reprint edition—e.g., *LJYS* 125:75.

LJZY. Liji zhengyi (Verification of meanings in the Record of Rites). 1980. In *Shisanjing zhushu* (Notes and commentaries on the thirteen classics), edited by Ruan Yuan. 1816 combined edition with collation notes. Beijing: Zhonghua shuju. Cited as traditional *juan*/modern volume and page number—e.g., *LJZY* 21/2:1416.

Loshantang chuanji (Complete collection from the Hall of Delight in Doing Good). By Hongli, the Qianlong emperor. Last preface 1737.

Loewe, Michael. 1994. *Divination, Monarchy and Mythology in Han China.* Cambridge: Cambridge University Press.

Lowe, Donald. 1982. *A History of Bourgeouis Perception.* Chicago: University of Chicago Press.

LQTS. Huangchao liqi tushi (Illustrations of dynastic ritual paraphernalia). 1759. Compiled by Yunda. Reprinted in the Sikushu zhenben series, vols. 122–29. Cited in traditional *juan* and page numbers.

Lui, Adam Yuen-chung. 1981. *The Hanlin Academy, Training Ground for the Ambitious.* Hamden, Conn.: Archon.

Lukes, Steven. 1975. "Political Ritual and Social Integration." *Sociology* 9, no. 2 (May): 289–308.

Luo Ming. 1986. "Cong Bishu shanzhuang tandao Qianlong huangdi" (A discussion of Qianlong from the purview of Bishu shanzhuang). In *Bishu shanzhuang luncong* (Collected essays on Bishu shanzhuang), edited by Ma Hongxian, 156–69. Beijing: Forbidden City.

Lu Wenchao. 1795. *Baojing tang wenji* (Collected works from the Hall of Classical Preservation). Reprint ed., Beijing: Zhonghua shuju, 1990.

Lynn, John. 1975. "Wang Shih-chen's Theory of Poetry." In *The Unfolding of Neo-Confucianism,* edited by W. Theodore De Bary. New York: Columbia University Press.

Mahoney, Robert Joseph. 1986. "Lu Hsiang-shan and the Importance of Oral Communication in Confucian Education." Ph.D. diss., Columbia University.

Major, John. 1984. "The Five Phases, Magic Squares, and Schematic Cosmography." In *Explorations in Early Chinese Cosmology,* edited by Henry Rosemont Jr., 133–66. Chico, Cal.: Scholar's Press.

Mann, Susan. 1991. "Grooming a Daughter for Marriage: Brides and Wives in the mid-Qing Period." In Watson and Ebrey 1991: 204–30.

———. 1987. "Widows in the Kinship: Class and Community Structures of Qing Dynasty China." *Journal of Asian Studies* 46, no. 1:37–56.

Mann Jones, Susan. 1975. "Scholasicism and Politics in the Eighteenth Century China." *Ch'ing-shih wen-t'i* 3, no. 4 (December): 28–49.

Mao Qiling. N. d. *Bianding jili tongsu pu* (Collection of interpretations and definitions of rites of sacrifice). In *Xihe heji* (Collected writings from Westlake). Woodblock ed.

March, Andrew. 1974. *The Idea of China: Myth and Theory in Geographic Thought.* New York: Praeger.

Marin, Louis. 1988. *Portrait of the King.* Translated by M. H. Houle. Minneapolis: University of Minnesota Press.

Maspero, Henri. 1981. *Taoism and Chinese Religion.* Translated by Frank A. Kierman, Jr. Amherst: University of Massachusetts Press.

McMahon, Keith. 1987. *Causality and Containment in Seventeenth Century Chinese Fiction.* Leiden: E. J. Brill.

McMullen, David. 1987. "Bureaucrats and Cosmology: The Ritual Code of T'ang China." In Cannadine and Price 1987: 181–236.

Meech, S. E. 1916. "The Imperial Worship at the Altar of Heaven." *The Chinese Recorder* 47, no. 2 (February): 112–17.

Meng Sen. 1981. *Ming Qing shi jiang* (Lectures on Ming Qing history) 2 vols. Beijing: Zhonghua shuju.

———. 1960. "Baqi zhidu kaoshi" (Investigation of the eight-banner system). In *Qingdai shi* (History of the Qing period), 20–100. Taipei: Zhengzhong.

Meyer, Jeffrey. 1976. *Peking as a Sacred City.* Asia Folklore and Social Life Monographs, no. 18. Taipei: Oriental Culture Service.

Mitchell, Timothy. 1991. *Colonizing Egypt.* Berkeley: University of California Press.

Miyazaki, Ichisada. 1981. *China's Examination Hell: The Civil Service Examination of Imperial China.* New Haven: Yale University Press.

Morris, Meaghan, and Paul Patton, eds. 1979. *Michel Foucault: Power, Truth, Strategy.* Sydney: Feral.

Mote, Frederick. 1987. "Reflections on the First Complete Printing of the Siku chuanshu." *Gest Library Journal* 1, no. 2 (Spring): 26–50.

———. 1977. "The Transformation of Nanking, 1350–1400." In Skinner 1977b.

Munn, Nancy. 1986. *The Fame of Gawa: A Symbolic Study of Value Transformation in a Massim (Papua New Guinea) Society.* Cambridge: Cambridge University Press.

Munro, Donald. 1985. *Individualism and Holism in Confucian and Taoist Values.* Ann Arbor: Center for Chinese Studies, University of Michigan.

Murphy, Robert. 1971. *The Dialectics of Social Life: Alarms and Excursions into Anthropological Theory.* New York: Columbia University Press.

Nakeseko, Kazua. 1957. "Symbolism in Ancient Chinese Music Theory." *Journal of Music Theory* 1, no. 2 (November): 140–62.

Naquin, Susan. 1981. *Shantung Rebellion: The Wang Lun Uprising of 1774.* New Haven: Yale University Press.

———. 1976. *Millenarian Rebellion in China: The Eight Trigrams Uprising of 1813.* New Haven: Yale University Press.

Naquin, Susan, and Evelyn Rawski. 1987. *Chinese Society in the Eighteenth Century.* New Haven: Yale University Press.

Needham, Joseph. 1978. *The Shorter Science and Civilization in China.* Cambridge: Cambridge University Press.

———. 1954. *Science and Civilization in China*. Cambridge: Cambridge University Press.

Neigetiben. Routine memorials in the Number One Historical Archives of the Palace Museum, Beijing. Cited with archive classification number followed by traditional reign date of year/month/day.

Nivison, David. 1966. *The Life and Thought of Chang Hsueh-ch'eng, 1738–1801*. Stanford: Stanford University Press.

Ortner, Sherry. 1984. "Theory in Anthropology since the Sixties." *Comparative Studies in Society and History* 26:126–46.

Parry, Jonathan, and Maurice Bloch. 1989. *Money and the Morality of Exchange*. Cambridge: Cambridge University Press.

Peacock, James L. 1987. *The Anthropological Lens: Harsh Light, Soft Focus*. New York: Cambridge University Press.

Perelmov, L. S. 1977. "Confucianism in the Political Life of Contemporary China." *Chinese Studies in History* 10, no. 4 (Summer): 73–94.

Peterson, Willard. 1988. "Another Look at Li," *Bulletin of Sung Studies* 18:13–31.

———. 1979. *Bitter Gourd: Fang Yi-Chih and the Impetus for Intellectual Change*. New Haven: Yale University Press.

Pi Xirui. 1961. *Jingxue lishi* (History of classical studies). Hong Kong: Zhonghua shuju.

Pirazolli-t'Serstevens, Michelle. 1971. *Living Architecture: Chinese*. New York: Grosset and Dunlap.

Plaks, Andrew. 1977. "Towards a Critical Theory of Chinese Narrative." In *Chinese Narrative: Critical and Theoretical Essays*, 309–52. Princeton: Princeton University Press.

Porkert, Manfred. 1974. *The Theoretical Foundations of Chinese Medicine: Systems of Correspondence*. Cambridge: Cambridge University Press.

Price, S. R. F. 1984. *Rituals and Power: The Roman Imperial Cult in Asia Minor*. Cambridge: Cambridge University Press.

Price, Simon. 1987. "From Noble Funerals to Divine Cult: The Consecration of Roman Emperors." In Cannadine and Price 1987: 56–105.

Priest, Quinton G. 1986. "Portraying Central Government Institutions: Historiography and Intellectual Accommodation in the High Ch'ing." *Late Imperial China* 7, no. 1 (June): 46–65.

Pu Gui. 1982. "Ji Qinggong de jiadian, jisi he jingshen" (Remembering occasions of congratulations, sacrifice, and Manchu Rites at the Qing court). In *Wan Qing gongting shenghuo jianwen* (Eyewitness accounts of life at court during the late Qing), 118–23. Beijing: Wenshi ziliao chubanshe.

Qian Mu. 1963. *Zhongguo jin sanbainian xueshu shi* (A history of scholarship in China in the last three hundred years). Taiwan: Commercial Press.

Qingchao wenxian tongkao. Juan 125, "Wangli." Reprint ed., Taiwan: Commercial Press, 1963.

Qingdai dihou xiang (Portraits of emperors and empresses in the Qing). 1934–35. Peiping.

Qingdai gongting huihua (Court painting during the Qing dynasty). 1992. Beijing: Palace Museum.

Qingdai gongting shenghuo (Life at court during the Qing dynasty). 1993. Taipei: Nantian shuju.

QSG. Qingshi gao. (Draft history of the Qing). 1976. Beijing: Zhonghua shuju. Cited with traditional *juan* and page, followed by modern page number—e.g., *QSG* 82.57/2486.

Rabinow, Paul. 1986. "Representations are social facts." In *Writing Culture: The Politics and Poetics of Ethnography,* edited by James Clifford and George Marcus. Berkeley: University of California Press.

Rawski, Evelyn. 1991. "Research Themes in Ming-Qing Socioeconomic History." *Journal of Asian Studies* 50, no. 1:84–112.

———. 1985. "Economic and Social Foundations of Late Imperial Culture." In Johnson, Rawski, and Nathan 1985: 3–33.

———. 1979. *Education and Popular Literacy in Ch'ing China.* Ann Arbor: University of Michigan Press.

Reiss, Timothy. 1982. *The Discourse of Modernism.* Ithaca, N.Y.: Cornell University Press.

Ren Ming. 1982. *Liji mulu hou'an* (Judgments on the bibliography of the Record of Rites). Jinan, Shandong: Jilu shushe.

Ricoeur, Paul. 1978a. "Can There Be a Scientific Concept of Ideology?" In *Phenomenology and the Social Sciences,* edited J. Bien, 44–59. The Hague: Martinus Nijihof.

———. 1978b. "Explanation and Understanding: On Some Remarkable Connections among the Theory of the Text, Theory of Action and Theory of History." In *The Philosophy of Paul Ricoeur,* edited C. Reagan. Boston: Beacon Press.

Robertson, Maureen. 1992. "Voicing the Feminine: Constructions of the Gendered Subject in Lyric Poetry by Women of Medieval and Late Imperial China." *Late Imperial China* 13, no. 1 (June): 63–110.

Rogers, Howard, and Sherman Lee. 1988. *Masterworks of Ming and Qing Painting from the Forbidden City.* Lansdale, Pa.: International Arts Council.

Rossiaud, Jacques. 1988. *Medieval Prostitution.* Translated by Lydia Cochrane. New York: Basil Blackwell.

Roth Li, Gertrude. 1975. "The Rise of the Early Manchu State: A Portrait Drawn from Manchu Sources to 1936." Ph.D. diss., Harvard University.

Rowe, William T. 1985. "Approaches to Modern Chinese History." In Zunz 1985: 236–96.

Rudolf, S. H. 1987. "State Formation in Asia—Prolegomenon to a Comparative Study." *Journal of Asian Studies* 46, no. 4 (November): 731–46.

RXJWK. Rixia jiuwen kao (revised edition of Zhu Yizun [Legends of old about the capital]). 1981. Originally printed by Zhu in 42 chapters in 1688, with additions by his son, Zhu Kuntian (1652–1699), the Qianlong revision of 160 chapters was printed ca. 1785. Cited as traditional *juan,* followed by modern volume and page number— e.g., *RXJWK* 9/1:129.

Sahlins, Marshall. 1995. *How Natives Think: About Captain Cook, For Instance.* Chicago: University of Chicago Press.

————. 1985. *Islands of History.* Chicago: University of Chicago Press.

Sakai, Tadao. 1970. "Confucianism and Popular Educational Works." In *Self and Society in Ming Thought,* edited by W. Theodore De Bary, 331–68. New York: Columbia University Press.

Samuels, David. 1995. "The Call of Stories." *Lingua Franca* 5, no. 4 (May–June): 35–43.

Sangren, P. Steven. 1987a. "Orthodoxy, heterodoxy and the structure of value in Chinese rituals." *Modern China* 13.3 (July): 63–89.

————. 1987b. *History and Magical Power in a Chinese Community.* Palo Alto: Stanford University Press.

————. 1984. "Great Tradition and Little Tradition Reconsidered: The Question of Cultural Integration in China." *Journal of Chinese Studies* 1:1–24.

Schiefflin, Edward L. 1985. "Performance and the Cultural Construction of Reality." *American Ethnologist* 12:700–715.

Segre, Caesera. 1978. "Culture and Modelling Systems." *Critical Inquiry* (Spring): 278–302.

Sheets-Johnstone, Barbara. 1992. *Giving the Body Its Due.* Albany: State University of New York Press.

Shaw, Shou–jyu Lu. 1983. *The Imperial Printing of Early Ch'ing China, 1644–1805.* Taiwan: Chinese Materials Center.

Shi Jin. 1973. "Qingzhong guxue yundong zaisheng de lishi yiyi" (The historical significance of the revival of classical learning in the mid-Qing). *Shi huo yuekan* 3, no. 3 (June).

Shi Meicen. 1966. *Zhongguo yinshua fazhan shi* (A history of Chinese printing). Taiwan: Commercial Press.

Shuntian fuzhi. (Gazetteer of Shuntian prefecture) 1886. Woodblock ed. *juan* 6.

Singer, Milton. 1966. "Culture." In *The International Encyclopedia of the Social Sciences,* 538–39.

Skinner, G. William. 1977a. "Regional Urbanization in Nineteenth-Century China." In Skinner 1977b: 211–49.

Skinner, G. William, ed. 1977b. *The City in Late Imperial China.* Stanford: Stanford University Press.

SKQSWYG. Siku quanshu (Library of the four treasuries). 1983. Facsimile of the Wenyuange edition. Taiwan: Commercial Press. Cited by volume and page numbers in the reprint edition—e.g., *SKQSWYG* 123:56.

SKQSZM. Siku quanshu zongmu (General catalogue of the Library of the Four Treasuries). 1963. 2 vols. Reprint ed., Beijing: Zhonghua shuju, 1983. Cited as traditional *juan* and modern volume and page numbers—e.g., *SKQSZM* 7/1:55.

Smith, Jonathan Z. 1987. *To Take Place: Toward Theory in Ritual.* Chicago: University of Chicago Press.

Smith, Paul. 1988. *Discerning the Subject.* Minneapolis: University of Minnesota Press.

Snellgrove, David. 1959. "The Notion of Divine Kingship in Tantric Buddhism." In *The Sacral Kingship,* 204–18. Leiden: E. J. Brill.

Snellgrove, David, and Hugh Richardson. 1980. *A Cultural History of Tibet.* Boston and London: Shambala.

Spence, Jonathan. 1990. *The Search for Modern China.* New York: W. W. Norton.

———. 1988. *The Death of Woman Wang.* New York: Penguin Books.

———. 1977. "Ch'ing." In *Food in Chinese Culture,* edited by K. C. Chang. New Haven: Yale University Press.

Stearns, Peter R. 1985. "Social History and History: A Progress Report." *Journal of Social History* 19:319–34.

Strong, Roy. 1973. *Art and Power.* Woodbridge, Suffolk: Boydell Press.

Sun Longji. 1983. *Zhongguo wenhua de shenceng jiegou* (The Deep Structure of Chinese Culture). Hong Kong: Taishan.

Sun Xidan. 1868. *Liji jijie* (Collected explanations of the Record of Rites). Wanyou wenku jianyao collection, 1868; reprint ed., Taipei: Commercial Press, n.d.

Tambiah, Stanley J. 1985a. "The Galactic Polity in Southeast Asia." In *Culture, Thought, and Social Action,* 252–86. Cambridge: Harvard University Press.

———. 1985b. "A Performative Approach to Ritual." In *Culture, Thought, and Social Action.* Cambridge: Harvard University Press.

———. 1976. *World Conqueror and World Renouncer: A Study of Buddhism and Polity in Thailand against a Historical Background.* London: Cambridge University Press.

Teng Ssu-yu and Knight Biggerstaff, ed. 1971. *An Annotated Bibliography of Selected Chinese Reference Works.* Cambridge: Harvard University Press.

Tie Yuqin and Wang Peihuan, eds. 1987. *Shenjing huanggong* (Imperial Shenjing). Beijing: Zijincheng chubanshe.

Tilly, Charles. 1985. "Retrieving European Lives." In Zunz 1985: 11–52.

Tjan Tjo-som, trans. 1949. *Po Hu-t'ung: The Comprehensive Discussions in White Tiger Hall.* Leiden: E. J. Brill.

Torbert, Preston. 1977. *The Ch'ing Imperial Household Department: A Study of Its Organization and Principal Functions, 1662–1796.* Cambridge: Harvard University Press.

Tsien, T. H. 1952. "A History of Bibliogrphical Classification in China." *Library Quarterly* 22, no. 4 (October): 307–24.

Tu Weiming. 1976. *Centrality and Commonality.* Monographs of the Society for Asian and Comparative Philosophy, no. 3. Honolulu: University of Hawaii Press.

Turner, Terence. 1980. "The Social Skin." In *Not Work Alone: A Cross-Cultural View of Activi-*

ties Superfluous to Survival, edited by Jeremy Cherfas and Roger Lewin. Beverly Hills: Sage.

Turner, Victor. 1969. *The Ritual Process.* Ithaca, N.Y.: Cornell University Press.

Valeri, Valerio. 1985. *Kingship and Sacrifice: Ritual and Society in Ancient Hawaii.* Chicago: University of Chicago Press.

van Gennep, Arnold. 1960. *The Rites of Passage.* Chicago: University of Chicago Press.

Vargas, Paul, ed. 1987. *A History of Private Life v. I: From Pagan Rome to Byzantium.* Cambridge: Belknap Press.

Vinograd, Richard. 1992. *Boundaries of the Self: Chinese Portraits, 1600–1900.* Cambridge: Cambridge University Press.

Vollmer, John E. 1977. *In the Presence of the Dragon Throne: Ch'ing Dynasty Costume in the Royal Ontario Museum.* Toronto: Royal Ontario Museum.

Volosinov, V. N. 1973. *Marxism and the Philosophy of Language.* Translated by Ladislav Matejka and I. R. Titunik. New York: Basic Books.

Wakeman, Fredrick. 1986. "China and the Seventeenth Century Crisis." *Late Imperial China* 7, no. 1 (June): 1–26.

————. 1985. *The Great Enterprise: The Manchu Reconstruction of Imperial Order in Seventeenth-Century China.* 2 vols. Berkeley: University of California Press.

————. 1975. *The Fall of Imperial China.* New York: Free Press.

Waltner, Ann. 1990. *Getting an Heir: Adoption and the Construction of Kinship in Late Imperial China.* Honolulu: University of Hawaii Press.

Wang Chunmao. 1982. "Qingdai diwang de jitian yu siyu" (Qing emperors sacrifice to Heaven and request rain). *Zijin cheng* (Forbidden City) 13. no. 3:17–27.

Wang Peihuan. 1993. *Qinggong houfei* (Qing court empresses and concubines). Liaoning: Liaoning daxue chubanshe.

Wang Shuqing. 1983. "Qingdai gongzhung shanshi" (Provisioning the palace under the Qing). *Gugong bowuyuan yuankan* no. 3:57–64.

Wang Yunying. 1985. *Qingdai Manzu fushi* (Qing daynasty Manchu costume). Liaoning: Liaoning minzu chubanshu.

Watson, James L., and Evelyn S. Rawski, eds. 1988. *Death Ritual in Late Imperial and Modern China.* Berkeley: University of California Press.

Watson, Rubie, and Patricia Ebrey, eds. 1991. *Marriage and Inequality in Chinese Society.* Berkeley: University of California Press.

Watt, John. 1977. "The Yamen and Urban Administration." In Skinner 1977b.

Weber, Max. 1951. *The Religion of China.* Translated by Hans Gerth. New York: Free Press.

Wechsler, Harold. 1985. *Offerings of Jade and Silk.* New Haven: Yale University Press.

Wei Yingqi. 1944. *Zhongguo shixue shi* (History of Chinese historiography). Chongqing: Commercial Press.

Wenmiao shangding yuebei kao (A study of music and preparation for the sacrifice in the Confucian Temple). 1870. Wujian woodcut, preface dated 1870.

Wheatley, Paul. 1971. *The Pivot of the Four Quarters.* Edinburgh: the University Press.

———. 1969. *The City as Symbol.* Edinburgh: T. A. Constable.

Williams, E. T. 1936. "Agriculatural rites in China." *Journal of the North China Branch, Royal Asiatic Society* 57:24–59.

———. 1913. "The State Religion of China during the Manchu Dynasty." *Journal of the North China Branch, Royal Asiatic Society* 44:11–45.

Williams, Raymond. 1986. "The Uses of Cultural Theory." *New Left Review* 158 (July–August): 1–32.

———. 1977. *Marxism and Literature.* Oxford: Oxford University Press.

WLTK. Wuli tongkao (A comprehensive investigation of the Five Rites). 1761. Edited by Qin Huitian. Taiwan photo-reprint, n.d. Cited as traditional *juan* and page number followed by continuous modern pagination—e.g., *WLTK* 5.12a/431.

Woodside, Alexander. 1990. "State, Scholars and Orthodoxy: The Ch'ing Academies, 1736–1839. In *Orthodoxy in Late Imperial China,* edited K. C. Liu. Berkeley: University of California Press.

Wolf, Arthur. 1974. "Gods, Ghosts and Ancestors." In *Religion and Ritual in Chinese Society,* edited by Arthur Wolf. Stanford: Stanford University Press.

Wright, Arthur. 1957. "The Formation of Sui Ideology, 581–604." In *Chinese Thought and Institutions,* edited John K. Fairbank, 71–104. Chicago: University of Chicago Press.

Wu Changguan. 1788. *Zhenyuan shilue.* Woodblock ed.

Wu Jingzi. 1981. *Rulin waishi.* Beijing: Renmin wenhua chubanshe. Translated as *The Scholars* by Gladys Yang. Beijing: Foreign Languages Press, 1977.

Wu Zhefu. 1970. *Siku chuanshu huiyao zuanxiu kao* (An analysis of the editing of the "Siku quanshu hui yao"). Taipei: Palace Museum.

Xiao Yishan. 1963. *Qingdai tongshi* (A complete history of the Qing). 3 vols. Taipei: Commercial Press.

Xie Mincong. 1980. *Ming-Qing Beijing de chengyuan yu gonque zhi yanjiu* (Research into the city and palaces of Ming-Qing Beijing). Taipei: Taiwan xuesheng shuju.

Xu Bihai. 1983. "Qing gong juxing dadianshi Wumen qiande jialuo chenshe" (The arrangements of standings of the cortege before Meridien Gate during important ceremonial occasions of the Qing palace). *Zijin cheng* (Forbidden City) 17.

Xu Qixian. 1980. "Qingdai huangdi yongshan" (Imperial meals in the Qing). *Forbidden City* 4:10–11.

Xu Yangda, ed. 1871. Preface to *Huangchao jiqi yuewu lu* (A record of dynastic sacrificial vessels, music and dances). Hubei, woodblock ed.

Yan Yuan. *Sishu zhengwu* (Correction of errors in the Four Books), 1.2b, in *Yanli congshu* 1.47.

Yang, C. K. 1967. "The Functional Relationship between Confucian Thought and Chinese Religion." In *Chinese Thought and Institutions,* edited by John K. Fairbank, 269–90. Chicago: University of Chicago Press.

Yang, Mayfair. 1994. *Gifts, Favors and Banquets: The Art of Social Relationships in China*. Ithaca, N.Y.: Cornell University Press.

———. 1989. "The Gift Economy and State Power in China." *Comparative Studies in Society and History* 31, no. 1 (January): 25–54.

Yao Mingda. 1974. *Zhongguo muluxue shi* (History of Chinese bibliography). Taipei: Commercial Press.

Yu Ying-shih. 1977. "Qingdai sixiang shi yige xin jieshi" (A new interpretation of the history of thought in the Qing period). In *Zhongguo zhexue sixiang lunji Qingdai pian* (Collected essays on Chinese philosophy and thought, Qing period volume), edited by Yu Ying-shih et al., 11–48. Taipei: Mutong chubanshe.

———. 1975. "Some Preliminary Observations on the Rise of Ch'ing Confucian Intellectualism." *Tsing Hua Journal of Chinese Studies* 11:105–46.

———. 1970. "Cong Song-Ming Ruxue di fazhan lun Qingdai sixiang shi" (Discussion of Qing history of thought from the perspective of Song-Ming Confucianism). *Zhongguo xueren* 2 (September): 19–41.

Yuan Hongqi 1991. "Qianlong shiqi de gongting jieqing huodong" (Celebrating holidays in the court during the Qianlong era). *Gugong bowuyuan yuankan* no. 3:81–87, 27.

Yun Jing (1757–1817). 1883. *Shier zhang tushuo* (Discussion of the Twelve Emblems). In *Zhijin zhai congshu*, edited by Yao Wentian. Woodblock ed.

Zelin, Madeleine. 1984. *The Magistrate's Tael: Rationalizing Fiscal Reform in Eighteenth Century China*. Berkeley: University of California Press.

Zeng Jiabao. 1990. "Ji feng gong—she wei ji—Qing Gaozong shichuan wugong di tuxiang jilu" (Commemorating abundant merit, narrating great achievements—a record of the paintings of Qing Gaozong's ten great military victories). *Gugong wenwu yuekan* 93:38–65.

Zhang Deyi. 1981. *Qingdai guojia jiguan kaolue* (Investigation of national offices in the Qing era). Beijing: Renmin chubanshe.

Zhang Shunwei. 1962. *Qingdai Yangzhou xueji* (Record of Yangzhou scholarship in the Qing period). Shanghai: Renmin chubanshe.

Zhang Xixin. 1981. "Huangdi yu jiu" (The emperor and "nine"). *Forbidden City* 10.

Zhang Xuecheng. 1985. *Zhang Xuecheng yishu* (Posthumous works of Zhang Xuecheng). Beijing: Wenwu chuban she.

Zheng Tianting. 1980a. "Manzhou ruguan qianhou jizhong lisu zhi bianqian" (Some changes in Manchu customs around the time they entered China). In *Tan wei ji* (Collected explorations of finer points). Beijing: Zhonghua Shuju.

———. 1980b. "Qing ruguan qian Manzu de shehui xingzhi xutan" (Further discussion of Manchu society before their entry into China). In *Tan wei ji*.

———. 1980c. "Qing shizu ru guan qian zhangzou chengshi" (Cities in the Manchu homeland before the Shunzhi emperor entered China). In *Tan wei ji*.

Zhongguo wenhua yenjiu jikan (Collection on research in Chinese cultural history). 1984. Shanghai: Commercial Press.

Zhongguo zongdai minghua ji (A collection of famous paintings of various dynasties). Vol. 3. Beijing: Renmin meishu chubanshe.

Zhou He. *Liji: Rujia de lixiang guo* (Record of Rites: Ideal domain of Confucianists). Taiwan: Qingshao nianban, 1981.

Zhou Yuanlian. 1991. *Qianlong dazhuan* (Biography of Qianlong). Henan renmin chubanshe.

Zhu Jiajin. 1988. "Castiglione's *Tieluo* Paintings." *Orientations* 19, no. 11:80–83.

Zhu Yizun. 1785. *Rixia jiuwen kao* (Revision of the "Legends of old about the capital"). 6 vols. Woodblock ed. Reprint ed., Beijing: Guji chubanshe, 1981.

Zijin cheng dihou shenghuo (Imperial life in the Forbidden City). 1981. Beijing: Gugong buowu yuan.

Zito, Angela. 1995. "The Imperial Birthday: Ritual Encounters between the Qianlong Emperor and the Panchen Lama in 1780." Paper presented at "The State and Ritual in Asia," College of France, Columbia University, Paris, June.

———. 1993. "Ritualizing *Li*: Implications for Studying Power and Gender." *positions: east asia cultures critique* 1, no. 2 (Fall): 321–48.

———. 1987. "City Gods, Filiality and Hegemony in Late Imperial China." *Modern China* 13, no. 3 (July): 333–71.

———. 1984. "Re-presenting Sacrifice: Cosmology and the Editing of Texts." *Ch'ing-shih wen-t'i* 5, no. 2 (December): 47–78.

Zito, Angela, and Tani E. Barlow, eds. 1994. *Body, Subject and Power in China*. Chicago: University of Chicago Press.

Zong Baihua. 1981. *Meixue sanbu* (Musings on aesthetics). Shanghai: Renmin chubanshe.

Zunz, Olivier, ed. 1985. *Reliving the Past: The Worlds of Social History*. Chapel Hill: University of North Carolina Press.

Zuo Buqing. 1989. "Manzhou guizu de shangwu jingshen ji qi minmie" (The martial spirit of the Manchu aristocracy and its disappearance). *Gugong bowuguan yuankan* 8, no. 3:32–37.

Index

2360093